THE HISTORY OF AL-ṬABARĪ

AN ANNOTATED TRANSLATION

VOLUME XXVI

The Waning of the Umayyad Caliphate

PRELUDE TO REVOLUTION

A.D. 738–745/A.H. 121–127

The History of al-Ṭabarī

Editorial Board

Ihsan Abbas, University of Jordan, Amman

C. E. Bosworth, The University of Manchester

Jacob Lassner, Wayne State University, Detroit

Franz Rosenthal, Yale University

Ehsan Yar-Shater, Columbia University (*General Editor*)

SUNY

SERIES IN NEAR EASTERN STUDIES

Said Amir Arjomand, Editor

The general editor acknowledges with gratitude the support received for the execution of this project from the Division of Research Programs, Translations Division of the National Endowment for the Humanities, an independent federal agency.

Bibliotheca Persica
Edited by Ehsan Yar-Shater

The History of al-Ṭabarī
(Ta'rīkh al-rusul wa'l-mulūk)

VOLUME XXVI

The Waning of the Umayyad Caliphate

translated and annotated
by

Carole Hillenbrand

University of Edinburgh

State University of New York Press

The preparation of this volume was made possible in part by a grant from the Division of Research Programs of the National Endowment for the Humanities, an independent federal agency.

Published by
State University of New York Press, Albany

Printed in the United States of America

For information, address State University of New York Press, State University Plaza, Albany, N.Y. 12246

Library of Congress Cataloging–in–Publication Data

Ṭabarī, 838?-923.
[Ta 'rīkh al-rusul wa-al-mulūk. English. Selections]
The waning of the Umayyad caliphate:prelude to revolution/ translated and annotated by Carole Hillenbrand.
p. cm.—(SUNY series in Near Eastern studies) (The history of al-Ṭabari = Ta'rīkh al-rusul wa'l-mulūk;v.26) (Bibliotheca Persica)
Translation of extracts from: Ta'rīkh al-rusul wa-al-mulūk.
Bibliography: p.
Includes index.
ISBN 0-88706-810-3. ISBN 0-88706-812-X (pbk.)
1. Islamic Empire—History—661-750. I.Hillenbrand, Carole. II.Title. III.Series. IV.Series: Ṭabarī. 838?-923. Ta'rīkh al-rusul wa-al-mulūk. English;v.9. V.Series: Bibliotheca Persica (Albany, N.Y.)
DS38.2.T313 1985 vol. 9 1987
[DS38.5]
909'.097671 s—dc19
[909'.097671] 87-33505
CIP

10 9 8 7 6 5 4 3 2 1

Preface

The History of Prophets and Kings (*Ta'rīkh al-rusul wa'l-mulūk*) by Abū Ja'far Muḥammad b. Jarīr al-Ṭabarī (839–923), here rendered as the *History of al-Ṭabarī*, is by common consent the most important universal history produced in the world of Islam. It has been translated here in its entirety for the first time for the benefit of non-Arabists, with historical and philological notes for those interested in the particulars of the text.

Ṭabarī's monumental work explores the history of the ancient nations, with special emphasis on biblical peoples and prophets, the legendary and factual history of ancient Iran, and, in great detail, the rise of Islam, the life of the Prophet Muḥammad, and the history of the Islamic world down to the year 915. The first volume of this translation will contain a biography of al-Ṭabarī and a discussion of the method, scope, and value of his work. It will also provide information on some of the technical considerations that have guided the work of the translators.

The *History* has been divided here into thirty-eight volumes, each of which covers about two hundred pages of the original Arabic text in the Leiden edition. An attempt has been made to draw the dividing lines between the individual volumes in such a way that each is to some degree independent and can be read as such. The page numbers of the original in the Leiden edition appear on the margins of the translated volumes.

Al-Ṭabarī very often quotes his sources verbatim and traces the chain of transmission (*isnād*) to an original source. The chains of transmitters are, for the sake of brevity, rendered by only a dash

(—) between the individual links in the chain. Thus, according to Ibn Ḥumayd—Salamah—Ibn Isḥāq means that al-Ṭabarī received the report from Ibn Ḥumayd who said that he was told by Salamah, who said that he was told by Ibn Isḥāq, and so on. The numerous subtle and important differences in the original Arabic wording have been disregarded.

The table of contents at the beginning of each volume gives a brief survey of the topics dealt with in that particular volume. It also includes the headings and subheadings as they appear in al-Ṭabarī's text, as well as those occasionally introduced by the translator.

Well-known place names, such as, for instance, Mecca, Baghdad, Jerusalem, Damascus, and the Yemen, are given in their English spellings. Less common place names, which are the vast majority, are transliterated. Biblical figures appear in the accepted English spelling. Iranian names are usually transcribed according to their Arabic forms, and the presumed Iranian forms are often discussed in the footnotes.

Technical terms have been translated wherever possible, but some, such as dirham and imām, have been retained in Arabic forms. Others that cannot be translated with sufficient precision have been retained and italicized as well as footnoted.

The annotation aims chiefly at clarifying difficult passages, identifying individuals and place names, and discussing textual difficulties. Much leeway has been left to the translators to include in the footnotes whatever they consider necessary and helpful.

The bibliographies list all the sources mentioned in the annotation.

The index in each volume contains all the names of persons and places referred to in the text, as well as those mentioned in the notes as far as they refer to the medieval period. It does not include the names of modern scholars. A general index, it is hoped, will appear after all the volumes have been published.

For further details concerning the series and acknowledgments, see Preface to Volume I.

Ehsan Yar-Shater

Contents

Preface / v
Abbreviations / xi
Translator's Foreword / xiii
Table I. Genealogy of the Later Umayyads / xix
Table II. Genealogy of the Prophet's Family (The Shī'ah and the 'Abbāsids) / xx
Map I. Khurāsān / xxi
Map II. Transoxiana / xxii
Map III. Syria in the Umayyad Period / xxiii
Map IV. Al-Kūfah and Its Environs / xxiv

The Caliphate of Hishām

The Events of the Year 121 (738/739) / 3

The Reason for [Zayd b. 'Alī's] Death, an Account of His Circumstances, and the Cause of His Rebellion / 4
The Raids of Naṣr b. Sayyār / 24

The Events of the Year 122 (739/740) / 36

The Killing of Zayd b. 'Alī / 36

The Events of the Year 123 (740/741) / 56

The [Treaty with the Soghdians] and the Reason for It / 56

The Reason for Yūsuf's Request and the Outcome of It / 58
An Account of [the Denunciation of Naṣr] and of the Part Played in It by Hishām and Yūsuf b. ʿUmar / 59

The Events of the Year 124 (741/742) / 66

The Reason Why Bukayr b. Māhān Bought Abū Muslim / 66

The Events of the Year 125 (742/743) / 70

The Malady That Caused Hishām's Death / 71
Some Biographical Details about Hishām / 72

The Caliphate of al-Walīd b. Yazīd b. ʿAbd al-Malik b. Marwān

The Events of the Year 125 (cont'd) (742/743) / 87

Some of the Reasons Why al-Walīd Acceded to the Caliphate / 87
What Transpired between Yūsuf and Naṣr in the Matter [of Tribute] / 116
The Killing of Yaḥyā b. Zayd b. ʿAlī / 120

The Events of the Year 126 (743/744) / 126

The Reason for Yazīd's Killing of al-Walīd and the Manner of His Killing / 126
Part of the Account of al-Walīd's Causing Disaffection among the Sons of His Two Uncles, Hishām and al-Walīd / 127
The Killing of Khālid al-Qasrī and the Reason for It / 166

The Caliphate of Yazīd b. al-Walīd

The Events of the Year 126 (cont'd) (743/744) / 183

The Discords That Occurred / 183
The Uprising in Ḥimṣ / 184
The Rebellion of the People of Palestine and Jordan and the Treatment They Received from Yazīd b. al-Walīd / 189

The Dismissal of Yūsuf b. ʿUmar and the Appointment of Manṣūr b. Jumhūr (as Governor of Iraq) / 196
The Text of Marwān's Letter to al-Ghamr / 214
The Dismissal of Manṣūr b. Jumhūr from the Post of Governor of Iraq / 219
The Discord between Naṣr and al-Kirmānī and What Had Caused It / 221
The Reason for Granting Safe-Conduct to al-Ḥārith b. Surayj / 235
The Account of [Marwān's Rebellion] and of the Reason That Prompted Marwān to Oppose (Yazīd) and Then to Give Allegiance to Yazīd / 239

The Caliphate of Abū Isḥāq Ibrāhīm b. al-Walīd and the Rise of Marwān II

The Events of the Year 126 (cont'd) (743/744) / 247

The Events of the Year 127 (744/745) / 249

The Account of Marwān's Journey and What Caused the Battle [at ʿAyn al-Jarr] / 249
The Account of the Cause of the Uprising of ʿAbdallāh (b. Muʿāwiyah) and of His Summoning the People to Himself / 254
The Account of the Affair of al-Ḥārith and Naṣr after al-Ḥārith Came to See Him / 263

Appendix I. Problems of Translation / 267

Appendix II. Al-Walīd's Letter Appointing His Two Sons, al-Ḥakam and ʿUthmān, as His Successors / 271

Bibliography of Cited Works / 275

Index / 283

Abbreviations

Arch. Or.: *Archiv Orientální*
BEO: *Bulletin d'Etudes Orientales de l'Institut Français de Damas*
EI[1]: *Encyclopaedia of Islām*, first edition.
EI[2]: *Encyclopaedia of Islam*, second edition.
JA: *Journal Asiatique*
JESHO: *Journal of the Economic and Social History of the Orient*
JHS: *Journal of Hellenic Studies*
JSS: *Journal of Semitic Studies*
RSO: *Rivista degli studi orientali*
SI: *Studia Islamica*

Translator's Foreword

The years 121–26 (738–44), which are covered in this volume, saw the outbreak of savage internecine struggles between members of the ruling Umayyad family in Syria. Once the towering figures of the Umayyad caliph Hishām, presented in the sources as a most able if somewhat unattractive and parsimonious figure, and his redoubtable governor in Iraq, Khālid al-Qasrī, had died, the process of decay at the center of Umayyad power, the ruling family itself, was swift and devastating. Al-Walīd II, his cousin Yazīd b. al-Walīd and Yazīd's brother Ibrāhīm all ruled as caliph within the space of little more than a year, and when finally their distant cousin, the shrewd and seasoned politician Marwān b. Muḥammad, made his move from Armenia to seize power in Syria, he was not able to arrest the impetus of the forces of opposition that were gathering momentum against the Umayyads and that were shortly to culminate in the ʿAbbāsid revolution.

In its account of these momentous years, al-Ṭabarī's history concentrates on three major areas of the Islamic world: Syria, the center of Umayyad power; the garrison town of al-Kūfah in Iraq; and the eastern provinces of Khurāsān and Transoxiana. It is worthy of note that Spain, North Africa, Egypt, and the Ḥijāz are barely mentioned at all.

Al-Ṭabarī records the end of Hishām's reign in exhaustive detail, and with a rich store of biographical anecdotes, before turning his attention to the notorious life-style of al-Walīd II, both before and after his accession to the caliphate. In spite of al-Ṭabarī's protestations that he has omitted many of the scabrous stories about al-Walīd (cf. p. 1775), he gives a detailed account of this talented, if slightly deranged, member of the Umayyad family on whom subsequent ʿAbbāsid anti-Umayyad propaganda fell with particular weight.

Al-Ṭabarī chronicles at great length the events surrounding the last years of the Prophet Muḥammad's great-great-grandson, Zayd b. ʿAlī, his various litigation proceedings, his unsuccessful rebellion and his death in al-Kūfah, and finally, the hounding and eventual murder in Khurāsān of Zayd's son, Yaḥyā. Turning further to the east, al-Ṭabarī records in detail the activities of the last Umayyad governor of Khurāsān, Naṣr b. Sayyār.

To what extent al-Ṭabarī's selection of his material for these five crucial years is dictated by the availability of historiographical, oral, and archival sources, or by a deliberate emphasis on these three geographical areas, it is impossible to say. The reader cannot, however, dispute the undeniable importance of the events chronicled by al-Ṭabarī for an understanding of the manifold elements of disaffection against the Umayyads which shortly afterward erupted into revolution.

What of the sources on which al-Ṭabarī draws for his account of the events in these three main geographical areas? For his coverage of the Umayyad caliphs—Hishām, al-Walīd II, and Yazīd III—in Syria, al-Ṭabarī relies heavily on reports from al-Madā'inī (died probably in 228/843), through the latter's pupil Aḥmad b. Zuhayr (died 279/892), a Ḥanbalī from Baghdad whose work *al-Ta'rīkh al-kabīr* (extant only in fragmentary form) was a direct source for al-Ṭabarī.

For his narrative of events in Iraq, for the torture and death of Khālid al-Qasrī at the hands of Yūsuf b. ʿUmar and especially for the lengthy accounts of the litigation and rebellion of Zayd b. ʿAlī, al-Ṭabarī's major source is Abū Mikhnaf (died 157/774), usually through reports transmitted by Hishām b. Muḥammad al-Kalbī (died 204 or 206/819 or 821). The importance accorded by Abū Mikhnaf to the rebellion of Zayd b. ʿAlī probably sprang more from geographical factors than religious conviction. The Kūfan historian naturally gave thorough coverage of local events without necessarily revealing a Shīʿite bias. Indeed, Abū Mikhnaf's account of Zayd's marriage in al-Kūfah (pp. 1685–86) could be construed as slightly derogatory to him. Nor, moreover, does al-Ṭabarī opt to omit this episode, as does al-Balādhurī.

Al-Ṭabarī uses reports of Hishām b. Muḥammad al-Kalbī, quoting either Abū Mikhnaf or other unspecified sources. Hishām al-Kalbī was also a Kūfan and had access to material both from Abū Mikhnaf and from his own father, Muḥammad al-Kalbī. Hishām's son, al-ʿAbbās, who is known to have been an informant for al-Balādhurī, may well have been the missing transmitter through whom al-Ṭabarī derived the information, if it was passed on orally.

For his material on Khurāsān and Transoxiana, all of al-Ṭabarī's attributed reports come from al-Madā'inī, a historian who was highly praised by ʿAbbāsid and later Muslim scholars as an authority on events in the eastern Islamic world. Much of the information provided by al-Madā'inī in al-Ṭabarī's coverage of these years is not extant in any other sources. The material is therefore difficult to assess: sometimes it is very lacunary and on other occasions the anecdotes are full and have the flavor of composite accounts or folk tales.

This section of al-Ṭabarī's history contains a number of interesting chancery or *inshā'* documents which, if authentic (and they probably are), have considerable value. These include the correspondence between the caliph Hishām and his heir-apparent, al-Walīd, which records the deterioration in their relationship (pp. 1746–49). For this correspondence there are parallel versions in the *Ansāb* and the *Aghānī*. By far the most challenging of these documents (and of daunting difficulty to the translator) is the elaborate and lengthy epistle of al-Walīd, designating his two young sons as his successors (pp. 1756–64). It is clear that the text is corrupt in a number of places and there is no other extant version with which to compare it. Nevertheless, in spite of its verbal conceits, contorted style, and tedious length, it is at times a *tour de force*, an arousing and persuasive piece of early Arabic rhetorical prose.

The poetry in this volume is of varying quality, most of it poor. The arrangement of the lines of verse is often unsatisfactory and probably on occasion out of sequence. Rising above the mediocre, however, is the fine poetry that is attributed to al-Walīd II himself and that was edited by Gabrieli from the texts of al-Ṭabarī, al-Iṣfahānī, and Ibn ʿAbd Rabbihi.

My remarks on the manuscripts of al-Ṭabarī's history, which form the basis of this section of the Leiden edition, must inevitably be limited, since I have not had the opportunity to view the manuscripts personally. M. J. de Goeje, who took over from D. H. Müller the task of editing these pages, used three manuscripts—those in Oxford (O), the British Museum (BM), and Berlin (B)—for most of this section of the text (pp. 1667–1811). Thereafter he was limited to only two (BM and B), since the Oxford manuscript had come to an end (pp. 1811–25). For the final pages he had only one manuscript (O), as the British Museum manuscript had also finished (p. 1825).

Considerable help is provided by other parallel sources at certain points in this section of al-Ṭabarī's text. The *Kitāb al-ʿuyūn wa-al-ḥadāʾiq fī akhbār al-ḥaqāʾiq*, edited by M. J. de Goeje and P. de Jong under the title *Fragmenta Historicorum Arabicorum* (and abbreviated in this volume as *Fragmenta*) covers much of the material on the Umayyad caliphs. Many of the details of the relationship between Hishām and al-Walīd and of the brief caliphate of al-Walīd, provided by al-Ṭabarī, are also to be found in al-Iṣfahānī's *Kitāb al-Aghānī* and al-Balādhurī's *Ansāb al-Ashrāf*. The wording of the *Ansāb* is almost always identical with that found in the later *Fragmenta*.

For the events concerning Zayd b. ʿAlī and his son Yaḥyā, there are parallel, often identical, accounts to be found in the *Ansāb* and in al-Iṣfahānī's *Maqātil al-Ṭālibiyyīn*. For Khurāsān and Transoxiana there is, however, a paucity of early extant sources which would help to clarify a number of obscurities in the relevant part of al-Ṭabarī's text. There are only Narshakhī's *History of Bukhārā*, which gives an account of the murder of the Bukhār Khudāh very like that of al-Ṭabarī (pp. 1693–94), and al-Dīnawarī's version of the exploits of al-Kirmānī (pp. 1858–66), which at times diverges considerably from al-Ṭabarī's account.

The basis of the translation provided here has been the Leiden text. Although there are a number of unsolved textual difficulties, de Goeje's editing achievement with its full critical apparatus still excites admiration even after the lapse of a century. The Cairo edition of al-Ṭabarī has also been consulted throughout. At times it has helped in the clarification of textual problems. On other occasions it has been found to make changes in the text without satisfactory explanation.

There is a considerable corpus of secondary scholarly literature which helps to throw light on this crucial section of Umayyad history. The general reader is directed to G. R. Hawting's recent book, *The First Dynasty of Islam: The Umayyad Caliphate. A.D. 661–750*, for a clear and balanced account of the Umayyads. Further detailed accounts can be found in the pioneer works of Wellhausen, Gibb, and Gabrieli and in the more recent studies of Shaban. For the topography of al-Kūfah, the work of Massignon is still useful, if taken in conjunction with the more recent researches of Djaït.

Several small miscellaneous points require brief mention. All quotations from the Qur'ān have been made from *The Meaning of the Glorious Koran*, translated by M. Pickthall (London, 1957). Often in the translation names or nouns have been provided instead of pronouns to clarify the narrative, and I have freely used synonyms for the ubiquitous 'said' and 'came.' Bolder changes of word order or other points of translation have been explained in the footnotes. It was not possible to identify all the personalities and place names mentioned in this section of al-Ṭabarī's text, but the notes cover the great majority of these.

Finally, I should like to thank those who have helped with the task of producing this volume. I am most grateful to Mrs. Mona Bennett for her meticulous and patient typing of the translation and footnotes. Warm thanks also go to Dr. ʿAbd al-Muʿnim al-Zubaydī, who gave unstintingly of his vast expertise and knowledge to help with the clarification of the substantial quantity of poetry in this volume. Without his help certain of the verses would have remained obscure. My colleague, Dr. M. F. El-Shayyal, read through the whole of the translation and made many valuable suggestions. I would also like to acknowledge the help given to me by Dr. James Allan; by my brother-in-law Dr. Peter Hillenbrand, who advised me on Hishām's alleged angina; by Dr. Ian Howard, who advised me on a number of points of detail; and by Dr. Martin Hinds and Dr. Patricia Crone, who gave me access, just before I completed this book, to the relevant sections of their new book, *God's Caliph.* Martin Hinds also gave me other helpful information on certain detailed points in the text. Above all, I should like to thank Professor Edmund Bosworth for his constant willingness to help with advice and moral support; and my husband, Dr. Robert Hillenbrand, for his most valuable criticisms and comments.

Carole Hillenbrand

Table I. Genealogy of the Later Umayyads

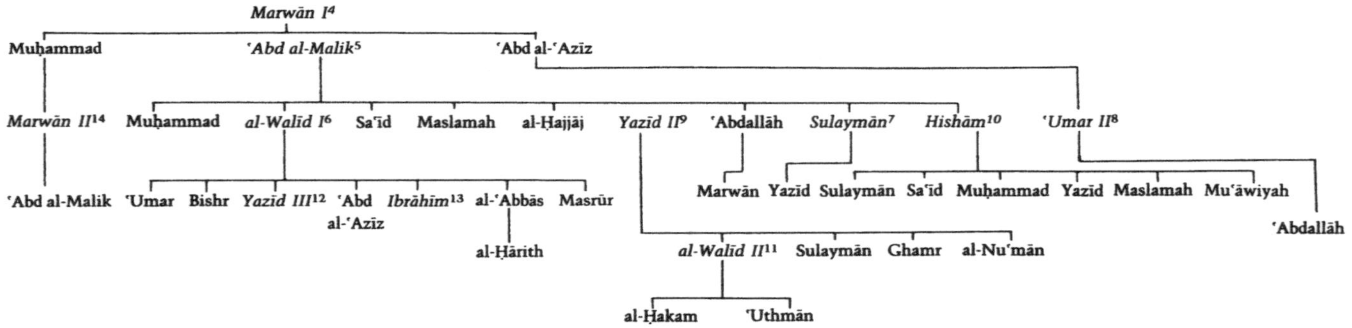

Notes:
Italics denote an Umayyad caliph.
The numbers by the names of the caliphs denote the chronological order of their rule.
This table is not comprehensive. It includes the names of those Umayyads mentioned in this volume of al-Ṭabarī's history.

Table II. Genealogy of the Prophet's Family (The Shīʿah and the ʿAbbāsids)

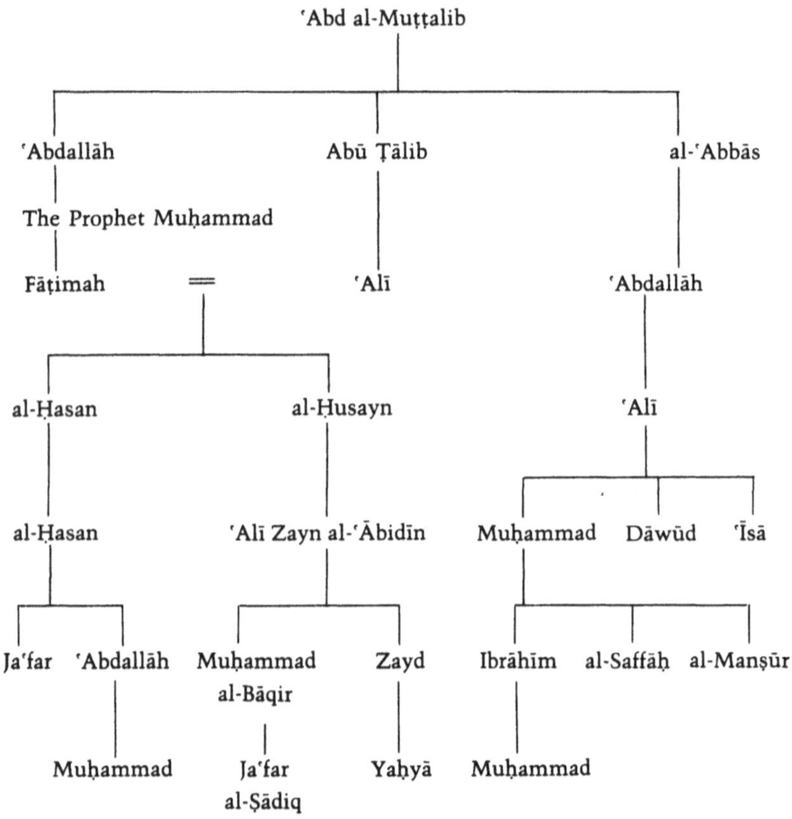

The names shown here are only those of importance to this volume of al-Ṭabarī's history.

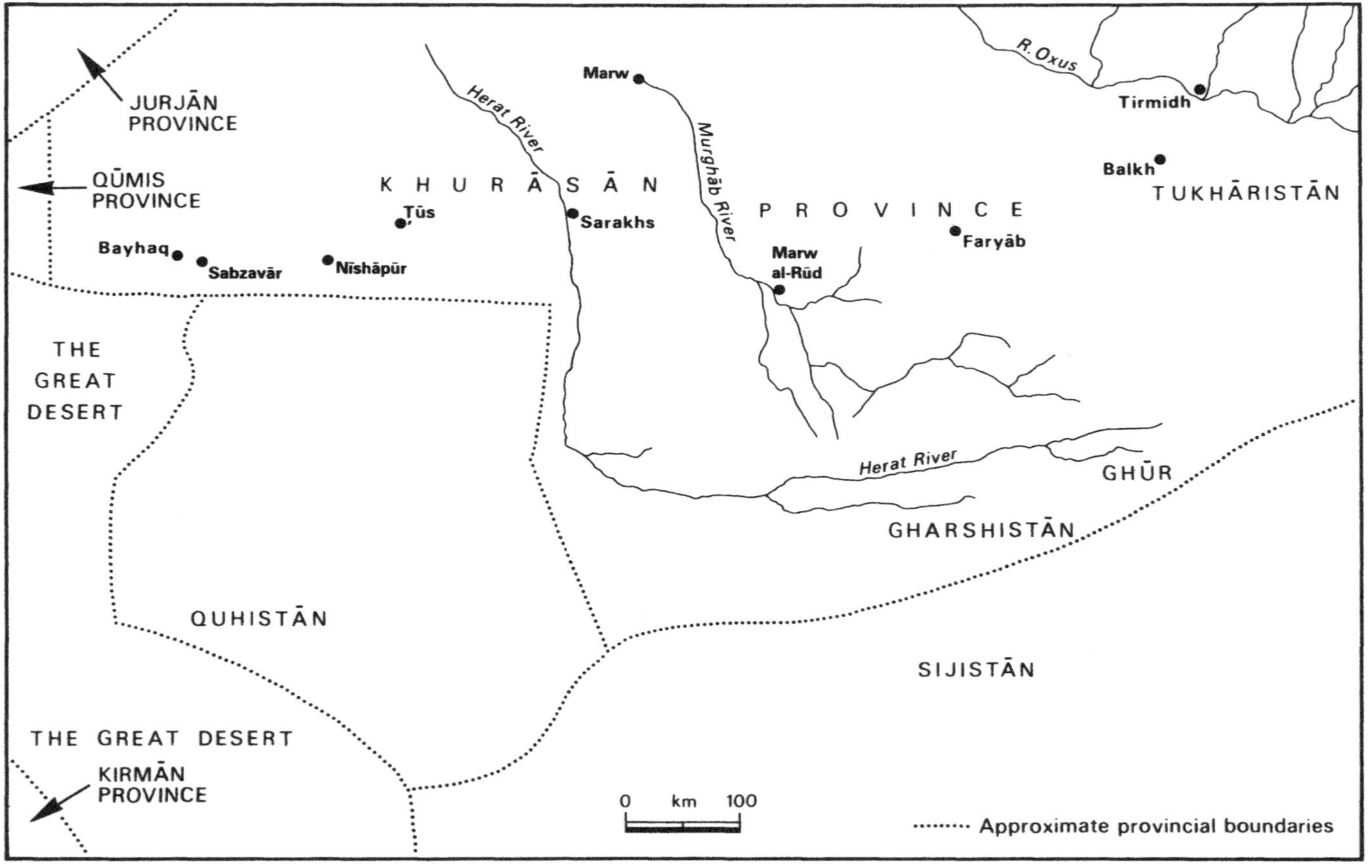

Map I. Khurāsān

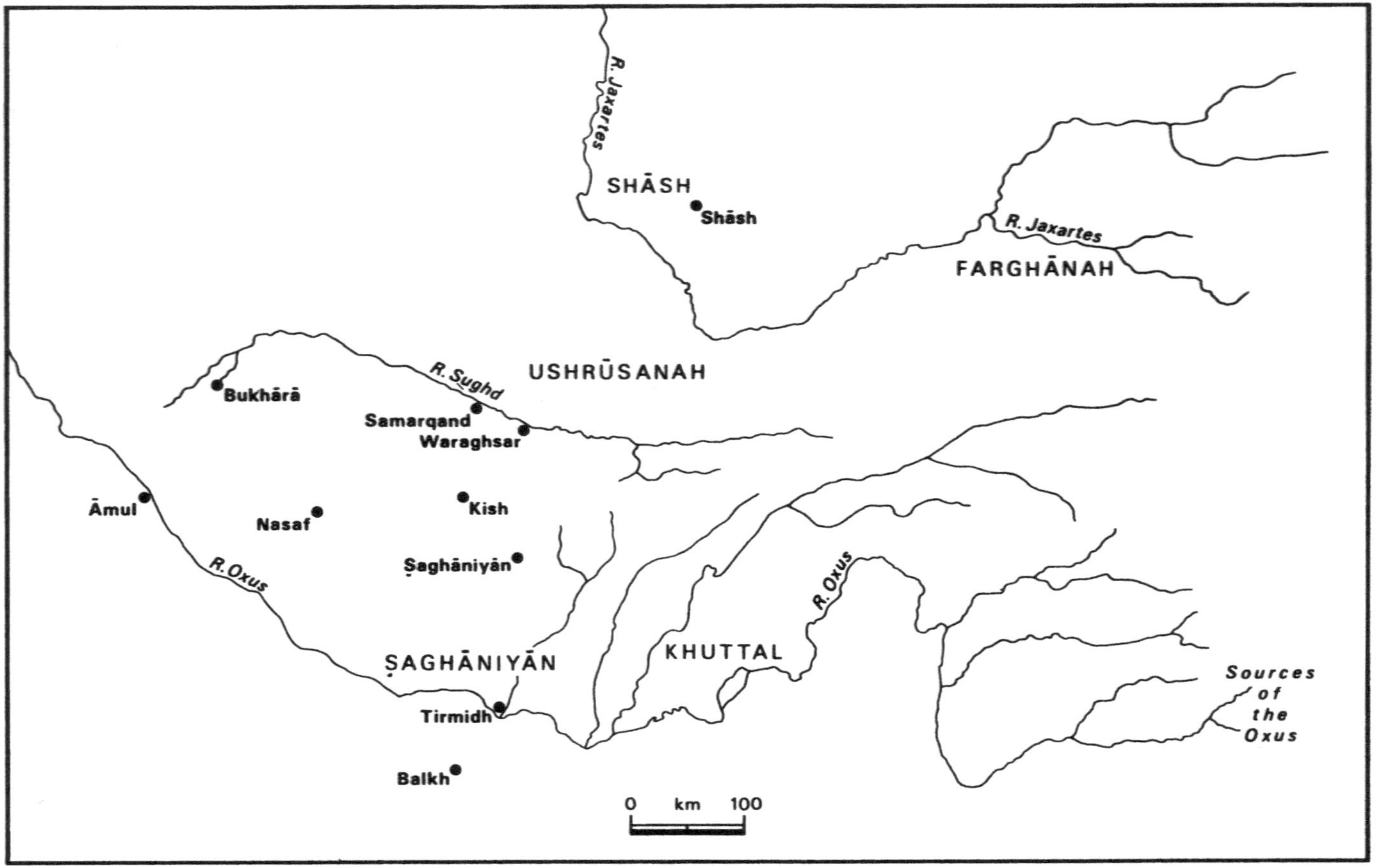

Map II. Transoxiana

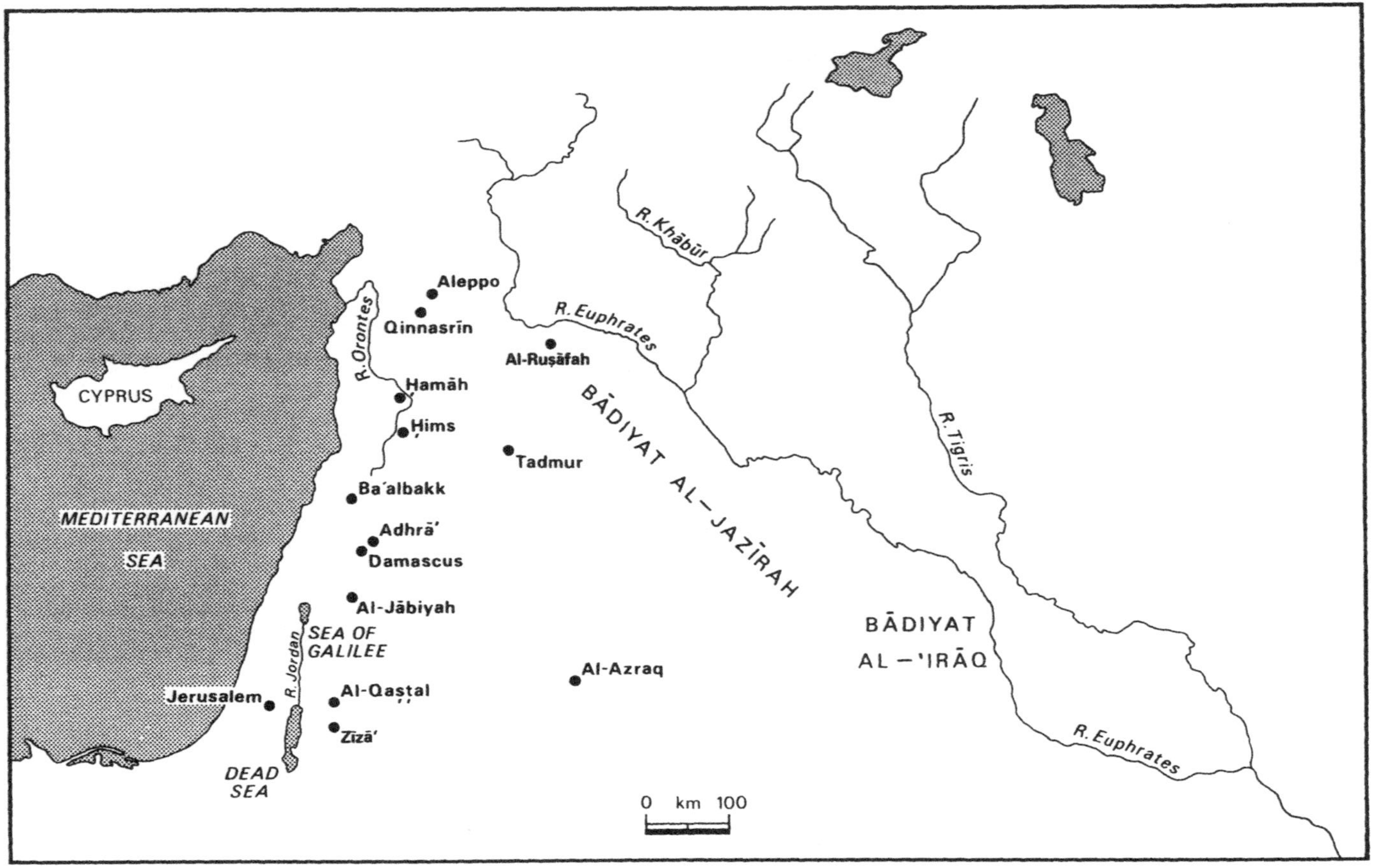

Map III. Syria in the Umayyad Period

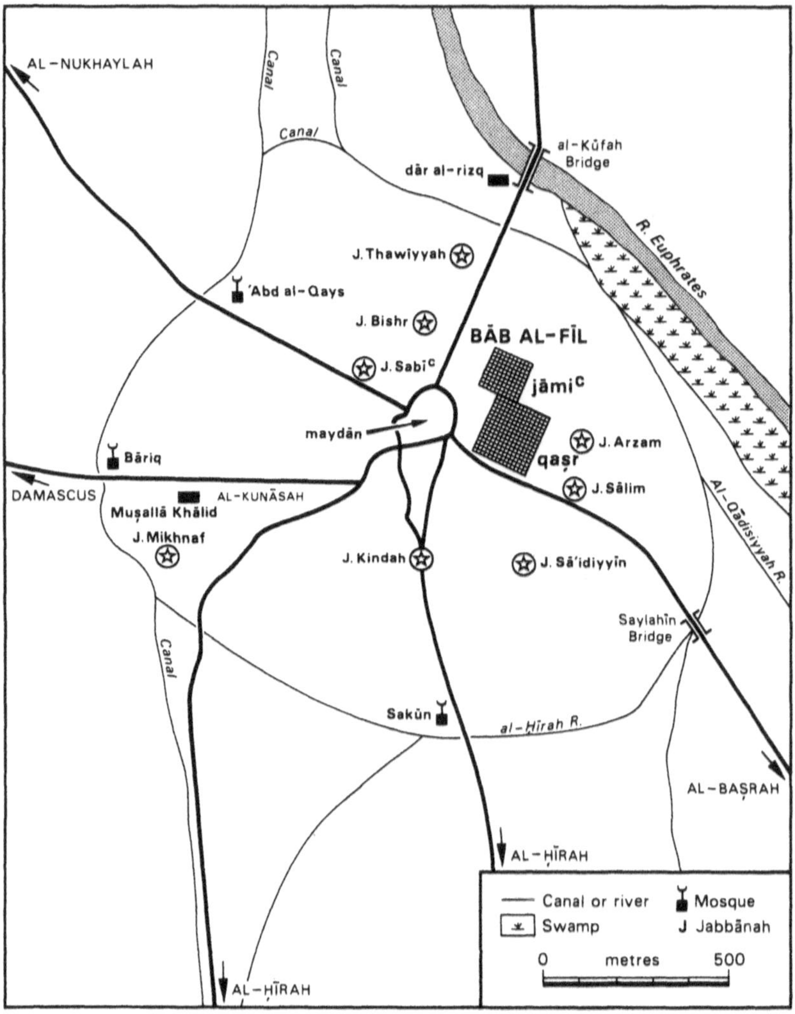

Map IV. Al-Kūfah and Its Environs

The Caliphate of Hishām

The Events of the Year 121 [1667]

(December 18, 738–December 6, 739)

Among the events taking place during this year were the raid into Byzantium of Maslamah b. ʿAbd al-Malik,[1] during which he conquered Maṭāmīr,[2] and the raid into the country of the Lord of the Golden Throne[3] by Marwān b. Muḥammad.[4] Marwān captured

---

1. There is some confusion in the sources as to which Maslamah conducted this raid. It is more likely that the Umayyad commander concerned here was the experienced Maslamah b. ʿAbd al-Malik who had conducted a number of campaigns into Asia Minor and Armenia and had been governor of the Jazīrah, Armenia, and Āzarbāyjān. This is the view of Ibn Khayyāṭ (II, 367) and al-Yaʿqūbī (*Historiae*, II, 395). For the career of Maslamah b. ʿAbd al-Malik, cf. Shaban, *Islamic History*, I, 136ff; Wellhausen, 316–19; Crone, 125.

2. The word *maṭāmīr* means underground caves or cellars, often used for storing corn (cf. Freytag, 381). Here, however, Maṭāmīr appears to be a specific place, probably identifiable with the famous caves in Cappadocia. This is the name given to them by E. Honigmann (*Die Ostgrenze des Byzantinischen Reiches*, 45–46). Brooks definitely thinks Maṭāmīr is a place name ("The Arabs in Asia Minor (641–750) from Arabic sources," *JHS* XVIII (1898): 201).

3. *Ṣāḥib sarīr al-dhahab*. The area of the Sarīr whom Wiet identifies as the Avars was visited by Ibn Rustah some time before 290 (902) and is to be identified as Daghestan. According to Ibn Rustah, "the king possesses a golden throne (*sarīr*) and a silver throne." The people were thus named because of the throne story. Cf. Ibn Rustah, *Les Atours*, trans. by G. Wiet, 165; *Ḥudūd*, 447–50; V. Minorsky, *A History of Sharvān and Darband*, 167–68.

4. Since 115 (733–34) Marwān b. Muḥammad b. Marwān had been governor of

his fortresses and laid waste his land. He submitted to Marwān, having agreed to give him as *jizyah*[5] one thousand slaves.[6] Marwān took a pledge from him on that basis and reinstated him in control of his territory.

In this year al-ʿAbbās b. Muḥammad was born.[7]

In this year Zayd b. ʿAlī b. al-Ḥusayn b. ʿAlī b. Abī Ṭālib was killed.[8] Al-Wāqidī[9] said this was in Ṣafar 121 (January 17–February 14, 739), whilst Hishām b. Muḥammad (al-Kalbī)[10] claimed that he was killed in Ṣafar 122 (January 6–February 4, 740).

The Reason for [Zayd b. ʿAlī's] Death, an Account of His Circumstances, and the Cause of His Rebellion[11]

According to al-Haytham b. ʿAdī[12]—ʿAbdallāh b. ʿAyyāsh:[13]
[1668] Zayd b. ʿAlī, Muḥammad b. ʿUmar b. ʿAlī b. Abī Ṭālib[14] and Dāwūd b. ʿAlī b. ʿAbdallāh b. al-ʿAbbās[15] went to see Khālid b. ʿAbdallāh,[16] when he was governor of Iraq. Khālid gave them

---

Armenia, whence he conducted raids into the Caucasus. Cf. Ibn Khayyāṭ, II, 367; al-Ṭabarī, II, 1431–32. For an account of his career, cf. Shaban, *Islamic History*, I, 144–45, 160–64; Wellhausen, 370–96.

5. Poll-tax payable to the Muslims by the "People of the Book." For a fuller definition, cf. *EI*², s.v. (C. Cahen). Cf. also n. 105 and n. 107.

6. Literally, "one thousand heads."

7. Al-ʿAbbās b. Muḥammad b. ʿAlī b. ʿAbdallāh, the brother of the ʿAbbāsid caliphs al-Saffāḥ and al-Manṣūr. Cf. *EI*², s.v. (K. Zettersteén).

8. Cf. the genealogical table of the ʿAlids.

9. Muḥammad b. ʿUmar al-Wāqidī (130–207/748–823), the famous historian and author of the *Kitāb al-Maghāzī*. Cf. Duri, 37; *EI*¹, s.v. (J. Horovitz).

10. Abū al-Mundhir Hishām b. Muḥammad al-Kalbī, an important and prolific scholar of history and genealogy. Cf. Ibn al-Nadīm, I, 205–13; Sezgin, I, 268, 271; Duri, 146–48.

11. For other accounts in primary sources of the rebellion of Zayd b. ʿAlī, the great-great-grandson of the Prophet, cf. al-Balādhurī, *Ansāb*, 229–59; al-Iṣfahānī, *Maqātil*, 127–51; Ibn Aʿtham, V, 108–25; al-Yaʿqūbī, *Historiae*, II, 390–91; *Fragmenta*, 92–100; al-Masʿūdī, *Murūj*, V, 467–71.

12. The famous historian and genealogist, d. 206 (821) or 207 (822). Cf. Ibn al-Nadīm, I, 216–19; Duri, 53–54; Sezgin, I, 272.

13. ʿAbdallāh b. ʿAyyāsh b. al-Rabīʿah, a *muḥaddith*. Cf. Ibn al-Nadīm, I, 68.

14. Cf. the genealogical table of the ʿAlids.

15. Cf. the genealogical table of the ʿAbbāsids.

16. Khālid b. ʿAbdallāh al-Qasrī had been appointed governor of Iraq in 105 (723–24) or 106 (724–25). Cf. al-Ṭabarī, II, 1471. He fell from power in 120 (738), so this incident must have occurred before that date.

money and they returned to Medina. When Yūsuf b. ʿUmar[17] became governor, he wrote to Hishām listing their names and telling Hishām what Khālid had given them.[18] Yūsuf also mentioned that Khālid had bought land in Medina from Zayd b. ʿAlī for ten thousand dīnārs and that he had then handed the land back to Zayd. Hishām[19] wrote to the governor of Medina[20] asking him to send the men to him. This he did. Hishām questioned them and they admitted that they had been given money, but they denied everything else. Then Hishām asked Zayd about the land (in Medina) and he denied the allegation. The men then took an oath before Hishām and he believed them.

According to Hishām b. Muḥammad al-Kalbī—Abū Mikhnaf:[21] The affair of Zayd b. ʿAlī began as follows. Yazīd b. Khālid al-Qasrī[22] claimed that he was owed money from Zayd b. ʿAlī, Muḥammad b. ʿUmar b. ʿAlī b. Abī Ṭālib, Dāwūd b. ʿAlī b. ʿAbdallāh b. al-ʿAbbās b. ʿAbd al-Muṭṭalib, Ibrāhīm b. Saʿd b. ʿAbd al-Raḥmān b. ʿAwf al-Zuhrī and Ayyūb b. Salmah b. ʿAbdallāh b. al-Walīd b. al-Mughīrah al-Makhzūmī. Yūsuf b. ʿUmar wrote about them to Hishām b. ʿAbd al-Malik. Zayd b. ʿAlī was at that time in al-Ruṣāfah[23] in litigation with the sons of al-Ḥasan b. ʿAlī b. Abī Ṭālib about the *ṣadaqah* of the Prophet of God[24] and Muḥammad b. ʿUmar b. ʿAlī was with Zayd. When the letters of Yūsuf b. ʿUmar reached Hishām b. ʿAbd al-Malik, he wrote to the men concerned

---

For Khālid's career, cf. Gabrieli, *Califfato,* 5–34; *EI²*, s.v. (G. R. Hawting); al-Iṣfahānī, *Aghānī,* VI, 53–63; Ibn ʿAbd Rabbihi, II, 275 ff.

17. Yūsuf became governor on the dismissal of Khālid al-Qasrī. Cf. Dīnawarī, 339; *Fragmenta,* 92. For the career of Yūsuf b. ʿUmar, cf. *EI¹*, s.v. (K. V. Zetterstéen); Hawting, 82–83, 96–97.

18. *Bi-mā ajazahum bihi.* Cf. line 2, *fa-ajāzahum.*

19. Umayyad caliph, ruled 105–25 (726–43). Cf. *EI²*, s.v. (F. Gabrieli).

20. Ibrāhīm b. Hishām al-Makhzūmī, the maternal uncle of the caliph Hishām.

21. The famous genealogist and historian (d. 157/774). Cf. U. Sezgin, *Abū Miḥ̮naf;* Duri, 43–44.

22. There is confusion in the sources as to whether it was Khālid, his son Yazīd, or both who made the allegations. Whichever of the two made the claims about the money did so under torture. Cf. Ibn Aʿtham, VIII, 108; al-Iṣfahānī, *Maqātil,* 133; *Fragmenta,* 93.

23. Hishām's preferred place of residence. Cf. the fuller discussion in n. 426.

24. *Fī ṣadaqat rasūl Allāh.* This phrase is used in other sources. Cf. Shaykh al-Mufīd, 402; *Fragmenta,* 92. Zayd was appointed by his brother Muḥammad to represent the Ḥusaynids in litigation against the Ḥasanids. Later on, al-Ṭabarī uses the term *wuqūf ʿAlī* when probably referring to the same litigation. Cf. n. 35. Cf. *EI²*, "Fadak" (L. Veccia Vaglieri); Hrbek, "Muḥammads Nachlass und die Aliden," 145, 148; *EI¹*, "Ṣadaḳa" (T. H. Weir).

stating that Yūsuf b. ʿUmar had written to him about a sum of money which Yazīd b. Khālid claimed they owed him. They denied it, so Hishām said to them: "We will send you to Yūsuf so
[1669] that he may bring you and your accusers together." Zayd b. ʿAlī said to Hishām: "I implore you by God and kinship not to send me to Yūsuf b. ʿUmar." Hishām said: "What is it that you fear from Yūsuf b. ʿUmar?" Zayd said: "I am afraid that he will act aggressively toward me."

Hishām replied, "Yūsuf cannot do that," called his scribe, and wrote to Yūsuf b. ʿUmar as follows:[25] "Now when these persons come to you, bring them and Yazīd b. Khālid al-Qasrī together; if they admit the allegations made against them, send them to me. If they deny them, ask Yazīd for proof. If he does not produce the proof, then following the afternoon prayer make them swear in the name of the One God that Yazīd b. Khālid al-Qasrī did not entrust them with any deposit and that he is entitled to nothing from them. Then let them go." They said to Hishām: "We are afraid that Yūsuf will go against your letter and will act aggressively toward us." Hishām said: "Not at all! I will send one of the guards with you to make sure that Yūsuf carries out this order and expedites the matter." They said: "May God reward you for honoring the ties of kinship! You have judged fairly." Then Hishām sent them to Yūsuf but he kept back Ayyūb b. Salmah, because Hishām's mother was the daughter of Hishām b. Ismāʿīl b. Hishām b. al-Walīd b. al-Mughīrah al-Makhzūmī, and Ayyūb was one of Hishām's maternal uncles. So the caliph did not want him involved at all in that suspicious matter.[26]

When they came to Yūsuf, they were ushered into his presence. Yūsuf sat Zayd b. ʿAlī near him and questioned him in a kindly manner. Then he asked the men about the money and they all denied it, saying: "Yazīd did not leave any money with us nor is he owed anything from us." Then Yūsuf brought Yazīd b. Khālid out (of prison) to them and he put him and them together. Yūsuf
[1670] said to Yazīd: "This is Zayd b. ʿAlī and this is Muḥammad b. ʿUmar b. ʿAlī and this is so-and-so and this is so-and-so against

25. Cf. al-Iṣfahānī, *Maqātil,* 135; Ibn Aʿtham, VIII, 109.

26. *Qarf.* The variant reading from MSS. BM and O, *qadhf* ("calumny"), also makes good sense.

whom you have made the allegations that you have made." Yazīd said: "I am not owed any sum, either small or great, from them." Yūsuf said: "Are you ridiculing me or the Commander of the Faithful?" Then Yūsuf tortured Yazīd so much that day that he thought he had killed him. He took the other men to the mosque when the afternoon prayer was over and made them take an oath. When they had sworn an oath to him, he ordered these men to be flogged, with the exception of Zayd b. ʿAlī, from whom he withheld his hand. He did not dare to do anything (more) with them and he wrote to Hishām informing him of the situation.[27] Hishām replied that he should make them swear an oath and release them. So Yūsuf set them free. They left and went to Medina but Zayd b. ʿAlī stayed in al-Kūfah.

According to ʿUbayd b. Jannād—ʿAṭā' b. Muslim al-Khaffāf: Zayd b. ʿAlī dreamt that he lit a fire in Iraq which he extinguished, and that thereafter he died. This frightened him and he said to his son Yaḥyā: "My son, I have had a dream that frightened me." So he told him about it. Then came the letter from Hishām b. ʿAbd al-Malik requesting his presence. Zayd went and Hishām said to him: "Go to your *amīr*,[28] Yūsuf." Then Zayd said to him: "I implore you, for God's sake, O Commander of the Faithful! By God, if you send me to him, I am not sure that you and I will ever again meet alive on the face of the earth." Then Hishām said: "Go to Yūsuf as you have been commanded to do." So Zayd went to him.[29]

Some reports said that Hishām b. ʿAbd al-Malik summoned Zayd from Medina only because of the letter from Yūsuf b. ʿUmar.

According to Abū ʿUbaydah:[30] The reason for Hishām's summoning Zayd was that when Yusuf b. ʿUmar tortured Khālid b. [1671]
ʿAbd Allāh, Khālid claimed that he had deposited a great deal of money with Zayd b. ʿAlī, Dāwūd b. ʿAlī b. ʿAbdallāh b. al-ʿAbbās and two men of the Quraysh, one of whom was a Makhzūmī and

27. Ibn al-Athīr's account is clearer (V, 172).

28. For the use of the term *amīr*, cf. *EI*², s.v. (A. A. Duri).

29. Cf. al-Balādhurī, *Ansāb*, 231.

30. Abū ʿUbaydah Maʿmar b. al-Muthannā (110–210/728–825) was a scholar of wide-ranging activities, highly praised by al-Iṣfahānī, Ibn al-Nadīm, and al-Jāḥiẓ. Cf. Duri, 55–56; Sezgin, I, 265.

the other a Jumaḥī. Yūsuf wrote to Hishām about this and Hishām thereupon wrote to his maternal uncle Ibrāhīm b. Hishām, who was his governor in Medina, ordering him to bring the men to him. Ibrāhīm b. Hishām summoned Zayd and Dāwūd and asked them about what Khālid had said. They swore that Khālid had not deposited anything with them. Ibrāhīm said: "In my view, you are telling the truth, but the letter from the Commander of the Faithful has come with these instructions and I am obliged to carry out his orders." He took them to Syria and they swore an inviolable oath that Khālid had never deposited anything with them. Dāwūd said: "I came to Khālid in Iraq and he ordered 100,000 dirhams[31] for me." Hishām said: "In my view the two of you are more truthful than Ibn al-Naṣrāniyyah.[32] Go to Yūsuf so that he may bring you and Khālid together; then expose him as a liar before Yūsuf."

It was said that Zayd only went to Hishām to litigate against his paternal cousin ʿAbdallāh b. Ḥasan b. Ḥasan b. ʿAlī. This account came from Juwayriyah b. Asmāʾ[33] who said: "I saw Zayd b. ʿAlī and Jaʿfar b. Ḥasan b. Ḥasan disputing[34] over the guardianship of the endowments (*wuqūf*) of ʿAlī.[35] Zayd was arguing on behalf of the Ḥusaynids and Jaʿfar was arguing on behalf of the Ḥasanids.
[1672] Jaʿfar and Zayd used all the arguments at their disposal[36] in the presence of the governor, and then they stood up and never spoke another word about the disagreement between them. When Jaʿfar died, ʿAbdallāh said: "Who will take on Zayd for us?" and Ḥasan b. Ḥasan b. Ḥasan said: "I will take him on for you." Then ʿAbdallāh said: "Not at all! We fear your tongue and your hand. I will do it." Ḥasan said: "In that case you will not achieve your aim or

31. Cf. *EI*², "Dirham" (G. C. Miles).

32. Khālid was often called Ibn al-Naṣrāniyyah and was accused *inter alia* of pro-Christian sympathies. He was said to have built a church for his Christian mother behind the mosque in al-Kūfah. Cf. Hawting, 81–82, and Hell, 33, quoting Farazdaq, *Dīwān*, 451: *bana biʿatan fīhā al-ṣalību li-ummihi* ("he built a church in which is the cross, for his mother").

33. Juwayriyah b. Asmāʾ b. ʿUbayd al-Baṣrī, d. 173 (789), who transmitted reports from his father. Cf. Sezgin, II, 94.

34. Jaʿfar argued the Ḥasanid case. After he died, his place was taken by ʿAbdallāh b. Ḥasan b. Ḥasan. Cf. al-Balādhurī, *Ansāb*, 231.

35. Cf. n. 24.

36. *Yatabālaghāni . . . ilā kulli ghayah.* An alternative translation might be: "They were extremely skillful in argument."

win your argument." ʿAbdallāh said: "As far as my argument is concerned, I will win it." Then Zayd and ʿAbdallāh went off to contest the dispute before the governor, who at that time, according to some reports, was Ibrāhīm b. Hishām.[37]

ʿAbdallāh said to Zayd: "Do you want to obtain this[38] when you are only the son of an Indian slave-girl?" Zayd retorted: "Ismāʿīl was the son of a slave-girl and he obtained more than that," and ʿAbdallāh fell silent. They both went to extremes in their arguments that day. On the morrow the governor summoned them together with the Quraysh and the Anṣār[39] and they contested their dispute afresh. One of the men of the Anṣār objected and intervened between them. Zayd said to him: "What are you doing intervening between us? You are a man from the Qaḥṭān."[40] He said: "By God, I am better than you not only as a person but also so far as my father and mother are concerned." Zayd fell silent but a man of the Quraysh intervened on his behalf and said: "In the name of God, you have lied! He is better than you as a person and also in respect to his father and mother, from beginning to end, above the earth and beneath it." The governor said: "What has this to do with you?" The Qurashī[41] took a handful of stones, threw them on the ground and said: "By God, I do not have any patience with this." At this point, ʿAbdallāh and Zayd realized that the governor harbored malicious intentions toward them. ʿAbdallāh made as if to speak but Zayd asked him not to do so and he was silent. Then Zayd said to the governor: "By God, you have brought us together on a matter for which neither Abū Bakr nor ʿUmar would have brought us together. I [1673]

37. The editor notes (1672, n. g) that Ibrāhīm b. Hishām was dismissed in 114 (732) and replaced by Khālid b. ʿAbd al-Malik, who governed until 118 (736).

38. *Attmaʿu an tanālahā.* This is either a reference to the *wilāyat wuqūf ʿAlī* (the guardianship of ʿAlī's endowments), which has already been mentioned, or to the caliphate. One of the accounts from al-Balādhurī refers specifically to the caliphate: *attmaʿu fī al-khilāfah* (*Ansāb,* 230).

39. "The Helpers." The term was originally used to designate the men of Medina who supported the Prophet. In Umayyad times, the Anṣār formed a "pious opposition" to the regime. Cf. *EI²*, s.v. (W. Montgomery Watt).

40. Qaḥṭān was the legendary forefather of the "Southern" tribes just as Quḍāʿah was the ancestor of the "Northerners." Cf. *EI²*, s.v. (A. Fischer-A. K. Irvine).

41. ʿAbdallāh b. Wāqid b. ʿAbdallāh b. ʿUmar b. al-Khaṭṭāb. Cf. p. 11.

call God to witness that I will not litigate before you again on this matter, either rightly or wrongly, as long as I live." Then Zayd said to 'Abdallāh: "Get up, cousin." So they stood up and the people dispersed.

Some sources said that Zayd continued litigating against Ja'far b. Ḥasan and then against 'Abdallāh after him until Hishām b. 'Abd al-Malik made Khālid b. 'Abd al-Malik b. al-Ḥārith b. al-Ḥakam governor of Medina. Zayd and 'Abdallāh were in litigation and 'Abdallāh spoke rudely to Zayd saying: "You son of a Hindu woman!"[42] Zayd laughed it off and said: "You've done it now, Abū Muḥammad." Then he retaliated by mentioning 'Abdallāh's mother in some (disparaging) connection.[43]

According to al-Madā'inī:[44] When 'Abdallāh said that to Zayd, Zayd said: "Yes, indeed. By God, she was patient after the death of her master. She never crossed her threshold, whilst other women[45] were not as patient." Zayd repented and was ashamed of what he had said about his aunt[46] and he did not go in to see her for a time. She sent a message to him saying: "I know, nephew, that you feel about your mother just as 'Abdallāh feels about his mother."

Some sources said that Fāṭimah sent a message to Zayd: "If 'Abdallāh has insulted your mother, then you insult his mother." She said to 'Abdallāh: "Did you say such-and-such about Zayd's mother?" He said: "Yes." She said: "O wretched man to have done that! By God, she was the best woman of our kinsfolk."

It is reported that Khālid b. 'Abd al-Malik said to Zayd and 'Abdallāh: "Give us a break until tomorrow morning, for I am not the son of 'Abd al-Malik if I cannot decide between you." During the night the city (Medina) seethed like a cauldron.[47] Some said

---

42. "You son of the Sindī woman": MS. B and Ibn al-Athīr, V, 172. In one report from al-Balādhurī, 'Abdallāh calls Zayd's mother "a witch" (*sāḥirah*) (*Ansāb*, 230). Zayd's mother was a slave given by al-Mukhtār to 'Alī Zayn al-'Ābidīn. Cf. al-Iṣfahānī, *Maqātil*, 127.

43. Al-Balādhurī quotes in the mouth of Zayd a scabrous story about 'Abdallāh's mother. Cf. *Ansāb*, 230.

44. Al-Madā'inī, the famous historian, d. 225 (839). Cf. Duri, 48; *EI*[1], s.v. (C. Brockelmann); *EI*[2], s.v. (U. Sezgin).

45. According to Ibn al-Athīr, Zayd is referring here to his aunt who married again after the death of her husband (V, 172).

46. Fāṭimah bint al-Ḥusayn b. 'Alī.

47. For an almost identical account, cf. *Fragmenta*, 92–93.

one thing and others another. Some said Zayd had said such-and-such and others said ʿAbdallāh had said such-and-such. The next [1674] morning Khālid held an audience in the mosque and the people assembled, some gloating, some grieving, and Khālid called the two of them, wanting them to insult one another. ʿAbdallāh made as if to speak, so Zayd said: "Don't hurry, Abū Muḥammad! Zayd will free all his slaves before he ever litigates with you in front of Khālid." Then Zayd went up to Khālid and said to him: "Khālid, you have assembled the descendants of the Prophet of God in a way in which Abū Bakr and ʿUmar would never have done." Khālid said: "Is there no one here to answer this fool?" Then one of the Anṣār from the family of ʿAmr b. Ḥazm spoke and said: "You descendant of the 'dustman' (ʿAlī)[48] and of that fool Ḥusayn! Can't you see that you have a duty to the governor and that you owe him obedience?" Zayd retorted: "Shut up, Qaḥṭānī, we don't reply to the likes of you." The man said: "Why are you shunning me? By God, I am better than you and my father is better than your father and my mother is better than your mother." Zayd laughed it off and said: "O tribe of Quraysh! This religion has gone, but has honorable lineage gone too? By God, the religion of the people may disappear, but their honorable lineage does not." Then ʿAbdallāh b. Wāqid b. ʿAbdallāh b. ʿUmar b. al-Khaṭṭāb said: "You are a liar, you Qaḥṭānī! By God, he is better than you as a person and in respect of his father and mother and in every way." He spoke about Zayd for a long time and the Qaḥṭānī said: "Leave us alone, Ibn Wāqid." Then Ibn Wāqid took a hand- [1675] ful of stones and threw them on the ground and said: "By God, I have no patience with this," and he stood up (and left).

Then Zayd went to Hishām b. ʿAbd al-Malik. Hishām began by not allowing Zayd into his presence, so Zayd complained in writing to Hishām, and whenever he did so Hishām wrote at the bottom of it: "Go back to your *amīr*." Zayd said: "By God, I won't go back to Khālid ever again. I am not asking for money. I am only a litigant." Then one day, after a long delay, Hishām allowed Zayd in to see him.

---

48. Literally, "O descendant of Abū Turāb" ("father of dust," "dustman"). This was a name given contemptuously to ʿAlī by his enemies, but it was later interpreted as an honorific and legends developed on this theme. Cf. *EI*², "ʿAlī b. Abī Ṭālib" (L. Veccia Vaglieri).

According to 'Umar b. Shabbah[49]—Ayyūb b. 'Umar b. Abī 'Amr[50]—Muḥammad b. 'Abd al-'Azīz al-Zuhrī: When Zayd b. 'Alī went to Hishām b. 'Abd al-Malik, his chamberlain (*ḥājib*)[51] informed the caliph that Zayd was there. Hishām went up to a long upper chamber of his, and then allowed Zayd in. He ordered a servant to walk behind Zayd and told this man not to let Zayd see him and to listen to what Zayd said. (The servant said): "I followed Zayd up the stairs. He was stout and he stopped on some of the stairs and said: 'By God, anyone who loves this world will be humiliated.'" When Zayd came to Hishām, the latter met Zayd's demands and Zayd departed for al-Kūfah.[52] Hishām forgot to ask the servant what had happened until a few days had elapsed. Then Hishām inquired and the servant told him. Hishām turned to al-Abrash,[53] who said: "By God, may the first news that reaches you be that of his removal!" That was the first news to reach Hishām, and it happened as al-Abrash had said it would.

It was reported that Zayd took an oath on some matter before
[1676] Hishām, who said to him: "I don't believe you." Zayd replied: "O Commander of the Faithful, God does not make it a prerequisite that He should be pleased with someone in order to elevate him nor does He make His displeasure a reason for bringing him low."[54] Hishām said to him: "I have heard that you are thinking of the caliphate and wanting it; but you will not obtain it, since you are the son of a slave girl." Zayd replied: "I have an answer for you, O Commander of the Faithful." Hishām said: "Speak." Zayd went on: "Nobody is closer to God nor more exalted in rank with Him than a prophet whom He has sent. Ismā'īl was amongst

49. Abū Zayd 'Umar b. Shabbah al-Numayrī (d. 264/877), historian and *muḥaddith*. Cf. Sezgin, I, 345; Rosenthal, 386.

50. 'Umar in the text. The editor later corrects it in *Introductio*, p. DCCX.

51. On the office of *ḥājib*, cf. *EI*², s.v. (D. Sourdel).

52. An important garrison town (*miṣr*) in early Islamic times. For a further discussion of al-Kūfah, cf. n. 221 and n. 233.

53. Al-Abrash Sa'īd b. al-Walīd al-Kalbī. For stories about his dealings with Hishām, cf. Ibn 'Abd Rabbihi, I, 74, 148; II, 124; al-Iṣfahānī, *Aghānī*, II, 121; X, 62; al-Jahshiyārī, 37.

54. Zayd is presumably implying that just because Hishām is caliph, God is not necessarily pleased with him. Cf. Shaykh al-Mufīd, 404; Ya'qūbī, *Historiae*, II, 67. Al-Mas'ūdī has "No one is too high or too humble to dispense with fearing God" (*Murūj*, V, 468).

the best of the prophets and was the ancestor of the best of them, Muḥammad. Ismāʿīl was the son of a slave girl and his brother was born of a pure woman, just as you were; but God chose Ismāʿīl in preference to his brother and caused the best of mankind to come forth from him and no one disputes that. A man whose ancestor was the Prophet of God should not therefore be ignored, whoever his mother was." Then Hishām said to him: "Get out." Zayd said: "I am leaving and you will not see me (again) except where you do not want to see me." Sālim[55] said to him: "O Abū Ḥusayn, this is certainly not what is expected of you."

The account now goes back to the narrative of Hishām b. Muḥammad al-Kalbī—Abū Mikhnaf: The Shīʿīs[56] began to rally behind Zayd and to put pressure on him to rebel, saying: "We hope that you will be *al-Manṣūr*[57] and that this will be the time when the Banū Umayyah will perish." Zayd stayed in al-Kūfah and Yūsuf b. ʿUmar began asking questions about him and was told that Zayd was there. Yūsuf sent a message to Zayd asking him to leave. Zayd said that he would do so, but he made the excuse that he was ill and he delayed a good while. Then Yūsuf asked about Zayd again, and he was told that he was still living in [1677]
al-Kūfah and that he had not gone away. Yūsuf sent a message to Zayd, urging him to come in person. Zayd fobbed him off with the excuse that he had things to buy and he told Yūsuf that he was preparing himself (for the journey). Zayd now realized how persistent was Yūsuf's interest in him, so he got ready and went as far as al-Qādisiyyah.[58]

Some sources say that Yūsuf sent a messenger with Zayd who took him as far as ʿUthayb.[59] The Shīʿīs joined him there and said

55. This is probably a reference to Sālim b. ʿAbd al-Raḥmān, Hishām's *kātib*, who was in charge of the *dīwān al-rasāʾil*. The Leiden index differentiates between Sālim the *kātib* and another Sālim, the mawlā of the ʿAnbasah. For a clear discussion of the names and identity of Sālim, cf. Grignasci, 12–13.

56. Cf. a similar account in Ibn Aʿtham, VIII, 110–11.

57. "The one to whom victory is given." Cf. n. 206.

58. Two towns bear this name. This is a reference to the large hamlet five leagues west of al-Kūfah, the first stage on the road to Mecca. Cf. Le Strange, *Lands*, 76, 83.

59. ʿUthayb was 6 *mīls* (12 km) from al-Qādisiyyah and was a fortified place in the desert. Cf. Ibn Rustah, 202.

to him: "Why are you leaving us, when you have 100,000 men of al-Kūfah fighting on your side tomorrow with their swords and there is only a small number of Syrians against you? Even if one of our tribes like Madhḥij or Hamdān or Tamīm or Bakr joined them, there would still be enough men for you to deal with them if God Almighty wills it so. We implore you by God to come back." They kept on urging Zayd until they brought him back to al-Kūfah.[60]

Accounts other than that of Abū Mikhnaf come from 'Ubayd b. Jannād—'Aṭā' b. Muslim: When Zayd b. 'Alī went to see Yūsuf, Yūsuf said to him: "Khālid has claimed that he has entrusted money to you." Zayd said: "How would anyone who cursed my ancestors from his pulpit entrust money to me?" Then Yūsuf sent a messenger to Khālid and the latter came to him wearing a cloak (*'abāh*). Yūsuf said: "This is Zayd. You have alleged that you deposited money with him and he has denied it." Khālid looked at both of them, and then he said (to Yūsuf): "Do you want to add to your crime against me a crime against this man? How would I entrust money to him when I curse him and his ancestors from the pulpit?" Yūsuf cursed him and sent him away.

Abū 'Ubaydah's account is as follows: Hishām believed Zayd
[1678] and the other men against whom Yūsuf had made accusations and he sent them to Yūsuf. Hishām said: "They have sworn oaths to me and I have accepted their oaths and have pronounced them innocent in regard to the money. I have sent them to you only so that you may bring them and Khālid together so that they may prove him a liar." Then Hishām gave them presents.

When they came to see Yūsuf, he received them hospitably and treated them well. He sent for Khālid, who was duly brought in. Yūsuf said to Khālid: "These people have sworn oaths and this is the letter from the Commander of the Faithful exonerating them. Do you have any proof about what you have alleged?" Khālid had no proof, and the men said to him: "What made you do what you did? Khālid said: "Yūsuf tortured me severely and I made the allegation that I made, hoping that God would give me relief before you arrived."[61] Then Yūsuf released them. The two men of

60. Cf. al-Iṣfahānī, *Maqātil,* 135.
61. Cf. *Fragmenta,* 94–95.

Quraysh, the Jumaḥī and the Makhzūmī, went to Medina and the two Hāshimīs, Dāwūd b. ʿAlī and Zayd b. ʿAlī, stayed behind in al-Kūfah.

It was reported that Zayd stayed in al-Kūfah for a period of four or five months. Yūsuf then ordered him to leave and wrote to his agent (*ʿāmil*)[62] in al-Kūfah—Yūsuf being at that time in al-Ḥīrah[63]—ordering him to harass Zayd. Zayd said that he was in litigation with some of the family of Ṭalḥah b. ʿUbaydallāh[64] about money in Medina. Yūsuf's agent wrote to him about this and Yūsuf let Zayd stay on a few days. Then the news reached Yūsuf that the Shīʿīs were rallying to Zayd. So Yūsuf wrote to his agent saying: "Send Zayd away and don't allow him to stay any longer. If he asserts that he is in litigation, then let him appoint an agent and choose a trustee to take his place in the legal pro- [1679]
ceedings." A group of people, amongst whom were Salamah b. Kuhayl, Naṣr b. Khuzaymah al-ʿAbsī, Muʿāwiyah b. Isḥāq b. Zayd b. Ḥārithah al-Anṣārī, Ḥujayyah b. al-Akhlaj al-Kindī,[65] and other Kūfan leaders, had given Zayd the oath of allegiance.

When Dāwūd b. ʿAlī discovered this, he said to Zayd: "Cousin, don't let these men make you delude yourself, for you should learn a lesson from the members of your family and the way in which these people (the Kūfans) let them down." Zayd said: "Dāwūd, the Umayyads have been inordinately proud and pitiless." Dāwūd continued speaking (to Zayd) in this way until Zayd decided to leave (al-Kūfah) and they both went as far as al-Qādisiyyah.

According to Abū ʿUbaydah: The Kūfans followed Zayd to al-Thaʿlabiyyah[66] and they said to him: "We are forty thousand. If

---

62. For this term, which was used for a variety of government officials, including the governor of a province and the director of finances in a provincial centre, cf. *EI*², s.v. (A. A. Duri).

63. Al-Ḥīrah, situated close to the Euphrates and to the southeast of present-day Najaf, was the center of Lakhmid power in the late Sasanian period. Cf. Le Strange, *Lands*, 75; *EI*², s.v. (I. Shahid).

64. One of the Companions of the Prophet. Cf. *EI*¹, s.v. (G. Levi della Vida).

65. The text has al-Akhlaj. This is emended by the editor to al-Ajlaḥ (*Introductio*, p. DCCX).

66. A town on the road from Iraq to Mecca, between Biṭāniyyah and Khuzaymiyyah. In ʿAbbāsid times it was one-third of the route from Baghdad to Mecca. Cf. Ibn Rustah, 204.

you return to al-Kūfah everyone will join you." They made covenants with him and swore inviolable oaths. Then Zayd began to remonstrate: "I am afraid that you will desert me and hand me over, as you did with my father and grandfather." So they swore further oaths to him (that they would not desert him). Then Dāwūd b. ʿAlī said: "Cousin! These men will let you down! Did they not desert someone who was dearer to them than you, your great-grandfather ʿAlī b. Abī Ṭālib, so that he was killed? Then they gave the oath of allegiance to al-Ḥasan[67]; after that they attacked him, snatched his cloak from round his neck, plundered his tent, and wounded him. Moreover, did they not force your grandfather al-Ḥusayn to rebel? They made binding oaths to him, then they deserted and abandoned him and were not satisfied until they had killed him. So don't do it and don't go back (to al-Kūfah) with them." Then the Kūfans said: "This man doesn't want you to be victorious. He is claiming that he and the members of his family are more entitled to this authority than you."
[1680] Zayd b. ʿAlī said to Dāwūd: "ʿAlī had Muʿāwiyah,[68] with his sagacity and cunning,[69] and the Syrians fighting against him and al-Ḥusayn had Yazīd b. Muʿāwiyah[70] fighting against him, and the situation went in their favor." Dāwūd said: "I am afraid that if you go back with them nobody will be more violent toward you than they will be, but you know best." Then Dāwūd went to Medina and Zayd returned to al-Kūfah.

According to ʿUbayd b. Jannād—ʿAṭā' b. Muslim al-Khaffāf: Hishām wrote to Yūsuf telling him to send Zayd to his own town, since whenever he lived in any other town and summoned his followers they responded to his call. So Yūsuf sent him away and when he had got as far as al-Thaʿlabiyyah or al-Qādisiyyah, the wretches, that is, the Kūfans, caught up with him, brought him back (to al-Kūfah), and gave the oath of allegiance to him. Salamah b. Kuhayl[71] came to him and asked permission to see him.

---

67. The Prophet's grandson. Cf. the genealogical table of the ʿAlids.
68. The first Umayyad caliph, who ruled from 41 to 60 (661–80).
69. *Bi-dahā'ihi wa-nakhrā'ihi.* The two words are synonyms. Cf. Ibn Manẓūr, *Lisān*, III, 715.
70. The second Umayyad caliph, who ruled from 60 to 64 (680–83). During his reign (in 61/680) the Prophet's grandson, al-Ḥusayn, was martyred at Karbalā'.
71. For the conversation between Salamah and Zayd, cf. also *Fragmenta*, 95–96.

This he was allowed to do. He mentioned Zayd's kinship with the Prophet of God and his rightful claim and he spoke well. Zayd replied and he too spoke well. Then Salamah said to him: "Give me permission to speak frankly." Zayd said: "God forbid that the likes of you should ask the likes of me for permission to speak." Salamah only wanted his companions to hear that. Then Zayd said: "You can go ahead." Salamah said: "I beseech you, by God! How many people have given the oath of allegiance to you?" Zayd replied: "Forty thousand." Salamah went on: "How many gave the oath of allegiance to your grandfather?" and Zayd replied "Eighty thousand." Then Salamah inquired: "How many remained with him?" and Zayd said "Three hundred." Then Salamah said: "I adjure you by God, is it you or your grandfather who is the better man?" and Zayd answered: "My grandfather." Then Salamah asked: "Who are the better men, the companions with whom you have rebelled or the companions with whom your grandfather rebelled?" Zayd replied: "The companions with [1681]
whom my grandfather rebelled." Salamah said: "Do you expect that these men will keep faith with you when those men acted treacherously with your grandfather?"

Zayd said: "They have given the oath of allegiance to me and the oath of allegiance is binding on me and them." Thereupon Salamah said: "Will you allow me to leave the town?" Zayd asked "Why?" Salamah responded: "I cannot guarantee that if anything happens to you I could control myself."[72] Zayd said: "I grant you permission (to leave)". Salamah then went to al-Yamāmah[73] and Zayd rebelled, was killed, and was put on a cross. Hishām wrote to Yūsuf blaming him for allowing Salamah b. Kuhayl to leave al-Kūfah, saying, "Salamah's staying (in al-Kūfah) would have been better for you than your having such-and-such a number of cavalry with you."

According to ʿUmar—Abū Isḥāq—a *shaykh* of the people of Iṣfahān: ʿAbdallāh b. Ḥasan wrote to Zayd b. ʿAlī as follows:

> Cousin! The Kūfans are puffed up with wind on the outside and weak inside. They are loud when circumstances are easy

---

72. *Lā amliku nafsī. Fragmenta*, 96, has *lā ahliku nafsī* ("I would not destroy myself").

73. District of Central Arabia. Cf. *EI*[1], s.v. (A. Grohmann).

and impatient when you meet them. Their tongues go ahead of them but their hearts do not accompany them. They do not spend their nights preparing for possible misfortunes nor will they bring about a hoped-for change of government. They have sent me a succession of letters inviting me, but I have remained deaf to their summons and in sheer despair and rejection of them have draped my heart with a cloth so as not to remember them. There is no way to describe them except in the words of ʿAlī b. Abī Ṭālib: "If you are left to your own devices you rush in (recklessly). If you are attacked,
[1682] you collapse. When people gather round an imām you join in (but) once you have answered the call to rebel, you (then) beat a retreat."[74]

It was related that Hishām b. ʿAbd al-Malik wrote to Yūsuf b. ʿUmar about Zayd b. ʿAlī as follows:[75]

Now to our topic. You know what love the Kūfans feel for the members of this family. You know that the Kūfans have placed them in positions where they should not be, because they have made obedience to them an obligation on themselves. They have put them in charge of the statutes of their religion and they have falsely attributed to them a knowledge of what is to come, until, thanks to the fragmented state of the community, they have brought them to a situation in which they have incited them to rebel. Zayd b. ʿAlī came to the Commander of the Faithful on the matter of the lawsuit of ʿUmar b. al-Walīd, and the Commander of the Faithful settled the matter between them. The Commander of the Faithful found Zayd argumentative, eloquent, able to embellish and mold speech, and to attract men by the sweetness of his tongue. (Zayd achieved this) by virtue of the many solu-

---

74. Cf. al-Balādhurī, *Ansāb*, 241. Parts of this are susceptible to more than one interpretation. The meaning of *ṭaʿantum* is especially difficult. However, in view of the fact that the other parts of ʿAlī's statements are in the form of sharp contrasts, *ṭaʿana* has been translated as "to join in" (Cf. Lane, I, 1855). Other possible translations would include "you defame (him)" or even "you go away." (Cf. Lane, loc. cit.).

75. Al-Balādhurī has a shorter version of this letter from Hishām to Yūsuf. Al-Balādhurī attributes the letter to Sālim (*Ansāb*, 238).

tions in arguments and the sharp, forceful (verbal) attacks he produces against his opponent to obtain victory. Send him quickly to the Ḥijāz[76] and do not let him stay with you. For if the people lend him their ears, so that he fills them, because of the softness of his speech and the sweetness of his diction as well as the appeal of his kinship with the Prophet of God, he will find the Kūfans inclined toward him, their hearts not [1683]
slow, their minds[77] far from tranquil, and their religious oaths no longer honored.

I would rather take repressive measures against Zayd which will harm him, and send him away and cast him off, thereby ensuring communal safety, the prevention of bloodshed, and security against division, than see a situation in which their (the people's) blood is shed, discord is spread amongst them, and their offspring cut down.[78] Communal unity is God's firm covenant, true obedience to Him and His most secure support.[79] So I am leaving the leaders of the Kūfans to you. Threaten them with flogging and confiscation of their wealth, and those of them who have any contract or covenant (with me) will be slow to join up with Zayd. The only people who will be swift to rally to him, delighting in strife, will be the rabble, the masses, people impelled by dire need and those who are in league with Satan and who have been enslaved by him. So threaten them publicly, lash them with your whip and unsheath your sword amongst them. Terrorize the leaders before those of middle rank and those of middle rank before the common people. Know that you stand at the door that leads to union, that you are summoning the people to obedience, that you are promoting unity and doing your utmost to maintain God's covenant. So do not flinch from their large numbers but make as your stronghold in [1684]
which you take refuge, and as your hiding place from which you emerge, your trust in your Lord, your zeal for your religion, your desire to preserve communal unity, and your

76. The northwestern part of the Arabian peninsula. Cf. *EI*², s.v. (G. Rentz).

77. *Aḥlāmuhum*. Cf. Qur'ān 52, v. 32.

78. *Qaṭ'u naslihim*. It is possible that the phrase has to do with *qaṭ'u raḥmihi* ("the severing of the ties of kinship"). Cf. Freytag, 509.

79. Cf. Qur'ān 2, v. 255.

hostility and animosity toward anyone who wants to break down this door through which God has commanded us to enter.

Indeed, the Commander of the Faithful has exonerated Zayd and has pronounced judgment, decreeing indemnity for him. Zayd's only chance of claiming a right that is his and of saying that he has been deprived of his own portion, either as permanent booty (*fay'*)[80] or as a gratuity for those related to him is, as the Commander of the Faithful fears, by causing the rabble to undertake something that would probably make them more wretched and misguided (i.e., rebellion). (The exonerating of Zayd) makes them more secure, (makes) the Commander of the Faithful stronger, and makes it easier for him to protect and preserve true religion.[81] For he does not want to see in his community a disruptive situation which could become the reason for their punishment and perdition. Therefore, he will consider long and carefully and will prepare himself to make the right decision; he will steer them away from the abodes of fear, draw them toward right paths, and turn them away from places of perdition, just as a tender father does with his child or a kind shepherd with his flock.

Know that a means to gain the upper hand over them and to render yourself worthy of assistance from God, if they do disobey, is to meet their demands in full, to give money to their children, and to forbid your army to attack their women
[1685] and their houses. So seize the chance to please God on the path on which He has placed you. There is no sin more quickly punished than injustice; the devil has ensnared these people and led them astray toward it and has guided them to it. He who sets his face against injustice approaches most closely to infallibility. The Commander of the Faithful calls on God for help against these people and against his other subjects of like mind, and he calls on his God and his Lord and his Friend to set to rights that which is corrupt in them and to bring them speedily to salvation and deliverance. Verily He is the Listener, the One near at hand.

---

80. In pre-Islamic times a term used for chattels taken as booty. For its usage in the early Islamic period, cf. *EI*², s.v. (F. Løkkegaard).

81. This passage is discussed at length in Appendix I.

The narrative returns to the account of Hishām (b. Muḥammad al-Kalbī):[82] Zayd returned to al-Kūfah and went into hiding. When he wanted to go back to al-Kūfah, Muḥammad b. ʿUmar b. ʿAlī b. Abī Ṭālib said to him: "May God grant you wisdom, O Zayd, when you rejoin your people. Do not accept the word of any of those who are inviting you to do as they suggest, for they will not keep faith with you." However, Zayd did not accept that advice from him and returned to al-Kūfah.

According to Hishām (b. Muḥammad al-Kalbī)—Abū Mikhnaf: When Zayd returned to al-Kūfah, the Shīʿīs came rallying round him and gave the oath of allegiance to him, until his register numbered fifteen thousand men. Zayd stayed in al-Kūfah some ten months, although he was in al-Baṣrah for about two months of that period and then he came to al-Kūfah where he stayed.[83] He sent men to the people of the Sawād[84] and of al-Mawṣil inviting them to join him.

When Zayd came to al-Kūfah, he married the daughter of Yaʿqūb b. ʿAbdallāh al-Sulamī, one of the Banū Farqad, and he also married the daughter of ʿAbdallāh b. Abī al-ʿAnbas al-Azdī. The reason for his marrying her was as follows:[85] her mother, Umm [1686]
ʿAmr, daughter of al-Ṣalt, was of the Shīʿī persuasion. She heard where Zayd was and she went to greet him. She was a corpulent, good-looking, fleshy woman who was already getting on in years, although she did not look her age. When she went in to see Zayd b. ʿAlī and greeted him, he thought that she was a young woman. She chatted to him and she was the most eloquent of people and most beautiful in appearance. Zayd asked her about her lineage and she told him about it and she informed him who her family were. Zayd then said to her: "May God's mercy be upon you, how would you like to marry me?" She said to him: "By God, may He have mercy on you, you are the one I would like to marry, if I were in a position to do so." Zayd rejoined: "What prevents you from doing so?" She said: "What prevents me from doing so is that I am too old." Zayd said to her: "Not at all! I am satisfied.

---

82. Cf. p. 13.

83. Al-Balādhurī's account is clearer: "He stayed in al-Kūfah about ten months and went to al-Baṣrah and stayed there for two months" (*Ansāb*, 237). Cf. also al-Iṣfahānī, *Maqātil*, 135.

84. The alluvial plain of southern Iraq. Cf. Le Strange, *Lands*, 24.

85. This anecdote is also given by Ibn Aʿtham, VIII, 112.

You are far from being too old."[86] She said: "May God have mercy on you! I know myself better than you do and I know better what time has done for me. If I were to marry one day, I would not prefer anyone else to you. But I do have a daughter, whose father was my paternal cousin and who is more beautiful than I am. I will give her to you in marriage, if you like." He said to her: "I will be satisfied if she is like you." She said: "Her Creator and Maker was not content to make her like me, so He made her whiter, more good-looking, more corpulent, and finer than me in coquettishness and form." Zayd laughed and said to her: "You have been blessed with your full share of eloquence and fine speaking. How does her eloquence compare with yours?" She said: "I am not sure about that, because I grew up in the Ḥijāz and
[1687] my daughter grew up in al-Kūfah, so I don't know. Perhaps my daughter speaks as the Kūfans do." Zayd said: "I don't object to that." Then he arranged a meeting with her, came to her, and contracted a marriage with her. Then he went in to her. She bore him a daughter, after which she died. As for Zayd, he was madly in love with her.

Zayd b. ʿAlī lived in various houses in al-Kūfah:[87] in his wife's house with the Azd on one occasion, with his Sulamī sons-in-law on another occasion, once with Naṣr b. Khuzaymah from the Banū ʿAbs, and once with the Banū Ghubar. Then he moved from the Banū Ghubar to the house of Muʿāwiyah b. Isḥāq b. Ḥārithah al-Anṣārī at the far end of the Jabbānah of Sālim al-Salūlī.[88] He also lived with the Banū Nahd[89] and the Banū Taghlib near the mosque of the Banū Hilāl b. ʿĀmir. He remained there, receiving the oath of allegiance from his followers. The oath of allegiance

86. An alternative translation might be: "I would be satisfied, as long as (*mā*) I could keep you (*ubʿiduki*) from growing old."

87. For the subsequent accounts of Zayd's revolt in al-Kūfah, the researches of Massignon and Djaït are invaluable in clarifying the topography and tribal organization of the town.

88. There were a number of *jabbānāt* at al-Kūfah. Massignon translates *jabbānah* as "tribal cemetery," but states that such open spaces were used for public ceremonies and for mobilizing troops ("Explication," 347–48). Djaït plausibly suggests that the *jabbānah* was not a cemetery but a space used for public prayer on special occasions and also for mobilizing the tribesmen (*Yamanites*, 176–77). The Jabbānah Sālim al-Salūlī mentioned here belonged to the Banū ʿĀmir of Qays (cf. Massignon, loc. cit.).

89. Ibn al-Athīr has the *Banū Hind* (*Kāmil*, V, 177).

which he made with the people was as follows:[90] "We summon you to the Book of God and the *sunnah*[91] of His Prophet, and to wage war against those who act tyrannically, to defend those who have been oppressed,[92] to give pensions to those who have been deprived of them, to distribute this booty (*fay'*) equally amongst those who are entitled to it, to make restitution to those who have been wronged, to bring home those who have been detained on the frontiers, and to help the *ahl al-bayt*[93] against those who have opposed us and disregard our just cause. Do you swear allegiance on that basis?" If they said "Yes," Zayd would place his hand on theirs[94] and he would say: "The pledge, treaty, and covenant of God and the covenant of His Prophet are upon you so that you keep your allegiance to me, fight my enemy, and act in good faith toward me both secretly and publicly." If they said "Yes," Zayd would rub his hand on their hands[95] and would say: "May [1688]
God be our witness." The situation remained like this for some ten months. When the time for his uprising drew near, he ordered his followers to make their preparations. Those who wanted to keep faith and rebel with him began to get ready and his activities became widely known amongst the people.

In this year Naṣr b. Sayyār[96] raided Transoxiana twice, then he raided it a third time[97] and killed Kūrṣūl.[98]

---

90. Versions of this oath are given by Ibn Aʿtham (VIII, 113) and al-Balādhurī (*Ansāb*, 237–38).

91. Muḥammad's *sunnah* comprises his deeds, sayings, and unspoken approval. Cf. *EI*[1], s.v. (A. J. Wensinck).

92. Cf. Qur'ān 28, vv. 4–5.

93. The family of the Prophet.

94. Literally, "on his hand."

95. Again the plural has been used here for consistency.

96. The last Umayyad governor of Khurāsān, appointed by Hishām in 120 (738).

97. It is likely that these three campaigns were spread out over a number of years (121–23/739–41); cf. Gabrieli, *Califfato*, 66.

98. For the career of Kūrṣūl, a Türgesh leader, cf. Gibb, 85, 91. Gibb believes that al-Ṭabarī's narrative here, which attributes the capture of Kurṣūl to Naṣr b. Sayyār, is later Muslim glorification of Arab achievements. He adds that if Kūrṣūl is to be identified with Bagha Ṭarkhān, he was executed by the Chinese in 126 (744). Gabrieli accepts al-Ṭabarī's account (*Califfato*, 66 ff.).

The Raids of Naṣr b. Sayyār[99]

According to ʿAlī (b. Muḥammad al-Madāʾinī)—his *shaykhs*: Naṣr raided Transoxiana from Balkh[100] in the region of the Gate of Iron,[101] then he returned to Marw[102] and delivered the following sermon (*khuṭbah*):

> Verily, Bahrāmsīs[103] was the protector of the Magians (*majūs*); he favored them, protected them and put their burdens[104] on the Muslims. Verily, Ashbdād son of Gregory was the protector of the Christians, just as Aqiva the Jew protected the Jews. But I am the protector of the Muslims. I will defend them and shield them and make the polytheists carry their burdens. Nothing less than the full amount of the *kharāj*[105] as written and recorded will be accepted by me. I have placed Manṣūr b. ʿUmar b. Abī al-Kharqā as agent (*ʿāmil*) over you and I have ordered him to act justly toward you. If there is a man amongst you who is a Muslim and from whom *jizyah* has been levied, or who has been charged an excessive amount of *kharāj*, thus lightening the burden for the poly-
> [1689] theists, then let him raise that with Manṣūr b. ʿUmar so that he may take the burden away from the Muslim and impose it on the polytheist.

By the following Friday, Manṣūr had dealt with thirty thousand Muslims who had been paying the *jizyah* and eighty thousand

99. For the activities of Naṣr b. Sayyār in Central Asia, cf. Gibb, 88–99; van Vloten, 71–72; Wellhausen, 473–86; Gabrieli, *Califfato*, 27–70.

100. A city now in Afghanistan. According to al-Yaʿqūbī, Balkh was the greatest city of Khurāsān (*Buldān*, trans. by G. Wiet, 100). Cf. Le Strange, *Lands*, 420–22.

101. *Bāb al-Ḥadīd*, the famous "Iron Gate," two marches to the north of Hāshimjird. This defile in the mountains was the thoroughfare between Samarqand and India. Cf. Le Strange, *Lands*, 441–42.

102. Marw al-Shāhijān, the important city of medieval Khurāsān. The epithet al-Shāhijān was used to distinguish it from Marw al-Rūd. Cf. Le Strange, *Lands*, 397–403; *EI*², s.v. (A. Yakubovski-C. E. Bosworth).

103. Bahrāmsīs had been appointed Marzubān of Marw by Muslim b. Saʿīd al-Kilābī in 105 (723–24). It was Muslim's policy to appoint officials acceptable to the Persians. Cf. al-Ṭabarī, II, 1462.

104. I.e. taxation.

105. It is difficult to define exactly the use of such terms as *kharāj* and *jizyah* in this period and area. Cf. Van Vloten, 72; *EI*², "Kharādj" (Cl. Cahen).

polytheists[106] who had been exempted from the *jizyah*. He imposed the *jizyah* on the polytheists and removed it from the Muslims. Then he readjusted the *kharāj*, allocating it properly, and reassessed the amount (of tribute) payable in accordance with the peace treaty (*ṣulḥ*). In the time of the Umayyads, the revenues of Marw amounted to one hundred thousand dirhams, not including the *kharāj*.[107]

Naṣr b. Sayyār made a second raid to Waraghsar[108] and Samarqand[109] and returned to Marw. He then went out on a raid from Marw a third time, to al-Shāsh,[110] but Kūrṣūl, accompanied by fifteen thousand men, prevented him from fording the river, which was the river at al-Shāsh. Kūrṣūl was paying each of his men per month one piece of silk, which at that time was worth twenty-five dirhams. The two armies remained a bowshot apart and Kūrṣūl prevented Naṣr from crossing to al-Shāsh. Al-Ḥārith b. Surayj was at that time in Turkish territory and he had come with the Turks[111] and was positioned opposite Naṣr. He shot a short arrow at Naṣr who was sitting on his litter (*sarīr*)[112] on the river bank. The arrow hit a servant of Naṣr's in the side of the mouth while he was performing Naṣr's ablutions. Naṣr got down from his litter and shot an arrow at a horse belonging to one of the Syrians and it fell dead.

---

106. Literally, "Thirty thousand Muslims who had been paying the *jizyah* and eighty thousand polytheists who had been exempted from the *jizyah* came to him."

107. For a clear summary of the preceding fiscal situation in Khurāsān and of this celebrated tax reform introduced by Naṣr b. Sayyār, cf. Hawting, 106. Cf. also Wellhausen, 477–82; Gabrieli, *Califfato*, 68. Here Naṣr established that all cultivators of taxable land, whatever their religious affiliation, would be liable to pay land tax (*kharāj*) and that non-Muslims only would pay poll tax (*jizyah*).

108. A large village between Banjīkath and Samarqand. Cf. Le Strange, *Lands*, 465, 467.

109. For this important Central Asian city, cf. *EI*¹, s.v. (H. H. Schaeder).

110. Nowadays Tashkent. The medieval city of al-Shāsh lay to the west of Farghānah, on the right bank of the Jaxartes. It was the greatest of the Arab towns beyond the Jaxartes. Cf. Le Strange, *Lands*, 480–82.

111. In 116 (734) al-Ḥārith b. Surayj from the Banū Tamīm had led a revolt of Arabs and Soghdian mawlās against the Umayyads and in support of the rights of the mawlās (non-Arab Muslims). Al-Ḥārith was willing to collaborate with the Türgesh with whom he eventually took refuge. Cf. Gibb, 76–85; Hawting, 86–88, 107–09; Shaban, *'Abbāsid revolution*, 118–22; *EI*², s.v. (M. J. Kister).

112. For the meanings of *sarīr*, cf. Sadan, 32–41.

[1690] Then Kūrṣūl crossed with forty men and made a night raid on Naṣr's camp, driving away some sheep which belonged to the people of Bukhārā. (This was possible because) the Bukhārans were at the rear and it was a dark night when Kūrṣūl went round the camp. Naṣr had with him men from Bukhārā, Samarqand, Kish,[113] and Ushrūsanah[114] and they numbered twenty thousand. Naṣr made the following proclamation to his tribal units:[115] "Let nobody leave his tent; hold firm to your positions."

ʿĀsim b. ʿUmayr, who was in charge of the *jund*[116] of the people of Samarqand, was outside (the camp) when the army of Kūrṣūl passed. The Turks had shouted (as they went) and the people in the camp thought that the Turks had all crossed (the river).[117] Then still more of Kūrṣūl's troops passed by, and ʿĀsim attacked the last of these. He captured a man who was one of their kings and the lord of four thousand tents (*qubbah*), and they took him to Naṣr. He was an old man who had a lifetime of fighting[118] behind him. He was wearing brocade gaiters with rings of metal in them and a silk *qabāʾ* hemmed with brocade. Naṣr asked him who he was and he told Naṣr that he was Kūrṣūl. Naṣr said to him: "Praise be to God who has enabled us to get hold of you, you enemy of God!" Kūrṣūl said: "What do you hope for by killing an old man? I will give you one thousand Turkish camels[119] and one thousand draft horses[120] with which to strengthen your army. So let me go." Naṣr asked the Syrians and the Khurāsānīs around him for their opinion and they said that he should let Kūrṣūl go. Then Naṣr asked Kūrṣūl: "How old are you?" He said: "I do not know." Naṣr said: "How many raids have you made?" and Kūrṣūl answered, "Seventy-two." Naṣr said: "Were you present at the

113. *Kiss* in the text. This should be identified as Kish (or Kishsh), which was later called Shahr-i Sabz and lies to the south of Samarqand. Cf. Le Strange, *Lands*, 469.

114. The province of Ushrūsanah lay to the east of Samarqand. There was a city of the same name. Cf. Le Strange, *Lands*, 474–76.

115. *Akhmās*, plural of *khums* ("fifths"). From 50 (670), Arab tribal settlements were divided into quarters or fifths. Cf. Crone, 31.

116. A regular regiment of soldiers under a *qāʾid*. Cf. Crone, 38.

117. The sequence of events in this passage is rather obscure.

118. Literally, "who had trailed his coat of mail for a (life-) span."

119. Ibn al-Athīr (V, 177) has four thousand camels.

120. *Birdhawn:* the heavy Persian warhorse.

Day of Thirst (*Yawm al-ʿAtash*)?"[121] and Kūrṣūl said: "Yes." [1691]
Naṣr said: "Even if you were to give me everything on which the sun rises, you would not escape me now that you have said that you were present at that battle." Naṣr said to ʿĀsim b. ʿUmayr al-Sughdī: "Get up, disarm and seize him." When Kūrṣūl realized that he was going to be killed, he said: "Who was it who took me prisoner?" Naṣr said laughing: "Yazīd b. Qurran al-Ḥanẓalī"[122] and he pointed to him. Kūrṣūl said: "He can't wash his backside properly"—or, according to another report, he said: "He cannot stop his urine,"[123]—"so how could he have taken me prisoner? Tell me who it really was who captured me, for I am worth killing seven times." He was then told that it was ʿĀsim b. ʿUmayr. Kūrṣūl said: "I will not feel the pain of death if the person who took me prisoner is a (true) Bedouin horseman." Then Naṣr killed him and crucified him upon the river bank. (The narrator said): ʿĀsim b. Umayr, who had the sobriquet al-Hazārmard,[124] was killed at Nihāwand[125] in the lifetime of Qaḥṭabah.[126]

When Kūrṣūl was killed, the Turks were in disarray.[127] They went to his quarters and burnt them. They cut their ears and tore the skin on their faces[128] and began weeping over him. When evening came and Naṣr wanted to leave he sent someone to Kūrṣūl with a bottle of naphtha (*nafṭ*), which he poured over him. He then set fire to the body lest people should take away his bones.

---

121. The defeat of Muslim b. Saʿīd al-Kilābī and the Arab troops in 106 (724) by the Türgesh and rebel Soghdians was called "The Day of Thirst." It was a major military disaster for the Arabs. Cf. Gibb, 64–67; Shaban, *ʿAbbāsid Revolution,* 106–07; al-Ṭabarī, II, 1480.

122. Cf. al-Ṭabarī, II, 1569.

123. These expressions denote contempt at a man's lack of manly qualities in war. Cf. *Gloss.*, p. CXLIV.

124. The word denotes either "having one thousand men under him" or "as strong as one thousand men." A number of other warriors were given this epithet. Cf. F. Justi, *Iranisches Namenbuch,* 128.

125. Nihāwand was a city some forty miles south of Hamadān. Cf. Le Strange, *Lands,* 196–97.

126. Qaḥṭabah b. Shabīb al-Ṭāʾī was appointed by the imām Ibrāhīm as military commander of the Hāshimiyyah. Qaḥṭabah and his son defeated the Umayyad forces at Nihāwand in Dhū al-Qaʿdah 131 (June 22–July 22, 749). Cf. Wellhausen, 540; al-Ṭabarī, III, 7–8.

127. *Takhaddarū:* cf. *Gloss.*, p. CCXIV.

128. *Wa-jarradū wujūhahum.* Nöldeke prefers a variant in the apparatus: *wa-khadadū wujūhahum.* Cf. *Gloss.*, p. CCXIV.

(The narrator commented): This action upset the people more than Kūrṣūl's killing. Then Naṣr went up to Farghānah[129] and took from there thirty thousand captives.

According to 'Anbar b. Bur'umah al-Azdī: Yūsuf b. 'Umar wrote
[1692] to Naṣr as follows: "Go to the man who has fixed himself in al-Shāsh,"[130] meaning al-Ḥārith b. Surayj. "If God gives you victory over him and the people of al-Shāsh, lay waste their country and take their children captive, but take care not to get into a situation from which the Muslims cannot extricate themselves."[131] Naṣr called the people, read the letter to them and asked them their opinion. Yaḥyā b. Ḥuḍayn said: "Fulfill the decree of the Commander of the Faithful and the order of the *amīr* (i.e., Yūsuf)." Naṣr said: "Yaḥyā, in the time of 'Āsim you said something[132] which reached the caliph and you obtained favor by that. He increased your salary, he gave stipends to the members of your family, and you achieved high rank. So you said to yourself: 'Why don't I say the same thing now?' Off you go, Yaḥyā. I have appointed you as my advance party." The people went up to Yaḥyā and reproached him. Naṣr then said: "What disaster[133] could be worse than that we should have to travel while they (the enemy) can stay where they are?" Then he went to al-Shāsh and al-Ḥārith b. Surayj came to him and set up two *'arrādah*s[134] against the Banū Tamīm. When he was told that they were the Banū Tamīm,[135] he moved the *'arrādah*s and set them up against the Azd.—Another report said that it was against Bakr b. Wā'il.

---

129. The city of Farghānah, otherwise known as Akhsīkath, lay on the north bank of the Jaxartes. There was a province of the same name. Cf. Le Strange, *Lands*, 477, and map opposite p. 433.

130. *Sir ilā hādhā al-ghāriz dhanabahu bi-al Shāsh* (lit., "go to that one who sticks his tail in al-Shāsh"). Cf. the example *aqāma bi-arḍinā wa-gharaza dhanabahu* ("he stayed in our land and remained fixed"). Cf. Lane, I, 980.

131. *Warṭat al-Muslimīn. Warṭah* means literally slime or thin mud into which sheep or goats fall and from which they cannot extricate themselves. Cf. Lane, I, 2938.

132. In 106 (724) Yaḥyā b. Ḥuḍayn al-Bakrī had advised 'Āṣim to stand firm against al-Ḥārith b. Surayj. Wellhausen describes him as "the most esteemed leader of the Bakr." Cf. Wellhausen, 467, 487.

133. Again the word used is *warṭah*. Naṣr is being sarcastic about the warning Yūsuf b. 'Umar has given him in his letter.

134. For a definition of *'arrādah* and *manjanīq*, both medieval artillery machines, cf. *EI²*, "'Arrādah" (C. Cahen).

135. I.e., al-Ḥārith's own people.

Al-Akhram, who was a Turkish horseman,[136] made a raid on them and the Muslims killed him, taking prisoner seven of his companions. Naṣr b. Sayyār ordered that al-Akhram's head should be shot amongst the enemy troops with a *manjanīq*. When they saw the head, they made a great din and fled in disarray. Naṣr went back and wanted to cross the river but he was prevented from doing so. Abū Numaylah Ṣāliḥ b. ʿAbbār said:

When Naṣr returned after his absence, we felt [1693]
like someone who watches a storm until the rain sheets down on him.
When it stopped, there abated with it a cold drenching climax[137]
which threatened the destiny of the people.

Naṣr went and attacked Samarqand in the year in which he fought al-Ḥārith b. Surayj. Then the Bukhār Khudāh[138] fled to his protection. The Muslims had the garrison[139] in their possession, and with them were two of the *dihqāns*[140] of Bukhārā, who had accepted Islam from the hand of Naṣr.[141] These men had resolved to kill both Wāṣil b. ʿAmr al-Qaysī,[142] who was the agent (*ʿāmil*) of Bukhārā, and the Bukhār Khudāh. They accused the Bukhār Khudāh, whose name was Ṭughshādah,[143] of injustice.[144] The

---

136. For a discussion of al-Akhram, cf. Gibb, p. 91.

137. *Awdā bi-ākhira minhu ʿāriḍun baridun.* Nöldeke prefers the reading *bi-Akhrama;* cf. *Add.*, p. DCCX. The Cairo edition of al-Ṭabarī (VII, 176) follows Nöldeke.

138. This episode, with similar details, is given by Narshakhī, 60–62. The Bukhār Khudāh was the local ruler of Bukhārā (ibid.).

139. *Wa-kānat al-maslaḥah ʿalayhim wa-maʿahum dihqānān.* The translation is only tentative. The meaning of *maslaḥah* is obscure in this context. Cf. *Gloss.*, p. CCXCV. As well as an arms depot, the word can denote the task of protecting the roads. Another possibility is the translation "they were armed." If the word is translated as "garrison," it is still not clear whether the use of the third person masculine plural suffix refers to the Muslims or to the Bukhār Khudāh and his followers.

140. *Dihqān:* a local Persian landlord. Cf. Morony, 529.

141. *Wa-kānā aslamā ʿalā yaday Naṣr,* rendered by Frye in his translation of the similar passage in Narshakhī as "Both had accepted Islam from Naṣr." Cf. Narshakhī, 61.

142. Cf. al-Ṭabarī, II, 1528.

143. The text has *Ṭūq Siyādah.* This is corrected by the editor on the basis of his reading of Narshakhī to Ṭūq Shādah. Cf. *Add.*, DCCX. A more likely reading is *Tughshādah,* as given by Gibb, 91.

144. He had seized their villages. Cf. Narshakhī, 61.

Bukhār Khudāh said to Naṣr: "May God bless the *amīr*. I have heard that the two of them have become Muslims in your presence, so why do they have daggers hanging on them?" So Naṣr said to the two *dihqāns*: "Why do you have daggers on you when you have become Muslims?" They said: "There is enmity between us and the Bukhār Khudāh, and we do not trust his intentions toward us." Naṣr gave orders to Hārūn b. al-Siyāwush, the mawlā[145] of the Banū Sulaym, who was in charge of the garrison,[146] and he seized the two men forcibly and removed their daggers.[147] The Bukhār Khudāh went up to Naṣr and spoke secretly to him about the two men. Then the two of them said: "We will die nobly." One of them attacked Wāṣil b. ʿAmr and stabbed him in the belly with a knife. Wāṣil struck him on the head with his sword, cleaving his skull, and killed him. The other (*dihqān*)
[1694] went in search of the Bukhār Khudāh. Prayer commenced[148] and the Bukhār Khudāh remained seated on a chair.[149] Naṣr stood up, went into the tent, and summoned the Bukhār Khudāh. He tripped at the door of the tent and the *dihqān* stabbed him. Al-Jūzjān b. al-Jūzjān[150] attacked the *dihqān*, striking him with an iron rod he had with him, and killed him. The Bukhār Khudāh was picked up and taken into Naṣr's tent. Naṣr ordered a cushion for him and he leaned back against it. Qarʿah,[151] the physician, came to him and began treating him. The Bukhār Khudāh made his will before Naṣr and then died soon afterward. Wāṣil was buried in the tent and Naṣr prayed over him. As for Ṭughshādah,

145. Mawlā: a client or protégé. Cf. Morony, 532.

146. *Al-rābiṭah* is given as a synonym for *al-maslaḥah*. Cf. *Gloss.*, p. CCLVI.

147. *Qaṭaʿahumā:* "he disarmed them." The words *their daggers* have been added, since in the following lines it is clear that the two *dihqāns* had other weapons on them.

148. Literally, "the *iqāmah* was performed." For the *iqāmah*, cf. I. K. A. Howard, "The Development of the *Adhān* and *Iqāma* of the *Ṣalāt* in Early Islam," 219–28.

149. Narshakhī adds, "He did not pray, for he was still an unbeliever in secret." Cf. Narshakhī, 61. For *kursī*, cf. Sadan, 123–37. Probably it was a stool, being more portable.

150. A *dihqān* who is mentioned in 116 (734) in the company of al-Ḥārith b. Surayj. Cf. al-Ṭabarī, II, 1569.

151. The vocalization of this name is uncertain. This same doctor in 118 (736) cut out the tongue of Khidāsh and put out his eye. Cf. al-Ṭabarī, II, 1589.

they removed the flesh from him and took his bones to Bukhārā.[152]

Naṣr made for al-Shāsh and when he came to Ushrūsanah, its *dihqān*, Abārākharrah,[153] gave him money. Then Naṣr went on to al-Shāsh. He made Muḥammad b. Khālid al-Azdī agent[154] (*ʿāmil*) of Farghānah and despatched him there with ten people. Muḥammad sent back from Farghānah Jaysh's[155] brother and those *dihqāns* who were with him, both from al-Khuttal[156] and from other areas. He took away many idols from there and put them in Ushrūsanah.

Some sources said that when Naṣr came to al-Shāsh, the ruler, Qadïr,[157] received him, offering peace terms, a gift, and a pledge. Naṣr imposed on him the condition that he should expel al-Ḥārith b. Surayj from his town. He therefore sent him away to Fārāb.[158] Then Naṣr appointed as the agent (*ʿāmil*) of al-Shāsh [1695]
Nīzak b. Ṣāliḥ, the mawlā of ʿAmr b. al-ʿĀṣ. Naṣr moved on and came down to Qubā,[159] which is in the region of Farghānah. The people there had heard that Naṣr was coming, so they burned the grass and stored away the provisions.

In the remaining part of the year 121, Naṣr sent people to the *walī ʿahd* of the ruler of Farghānah[160] and they besieged him in one of its citadels. The Muslims were caught unprepared by the people in the citadel, who seized and drove away their horses and

---

152. For a bibliography on Zoroastrian burial customs, cf. Frye's n. 223 in his translation of Narshakhī, 141.

153. *Abārākharahh* in the text is corrected by the editor to Abārākharrah. Cf. *Add.*, p. DCCX.

154. Al-Ṭabarī mentions this name here only.

155. Cf. al-Ṭabarī, II, 1593, 1618, where the form given is al-Jaysh.

156. The mountainous tract on the upper course of the Oxus, between the rivers Panj and Wakhshāb. The term was also vaguely applied to all lands of the infidel to the east and north of Khurāsān. Cf. *EI*[2], s.v. (C. E. Bosworth); Marquart, *Ērānšahr*, 299–303; Le Strange, *Lands*, 437–39.

157. Q.d.r.: the form of this name is unclear. In the apparatus it is suggested that the person may be B.d.r Ṭurkhān (cf. al-Ṭabarī, II, 1629). The editor later suggests another form, Tudun. Cf. *Add.*, p. DCCX.

158. Fārāb: the city on the east bank of the Jaxartes, later known as Utrār. This city should not be confused with Fāryāb in Khurāsān. Cf. Le Strange, *Lands*, 484–85.

159. A city in the province of Farghānah. Cf. Yāqūt, IV, 24–25; Ibn Ḥawqal, 490.

160. *Walī ʿahd:* the appointed heir and successor. Ibn al-Athīr has *walī ṣāḥib Farghānah* (V, 179).

took a number of them captive. Then Naṣr sent them reinforcements from the Banū Tamīm[161] accompanied by Muḥammad b. al-Muthannā,[162] who was a cavalryman. The Muslims laid a trap for the people in the citadel by abandoning their horses and lying in wait for them. The people in the citadel duly came out and took some of the horses. Then the Muslims emerged against them, put them to flight, killed the *dihqān*, and took some of the enemy prisoner. [163] The son of the slain *dihqān*, who was a beardless youth, attacked Ibn al-Muthannā. Muḥammad b. al-Muthannā tricked him and took him prisoner. He brought him to Naṣr, who beheaded him.

Naṣr sent Sulaymān b. Ṣūl[164] to the lord of Farghānah with the peace treaty between them (the Muslims and the people of Farghānah). Sulaymān gave the following account: I went in to the lord of Farghānah and he asked me who I was. I said: "I am a hired servant (*shākir*) and the *amīr*'s deputy scribe." He said (to his servants): "Take him into the storehouse, so that he can see what preparations we have made and tell him to stand up." I said: "I cannot walk (there)." He replied: "Give him a beast to ride." So I went into his storehouses and I said to myself: "Sulaymān, may Isrā'īl and Bishr b. 'Ubaydah rejoice at your misfortune! All this can only mean that he does not want peace and I will go away empty-handed."[165] I went back to the lord of Farghānah and he
[1696] said: "How did you find the road between us and you?" I said: "Easy, with plentiful water and pasturage." He was not pleased with what I told him, so he said: "How do you know?" I said: "I have gone on raids into Gharshistān,[166] Ghūr,[167] al-Khuttal, and

161. Cf. Ibn al-Kalbī, I, tables 59–84; and II, 7–10.

162. Muḥammad b. al-Muthannā al-Azdī. Cf. al-Ṭabarī, II, 1761–62.

163. The narrative only sometimes mentions explicitly who is performing what action here. To clarify the passage the phrase "the people in the citadel" has been adopted for one group of the protagonists.

164. This may be the son of a Turkish leader, Ṣūl, who was active against Yazīd b. Muhallab in 98 (716–17). Cf. Wellhausen, 446–47.

165. *Bi-khuffay Ḥunayn*. Cf. Freytag, *Proverba*, I, 539.

166. Gharshistān (or Gharistān) or more usually Gharjistān is the mountainous region to the east of Bādghīs, at the headwaters of the Murghāb river. Cf. Le Strange, *Lands*, 415.

167. The mountainous area to the east and south of Gharjistān was called Ghūr (or Ghūristān); it stretched from Herat to Bāmiyān and the borders of Kābul and Ghaznah. Cf. Le Strange, *Lands*, 416; *EI*², s.v. (A. D. H. Bivar); *Ḥudūd*, 342–44.

Ṭabaristān,[168] so how can I not know?" He said: "What did you think of the preparations we have made?" I said: "I saw good supplies, but did you not know that even the lord of a citadel[169] is not proof against all perils?"[170] He said: "What are they?" I said: "He is not free from the fear that those closest to him, most liked by him and most trusted by him might attack him, coveting his position, and advance themselves thereby. Then (there is the fear) that what he has hoarded will melt away and that he will be utterly ruined. Or an illness could afflict him and he might die." He scowled and did not like what I had said to him. He told me to go to my house, so I went off and stayed for two days, not doubting that he would reject the idea of peace. Then he summoned me. I gave the peace treaty to my slave and I said to him: "If a messenger comes from me to you asking for the treaty, go to the house and do not show the treaty, and say[171] that I have left the treaty in the house."[172] I went in to see the lord of Farghānah and he asked me about the letter, so I said: "I have left it behind in the house." He said: "Send someone to bring it to you." Then he accepted the (offer of) peace and gave me a fine reward. He sent his mother with me and she was in charge of his affairs. When I went in to see Naṣr, he looked at me and said: "The saying of an ancient is most appropriate for you:

> Send a wise man and you will not need to give him any orders."

I told Naṣr what had happened and he said: "You did well." Then he gave permission for the mother of the ruler of Farghānah to come in. She came in to him and he began talking to her, with the interpreter explaining what she was saying. Then Tamīm b.

---

168. The well-known province to the south of the Caspian Sea. Cf. Le Strange, *Lands*, 368–76.

169. Ibn al-Athīr has al-Maḥṣūr "the one under siege" (V, 179).

170. *Khiṣāl:* literally, "good or bad qualities." Cf. Lane, I, 751.

171. The variant *qul* in the apparatus has been preferred here since it makes better sense than *qul lī* in the text.

172. This seems a rather obscure narrative. Presumably, if the text is not faulty, which it may well be, Sulaymān's elaborate *démarche* was aimed at giving an impression of surprise if the *amīr* of Farghānah should decide after all to sign the treaty.

[1697] Naṣr[173] came in and said[174] to the interpreter: "Ask her: 'Do you know who this is?'" She said: "No." He said: "This is Tamīm b. Naṣr." She said: "By God, I see in him neither the sweetness of youth nor the nobility of age."

According to Abū Isḥāq b. Rabī'ah:[175] She said to Naṣr: "Every king is not a king unless he possesses six things: a vizier to whom he may divulge his secret intentions and from whom he may seek advice and receive trustworthy counsel in every contentious issue within his bosom that he wishes to discuss; a cook who, whenever the king does not fancy food, will bring him what he does like; a wife who, whenever he goes in with troubled mind to see her and he looks at her face, causes his trouble to disappear;[176] a fortress to which he betakes himself when he is afraid or in trouble and it rescues him [she meant his horse]; a sword which will not fail him when he fights the enemy; and a storehouse sufficient to live off no matter where in the world he takes it."

Then Tamīm b. Naṣr came in with a large group of people.[177] She said: "Who is this?" They said: "This is the hero of Khurāsān. This is Tamīm b. Naṣr." She said: "He has neither the nobility of old men nor the sweetness of young ones." Then al-Ḥajjāj b. Qutaybah came in and she said: "Who is this?" They said: "Al-Ḥajjāj b. Qutaybah." She greeted him and asked about him. Then she said: "You Arabs, you don't keep faith nor do you behave properly with one another. It was Qutaybah[178] who laid the foun-

---

173. Tamīm b. Naṣr was killed in 130 (748) fighting the Hāshimiyyah near Ṭūs. Cf. al-Ṭabarī, II, 2016.

174. It is not clear whether Tamīm or Naṣr asks the woman this question.

175. Cf. al-Ṭabarī, II, 1456.

176. Literally, "his trouble disappears."

177. The text has *fī mirfalatin wa jamā'atin*. For *mirfalah*, a long flowing garment, cf. *Gloss.*, p. CCLXVII. Lane (I, 1128) suggests that the term denotes a conceited gait. If this reading is accepted, a possible translation would be: "with conceited gait and a group of people." The Cairo edition (VII, 187) interprets the variant in the apparatus as *azfalah* ("a group or collection of people"), which makes good sense here.

178. Qutaybah b. Muslim al-Bāhilī became governor of Khurāsān in 85 (704). He was killed when he tried to rebel at the time of Sulaymān's succession in 96 (714–15). During his governorship he undertook many campaigns beyond Khurāsān. Cf. Wellhausen, 429–44; Gibb, 31–57. Qutaybah laid the foundations on which Islamic rule in Central Asia was built. Although many of his family held high office later, al-Ḥajjāj apparently did not. Cf. Crone, 137–38.

dations of your power,[179] as I myself saw. This is his son and yet you make him sit down below you. It is your duty to raise him to this position (*majlis*) and you should sit where he is."

In this year Muḥammad b. Hishām b. Ismā'īl al-Makhzūmī[180] led the pilgrimage. This report came from Abū Ma'shar[181]—Aḥmad b. Thābit[182]—his informants—Isḥāq b. 'Īsā—his father. Al-Wāqidī and others also gave the same report. [1698]

The governor (*'āmil*) of Hishām b. 'Abd al-Malik in charge of Medina, Mecca, and al-Ṭā'if in this year was Muḥammad b. Hishām. Hishām's *'āmil* over the whole of Iraq was Yūsuf b. 'Umar, his *'āmil* in Āzarbāyjān and Armenia was Marwān b. Muḥammad, and his *'āmil* in Khurāsān was Naṣr b. Sayyār. In the post of *qāḍī* in al-Baṣrah was 'Āmir b. 'Ubaydah[183] and the *qāḍī* of al-Kūfah was Ibn Shubrumah.[184]

---

179. *Waṭṭana lakum.*
180. Hishām's *'āmil* in Medina.
181. Abū Ma'shar Nājiḥ b. 'Abd al-Raḥmān al-Sindī al-Madanī (d. 170/786–87) was a younger contemporary of Ibn Isḥāq. Cf. Sezgin, I, 291–91; *EI²*, s.v. (J. Horovitz-F. Rosenthal); Brockelmann, I, 207; Ibn Ḥajar, *Tahdhīb*, X, 419–22.
182. Aḥmad b. Thābit b. 'Attāb al-Rāzī. Cf. Sezgin, I, 292, 796.
183. 'Āmir b. 'Ubaydah al-Bāhilī. Cf. Ibn Khayyāṭ, 378.
184. 'Abdallāh b. Shubrumah al-Ḍabbī. Cf. ibid.

The Events of the Year

122

(December 7, 739–November 25, 740)

The Killing of Zayd b. ʿAlī

According to Hishām (b. Muḥammad al-Kalbī)—Abū Mikhnaf: When Zayd b. ʿAlī commanded his followers to get ready to rebel and to make preparations, those who wanted to adhere to their pledge of allegiance to him began what he had ordered them to do in that eventuality. Sulaymān b. Surāqah al-Bāriqī[185] went to Yūsuf b. ʿUmar and gave him the information[186] that Zayd was making repeated visits to a man from amongst their number called ʿĀmir and to a man from the Banū Tamīm called Ṭuʿmah,
[1699] the nephew of Bāriq,[187] and that Zayd was living with them. Yūsuf sent people to their house in search of Zayd b. ʿAlī, but he was not to be found there. Then the two men were seized and brought to Yūsuf. When he had spoken to the two of them, the situation with Zayd and his followers became clear to him.

185. This man is also mentioned in a similar context by Ibn Aʿtham (VIII, 114) and al-Iṣfahānī (*Maqātil,* 135).

186. Literally, "gave him news about him and informed him that. . . ."

187. Literally, "the son of a sister of Bāriq."

Zayd[188] became afraid that he would be arrested, so he put forward the date that he had fixed between himself and the people of al-Kūfah (for the insurrection to begin).

In charge of the people of al-Kūfah at that time was al-Ḥakam b. al-Ṣalt.[189] In charge of his police force was ʿAmr b. ʿAbd al-Raḥmān, a man from the Qārah;[190] he was with the Thaqīf, who were his maternal uncles. He also had with him ʿUbaydallāh b. al-ʿAbbās al-Kindī[191] with some groups of Syrians. Yūsuf b. ʿUmar was in al-Ḥīrah.

When those supporters of Zayd b. ʿAlī who had given him the oath of allegiance found out that Yūsuf b. ʿUmar had heard about Zayd's activities, was scheming against Zayd, and was making inquiries about him, a group of their leaders assembled in his presence and said:[192] "May God have mercy on you! What do you have to say on the matter of Abū Bakr and ʿUmar?"[193] Zayd said: "May God have mercy on both of them and forgive them both! I have not heard anyone in my family renouncing them both nor saying anything but good about them."[194] They said: "In that case, why are you seeking the blood of the members of this family? Is it not perhaps because they have disputed your power and seized it from your hands?" Zayd replied: "My strongest argument against you is that we were more entitled than anyone else
to assume the authority of the Prophet of God and that they [1700]
appropriated our power for themselves and deprived us of it. In our opinion, that did not amount to unbelief (*kufr*) on their part,

---

188. Literally, "Zayd b. ʿAlī."

189. Al-Ḥakam b. al-Ṣalt al-Thaqafī. He was related to Yūsuf b. ʿUmar. Cf. Ibn Khayyāṭ, 536.

190. A tribal group that included some branches of al-Hawn b. Khuzaymah. Cf. Ibn al-Kalbī, II, 465.

191. For a discussion of this man's career, cf. Crone, 152–53. He later became governor of al-Kūfah. Cf. al-Ṭabarī, II, 1855.

192. This incident is also recorded in *Fragmenta*, 96–97, and al-Balādhurī, *Ansāb*, 240.

193. Ibn Aʿtham (VIII, 116) writes, "those two tyrannical men, Abū Bakr and ʿUmar."

194. This acceptance by Zayd of Abū Bakr and ʿUmar is an instance of the *imāmat al-mafḍūl*, the "imamate of the inferior." If this passage is an accurate reflection of Zayd's view, he was trying here to mobilize a wide spectrum of support to overthrow the Umayyads. For a general discussion of the *imāmat al-fāḍil* and the *imāmat al-mafḍūl*, cf. Watt, *Formative Period*, 226–27.

(for) when they were entrusted with government they behaved justly with the people and acted according to the Qur'ān and the *sunnah*." They said: "Then these men have not acted tyrannically toward you if (in your view) those did not do so. So why are you summoning people to fight those who are not tyrannical to you?" Zayd said: "These men are not like those others. These are tyrannical to me, to you, and to themselves. We are only summoning you to the Book of God and the *sunnah* of His prophet so that God's ordinances (*sunan*) may be revived and innovations (*bida'*) may be wiped out. If you answer our call, you will prosper; but if you refuse, I will not be responsible for you."

Then the group left him and broke their allegiance to him, saying: "The real imām has precedence." They were claiming that it was Abū Ja'far Muḥammad b. 'Alī, the brother of Zayd b. 'Alī, who was the imām. Muḥammad had died by that time[195] but his son, Ja'far b. Muḥammad, was still alive. They said: "Today Ja'far is our imām in succession to his father. He is the person most entitled to rule after his father. We will not follow Zayd b. 'Alī. He is not an imām."

This is the group that Zayd called Rāfiḍīs.[196] Today this group claims that the person who called them Rāfiḍīs when they broke with Zayd was al-Mughīrah.[197] Before Zayd's revolt, a group of them had gone to Ja'far b. Muḥammad b. 'Alī and said to him: "Zayd b. 'Alī is among us, asking us to give him the oath of allegiance. Do you think it right that we should do so?" Ja'far said to them: "Yes, give your oath of allegiance to him, for, by God, he is the most excellent of us. He is our master and the best of us."
[1701] But they came back and kept secret what it was that Ja'far had instructed them to do.[198]

Arrangements were made for the revolt of Zayd b. 'Alī, and he fixed the time with his followers as the night of Wednesday, the first night of Ṣafar, 122 (Wednesday, January 6, 740). When Yūsuf b. 'Umar heard that Zayd had resolved on rebellion, he sent word

---

195. Muḥammad b. 'Alī b. al-Ḥusayn. Cf. the 'Alids' genealogical table.

196. For this group, cf. Ibn 'Abd Rabbihi, who writes: "They are called al-Rāfiḍah only because they deserted (the claims of) Abū Bakr and 'Umar." (*'Iqd*, I, 217).

197. Al-Mughīrah b. Sa'īd al-'Ijlī. Cf. Watt, *Formative Period*, 51.

198. Cf. al-Balādhurī, *Ansāb*, 240.

to al-Ḥakam b. al-Ṣalt, ordering him to assemble the people of al-Kūfah in the Great Mosque[199] and to detain them there. Al-Ḥakam sent for the *'urafā'*,[200] the police, the *manākib*,[201] and the soldiers, and stationed them in the mosque. Then he issued the following proclamation: "Verily, the *amīr* says: 'We will not be responsible for the consequences for those whom we find in their houses, so go to the Great Mosque.'" So the people went to the mosque on the Tuesday, one day before Zayd's rebellion.[202]

They searched for Zayd b. 'Alī in the house of Mu'āwiyah b. Isḥāq b. Zayd b. Ḥārithah al-Anṣārī[203] but he left there during the night before the Wednesday.[204] It was a night of extreme cold.[205] Then the rebels raised burning torches and shouted: "O Manṣūr, kill! Kill, O Manṣūr!"[206] Whenever fire had consumed one torch they raised up another, and they continued like this until sunrise. In the morning, Zayd b. 'Alī sent al-Qāsim al-Tin'ī,[207] who was later called al-Ḥaḍramī, and another of his followers to proclaim their war-cry (*shi'ār*). When they were in the Jabbānah of 'Abd al-Qays, Ja'far b. al-'Abbās al-Kindī[208] met them. They attacked him and his companions.[209] The man who was with al-Qāsim al-Tin'ī

---

199. For the background history of the Great Mosque of al-Kūfah, cf. Massignon, 353.

200. *'Arīf*, plural *'urafā'*: an official in charge of a military division in the garrison towns. Cf. *EI*², "'Arīf" (S. el-Ali and C. Cahen).

201. *Mankib*, plural *manākib*: an official below the *'arīf*. Cf. Lane, I, 2846.

202. Cf. al-Balādhurī, *Ansāb*, 243; al-Iṣfahānī, *Maqātil*, 136.

203. Cf. p. 22.

204. One report from al-Iṣfahānī adds that this was seven nights before the end of al-Muḥarram. Cf. *Maqātil*, 136.

205. The translation has simplified the repetitiveness of the original. A literal translation would read: "They searched for Zayd in the house of Mu'āwiyah b. Isḥāq b. Zayd b. Ḥārithah al-Anṣārī. He (Zayd) left the house of Mu'āwiyah b. Isḥāq in the night, which was the night of Wednesday, on an extremely cold night."

206. *Yā Manṣūr, amit, amit ya Manṣūr* ("Kill, kill, you who are given victory"). This was the Prophet's war-cry on the Day of the Banū al-Muṣṭaliq. Cf. Ibn Hishām, 2, 218.

207. Other sources give al-T. b. 'ī. Cf. Ibn al-Athīr, V, 182; al-Iṣfahānī, *Maqātil*, 136; *Fragmenta*, 97.

208. Later he was to become governor of Armenia. In 127 (745) he fell in battle against the Khārijite al-Ḍaḥḥāk b. Qays b. al-Ḥusayn. Cf. Ibn al-Kalbī, II, 253.

209. Al-Ṭabarī's account is ambiguous: *shaddū 'alayhi wa aṣḥābihi. Fragmenta*, 97 has *shadda 'alayhimā* ("he attacked the two of them"). This latter version seems to suggest that it was Ja'far who began the fight against the two supporters of Zayd. Al-Iṣfahānī's account is clear: "Ja'far met them; they attacked him and his companions" (*Maqātil*, 136).

was killed and al-Qāsim himself was wounded and taken to al-Ḥakam. The latter questioned him, but al-Qāsim gave him no reply. Then al-Ḥakam gave orders as to his fate and he was executed at the gate of the citadel. Al-Qāsim and his companion were the first of the followers of Zayd b. ʿAlī to be killed.

[1702] Al-Ḥakam b. al-Ṣalt gave orders concerning the entrances to the market and they were shut and the doors of the mosque were locked on the Kūfans.

The following people were in charge of the quarters[210] of al-Kūfah at that time: Ibrāhīm b. ʿAbdallāh b. Jarīr al-Bajalī[211] was in charge of the Medinans; ʿAmr b. Abī Badhl al-ʿAbdī was in charge of Madhḥij[212] and Asad;[213] al-Mundhir b. Muḥammad b. al-Ashʿath b. Qays al-Kindī[214] was in charge of Kindah[215] and Rabīʿah;[216] and Muḥammad b. Mālik al-Hamdānī,[217] who was later called al-Khaywānī, was in charge of Tamīm[218] and Hamdān.[219]

Al-Ḥakam b. al-Ṣalt sent word to Yūsuf b. ʿUmar informing him of what was going on. Then Yūsuf gave orders to his herald, who proclaimed to the Syrians: "Who will go to al-Kūfah, approach the rebels, and bring me back news of them?" Jaʿfar b. al-ʿAbbās al-Kindī[220] responded: "I will," and he rode off with fifty horsemen. When he reached the Jabbānah of Sālim al-Salūlī,[221] he asked for information about the rebels. He then returned to Yūsuf b. ʿUmar and told him the news. The next morning Yūsuf went out to a hill near al-Ḥīrah and camped there. He was accompanied by some Quraysh and by leaders (*ashrāf*) of the people. In charge of his

---

210. For the tribal organization of al-Kūfah, cf. Djaït, 154–55; Massignon, 345; Crone, 31.
211. Cf. ibid., 115.
212. Cf. Ibn al-Kalbī, I, 176; II, 381–82.
213. Cf. ibid., II, 194.
214. For his family history, cf. Crone, 111.
215. Cf. Ibn al-Kalbī, II, 371–72.
216. Cf. ibid., II, 481.
217. For his family tree, cf. ibid., I, 228.
218. Cf. ibid., II, 544.
219. Cf. ibid., II, 277.
220. One report from al-Iṣfahānī has *ʿAbdallāh b. al-ʿAbbās al-Hamdānī.* Cf. *Maqātil,* 137.
221. For the function of the *jabbānah*s of al-Kūfah, cf. Djaït, 176–77.

shurṭah that day was al-ʿAbbās b. Saʿīd al-Murrī.[222] Then Yūsuf despatched al-Rayyān b. Salamah al-Arāshī[223] with two thousand men.[224] He had with him three hundred Qīqāniyyah[225] foot soldiers armed with arrows.

In the morning, Zayd b. ʿAlī found that the total of those who had come to him that night numbered only 218 men. He said: "Good God! Where are the people?" and he was told: "They are shut in the Great Mosque." Zayd said: "For God's sake, what sort [1703]
of excuse is that for people who gave us their oath of allegiance?"[226]

Naṣr b. Khuzaymah heard the shouting and went toward it. Then he encountered ʿAmr b. ʿAbd al-Raḥmān, the police chief of al-Ḥakam b. al-Ṣalt, accompanied by his cavalry from the Juhaynah,[227] near the house of al-Zubayr b. Abī Ḥakīmah on the road that led to the mosque of the Banū ʿAdī. Naṣr b. Khuzaymah said: "O Manṣūr, kill!" but ʿAmr b. ʿAbd al-Raḥmān vouchsafed him no reply, so Naṣr and his companions attacked him. ʿAmr b. ʿAbd al-Raḥmān was killed and those with him fled.

Zayd b. ʿAlī came from the Jabbānah of Sālim to the Jabbānah of al-Ṣāʾidiyyīn,[228] where five hundred Syrians were stationed. Zayd b. ʿAlī and the men he had with him attacked the Syrians and he put them to flight. That day Zayd b. ʿAlī was riding a jet-black horse which a man from the Banū Nahd b. Kahmas b. Marwān al-Najjārī had sold him for 25 dīnārs. Later, when Zayd was killed, al-Ḥakam b. al-Ṣalt took it.

Zayd b. ʿAlī went to the door of the house belonging to a man from Azd who was called Anas b. ʿAmr. He was one of the people who had given the oath of allegiance to Zayd. They shouted out-

---

222. The text has al-Muzanī, as elsewhere in al-Ṭabarī's history. Cf. II, 1707, 1711. The name should be read as al-Murrī. Cf. *Fragmenta*, 99; Ibn Khayyāṭ, 556; Ibn al-Kalbī, II, 103.

223. This person is called al-Arrānī by Ibn al-Athīr, V, 182.

224. These are specified as cavalry in *Fragmenta*, 98.

225. A well-known regiment of archers from Qīqān.

226. Cf. al-Iṣfahānī, *Maqātil*, 137.

227. For this tribal group, cf. *EI*², "Ḳudaʿa" (M. J. Kister).

228. Cf. al-Ṭabarī, II, 614; Massignon, 347. This *jabbānah* was for the Banū Asad.

side his house, and although he was there he remained silent.[229] Then Zayd called to him: "Anas, come out and join me! May God have mercy on you! Truth has come and falsehood has vanished away. Lo! falsehood is ever bound to vanish."[230] But still Anas did not go out to him. Then Zayd said: "What made you break your
[1704] promise? You have indeed acted (iniquitously)[231] and God will take account of this behavior of yours."[232]

Zayd went to al-Kunāsah,[233] attacked a group of Syrians who were there, and put them to flight. He then went into the *jabbānah* where Yūsuf b. ʿUmar was on the hill looking down at him and his followers.[234] In front of Zayd was Ḥizām b. Murrah al-Muzanī[235] and Zamzam b. Sulaym al-Thaʿlabī, who were in charge of a group of men wearing armor (*al-mujaffafah*). Zayd had about two hundred men with him and by God, if he had approached Yūsuf then, he could have killed him[236] while al-Rayyān b. Salamah was away with the Syrian troops looking for Zayd in al-Kūfah. Then Zayd bore right by the oratory (*muṣallā*) of Khālid b. ʿAbdallāh and he went into al-Kūfah.[237]

When Zayd had gone to al-Kunāsah, one group of his followers split off and went toward the Jabbānah of Mikhnaf b. Sulaym.[238] Then one of them suggested to the others that they should go to the Jabbānah of Kindah.[239] The man had no time to say more than that before the Syrians appeared. When Zayd's men saw them,

229. Literally, "he was shouted to while he was in the house and he began by not answering."

230. Qur'ān, 17, v. 81. These words were recited by the Prophet when he witnessed the destruction of the Kaʿbah after the conquest of Mecca. Cf. Pickthall, 290, n. 1.

231. *Fa ʿaltumūhā. Fragmenta*, 98, has *faʿaltumūhā Ḥusayniyyatan* ("You have behaved in the same way as [other Kūfans did] with al-Ḥusayn").

232. Literally, "God is your Reckoner."

233. "The Place of Sweepings," one of the chief quarters of al-Kūfah which lay to the western side of the town. It was in al-Kunāsah that the town's gibbet was situated. Cf. Le Strange, *Lands*, 75; Massignon, 354–55; Yāqūt, IV, 481.

234. *Wa-Yūsuf b. ʿUmar ʿalā al-talli yanẓuru ilayhi huwa wa-aṣḥābihi.* An alternative translation might be: "Yūsuf b. ʿUmar *and his followers* were looking down at Zayd," reading *aṣḥābuhu*.

235. This *nisbah* may also be al-Murrī. Cf. n. 222 above.

236. Cf. al-Iṣfahānī, *Maqātil*, 138.

237. For this route, cf. Massignon's map.

238. Cf. Massignon, 347.

239. Cf. Massignon, loc. cit.

they went into a lane and walked down it. One of Zayd's men hung back and went into the mosque, where he prayed two *rak'ahs*.[240] He then went out to the Syrians, whom he fought for some time. They got him on the ground and began striking him with their swords. One of them, who was a horseman wearing an iron helmet, shouted out: "Take off the helmet and then hit him on the head with iron bars." They did that and he was killed. The man's companions attacked the Syrians and pulled them away from him but he was already dead. Then the Syrians went away. They had taken one of Zayd's men but the rest of them got away. The man (they captured) had gone into the house of 'Abdallāh b. 'Awf and the Syrians went in after him and took him prisoner. [1705]
They brought him to Yūsuf b. 'Umar, who killed him.[241]

When Zayd b. 'Alī came and saw how the Kūfans had forsaken him, he said: "Naṣr b. Khuzaymah, are you afraid[242] that they will behave as they did with al-Ḥusayn?" Naṣr said: "May God make me a ransom for you! By God, I shall certainly fight by your side with this sword of mine until the death!" (His fight in fact took place that very day in al-Kūfah). Then Naṣr b. Khuzaymah said to Zayd b. 'Alī: "May God make me a ransom for you! The Kūfans are detained in the Great Mosque. So come with us to them."

Zayd went with them toward the mosque and he passed the house of Khālid b. 'Urfuṭah.[243] 'Ubaydallāh b. al-'Abbās al-Kindī heard that Zayd was coming, so he sallied forth with the Syrian troops. Zayd approached and the two sides met at the door of (the house of) 'Umar b. Sa'd b. Abī Waqqāṣ.[244] The standard-bearer[245] of 'Ubaydallāh, who was Salmān, his mawlā, recoiled in fear.

---

240. I.e., he performed two bowings of the head and body in prayer. Cf. Lane, I, 1147.

241. For a similar account, cf. al-Iṣfahānī, *Maqātil,* 138.

242. Ibn al-Athīr has: "I am afraid that . . ." (V, 183).

243. Khālid b. 'Urfuṭah fought at the battle of al-Qādisiyyah against the Persians and at al-Nukhaylah near al-Kūfah against the Khārijites. He was put in charge of the Banū Tamīm and the Banū Hamdān in 51 (671). Cf. al-Ṭabarī, II, 131; Shaykh al-Mufīd, 249; Ibn al-Kalbī, II, 343. His house was a well-known landmark in al-Kūfah for a long time. Cf. al-Ṭabarī, II, 615.

244. He led the Umayyad army against al-Ḥusayn in 61 (680). Cf. Shaykh al-Mufīd, 341–45.

245. *Ṣāḥib liwā'i 'Ubaydallāh.* The *liwā'* was the banner of a particular commander. Cf. Lane, I, 3015.

When ʿUbaydallāh wanted to attack and saw that Salmān was holding back in fear, he said: "Attack, you son of a trollop." Then Salmān launched an attack on Zayd's men and he did not withdraw until his banner was stained with blood.

Then ʿUbaydallāh himself came forth to fight[246] and Wāṣil al-Ḥannāṭ[247] went out against him and they struck each other with their swords. Wāṣil said to ʿUbaydallāh, who had a squint:[248] "Take this from me: I am the boy who sells wheat." The other
[1706] said: "May God cut off my hand if you ever manage to measure a *qafīz*[249] again," and Wāṣil struck ʿUbaydallāh but ʿUbaydallāh did not retaliate,[250] and he and his men fled until they came to the house of ʿAmr b. Ḥurayth.[251]

Zayd and his followers proceeded as far as the Bāb al-Fīl.[252] His men began placing their flags above the doors and saying: "You people in the mosque, come out!" Naṣr b. Khuzaymah began shouting to them saying: "Kūfans, forsake ignominy for glory! Come forth for your own good in both this world and the next.[253] (In your present position) you have the blessings neither of this world nor of the next." The Syrian troops looked down on them and they began throwing stones at them from the top of the mosque.

There was that day a large gathering of people in the environs of al-Kūfah—some reports say it was in the Jabbānah of Sālim. Al-

---

246. I.e., in individual combat.

247. "The wheat-seller."

248. *Fa-qāla liʾl-aḥwali* ("he said to the squint-eyed man"). The apparatus indicates that there are words missing here, but the editor believes the protagonist is al-Aḥwal, the mawlā of al-Ashʿariyyīn. Cf. al-Ṭabarī, II, 1711. It seems unlikely, however, that there is a third person involved here. Al-Balādhurī, whose account has been followed here, makes it clear that ʿUbaydallāh was the man with a squint: *ḍaraba Wāṣil al-Ḥannāṭ al-Aḥwala ʿUbaydallāh b. ʿAbbās al-Kindī.* Cf. *Ansāb,* 247.

249. *Qafīz:* a measure of capacity. Cf. Hinz, 48–49.

250. *Thumma ḍarabahu fa-lam yaṣnaʿ shayʾan.* This translation is only tentative. Cf. al-Balādhurī, *Ansāb,* 247.

251. The text has *ʿAmr min Ḥurayth.* Citing this reference, the index gives ʿAmr b. Ḥurayth al-Makhzūmī, 415–16. ʿAmr b. Ḥurayth (d. 98/716–17) was a leader of the Kūfans and an opponent of the Shīʿīs. Cf. Shaykh al-Mufīd, 244; Ibn al-Kalbī, II, 176.

252. The Bāb al-Fīl was situated near the Friday mosque and the citadel. Cf. Massignon's map.

253. On *dīn,* cf. *EI²,* s.v. (L. Gardet). On *dunyā,* cf. *EI²,* s.v. (A. S. Tritton).

Rayyān b. Salamah left for al-Ḥīrah in the evening and Zayd b. ʿAlī went away with his men. Some of the Kūfans went out to Zayd and he settled in the *dār al-rizq.*[254] (Before he left for al-Ḥīrah)[255] al-Rayyān b. Salamah came to Zayd and fought fiercely with him at the *dār al-rizq.* A large number of the Syrian troops were wounded and killed and Zayd's men pursued them from the *dār al-rizq* as far as the mosque. The Syrian troops returned home on the Wednesday evening with the worst possible forebodings. The following day, the Thursday morning, Yūsuf b. ʿUmar summoned al-Rayyān b. Salamah but he was not to be found at that time.

Some reports say: Al-Rayyān did go to Yūsuf. Al-Rayyān was [1707] not wearing his weapons and Yūsuf reproached him, saying: "Fie on you! Who is supposed to be the head of the cavalry round here? Sit down."[256] Then Yūsuf called al-ʿAbbās b. Saʿīd al-Murrī,[257] his chief of police, and sent him off with the Syrian troops. Al-ʿAbbās made for Zayd b. ʿAlī in the *dār al-rizq.* There was a lot of wood piled up for the carpenter and this made the road difficult to pass through. Zayd came out with his men. On his right and left wings he had Naṣr b. Khuzaymah al-ʿAbsī and Muʿāwiyah b. Isḥāq al-Anṣārī. When al-ʿAbbās saw them—and he himself did not have foot soldiers with him—he shouted, "You Syrian troops, get down on the ground, the ground." Many of his men did dismount and they fought fiercely in the battle.

One of the Syrians from the Banū ʿAbs[258] who was called Nā'il[259] b. Farwah had said to Yūsuf b. ʿUmar: "By God, if I set eyes on Naṣr b. Khuzaymah I will surely kill him or he will surely kill me." Yūsuf said to him: "Take this sword," and he gave him a sword that would cut through anything it touched. When the soldiers of al-ʿAbbās b. Saʿīd and those of Zayd met and fought each other, Nā'il b. Farwah caught sight of Naṣr b. Khuzaymah.

---

254. The army storehouse which was near the bridge over the Euphrates. Cf. Massignon, 349.

255. The sequence of events is clearer in *Fragmenta,* 99.

256. Al-Iṣfahānī gives a similar conversation between Yūsuf and al-Rayyān. Cf. *Maqātil,* 139.

257. Cf. n. 222 above.

258. For the Banū ʿAbs, cf. Ibn al-Kalbī, II, 135–36.

259. Ibn al-Athīr calls him Nabīl (V, 184).

He went toward him, struck him, and cut his thigh. Then Naṣr dealt him a blow which killed him. Naṣr also died soon afterward. The battle raged on fiercely and Zayd b. ʿAlī put the Syrians to flight, killing about seventy of them. The Syrians departed in a sorry state after al-ʿAbbās b. Saʿīd had called out to them: "Get back on your horses. In a narrow place cavalry can't do anything against foot soldiers." So they got back on their horses.

[1708] In the evening Yūsuf b. ʿUmar prepared them for battle again and sent them off. They came and met up with Zayd's men. Zayd launched an attack on them and routed them. Then he pursued them, driving them into the swamp (*sabkhah*).[260] He attacked them in the swamp, pushing them toward the Banū Sulaym.[261] Then he followed them with his horsemen and foot soldiers until he and his men had taken possession of the dam.

Zayd then sallied forth[262] against the Syrians in the area between the Bāriq[263] and the Ru'ās,[264] and there he engaged in a fierce battle with them. His standard-bearer that day was a man called ʿAbd al-Ṣamad b. Abī Mālik b. Masrūḥ from the Banū Saʿd b. Zayd, the ally (*ḥalīf*)[265] of al-ʿAbbās b. ʿAbd al-Muṭṭalib.[266] Masrūḥ al-Saʿdī had married Ṣafiyyah, the daughter of al-ʿAbbās b. ʿAbd al-Muṭṭalib. The Syrian cavalry began by breaking in the face of Zayd's cavalry and his foot soldiers. Then al-ʿAbbās b. Saʿīd al-Murrī[267] sent to Yūsuf b. ʿUmar informing him of this and asking him to send him archers. So Yūsuf sent them Sulaymān (b. Sulaym) b. Kaysān al-Kalbī[268] with the Qīqāniyyah and the Bukhāriyyah[269] who were archers. They began shooting at Zayd

260. The word is vocalized in the text as *sabkhah* but is later corrected to *sabakhah*; the lexica give both forms as correct. Cf. *Add.*, p. DCCX. For the location of the swamp, cf. Massignon's map.

261. Cf. Ibn al-Kalbī, II, 517.

262. The text has *aẓhara lahum*. The Cairo edition (VII, 185) has *ẓahara lahum*, which is followed here. This reading is supported by al-Iṣfahānī, *Maqātil*, 140.

263. Many of the Banū Bāriq had settled in al-Kūfah. Cf. Ibn al-Kalbī, II, 489.

264. For the Banū Ru'ās, cf. Ibn al-Kalbī, II, 489.

265. *Ḥalīf:* one who unites in a confederacy or covenant. Cf. Lane, I, 627.

266. The uncle of the Prophet. Cf. *EI*², s.v. (W. M. Watt).

267. Cf. n. 222 above.

268. Properly Sulaymān b. Sulaym b. Kaysān al-Kalbī. Cf. *Index*, 249; Crone, 139.

269. This group had been formed by ʿUbaydallāh b. Ziyād when he had taken four thousand Bukhārans prisoner in 53–54 (673–74). Cf. Narshakhī, 37; Crone, 230, n. 271.

and his men. (In fact), Zayd had wanted to send his men away when they reached the swamp but they had refused. Mu'āwiyah b. Isḥāq al-Anṣārī fought fiercely in front of Zayd b. 'Alī and was killed.[270] Zayd b. 'Alī and his men held firm until, when night was at hand, someone shot an arrow which struck him on the left side of his forehead and lodged in his head. Zayd then withdrew with his men. The Syrians, however, thought they had with- [1709] drawn only because night was falling.[271]

Salamah b. Thābit al-Laythī, who was with Zayd b. 'Alī and who, together with a slave belonging to Mu'āwiyah b. Isḥāq, was the last person to leave that day, said: I went with my companion, following in close behind Zayd b. 'Alī, and we found that he had been lifted down from his horse and taken into the apartment (*bayt*) of Ḥarrān b. Karīmah,[272] a mawlā of one of the Arabs in the *sikkah al-barīd*,[273] into the living area (*dūr*) of Arḥab[274] and Shākir.[275] [Salamah b. Thābit went on:] I came into the presence of Zayd and I said to him: "May God make me your ransom, Abū al-Ḥusayn!" His companions went off and fetched a physician called Shuqayr,[276] a mawlā of the Banū Ru'ās. This man took the arrow out of his forehead while I was watching him and, by God, hardly had he taken it out before Zayd began screaming and it was not long before he died. The people around said: "Where shall we bury him and where can we conceal him?" One of his companions said: "Let's dress him in his coat of mail and throw him in the water." Another of them said: "No, let's cut off his head and put it amongst those slain in battle." Zayd's son, Yaḥyā, said: "No, by God, the dogs shall not eat the flesh of my father." Another of them said: "Let's take him to al-'Abbāsiyyah and bury him."[277]

---

270. Literally, "He was killed in front of him."
271. Cf. al-Balādhurī, *Ansāb*, 250; al-Iṣfahānī, *Maqātil*, 141.
272. Al-Iṣfahānī has Ḥarrān b. Abī Karīmah. Cf. ibid.
273. "The street of the post."
274. The Banū Arḥab were the clan of Yazīd b. Qays, the police chief of 'Alī. Cf. Djaït, 159.
275. The Banū Shākir were a big clan from whom Ibn Kāmil, one of Mukhtār's associates, recruited men. Cf. Djaït, loc. cit.
276. The doctor's name in some sources was Sufyān. Cf. al-Balādhurī, *Ansāb*, 251; al-Iṣfahānī, *Maqātil*, 142.
277. Ibn A'tham, VIII, 121, relates that Zayd was buried in the swamp.

[Salamah continued]: I suggested to them that we should take him to the clay pit and bury him there. They accepted my advice and we went and dug a grave for him between two ditches, where there was at that time a lot of water. When we had prepared the
[1710] grave properly for him, we buried him and allowed the water to flow over him. There was a Sindī slave of his with us.

Then we went with Zayd's son as far as the Jabbānah of al-Sabīʿ, where we remained, and at that point the people left us. I stayed with Yaḥyā in a group of less than ten men. I said to Yaḥyā: "Where do you intend to go now that daybreak is upon you?" He had with him Abū al-Ṣabbār al-ʿAbdī. Yaḥyā replied: "The two rivers (*al-nahrayn*)." I said to him: "So you only want to go to the two rivers?"—I thought that he wanted to go alongside the Euphrates and fight them. Then I said to him: "Don't leave your position. Fight them until you are killed or until God decrees what He will." Yaḥyā said to me: "I want to go to the two rivers of Karbalā.'"[278] So I replied: "Well, then, flee before daybreak." Accordingly he left al-Kūfah, accompanied by me, Abū al-Ṣabbār, and a small group of men. As we left al-Kūfah we heard the call to prayer of the muezzins and we performed the dawn prayer at al-Nukhaylah.[279] Then we made off quickly in the direction of Nineveh.[280] Yaḥyā said to me: "I want to see Sābiq, the mawlā of Bishr b. ʿAbd al-Malik b. Bishr, so hurry up." Whenever I met people I would ask them for food and I would be given loaves. These I gave to Yaḥyā and he ate them and we ate with him. We reached Nineveh when darkness had already fallen. We arrived at Sābiq's house, I called through the door, and he came out to us. I said to him: "I'm going to al-Fayyūm[281] and I'll be staying there, so if you want to communicate with me, you know where to find me." Then I went away, leaving Yaḥyā with Sābiq, and that was the last time I ever saw him.

---

278. Karbalā' lies to the northwest of al-Kūfah and marks the place where al-Ḥusayn was martyred in 61 (680). Cf. Le Strange, *Lands*, 78. For al-Nahrayn, cf. Massignon's map.

279. A place near al-Kūfah. Cf. Yāqūt, IV, 771; Wellhausen, 76–77.

280. Nīnawā: the village where the prophet Job lived. According to Yāqūt (IV, 870–71), it was in the Sawād of al-Kūfah. Cf. *EI*[1], s.v. (M. Streck).

281. Besides the well-known town of this name in Egypt, there was a place called al-Fayyūm near Hīt in Iraq, which is probably meant here. Cf. Yāqūt, III, 933.

Then Yūsuf b. ʿUmar sent the Syrian troops to carry out a search for the wounded in the houses of the Kūfans. The troops [1711] brought the women out into the courtyard of the house while they went around the inner apartments looking for the wounded. Then on the Friday the Sindī slave of Zayd b. ʿAlī revealed where Zayd was to be found. Al-Ḥakam b. al-Ṣalt dispatched al-ʿAbbās b. Saʿīd al-Murrī[282] and Ibn al-Ḥakam b. al-Ṣalt, and they went off and took Zayd away. Al-ʿAbbās did not want Ibn al-Ḥakam to get in first,[283] so he parted company with him. Early on the Friday al-ʿAbbās sent a messenger, accompanied by al-Ḥajjāj b. al-Qāsim b. Muḥammad b. al-Ḥakam b. Abī ʿAqīl, to take the head of Zayd b. ʿAlī to Yūsuf b. ʿUmar.

Abū al-Juwayriyah, the mawlā of the Juhaynah,[284] composed the following lines:

Say to those who have dishonored women
    and who have set up candles in the desert of Sālim:
How did you find the fight against noble men,
    O Yūsuf b. al-Ḥakam b. al-Qāsim?

When the messenger came to Yūsuf b. ʿUmar, the latter gave orders concerning Zayd. His body was crucified at al-Kunāsah, together with Naṣr b. Khuzaymah, Muʿāwiyah b. Isḥāq b. Zayd b. Ḥārithah al-Anṣārī, and Ziyād al-Nahdī. Yūsuf had proclaimed that anyone who brought a head would receive five hundred dirhams. Muḥammad b. ʿAbbād brought the head of Naṣr b. Khuzaymah and Yūsuf b. ʿUmar ordered that he should have one thousand dirhams. When al-Aḥwal, the mawlā of al-Ashʿariyyīn, brought the head of Muʿāwiyah b. Isḥāq, Yūsuf said to him: "Did you kill him?" Al-Aḥwal replied: "May God make the *amīr* prosper! It was not I who killed him but I saw him and recognized him." Yūsuf said: "Give him seven hundred dirhams." The only thing that prevented al-Aḥwal from having the full one thousand

---

282. Cf. n. 222 above.

283. That is, to receive the reward.

284. This poet is probably the same Abū al-Juwayriyah ʿĪsā b. ʿIṣmah whose verses are quoted under the year 116 by al-Ṭabarī, II, 1565; al-Iṣfahānī, *Aghānī*, VI, 130, 137; Sezgin, II, 342.

dirhams was the fact that he asserted that he had not killed Muʿāwiyah.

[1712] Other reports say that it was only when Yūsuf b. ʿUmar was so informed by Hishām b. ʿAbd al-Malik that he heard about Zayd's activities and how, having left al-Kūfah and gone some distance, Zayd had gone back there.[285] That came about because a man from the Banū Umayyah wrote—according to the reports—to Hishām, mentioning Zayd's activities to him. Then Hishām wrote to Yūsuf, reproaching him, calling him ignorant and saying: "You are being negligent while Zayd has fixed himself at al-Kūfah and the oath of allegiance is being given to him. Keep on[286] searching for him. Give him a guarantee of safe conduct and, if he does not accept, fight him." Yūsuf wrote to al-Ḥakam b. al-Ṣalt, who was of the family of Abū ʿAqīl and was Yūsuf's deputy in al-Kūfah, asking him to look for Zayd. Al-Ḥakam looked for Zayd but he could not find where he was hiding. Then Yūsuf secretly summoned a Khurāsānī *mamlūk* of his who was a stutterer. He gave him five thousand dirhams and ordered him to ingratiate himself with some of the Shīʿah. Yūsuf told him to tell them that he had come from Khurāsān out of love for the family of the Prophet (*ahl al-bayt*) and that he had money that he wished to use to support their cause. After the *mamlūk* had met the Shīʿah on a number of occasions and told them about the money that he had with him, they took him in to see Zayd. Then the *mamlūk* went away and told Yūsuf where Zayd was to be found. Yūsuf sent out cavalry to Zayd. Zayd's men raised their war cry but only three hundred or less of them gathered to him. Zayd said: "Dāwūd b. ʿAlī knew you (Kūfans) better. He warned me that you would desert me but I took no heed."[287]

Other reports say that the person who revealed the place where Zayd was buried—and he was buried, according to these reports, in the river of Yaʿqūb, where his followers had blocked the river,

285. The text is very obscure here. The translation has attempted to clarify it. The literal translation would be: "Yūsuf b. ʿUmar knew about the affair of Zayd and his going back from the road to al-Kūfah after he had set out only by being informed about it by Hishām b. ʿAbd al-Malik."

286. The text has *fa-iljaj fī ṭalabihi*. This is emended later to *fa-alḥiḥ*; cf. *Add.*, p. DCCX. There is no great difference in meaning between the two.

287. Cf. also al-Balādhurī, *Ansāb*, 244.

dug a grave for him in the riverbed, buried him in his clothes, and allowed the water to flow over him—was the slave[288] of a fuller who happened to be there. The slave, having first agreed on a price to show Yūsuf's men where Zayd was laid, showed them the place. They took Zayd away, cut off his head, and crucified his body. They ordered that a guard should be posted over him in case anyone should try to take down the body, and a guard was indeed posted over him for some time. [1713]

Some reports say that Abū Khaythamah Zuhayr b. Muʿāwiyah[289] was amongst the people guarding Zayd. Zayd's head was sent to Hishām, who gave orders that it should be put up on the gate of the city of Damascus. Then it was sent to Medina. The body remained on the gibbet until Hishām died.[290] Then al-Walīd ordered that it should be taken down and burned.[291]

Other reports say that it was Ḥakīm b. Sharīk who informed on Zayd to Yūsuf.

Abū ʿUbaydah Maʿmar b. al-Muthannā gave the following report about Yaḥyā b. Zayd: When Zayd was killed, one of the Banū Asad went to Yaḥyā b. Zayd and said to him: "Your father has been killed. The people of Khurāsān will give you their support. I think you should go to them." Yaḥyā said: "How can I do that?" The man said: "Hide yourself until the search for you has been called off, then leave." So the man hid Yaḥyā in his house for one night. Then he lost his nerve and went to ʿAbd al-Malik b. Bishr b. Marwān,[292] saying to him: "Zayd was a close kinsman of yours. It is your duty to uphold his rights." ʿAbd al-Malik said: "Yes, but it would have been a more pious act to pardon him." The man said: "Zayd has been killed and this is his son, a young boy who has committed no crime. If Yūsuf b. ʿUmar finds out where he is he will kill him, so you must protect him and hide him with

288. *ʿAbdu qaṣṣārin.* The text itself has *ʿinda qaṣṣārin,* which makes little sense. Nöldeke emends the reading to *ʿabdu,* which is a variant in the apparatus. Cf. *Add.*, p. DCCX. This reading has been followed in the translation. According to *Fragmenta,* 100, it was the fuller himself who revealed where Zayd's body was.

289. Cf. Ibn al-Kalbī, I, 269.

290. According to al-Masʿūdī, Zayd's body remained attached to the gibbet in al-Kūfah for five years. Cf. *Murūj,* V, 472–73.

291. Zayd was forty-two when he died. Cf. al-Iṣfahānī, *Maqātil,* 130; Ibn Saʿd, V, 240.

292. He was an Umayyad. Cf. Ibn al-Kalbī, I, 10.

[1714] you." ʿAbd al-Malik said: "Yes, with great pleasure." So the man brought Yaḥyā to him and he hid him in his house. This came to the ears of Yūsuf and he sent the following message to ʿAbd al-Malik: "I have heard that this boy is with you. I swear to God, if you do not bring him to me I will certainly inform the Commander of the Faithful about you." ʿAbd al-Malik said to him: "This is a tissue of falsehood and lies. Would I hide somebody who would challenge my authority and have a better claim to it than I have myself? I would never have thought that you could believe such a thing of me nor that you would listen to the author of such lies." Yūsuf said: "He's telling the truth. By God, Ibn Bishr is not the sort of person to hide away the likes of Yaḥyā." So Yūsuf called off the search for Yaḥyā and when the hue and cry had died down, Yaḥyā escaped with a number of Zayd's supporters to Khurāsān.

After the killing of Zayd, Yūsuf delivered the following exhortation in al-Kūfah: "O people of al-Kūfah! Verily Yaḥyā b. Zayd has entered the bridal chambers of your women just as his father did. By God, if he were to show his face to me, I would rip off his testicles just as I ripped off the testicles of his father!"

The following report came from one of the Anṣār: When the head of Zayd was brought and displayed[293] in Medina in the year 123 [November, 26, 740–November 14, 741], one of the Anṣār poets came and stood before Zayd and said:

O violator of the covenant,
    rejoice in what has brought you disaster!
You have violated the trust and the covenant.
    You are steeped in wrongdoing.
Satan has broken faith
    over what he promised you.[294]

[1715] People said to the poet: "Woe on you! How dare you say this about the likes of Zayd?" He replied: "The *amīr* is angry and I wanted to please him." Then one of their poets gave him the following response:

---

293. The text has *ṣuliba*. The apparatus suggests an alternative, *nuṣiba*, which makes better sense.

294. The meter is *hazaj*.

You poet of evil,
    you have become a liar!
Are you reviling[295] the son of the messenger of God,
    just to gratify those who govern over you?

May God confound you,
    morning and evening!
And on the Day of Gathering, make no mistake,[296]
    the fire will be your abode!

Some reports say that Khirāsh b. Ḥawshab b. Yazīd al-Shaybānī was head of police for Yūsuf b. ʿUmar and that it was he who dug up Zayd and crucified him. Al-Sayyid[297] recited the following:

I spent the night sleepless
    and wakeful, composing poetry.
After reciting,
    I remained for a long time in a state of perplexity.
(I said) "May God shower on Ḥawshab
    and Khirāsh and Mazyad—
And Yazīd, for he
    was still more insolent and rebellious—
A million million
    curses for ever and ever,
For it was they who waged war on
    God and wrought harm on Muḥammad.
Rebelliously they have shared in shedding the blood
    of the pure one,[298] Zayd,
Then they raised him high on a rood,[299]
    stark naked and stripped to the skin.
O Khirāsh b. Ḥawshab,
    tomorrow it is you who will be the most wretched of men!"[300]

---

295. The text has *atashtimu ibna al-rasūl,* which breaks the meter (*hazaj*). The editor emends this later to read: *ashatmu ibna rasūli Allāhi;* cf. *Add.,* DCCXI. The Cairo edition (190) follows this emendation.

296. Literally, "there is no doubt that."

297. Ismāʿīl b. Muḥammad al-Ḥimyarī, whose *laqab* was al-Sayyid. Cf. Ibn Aʿtham, VIII, 205; Ibn al-Athīr, V, 185; al-Iṣfahānī, *Aghānī,* VII, 229.

298. *Al-Muṭahhar.* Ibn al-Athīr has al-Ḥusayn (V, 1815).

299. Literally, "a tree stump."

300. The meter is *muqtaḍab.*

[1716] According to Abū Mikhnaf: When Yūsuf had killed Zayd b. ʿAlī, he went into al-Kūfah, mounted the *minbar*, and said:

> O you citizens of an abominable city! By God, even a refractory camel can achieve nothing against me;[301] I am neither daunted by the clattering of worn-out water-skins[302] nor am I frightened by the wolf. Far from it! I was endowed with the mightiest of forearms. Lament, O men of al-Kūfah, your disgrace and degradation. Expect neither stipend nor allowance for yourselves from us. Indeed, I am resolved to destroy your city and your homes and to despoil your possessions. I have mounted[303] my *minbar* only to make you understand what repressive measures will be taken against you.[304] You are a people of violence and contumacy. All of you, except Ḥakīm b. Sharīk al-Muḥāribī, wage war against God and His Prophet. I have asked the Commander of the Faithful to give me permission to take action against you. If he gives me a free hand, I shall kill your fighting men and enslave your children.[305]

In this year Kulthūm b. ʿIyāḍ al-Qushayrī[306] was killed. He was the man whom Hishām b. ʿAbd al-Malik had sent with the Syrian cavalry to Ifrīqiyah[307] when strife broke out amongst the Berbers.

---

301. *Mā tuqarranu bī al-ṣaʿbatu.* Cf. *Gloss.*, p. CDXXI; Freytag, *Prov.*, II, 589.

302. *Lā yuqaʿqaʿu lī bi-al-shinānī* ("a confused and clattering noise will not be made for me with the old and worn-out water skins"). Cf. Lane, I, 1602. Yūsuf is suggesting that he is frightened by nothing.

303. An alternative translation could be: "I will never mount my *minbar* again until I have made you understand what repressive measures will be taken against you."

304. *Mā tukrahūna ʿalayhi* (lit., "what you will be forced to do"). Cf. Ullmann, 152.

305. Other versions of this *khuṭbah* can be found in *Fragmenta*, 100, and al-Balādhurī, *Ansāb*, 258–59.

306. According to Ibn Khayyāṭ, Kulthūm was sent as governor of Ifrīqiyah at the beginning of Shaʿbān 123 (June 21–July 19, 741) and he died in 124 (741–42) (*Taʾrīkh*, 369–70). For an analysis of Kulthūm's career, cf. Crone, 128; Gabrieli, *Califfato*, 98–101. It was in 124 (741–42) that the great Berber revolt occurred in Spain.

307. For definitions of the boundaries of the province of Ifrīqiyah, cf. *EI*², s.v. (M. Talbi).

Also in this year ʿAbdallāh al-Baṭṭāl was killed with a group of Muslims in Byzantine territory.[308]

In this year were born al-Faḍl b. Ṣāliḥ[309] and Muḥammad b. Ibrāhīm b. Muḥammad b. ʿAlī.[310]

Also in this year Yūsuf b. ʿUmar sent Ibn Shubrumah to govern Sijistān[311] and he appointed Ibn Abī Laylā as *qāḍī* (of al-Kūfah). [1717]

According to Aḥmad b. Thābit—his narrators—Isḥāq b. ʿIsā—Abū Maʿshar: In this year Muḥammad b. Hishām al-Makhzūmī led the people on the pilgrimage. Al-Wāqidī and others also gave the same account.

The agents (*ʿummāl*) of the garrison cities in this year were the same as in the previous year, and their names have already been mentioned, except that the *qāḍī* of al-Kūfah in this year is reported to have been Muḥammad b. ʿAbd al-Raḥmān b. Abī Laylā.

---

308. ʿAbdallāh al-Baṭṭāl b. al-Ḥusayn, the semilegendary hero to whom are attributed many raids into Byzantine territory. Cf. *Fragmenta*, 100; Ibn Khayyāṭ, 367. Ibn Khayyāṭ puts al-Baṭṭāl's death in 121 (738–39). Cf. also Brooks, "Arabs in Asia Minor," 198–200.

309. Al-Faḍl b. Ṣāliḥ b. ʿAlī b. ʿAbdallāh b. ʿAbbās, governor of Cairo in 169 (785–86). Cf. Zambaur, 26, and genealogical table 9, n. 206.

310. A member of the ʿAbbāsid family who was twice governor of Mecca, the first time from 149 to 158 (766–67 to 774–75) and the second from 178 to 184 (794–95 to 800). Cf. Zambaur, 20.

311. The province of Sijistān (or Sīstān) lay to the south of Khurāsān. Its capital in medieval times was Zaranj. Cf. Le Strange, *Lands*, 334–51. ʿAbdallāh b. Shubrumah al-Ḍabbī is not mentioned amongst the governors of Sijistān by Ibn Khayyāṭ (*Taʾrīkh*, 375).

312. The leader of the Turks. Cf. Wellhausen, 433.

The Events of the Year 123 (November 26, 740–November 14, 741)

Amongst the events taking place during this year was the drawing up of a peace treaty between Naṣr b. Sayyār and the Soghdians.

The [Treaty with the Soghdians] and the Reason for It

According to ʿAlī b. Muḥammad (al-Madāʾinī)—his *shaykh*s: When the *khāqān*[312] was killed during the governorship of Asad,[313] the Turks scattered in disarray, making forays against each other. The Soghdians wanted to return home and a group of them withdrew to al-Shāsh.[314] When Naṣr b. Sayyār became gov-

---

312. The leader of the Turks. Cf. Wellhausen, 433.

313. Asad b. ʿAbdallāh al-Qasrī, Khālid's brother, was appointed governor of Khurāsān for the second time in 117 (735). He defeated the Türgesh in 119 (737) at the battle of Kharistān. Cf. *EI*², s.v. (H. A. R. Gibb); Gibb, 81–85; Wellhausen, 467–74.

314. Judayʿ al-Kirmānī had routed most of the Khāqān's forces; just one band of Soghdians managed to retreat. Cf. Hawting, 88.

ernor, he sent messages to the Soghdians inviting them to return home and he complied with all their requests. They had asked for conditions that (previous) *amīrs* of Khurāsān had rejected:[315] namely, that those who had been Muslims and then apostasized from Islam should not be punished; that no excessive demands for repayment of debts should be inflicted on any of the people; that they should not be required to pay any tax arrears (*qabālah*) which they owed to the treasury;[316] and that they should have to [1718] return Muslim prisoners only at the decree of a *qāḍī* and on the testimony of trustworthy witnesses. People reproached Naṣr for having made this agreement and they taxed him about it. He replied: "Verily, by God, if you had seen with your own eyes—as I have done—the military prowess that the Soghdians displayed toward the Muslims and the havoc that they wrought amongst them, you would not have disapproved of this agreement." Then Naṣr sent a messenger to inform Hishām about that matter. When the messenger arrived, the caliph refused to support Naṣr in that affair.[317] So the messenger said: "O Commander of the Faithful, you have had experience of us in war and in peace alike, so decide for yourself." Hishām became angry. Then al-Abrash al-Kalbī said: "O Commander of the Faithful, win the people over with kindness and use forbearance toward them, for you know the havoc they have wrought amongst the Muslims." Thereupon Hishām endorsed the action that Naṣr had taken.[318]

In this year Yūsuf b. ʿUmar sent al-Ḥakam b. al-Ṣalt to Hishām b. ʿAbd al-Malik, asking him to put Khurāsān under his jurisdiction and to dismiss Naṣr b. Sayyār.

---

315. Cf. the discussion in Barthold, *Turkestan*, 192.

316. For the term *qabālah*, cf. *Gloss.*, p. CDXII; *EI*², "Ḳabāla" (Cahen). As Cahen says, it is difficult to define this term precisely. It would appear that the term generally refers to a practice whereby, when individuals had difficulty in paying the full amount of land tax, a local notable would advance the sum needed and would have to ensure future reimbursement. In this passage, however, the word may well mean simply "arrears."

317. *Fa-lammā qadima al-rasūl abā an yunfidha dhālika* ("When the messenger arrived, he refused to endorse that"). This sentence is ambiguous. The subject of the main clause could be the messenger or Hishām.

318. *Fa-anfadha Hishām mā sa'ala* (lit., "Hishām ratified what he (Naṣr) asked").

The Reason for Yūsuf's Request and the Outcome of It

According to 'Alī (al-Madā'inī)—his *shaykhs*: After Naṣr b. Sayyār had been governor for a long time and Khurāsān was well under his control, Yūsuf b. 'Umar, who was envious of Naṣr, wrote to Hishām saying: "Khurāsān is indeed a running sore![319] If the Commander of the Faithful deems it appropriate to annex Khurāsān to Iraq, I will send al-Ḥakam b. al-Ṣalt there, for he was with al-Junayd,[320] he governed the bulk of the (eastern) provinces, and he made the lands of the Commander of the Faithful prosper with good government. I am sending al-Ḥakam b. al-Ṣalt to the
[1719] Commander of the Faithful, for he is cultured and wise. Al-Ḥakam's counsel to the Commander of the Faithful will be like our own counsel, just as his love for the *ahl al-bayt* is like our own."

When Yūsuf's letter reached Hishām, he sent people to the public guesthouse (*dār al-ḍiyāfah*) where Muqātil b. 'Alī al-Sughdī[321] was lodging. They brought him to Hishām, who said: "Are you from Khurāsān?" Muqātil said: "Yes, and I am a friend of the Turks." (He had come to Hishām with one hundred and fifty Turks.)[322] Hishām said: "Do you know al-Ḥakam b. al-Ṣalt?" Muqātil said "Yes." Hishām said: "What were his responsibilities in Khurāsān?" Muqātil said: "He was in charge of a borough (*qaryah*) called al-Fāryāb;[323] its *kharāj*[324] amounts to seventy thousand [dirhams]. Then al-Ḥārith b. Surayj took him

---

319. The text has *dabiratun dabiratun*. This is emended to *dabaratu dabiratin* ("the sore of an ulcerated camel"). Cf. *Add.*, p. DCCXI. The Cairo edition (193) has *dabaratun dabiratun* and its editor explains in a footnote that the phrase means a disturbed area.

320. Al-Junayd b. 'Abdallāh al-Murrī was governor of Khurāsān from 111 (730) to 115 (733). He died in 116 (734). Cf. *EI*², "Al-Djunayd b. 'Abdallāh" (Veccia Vaglieri); Gibb, 72–76; Wellhausen, 459–62; Ibn Khayyāṭ, 375.

321. The text has al-Sa'dī, as does Ibn al-Athīr, V, 189. The name is later emended to al-Sughdī. Cf. *Add.*, p. DCCXI.

322. This is a comment by the narrator.

323. For al-Fāryāb, cf. *EI*², Faryāb (R. Frye). Of the various possible locations, the most likely is that it is a village in Sughd.

324. *Kharāj:* usually, land tax. For more precise definitions of the term, cf. *EI*², s.v. (Cahen); Morony, 99–106.

prisoner." Hishām said: "Oh dear! How did he escape from al-Ḥārith?" Muqātil said: "Al-Ḥārith twisted his ear, slapped him on the back of his head, and let him go."[325]

Later on, al-Ḥakam brought the *kharāj* revenues of Iraq to Hishām. Hishām found that al-Ḥakam was handsome and eloquent, so he wrote to Yūsuf saying: "Al-Ḥakam has arrived. He is as you described. In the area you govern there is ample scope for him. Dismiss al-Kinānī[326] (i.e., Naṣr) and make al-Ḥakam agent (*ʿāmil*) (in his place)."

In this year Naṣr made a second raid on Farghānah and he sent Maghrā' b. Aḥmar to Iraq. The latter, however, denounced him to Hishām.

An Account of [the Denunciation of Naṣr] and of the Part Played in It by Hishām and Yūsuf b. ʿUmar

It is reported that Naṣr sent Maghrā' b. Aḥmar as his envoy to Iraq after Naṣr had returned from his second raid on Farghānah. Yūsuf [1720]
b. ʿUmar said to Maghrā': "Ibn Aḥmar! Is Ibn al-Aqṭaʿ[327] [meaning Naṣr] getting a hold over you, you men of Qays?"[328] Ibn Aḥmar replied: "That has been so, may God make the *amīr* prosper!" Then Yūsuf said: "When you go to see the Commander of the Faithful, destroy Naṣr." So the delegation went to Hishām, who questioned them about the situation in Khurāsān. Maghrā' began to speak, giving praise and thanks to God and then referring to Yūsuf b. ʿUmar in the most fulsome terms. Hishām said: "Enough of that! Tell me about Khurāsān". Then Maghrā' said: "O Commander of the Faithful, there is no army (*jund*) of yours that can march faster[329] than they can and there are no falcons in the sky

325. Ibn al-Athīr (loc. cit.) adds that al-Ḥārith told al-Ḥakam that he was too contemptible for him to kill him.

326. The *nisbah* of Naṣr b. Sayyār. For the Banū Kinānah, cf. Ibn al-Kalbī, II, 371. They were a "small and almost neutral tribe" (Gibb, 89).

327. This term of abuse, probably meaning "son of a man with an amputated hand," would suggest thieving, for which the fixed penalty is well known.

328. Ibn al-Athīr (V, 189) has *Quraysh.*

329. *Aghaththu* ("more speedy"). There is some doubt about this reading. The apparatus cites two variants, *aʿaddu* and *aghazzu.*

more courageous[330] than they are; their cavalry[331] are like elephants; they have adequate supplies of men and equipment—but they have no leader." Then Hishām said: "Shame on you! What has al-Kinānī (Naṣr) been doing?" Maghrā' said: "Naṣr is so old that he does not even recognize his own son." But Hishām did not accept Maghrā''s statement. He sent someone to the public guesthouse and Shubayl b. 'Abd al-Raḥmān al-Māzinī[332] was brought to him. Hishām said to him: "Tell me about Naṣr." Shubayl said: "There is no need to fear that he is so old as to be in his dotage nor that he is too young to possess sound judgment. He is experienced and tried. He was in charge of all the borders and wars in Khurāsān even before he became governor."

Yūsuf was told by letter about what had happened and he posted spies. When Naṣr's delegation reached al-Mawṣil, they left the road taken by the postal service[333] and instead used byways until they reached Bayhaq.[334] Naṣr had also been informed by letter about what Shubayl had said. Now Ibrāhīm b. Bassām was in the delegation. Yūsuf practiced a deception on him, telling him that Naṣr was dead and that accordingly he had himself appointed
[1721] al-Ḥakam b. al-Ṣalt b. Abī 'Aqīl as governor of Khurāsān. So Ibrāhīm suggested to him the people to whom he should allocate all the provinces of Khurāsān.[335] Then Ibrāhīm b. Ziyād, the envoy of Naṣr, came to Ibrāhīm b. Bassām and told him that Yūsuf had tricked him. Ibrāhīm b. Bassām replied: "Yūsuf has destroyed me."

It is said that Naṣr sent Maghrā' together with Ḥamlah b. Nu'aym al-Kalbī (to Hishām). When they came to Yūsuf, Yūsuf aroused ambition in Maghrā', promising that if Maghrā' impugned Naṣr's reputation in front of Hishām, he (Yūsuf) would make Maghrā' governor of Sind. When Maghrā' and Ḥamlah came to

330. *Anjadu* ("more courageous"). The apparatus has a variant, *aḥaddu* ("more sharp"), which is followed by the Cairo edition (194).

331. *Firāsiyyah.* It is suggested tentatively in the glossary that this is a collective term for men skilled in horsemanship. This meaning is followed here.

332. Presumably this man was a visitor from Khurāsān.

333. For the route taken by the postal service, cf. Sprenger, *Die Post- und Reiserouten des Orients.*

334. The district of Bayhaq lay four days' march west from Nishāpūr. The town of Sabzavār was also known in medieval times as Bayhaq. Cf. Le Strange, *Lands,* 391.

Hishām, Maghrā' mentioned Naṣr's courage, valor, and skill in affairs, and he was profuse in his praise. Then he continued: "Would that God would allow us to enjoy (for a while longer) what is left of him!" Hishām sat up straight and said: "What do you mean by 'what is left of him'?" Maghrā' said: "Naṣr can recognize a man only by his voice, he only understands what is said to him if people get up close to him, and his own voice is so faint that it is scarcely intelligible because he is so old." Then Ḥamlah al-Kalbī stood up and said: "O Commander of the Faithful, Maghrā' is lying. By God, Naṣr is not as he said he is. He is as he is."[336] Hishām said: "Naṣr is not as Maghrā' has described him. This is the doing of Yūsuf b. 'Umar, who is motivated by envy of Naṣr."

Yūsuf had written to Hishām mentioning that Naṣr was old and infirm, recommending Salm b. Qutaybah to him.[337] Hishām wrote back to him: "Stop talking about al-Kinānī." Then on his return to Yūsuf, Maghrā' said: "You are aware of what Naṣr has suffered at my hand and you know how (badly) I have behaved [1722]
toward him. So there is no future[338] for me in being with him and there is no point in my staying on in Khurāsān. Therefore give orders for me to stay here." Yūsuf accordingly wrote to Naṣr saying: "I have transferred Maghrā''s name (from the Khurāsān register to that of Iraq).[339] So send me those of his family who are with you."

It is said that when Yūsuf ordered Maghrā' to give false witness against Naṣr, Maghrā' said: "How can I run him down after the difficult times he has been through and his kind actions toward me and my family?" But Yūsuf continued to press him, so

335. *Qassama lahu Ibrāhīm Khurāsāna kullahu.* This seems to mean that Ibrāhīm made suggestions as to who should assume rule over the individual parts of Khurāsān now that he believed Naṣr was dead. Cf. *Gloss.*, p. CDXXIII.

336. *Mā huwa kamā qāla huwa wa huwa.* The Cairo edition (194) punctuates this phrase to make better sense and omits the *wa*: *mā huwa kamā qāla; huwa huwa.* This reading has been followed in the translation.

337. Salm b. Qutaybah was not the only member of his family who was a contender for the governorship of Khurāsān. His brother Qaṭan and his cousin Muslim b. 'Abd al-Raḥmān were also in the running. For Salm's career, cf. Crone, 137.

338. *Khayr* (lit., "benefit").

339. *Qad ḥawwaltu ismahu.*

Maghrā' said: "With what can I reproach him? Should I find fault with his experience, his obedience, his good fortune in affairs, or his skillful government?" Yūsuf said: "Reproach him for being old." When Maghrā' went in to see Hishām, he spoke about Naṣr in the most glowing terms, and then, at the end of his speech, he said: "If only. . ." Then Hishām sat up straight and said: "What do you mean by 'If only'?" Maghrā' said: "If only old age had not overtaken him." Hishām said: "Come on now! Old age has not yet overtaken him." Maghrā' said: "Naṣr only recognizes a man close up and then only by his voice. He has become too weak to raid and ride." This distressed Hishām but then Ḥamlah b. Nu'aym spoke up.

When Naṣr heard about what Maghrā' had said he sent Hārūn b. al-Siyāwush to al-Ḥakam b. Numaylah, who was in the saddlers' quarter (*al-sarrājīn*) reviewing the troops (*jund*). Hārūn grabbed him by the foot, dragged him from a carpet on which he was sitting, and broke his flag on his head. Then he hit him in the face with his carpet and said: "This is how God deals with traitors."

According to 'Alī b. Muḥammad (al-Madā'inī)—al-Ḥārith b.
[1723] Aflaḥ b. Mālik b. Asmā' b. Khārijah: When Naṣr became governor of Khurāsān he made particular favorites of Maghrā' b. Aḥmar b. Mālik b. Sāriyah al-Numayrī,[340] al-Ḥakam b. Numaylah b. Mālik, and al-Ḥajjāj b. Hārūn b. Mālik. Maghrā' b. Aḥmar al-Numayrī was the leader of the people of Qinnasrīn.[341] Naṣr gave preference to Maghrā', appointed him to a privileged position,[342] and accepted his intercessions in respect of what he needed.[343] Naṣr appointed Maghrā''s nephew, al-Ḥakam b. Numaylah, as agent (*'āmil*) of al-Jūzajān (Jūzjān).[344] Then he put him in charge of the *ahl al-'āliyah*.[345] This was a responsibility that his father in al-

340. Some of the Banū Numayr had settled in Northern Syria in the early Islamic period. Cf. Ibn al-Kalbī, II, 450.

341. A town in northern Syria. The medieval geographers speak of its former greatness and comment on its insignificance in their own time. Cf. Yāqūt, IV, 184–87; Ibn Ḥawqal, 118; *EI*², "Ḳinnasrīn" (N. Elisséeff); Le Strange, *Palestine*, 486.

342. *Sannā manzilatahu*. Cf. *Gloss.*, p. CCXCIX.

343. *Wa-shaffa'ahu fī ḥawā'ijihi*.

344. A district in Afghan Turkestan between the Murghāb and the Oxus. Cf. *EI*², "Djūzdjān" (R. Hartmann); Le Strange, *Lands*, 423; *Ḥudūd*, 328–32.

345. The *ahl al-'āliyah* were a group consisting predominantly of Qays who are mentioned as one of the divisions (*akhmās*, "fifths") in al-Baṣrah. Cf. Djaït, 163.

Baṣrah had had before him; and 'Ukabah b. Numaylah took it on after him. Later on, Naṣr dispatched a delegation of Syrians and Khurāsānīs, and he appointed Maghrā' to be in charge of them. Ḥamlah b. Nu'aym al-Kalbī was also in the delegation. 'Uthmān b. Ṣadaqah b. Waththāb said to Muslim b. 'Abd al-Raḥmān b. Muslim,[346] the agent (*'āmil*) of Ṭukhāristān:[347]

Muslim gave me a choice of his riding animals
and I said: "It is enough for me to have Muslim as my judge;
This is the hero and lord of the Banū 'Āmir.
It is honor enough for anyone to rule over the Banū 'Āmir."

The poet was referring to al-Ḥakam b. Numaylah. Naṣr's attitude toward the Qays altered for the worse and he was troubled by what Maghrā' had done.

Abū Numaylah Ṣāliḥ al-Abbār, the mawlā of the Banū 'Abs, had left (al-Kūfah) with Yaḥyā b. Zayd b. 'Alī b. Ḥusayn and he stayed with Yaḥyā until the latter was killed in Jūzjān. Naṣr had been angry with Abū Numaylah because of this, so the latter approached 'Ubaydallāh b. Bassām, Naṣr's friend, and recited as follows:

I was in distress, perplexed and troubled
until 'Ubaydallāh removed my anxiety from me. [1724]
I cried out to him and he rose joyfully to the honor
just as the whiteness of the full moon illuminates the darkness.[348]
So rise up with the judgment and the springing leap of a lion!
If on the day of battle you act like a high-minded man,
You will win to your side one whose courage (*muruwwah*) has reached its zenith
and whose Lord has singled him out for His favor.
Steadfast in resolution, striking blows like a lion,
he advances against death on the day of fear.

346. Muslim b. 'Abd al-Raḥmān b. Muslim al-Bāhilī had been governor of Balkh for Junayd. He was the nephew of Qutaybah b. Muslim. Cf. al-Ṭabarī, II, 1529–32, 1663–64.

347. The area to the east of Balkh which stretched along the south side of the Oxus as far as the frontiers of Badakhshān. Cf. Le Strange, *Lands*, 426–27.

348. The text has *aẓlāmi*. The Cairo edition (196) has *iẓlāmi*, which seems better.

He is not one to prattle in the assembly, nor to blab his secrets
in his speech. Nor is he one who argues his opponents into silence.
The garment and seat of forbearance are his,
at a time when men of understanding are dishonored by public assemblies.

So ʿUbaydallāh took Abū Numaylah in to see Naṣr. Then Abū Numaylah said: "May God order your affairs aright! Indeed, I am weak. If you think it appropriate, give me permission to recite." Naṣr gave him permission and Abū Numaylah recited the following:

The gaming arrow of al-Kalbī has won the day, but as for
Maghrā', his efforts were impeded by his ignoble descent.
O sons of Numayr, make it clear and then make it clear again,
was Maghrā' born a slave or was he of pure parentage?
If he is to you as treason
and faithlessness are to the character of an honorable man,
[1725] And if he is a descendant of slaves,
then no blame will attach to you because of his treason.
The sons of Layth gave him their patronage—and what great patronage it was!—
granting him unsolicited favors and an important position.
They fattened him up and when he had attained an enviable state of well-being
through the kindness[349] they had accorded him,
He betrayed his patrons as easily as
the wild striped ass brays in the wilderness.
So, as a warning to others and in censure of him, we likened him
to a dog[350]—for blame should go to him who is worthy of it—
And we praised the sons of Layth, for excellence

349. The text has *min sabīhā al-maqsūmi*. This is corrected in the Cairo edition (196) to *min saybihā al-maqsūmi*, which makes better sense.

350. Cf. Qur'ān 7, 176: *fa-mathaluhu ka-mathali al-kalbi*. Cf. also the saying: "Fatten up your dog and he will eat you," quoted in G. R. Smith and M. A. S. Abdel Haleem, *The Book of the Superiority of Dogs over many of Those who wear Clothes*, Warminster, 1978, p. xxx.

is the exclusive mark of men of liberality, generosity, and good judgement.
Learn, then, you sons of mighty, victorious lions,
and you people of al-Ṣafāh and of al-Ḥatīm,[351]
That the gratitude of pious men is enough to outweigh
the words of one who is suspected of evil conduct and whose honor is impugned.[352]
God has seen what you have done and
the barking of dogs[353] will never stop the stars shining.[354]

When Abū Numaylah had finished, Naṣr said: "You have spoken truly." The Qays then spoke and asked for pardon.

Naṣr scorned the Qays and sent them away because of what Maghrā' had done. In this context, a poet recited the following:

God has made the noble ones hateful to you
just as the Merciful One made the Qays hateful to Naṣr.
I saw Abū Layth scorning their leaders
and bringing close to him all those who have only tenuous links with him.[355]

In this year Yazīd b. Hishām b. 'Abd al-Malik led the people on the pilgrimage.[356] I was told this by Aḥmad b. Thābit from his informants on the authority of Isḥāq b. 'Īsā from Abū Ma'shar. The same report was also given by al-Wāqidī.

The agents (*'ummāl*) of the garrison cities in this year were the same as in the preceding one, and I have already mentioned them.

---

351. Evocative place names from the Ḥijāz.

352. *Mawṣūm* ("one whose honor is subjected to envious detracting"). Cf. *Gloss.*, p. DLVIII.

353. There may well be an astronomical allusion here. Cf. Sirius, Procyon, and the *kilāb al-shitā'* (stars that set aurorally in winter).

354. The text wrongly has *lan yanquṣu*. This is corrected to *lan yanquṣa* in *Add.*, p. DCCXI.

355. *Wa-yudnā ilayhi kulla dhī wālithin ghumri.* This seems to be analogous to the phrase *dhū 'ahdin wālithin* ("he who has a weak covenant"). Cf. *Gloss.*, p. DLXV.

356. Cf. al-Ya'qūbī, *Historiae*, II, 394. Yazīd b. Hishām was given the nickname of al-Afqam. Cf. Ibn Khayyāṭ, 370.

[1726]

The Events of the Year 124

(November 15, 741–November 3, 742)

Amongst the events taking place during this year was the arrival in al-Kūfah of a group of ʿAbbāsid supporters who were making for Mecca.[357] According to some historians, Bukayr b. Māhān bought Abū Muslim, the leader of the ʿAbbāsid *daʿwah*, from ʿĪsā b. Maʿqil al-ʿIjlī.

The Reason Why Bukayr b. Māhān Bought Abū Muslim

The sources differ on this matter. According to ʿAlī b. Muḥammad (al-Madāʾinī)—Ḥamzah b. Ṭalḥah al-Sulamī—his father: Bukayr b. Māhān[358] was scribe to one of the agents (*ʿummāl*) of Sind. He went to al-Kūfah and the ʿAbbāsid supporters assembled in a house there. Then mischievous rumors circulated about

357. These men were the leaders (*nuqabāʾ*) of the ʿAbbāsids in Khurāsān.

358. Bukayr b. Māhān came originally from Sijistān and had served the governor of Sind, al-Junayd b. ʿAbd al-Raḥmān. He was won over to the Hāshimiyyah in 102 (720–21). He had visited Khurāsān twice on behalf of the imām Muḥammad. Cf. *EI*², s.v. (D. Sourdel); al-Ṭabarī, II, 1639.

them and they were arrested. Bukayr was imprisoned and the others were released. Also in the prison were Abū ʿĀṣim Yūnus and ʿĪsā b. Maʿqil al-ʿIjlī, who had Abū Muslim[359] with him as his servant. Then Bukayr invited them to support the ʿAbbāsid cause and they were won over to his views. Then Bukayr said to ʿĪsā b. Maʿqil: "Who is this young man?" ʿĪsā replied: "He is a slave." Bukayr inquired: "Will you sell him?" ʿĪsā responded: "He is yours." Bukayr said: "I would like you to take a proper price for him." ʿĪsā replied: "He is yours for whatever price you want," so Bukayr gave ʿĪsā four hundred dirhams. Then they were released from prison and Bukayr sent Abū Muslim to Ibrāhīm,[360] who gave him to Mūsā al-Sarrāj.[361] Abū Muslim learned (much) from Mūsā and memorized what the latter told him. Then he began making repeated journeys to Khurāsān.

Other reports said: In the year 124 [November 15, 741–November 3, 742] Sulaymān b. Kathīr,[362] Mālik b. al-Haytham, Lāhiz b. Qurayẓ,[363] and Qaḥṭabah b. Shabīb[364] left Khurāsān, [1727] making for Mecca. When they entered al-Kūfah, they went to ʿĀṣim b. Yūnus al-ʿIjlī, who was in prison under suspicion of spreading propaganda on behalf of the ʿAbbāsids. With ʿĀṣim were ʿĪsā and Idrīs, the sons of Maʿqil, whom Yūsuf b. ʿUmar had imprisoned, and those agents (*ʿummāl*) of Khālid b. ʿAbdallāh whom he had also put in prison. ʿĪsā and Idrīs were accompanied by Abū Muslim, who was their servant. The Khurāsānīs recognized unusual qualities (*ʿalāmāt*) in Abū Muslim, and they said: "Who is this?" The people in the prison replied: "A young man from al-Sarrājīn[365] who is with us." Abū Muslim had listened to ʿĪsā and

359. The future leader of the revolutionary ʿAbbāsid movement in Khurāsān. Cf. *EI*², s.v. (S. Moscati); Wellhausen, 518 ff; Shaban, *ʿAbbāsid revolution*, 153–57.
360. Ibrāhīm succeeded his father as ʿAbbāsid imām in 125 (743).
361. Ibn al-Athīr has *Abū* Mūsā al-Sarrāj (V, 191).
362. After the death of Khidāsh in 118 (736), Sulaymān b. Kathīr was appointed by the ʿAbbāsid imām, Muḥammad, to take charge of the ʿAbbāsid organization in Khurāsān. He is named as one of the six ʿAbbāsid chiefs in Marw. Cf. al-Ṭabarī, II, 1586; Shaban, *ʿAbbāsid Revolution*, 151–54.
363. Mālik b. al-Haytham and Lāhiz b. Qurayẓ were amongst a group of ʿAbbāsid supporters who had been imprisoned by Asad al-Qasrī in 117 (735). Cf. al-Ṭabarī, II, 1586.
364. Cf. *EI*², Ḳaḥṭaba (M. Sharon).
365. Abū Muslim learned the trade of saddler from Abū Mūsā al-Sarrāj and would take saddles to Iṣfahān, Mosul, and other places to sell them. Cf. Ibn al-

Idrīs talking about the ʿAbbāsid cause[366] and when he heard them he wept. When they saw him reacting in this way, they invited him to join their movement and he agreed.[367]

In this year Sulaymān b. Hishām[368] went on a summer raiding expedition. In battle he met Leo, the king of Byzantium, and he returned safely, having taken plunder.[369]

According to al-Wāqidī: In this year Muḥammad b. ʿAlī b. ʿAbdallāh b. ʿAbbās died.[370] According to Aḥmad b. Thābit—his informants—Isḥāq b. ʿĪsā—Abū Maʿshar: Muḥammad b. Hishām b. Ismāʿīl led the people on the pilgrimage in this year.[371] Al-Wāqidī gave the same report.

Also in this year ʿAbd al-ʿAzīz b. al-Ḥajjāj b. ʿAbd al-Malik[372] went on the pilgrimage, accompanied by his wife, Umm Salamah, the daughter of Hishām b. ʿAbd al-Malik.

According to Muḥammad b. ʿUmar (al-Wāqidī)—Yazīd, the
[1728] mawlā of Abū al-Zinād: I saw Muḥammad b. Hishām at Umm Salamah's door.[373] He was sending in his greetings and there were many gifts from him at her door. He begged her to accept

---

Athīr, V, 191–92. Al-Sarrājīn (the saddle makers' [quarter]) was apparently in Marw.

366. Literally, "this viewpoint."

367. For other reports on Abū Muslim in Yūsuf's prison, cf. al-Dīnawarī, 339–41; al-Yaʿqūbī, *Historiae*, II, 392–93.

368. This son of the caliph Hishām was later to play an important role at the time of the coup of Marwān b. Muḥammad in 127 (744). Cf. Hawting, 96–99. He had considerable military experience on the Byzantine frontier and was at the head of an armed force known as the Dhakwāniyyah, which numbered several thousand men. Cf. Crone, 53.

369. There is a similar report in al-Yaʿqūbī, *Historiae*, II, 395. According to Christian sources, however, it was Leo's son whom Sulaymān met in battle, since Leo III had died on June 18, 741 (i.e., in the preceding Muslim year, 123 A.H.). Cf. Brooks, "Arabs in Asia Minor," 202.

370. Cf. Ibn Khayyāṭ, 372; Ibn al-Athīr, V, 195. Muḥammad b. ʿAlī b. ʿAbdallāh b. ʿAbbās had come to prominence on the death of Abū Hāshim in 98 (716), when one group known as the Hāshimiyyah held him to be their imām. Muḥammad sent out missionaries to Khurāsān from around 100 (718). Cf. *EI*², "ʿAbbāsids" (B. Lewis); and n. 395.

371. Cf. Ibn Khayyāṭ, 372.

372. The caliph Hishām's nephew. Cf. the Umayyad genealogical table.

373. The inclusion of this anecdote probably suggests that Muḥammad b. Hishām was acting in an improper way toward Umm Salamah. Presumably the Muḥammad b. Hishām mentioned here is the man mentioned as being in charge of the pilgrimage.

them and she refused. Finally, when he had given up hope of her accepting his presents, she gave orders that they should be taken in.[374]

The agents (*ʿummāl*) of the garrison cities in this year were the same as in the years 122 [December 7, 739–November 25, 740] and 123 [November 26, 740–November 14, 741], and they have already been mentioned.

---

374. Literally, "When he had given up hope of her accepting his present, she gave orders that it should be taken in."

The Events of the Year

125

(November 4, 742–October 24, 743)

Amongst the events taking place during this year was a summer raid made by al-Nuʿman b. Yazīd b. ʿAbd al-Malik.[375]

Also in this year occurred the death of Hishām b. ʿAbd al-Malik b. Marwān. According to Abū Maʿshar: Hishām died after six nights had elapsed of the month of Rabīʿ II [February 6, 743]. The same report was given by Aḥmad b. Thābit—his informants—Isḥāq b. ʿĪsā. Al-Wāqidī, al-Madā'inī, and others gave the same report, but they said that Hishām's death occurred on a Wednesday, after six nights had elapsed of the month of Rabīʿ II [Wednesday, February 6, 743].

The length of Hishām's caliphate, according to all reports, was nineteen years. According to al-Madā'inī and Ibn al-Kalbī: Hishām ruled for nineteen years, seven months and twenty-one days. According to Abū Maʿshar: (nineteen years) and eight and one-half months. According to al-Wāqidī: (nineteen years,) seven months and ten nights.

---

375. For this expedition, cf. al-Yaʿqūbī, *Historiae*, II, 395. For al-Nuʿmān, cf. the Umayyad genealogical table.

There was some divergence of opinion over Hishām's age. According to Hishām b. Muḥammad al-Kalbī: Hishām died when he [1729] was fifty-five years old. Some reports said: Hishām died when he was fifty-two years old. According to Muḥammad b. ʿUmar (al-Wāqidī): On the day Hishām died he was fifty-four years old. His death occurred at al-Ruṣāfah, where his grave is to be found. His *kunyah* was Abū al-Walīd.[376]

The Malady That Caused Hishām's Death

According to Aḥmad b. Zuhayr[377]—ʿAlī b. Muḥammad (al-Madāʾinī)—Shaybah b. ʿUthmān—ʿAmr b. Kalīʿ[378]—Sālim Abū al-ʿAlāʾ:[379] One day, Hishām b. ʿAbd al-Malik came out to us.[380] His appearance betrayed the fact that he was in melancholy mood. His clothes were hanging loosely on him and he had slackened the reins of his steed. He rode for an hour [in this state] and then he roused himself from his listlessness, arranged his clothes, took the reins of his horse, and said to al-Rabīʿ: "Call al-Abrash." Al-Abrash was summoned and Hishām walked between me and al-Abrash. Al-Abrash said to him: "O Commander of the Faithful, I saw you doing something that troubled me." Hishām said: "What is that?" Al-Abrash said: "I saw you go out in a state of mind that troubled me." Hishām replied: "Come on now, Abrash! How can I not be troubled when men of wisdom (*ahl al-ʿilm*) have claimed that I will be dead in thirty-three days' time?"

---

376. For the length of Hishām's rule, the date of his death and his age, cf. also Ibn Khayyāṭ, 372; Ibn Qutaybah, 185; al-Yaʿqūbī, *Historiae*, II, 394; *Fragmenta*, 107; al-Masʿūdī, *Murūj*, 456–57; al-Masʿūdī, *Tanbīh*, 295; Ibn ʿAbd Rabbihi, II, 286; Hamzah, 129.

377. Aḥmad b. Zuhayr, also known as Aḥmad b. Abī Haythamah, d. 279 (892–93), was a Ḥanbalī jurist. He was one of al-Ṭabarī's authorities for the Baṣran and Medinan historical traditions, which he reported from his father. Cf. Pedersen, *ʿAlī and Muʿāwiya*, 110; Ibn Ḥajar, *Mīzān*, I, 174; Ibn al-Nadīm, I, 174.

378. The reading Kalīʿ is uncertain. Other variants, Wakīʿ and Dulayʿ, are cited in the apparatus.

379. According to the Leiden index, this Sālim is not Hishām's famous *kātib*, who was in charge of the *dīwān al-rasāʾil*. The index is probably wrong. Grignasci, who presents a clear discussion of the identity of Sālim, the *kātib*, calls him Sālim Abū al-ʿAlā; cf. *Rasāʾil*, 12–13.

Sālim continued: I went back to my house and I wrote on a scroll: "The Commander of the Faithful said on such-and-such a day that he would die[381] in thirty-three days." On the night when the thirty-three days were up, a slave came knocking at my door saying: "Come to the Commander of the Faithful and bring with you the medicine for diphtheria (*dhubaḥah*)."[382] Hishām had
[1730] taken the medicine once before, had treated himself with it,[383] and had regained his strength. So I left, taking the medicine with me. Hishām gargled with it. The pain increased in intensity and then subsided. Hishām said to me: "Sālim, some of the pain I was feeling has eased, so go to your family and leave the medicine with me." Then I went away and hardly had an hour passed before I heard loud voices lamenting: "The Commander of the Faithful is dead."

As soon as Hishām had died, the treasurers shut the doors. People looked for a copper pan in which to heat some water to wash Hishām's body, but they could not find one until they asked a neighbor to lend them one. One of the people present on that occasion said: "There is a warning in this for anyone who heeds it."[384] Hishām died of diphtheria. When he died, his son, Maslamah b. Hishām, prayed over him.

Some Biographical Details about Hishām

According to Aḥmad b. Zuhayr—ʿAlī b. Muḥammad (al-Madā'inī)—Wasnān al-ʿArajī[385]—Ibn Abī Nuhaylah—ʿAqqāl b. Shab-

---

380. A similar story is also given in *Fragmenta,* 106.

381. *Yusāfiru.* Cf. *Gloss.,* p. CCXCI.

382. Although *dhubaḥah* is used in modern Arabic to denote angina pectoris, it may well not be the illness that is meant here. Gabrieli states that Hishām died of angina, cf. *Califfato,* 140. *Dhubaḥah* most probably denotes a throat obstruction caused by diphtheria or quinsy, hence Hishām's gargling with the medicine.

383. *Fa-taʿālaja.*

384. Hishām's avarice was legendary. Cf. Ibn ʿAbd Rabbihi, I, 233; al-Jāḥiẓ, *Bukhalā',* 28, 214. Alternatively, this may be a sententious comment to the effect that death is no respecter of persons.

385. The reading Wasnān is uncertain. The apparatus has two variants, Rasnān and Rasyān. This appears to be the only place where this person is mentioned by al-Ṭabarī.

bah:[386] I went in to see Hishām, who was wearing a tunic (*qabā'*) made of green fur. Hishām was sending me to Khurāsān and he began to give me my instructions. I kept looking at the cloak and he became aware of this and inquired: "What is the matter with you?" I said: "Before you become caliph, I saw you wearing a tunic made of green fur. I was wondering if this is the same one or a different one." Hishām said: "By the One God, this is the same [1731] one. I do not possess any other tunic. But this money that you see me collecting and hoarding is for you all." ʿAqqāl was in the service of Hishām. As for Shabbah, ʿAqqāl's father, he worked for ʿAbd al-Malik b. Marwān.[387] ʿAqqāl used to say: "When I went in to see Hishām, I found him a man chock-full[388] of intelligence."

According to Aḥmad b. Zuhayr—ʿAlī (al-Madā'inī)—Marwān b. Shujāʿ, a mawlā of Marwān b. al-Ḥakam:[389] I was in the service of Muḥammad b. Hishām b. ʿAbd al-Malik. He sent for me one day and I went in to see him. He was angry and sorrowful, so I said: "What is the matter with you?" Muḥammad said: "A Christian hit my servant on the head," and he began railing against the Christian. I said to him: "Take it easy." He said: "What can I do?" I replied: "Arraign him before the judge." He said: "Is there nothing else I can do?" I replied: "No." Then a eunuch of his said to him: "I will settle this for you." So the eunuch went and gave the Christian a beating. When Hishām heard about this, he sought out the eunuch, who called on Muḥammad for protection. Muḥammad b. Hishām said: "I gave you no orders." The eunuch retorted: "Yes, by God, you certainly did give me orders!" Then Hishām gave the eunuch a beating and rebuked his son.

According to Aḥmad (b. Zuhayr)—ʿAlī (al-Madā'inī): In the time of Hishām nobody went around with a retinue except Maslamah b. ʿAbd al-Malik. One day Hishām saw Sālim with a retinue, so he forbade him to do so and warned him: "I shall certainly find out if you go around with a retinue!" Thereafter, whenever a stranger came up and walked along with him, Sālim would stop and say, "What do you want?" and he would prevent the man from walk-

---

386. ʿAqqāl b. Shabbah al-Tamīmī al-Khaṭīb. Cf. al-Ṭabarī, II, 1755–56, 1820.
387. Umayyad caliph who ruled 65–86 (685–705).
388. Literally, "stuffed."
389. Umayyad caliph who ruled 64–65 (684–85).

ing along with him. Yet it seems that it was Sālim who dominated Hishām.[390]

None of the Marwānids[391] used to draw an army stipend[392]
[1732] unless they had to go on raids. Some of them raided in person and some of them sent out a substitute. Hishām b. ʿAbd al-Malik had a mawlā called Yaʿqūb, who used to take Hishām's stipend, i.e. two hundred and one dīnārs, for he was treated to an extra dīnār. Yaʿqūb would take the money and go out on raids. The Marwānids used to make themselves *dīwān* guards[393] and gave themselves other posts which allowed them to stay put and which exempted them from the obligation of going out on raids. Dāwūd and ʿĪsā,[394] the two sons of ʿAlī b. ʿAbdallāh b. ʿAbbās[395] by the same mother, served as guards to Khālid b. ʿAbdallāh[396] in the east, in Iraq.[397] They stayed with Khālid and he gave them money. If that had not been the case, he would not have been able to detain them.[398] Khālid made them guards and they spent their nights talking to Khālid and engaging him in their conversations.

Hishām entrusted an estate of his to one of his mawlās. The mawlā made it flourish and the estate yielded a large income. He continued to make the estate prosper and its income was doubled. The mawlā sent his son to take the income; the latter presented it to Hishām and told him how the estate was faring. Hishām re-

390. *Wa-kāna Sālimun ka-annahu huwa ammara Hishāman.* Literally: "it was as if Sālim had made Hishām *amīr.*" This translation is only tentative.

391. The Banū Marwān, the descendants of Marwān I (cf. n. 389 above), from whose number the Umayyad caliphs were drawn from 65 (685) until the fall of the dynasty in 132 (750).

392. *ʿAṭāʾ*. Cf. *EI*², s.v. (C. Cahen).

393. *Fī aʿwāni al-dīwāni.* Cf. *Gloss.*, p. CCCLXXXIII.

394. Prominent members of the ʿAbbāsid family who were subsequently involved in the overthrow of the Umayyads. Cf. Wellhausen, 543–44.

395. The grandson of al-ʿAbbās, the Prophet's uncle. ʿAlī was the father of the imām Muḥammad. Cf. n. 370.

396. Khālid al-Qasrī.

397. *Fī aʿwāni al-sharqi bi-al-ʿIrāqi.* This translation is only tentative. The apparatus has a variant reading, *fī al-sūqi* ("in the market"), which is preferred in the Cairo edition, 202. Neither version is very satisfactory when followed by "in Iraq."

398. *Fa-aqāmā ʿindahu fa-waṣalahumā wa-lawlā dhālika lam yastaṭiʿ an yaḥbisahumā.* This is rather obscure. *Waṣalahumā* has been translated as "he gave them money," and the verb *ḥabasa* as "to detain," rather than "to imprison." Presumably, Khālid made guards of the two ʿAbbāsids as a device to keep them close to him.

warded him well and the boy saw that Hishām was pleased, so he said: "O Commander of the Faithful, I have a request." Hishām said: "What is it?" The boy said: "Ten more dīnārs in my stipend." Hishām said: "You all seem sure that ten dīnārs in the stipend are a mere trifle.[399] No, by my life, I will not do it!"

According to Aḥmad (b. Zuhayr)—ʿAlī (al-Madāʾinī)—Jaʿfar b. Sulaymān[400]—ʿAbdallāh b. ʿAlī:[401] I scrutinized the registers (*dawāwīn*) of the Marwānids and I have never seen a more sound register than that of Hishām nor one which was more beneficial both to the common people and to the government. According to Aḥmad (b. Zuhayr)—ʿAlī (al-Madāʾinī)—Ghassān b. ʿAbd al-Ḥamīd:[402] Nobody amongst the Marwānids was more avaricious [1733] in dealing with his associates and registers than Hishām nor did any of the Marwānids investigate (the activities of) his officials with such extreme thoroughness as did Hishām.[403]

According to Aḥmad (b. Zuhayr)—ʿAlī (al-Madāʾinī)—Ḥammād al-Abaḥḥ: Hishām said to Ghaylān:[404] "Fie on you, Ghaylān! People have been spreading gossip about you, so let's hear your side of the argument. If it is the truth, we shall support you; and if it is false you will be made to stop thinking that way." Ghaylān agreed, so Hishām called Maymūn b. Mihrān[405] to question

---

399. Literally, "the value of an almond."

400. Jaʿfar b. Sulaymān b. ʿAlī al-Hāshimī was governor of Medina under al-Manṣūr (r. 136–58/745–75). Cf. Ibn al-Nadīm, I, 106, 277, 494; al-Ṭabarī, III, 247, 249.

401. This may well be a reference to ʿAbdallāh b. ʿAlī b. ʿAbdallāh, the uncle of the ʿAbbāsid caliph, al-Manṣūr. Cf. Ibn al-Nadīm, I, 259, 330; al-Masʿūdī, *Murūj*, VI, 73–77, 176–77, 214–18.

402. Perhaps this is the son of Sālim's successor, the *kātib* ʿAbd al-Hamīd. Cf. *EI*², "ʿAbd al-Ḥamīd b. Yaḥyā" (H. A. R. Gibb), and Ibn ʿAbd Rabbihi, III, 89. Ghassān b. ʿAbd al-Ḥamīd was the secretary of Jaʿfar b. Sulaymān. Cf. Ibn al-Nadīm, I, 274, 277.

403. Hishām was apparently interested in the administrative methods of the ancient empires. Cf. Gibb, *Studies*, 63. According to al-Masʿūdī, al-Manṣūr followed the fine precedents established by Hishām, whom he admired as one of the three great Umayyad leaders; the other two were Muʿāwiyah and ʿAbd al-Malik.

404. Abū Marwān Ghaylān b. Muslim (or b. Marwān) al-Qibṭī al-Dimashqī was one of the Qadariyyah who advocated free will in Islam. For Ghaylān's career and writings, cf. Ibn al-Nadīm, I, 257, 274, 388; Ibn Qutaybah, 244; Cook, 81, 141, 232; Van Ess, *Anfänge*, 45; Watt, *Formative Period*, 85–86.

405. Maymūn b. Mihrān was in charge of justice in the Jazīrah under the caliph ʿUmar II (r. 99–101/717–20). For an analysis of this discussion in front of Hishām, cf. Watt, 86.

Ghaylān. Maymūn said to Ghaylān: "You ask first, since the case is strongest if you ask first." So Ghaylān said to Maymūn: "Has God willed that he should be disobeyed?" Then Maymūn replied to Ghaylān: "Was God disobeyed if He did not will it so?" Ghaylān was silent and Hishām said: "Give him an answer." But Ghaylān still did not answer him. Then Hishām said to Maymūn: "God will not forgive me for my errors if I forgive Ghaylān his." So Hishām gave orders that Ghaylān's hands and feet should be cut off.

According to Aḥmad (b. Zuhayr)—'Alī (al-Madā'inī)—a man of Banū Ghanī[406]—Bishr, the mawlā of Hishām: A man who had singing girls, wine, and a guitar in his home was brought to Hishām. Hishām said: "Break the lute over his head." The instrument struck the *shaykh*, who wept. Bishr (the narrator) said: "I said to him, by way of consolation: 'Be patient.' He retorted: 'Do you think I am crying because I was struck? I am only crying because of the contempt which Hishām showed toward the guitar when he called it a lute!' "

A man spoke rudely to Hishām, and Hishām said to him: "You should not speak rudely to your imām."

Hishām went in search of one of his sons who had not attended the Friday prayer. Hishām said to him: "What prevented you from performing the prayer?" His son said: "My horse has died." Hishām said: "Why didn't you walk instead of missing the Friday prayer?" Then he deprived his son of a horse for a year.

Sulaymān b. Hishām wrote to his father as follows:[407] "My mule is too weak to carry me. If the Commander of the Faithful
[1734] thinks it appropriate to issue orders for me to be given a horse, then let him do so." Hishām wrote back to Sulaymān as follows: "The Commander of the Faithful has understood your letter and what you have said about the weak condition of your riding animal. The Commander of the Faithful thinks that this situation has arisen from your negligence in feeding the animal, and that its fodder is being wasted. So see to the maintenance of your animal personally and the Commander of the Faithful will further consider the matter of your transport."[408]

406. On the Banū Ghanī, cf. Ibn al-Kalbī, II, 272.
407. Al-Mas'ūdī relates the same story. Cf. *Murūj*, V, 478.
408. *Fī ḥumlānika:* Literally, "your riding beast." Cf. *Gloss.*, p. CCX.

One of Hishām's finance officials wrote to him as follows: "I have sent the Commander of the Faithful a basket of peaches.[409] Let the Commander of the Faithful write and tell me that it has arrived safely." Hishām wrote back to him: "The peaches which you sent have reached the Commander of the Faithful and he liked them. So send him some more and close the receptacle tightly."

Hishām wrote to one of his finance officials as follows: "The truffles which you sent the Commander of the Faithful have arrived. There are forty of them and some of them have gone bad. The only reason they got like that was because of the way they were packed. If you send any more of them to the Commander of the Faithful, fill with sand the jar in which you put them so that they will not move about and knock against each other."

According to Aḥmad (b. Zuhayr)—ʿAlī (al-Madāʾinī)—al-Ḥārith b. Yazīd—a mawlā belonging to Hishām: A mawlā belonging to Hishām who was on one of his estates sent me with two fine birds. I then went in to see Hishām, who was sitting on a sofa[410] in the courtyard of the house. Hishām said: "Put them in the house." So I did so and he looked at them. Then I said: "O Commander of the Faithful, what about my reward?" Hishām said: "Shame on you! What is a suitable reward for two birds?" I said: [1735] "Whatever you think." Hishām said: "Take one of the birds," so I ran into the house to look at the birds. Hishām said: "What are you doing?" I replied: "I am choosing the better of the two birds." Hishām said: "Are you choosing the better of the two and leaving me with the worse one? Leave them both and we will give you forty or fifty dirhams."[411]

(Before becoming caliph) Hishām was assigned a piece of land called Dawrīn. He sent people to take possession of it and they found it in a state of ruin. Hishām said to Dhuwayd, a scribe who was (working) in Syria: "Now then, what strategem can we use here?" Dhuwayd said: "What will you do for me in return?" Hishām said: "Four hundred dīnārs." So Dhuwayd set down the words "Dawrīn and its villages" in the registers. Hishām drew a lot of income (from this estate). Later, when Hishām became

---

409. *Durrāqin:* "Syrian peaches." Cf. *Lisān,* I, 971.

410. For a discussion of *sarīr,* cf. n. 112.

411. This story is also told by al-Masʿūdī, *Murūj,* V, 477.

caliph, Dhuwayd went in to see him. Hishām said: "Dawrīn and its villages. No, by God, you will never govern a province for me," and he banished Dhuwayd from Syria.

According to Aḥmad (b. Zuhayr)—ʿAlī (al-Madāʾinī)—ʿUmayr b. Yazīd—Abū Khālid—al-Walīd b. Khulayd: Hishām b. ʿAbd al-Malik saw me riding a Ṭukhārī horse, and he said to me: "O Walīd b. Khulayd, what is this horse?" I said: "Al-Junayd gave it to me." Hishām was envious of me and he said: "By God, there are too many of these Ṭukhārī horses around." Yet when ʿAbd al-Malik had died, we found amongst his riding-animals only one single Ṭukhārī horse. His sons vied with one other as to which of them should take it, and each of them thought that if he did not possess it himself he had not inherited anything worth having from ʿAbd al-Malik.[412]

One of the family[413] of Marwān[414] said to Hishām: "How can
[1736] you, who are miserly and cowardly, want the caliphate?" Hishām replied: "Why should I not want it, seeing that I am forbearing and decent?"[415]

One day Hishām said to al-Abrash: "Have your she-goats given birth yet?" Al-Abrash said: "By God, yes." Hishām said: "But my she-goats are late in giving birth. Take me out to see your she-goats and let me have some of their milk." Al-Abrash said: "Yes. Shall I send people on in advance (to make preparations)?" Hishām said "No." Al-Abrash said: "Shall we send a tent ahead so that it can be put up for us?" Hishām said "Yes." Accordingly, al-Abrash sent out two men with a tent and it was put up. Early the next morning, Hishām, al-Abrash and the people went out, Hishām and al-Abrash each seated themselves on a stool, and an ewe was brought to each of them. Hishām milked the ewe with his own hand and said: "Take note, Abrash, that I had no difficulty in

412. It is possible that this was the type of horse that had been much in demand for the Sasanian armored cavalry and had also been exported for centuries to China—the celebrated "blood-sweating" horse of the Oxus. Cf. Watson, *Genius*, 110, 119–20. A similar story is told by al-Masʿūdī, *Murūj*, V, 478–79.

413. The text has *ālī*. This is corrected later to *āli*. Cf. *Add.*, p. DCCXI. The Cairo edition (VII, 205) has the corrected form.

414. According to al-Masʿūdī, it was Maslamah, the brother of Hishām, who teased Hishām in this way. Cf. *Murūj*, V, 479.

415. *Anā ḥalīmun ʿafīfun*. Al-Masʿūdī has *anā ḥakīmun wa-ʿālimun* ("I am wise and knowledgeable"). Cf. *Murūj*, loc. cit.

getting the milk to flow."[416] Then Hishām ordered that the bread dough should be brought and it was kneaded.[417] Then Hishām lit the fire himself, made a hollow in it for the bread, and threw in the bread. He began turning it over with the poker and said: "Well Abrash, what do you think of my expertise?" When the bread was cooked thoroughly Hishām removed it. He began hitting it with the poker, saying: "This is just for you!" And al-Abrash would reply "Here I am"[418] (this is what young boys say when bread is being baked for them). Then Hishām and the people ate lunch and he returned home.

'Ilbā' b. Manẓūr al-Laythī came to Hishām and recited the following to him:

'Ulayyah said, when I decided to undertake a journey
  on a bewildered she-camel flapping her ears:
"How can you contemplate a journey when all the people of
  your family,
  old and young alike, are dependent on you?
The young ones are like little sand-grouse,
  wealthy neither in property nor in kinsfolk."

(I replied): "I am traveling to the king of Syria, the one to whom every care-burdened man[419] makes his way.

I will certainly leave you rich, provided I stay alive, [1737]
  through the gifts of the caliph, that dispenser of glittering
  largesse.
We are indeed a people whose court is dead;[420]

---

416. *Lam abuss al-ḥalaba*. Cf. *Lisān*, I, 212. Hishām is clearly proud of his prowess in milking.

417. *Amara bi-mallaṭin fa-'ujinat*. The *mallah* can mean the hollow made in the fire for baking bread, or the hot dust and ashes in which the bread is cooked. *Khubzu mallatin* is bread baked in hot ashes. Cf. Lane, I, *Supplement*, 3023. In view of the following verb, *'ujinat* ("it was kneaded"), the word *mallah* has been translated as "bread dough." Cf. *EI*², "Khubz" (C. Pellat).

418. *Yaqūlu jabīnaka, jabīnaka wa-al-Abrash yaqūlu labbayka, labbayka*. This translation is only tentative. *Jabīnaka* may be analogous to the phrase *min jabīnī*, "I alone."

419. The text has *muwaqqari*. Nöldeke prefers the reading *mūqari*. Cf. *Add.*, p. DCCXI. This emendation is followed by the Cairo edition, VII, 206.

420. *Mayyitun dīwānunā*. An alternative translation is provided in the *Gloss.*, p. CCXLVII: "We accept no stipends."

> but once it is touched by the generosity of the caliph it will be raised to life again."

Hishām said to ʿIlbāʾ: "You have tried hard and petitioned well." So he gave orders that ʿIlbāʾ should receive five hundred dirhams and gave him an increase in his stipend.

Muḥammad b. Zayd b. ʿAbdallāh b. ʿUmar b. al-Khaṭṭāb[421] came to Hishām, who said: "I have nothing for you." Then he added, "Take care lest anyone deceive you and say that the Commander of the Faithful has failed to recognize you. I have indeed recognized you. You are Muḥammad b. Zayd b. ʿAbdallāh b. ʿUmar b. al-Khaṭṭāb. Do not stay and spend what money you already have, for you will get no gift from me. So go back to your family!"

One day, Hishām stopped near a walled garden of his in which there was an olive tree. With him was ʿUthmān b. Ḥayyān al-Murrī.[422] ʿUthmān was standing with his head almost at a level with the head of the Commander of the Faithful, who was talking to him. Then Hishām heard the olive tree shaking and he said to someone: "Go to them and tell them to pick the olives properly and not to shake the tree; otherwise its fruit will burst open and its branches will break."

Hishām went on the pilgrimage. Al-Abrash took along some *mukhannaths*[423] who had guitars with them. Hishām said: "Imprison them and sell their possessions"—Hishām was not aware of what their goods were—"and put the proceeds in the treasury. If they mend their ways, return the money to them."

Hishām b. ʿAbd al-Malik lived at the Ruṣāfah which is reported to have been in the area of Qinnasrīn.[424] According to Aḥmad b.
[1738] Zuhayr b. Ḥarb—ʿAlī b. Muḥammad (al-Madāʾinī): The reason why Hishām lived at al-Ruṣāfah was that the caliphs and their sons used to seclude themselves[425] to escape the plague. So they

---

421. The great-grandson of the caliph ʿUmar (r. 13–23/634–44).

422. ʿUthmān b. Ḥayyān al-Murrī was made governor of Medina in 93 or 94 (711–712 or 712–713) and dismissed in 96 (715). Cf. al-Ṭabarī, II, 1282; Ibn ʿAbd Rabbihi, I, 93; II, 51; III, 43.

423. The term *mukhannath* is difficult to define precisely. It denotes an effeminate man or someone who is neither entirely male or female. Cf. *Lisān*, I, 908.

424. For a discussion of al-Ruṣāfah, cf. n. 426.

425. *Yantabidhūna:* "They would retire apart." The apparatus has a variant reading, *yatabaddūna*, "they would go into the desert," which is adopted by the Cairo edition (VII, 207).

lived in the desert far away from people. When Hishām wanted to move to al-Ruṣāfah, he was told: "Do not leave! Caliphs are not touched by plague. It is unheard of for a caliph to catch the plague." Hishām said: "Do you want to experiment with me?" So he moved to al-Ruṣāfah, which is a desert place, and he built two castles there. Al-Ruṣāfah is a Byzantine city built by the Byzantines.[426]

Hishām had a squint (*aḥwal*). According to Aḥmad (b. Zubayr)—ʿAlī (al-Madāʾinī): Khālid b. ʿAbdallāh[427] sent a camel-driver (*ḥādī*) to Hishām b. ʿAbd al-Malik, and he recited[428] before Hishām a poem of Abū al-Najm (al-ʿIjlī)[429] in the *rajaz* meter:

The sun on the horizon is descending like the eye of a man
with a squint.
It intends to set but has not yet done so.

At this Hishām became angry and dismissed him.

According to Aḥmad b. Zuhayr—ʿAlī b. Muḥammad (al-Madāʾinī)—Abū ʿĀṣim al-Ḍabbī: I noticed Muʿāwiyah b. Hishām pass me when I was in the clearing (*raḥbah*) of Abū Sharīk. Abū Sharīk was a Persian after whom the clearing—which was a field under cultivation—was named. I had been baking bread. Muʿāwiyah stopped near me and I said: "Have some lunch." He dismounted and I took out the bread, put it on some bricks,[430] and he ate. Then other people came along and I asked, "Who is this?" They replied: "Muʿāwiyah b. Hishām." Muʿāwiyah ordered that I

---

426. There has been a long controversy about the interpretation of this passage. The reference to "two castles" (*qaṣrayn*) was interpreted by Sauvaget ("Remarques", 2–13) and by Creswell (*Architecture*, 513, 537–38) as denoting Qaṣr al-Ḥayr al-Sharqī in the Palmyrene steppe, which has two adjoining enclosures of Umayyad date. One of these, however, is a city and the other apparently a *khān*; for neither of them does the term *qaṣr* seem appropriate. Moreover, subsequent excavations on the site have revealed no traces of a Roman or Byzantine city (Grabar, *City*, 13). It seems preferable, therefore, to assume with Grabar that the Ruṣāfah mentioned by al-Ṭabarī is Ruṣāfat al-Shām/Sergiopolis, the major Byzantine city of northeastern Syria, situated in the desert some twenty-five miles south of the Euphrates. Cf. *EI*[1], "Al-Ruṣāfa" (E. Honigmann).

427. Khālid al-Qasrī.

428. *Ḥadā:* to urge on a camel by reciting verses to it in the *rajaz* meter. Cf. Lane, I, 532–33.

429. Abū al-Najm al-Faḍl (or al-Mufaḍḍal) b. Qudāmah al-ʿIjlī was a well-known *rajaz* poet. He enjoyed particular success under Hishām. Cf. Sezgin, II, 371–72.

430. The text has *fī labinin*, "on bricks." An alternative reading could be *fī labanin*, "in milk."

should be given a present and then he rode off. Suddenly a fox appeared in front of him and he chased after it. He had not fol-
[1739] lowed it for more than a bow-shot's distance when his horse unseated him and he fell. They took him away dead. Hishām said: "By God, I had resolved to choose him for the caliphate but here he is, chasing after a fox!" Muʿāwiyah b. Hishām had with him the daughter of Ismāʿīl b. Jarīr and another woman. Hishām settled on each of them one-half of the eighth (i.e., their legal inheritance), namely, forty thousand (dīnārs).

According to Aḥmad b. Zuhayr—ʿAlī (al-Madāʾinī)—Qaḥdam, Yūsuf's secretary: Yūsuf b. ʿUmar sent me to Hishām to take him a red ruby,[431] the sides of which were bigger than my palm, and a pearl as large as could be.[432] I went in to see Hishām and approached him, but I could not see his face because the couch was so long and there were so many cushions.[433] He reached out for the stone and the pearl and asked: "Did you bring papers indicating what weight they are?" I replied: "O Commander of the Faithful, they are too heavy for anyone to write down their weight. Where can the likes of them be found?" Hishām said: "You are right." The ruby had belonged to al-Rāʾiqah, the slave girl of Khālid b. ʿAbdallāh. She had bought it for seventy-three thousand dīnārs.

According to Aḥmad b. Zuhayr—Ibrāhīm b. al-Mundhir al-Ḥizāmī[434]—Ḥusayn b. Yazīd—Shihāb b. ʿAbd Rabbihi—ʿAmr b. ʿAlī: I was walking along with Muḥammad b. ʿAlī[435] to his house, which was near the bathhouse, and I said to him: "Hishām's rule and authority have lasted a long time. It is nearly twenty years.

---

431. According to another source, the ruby was one and one-half *qabḍah*s in length. Cf. *Fragmenta*, 101. The *qabḍah* was usually measured as one-sixth of a cubit. Cf. Hinz, 63.

432. The pearl weighed three and one-half *mithqāl*s. Cf. *Fragmenta*, 101. For the weight of the *mithqāl* in various parts of the Islamic world, cf. Hinz, 1–7.

433. *Fursh*. This usually means "carpets." Given the common Sasanian royal custom of piling cushions one upon another beside the monarch as he reclined (Grabar, *Sasanian Silver*, plates 13–14) and Hishām's readiness to favor Persian culture and customs, it seems probable that he had adopted this aspect of Sasanian court ceremonial. Even if *fursh* were to be translated as "carpets," the context (and the Sasanian silver dishes published by Grabar) establishes that such carpets were being used as cushions in this instance.

434. Ibrāhīm b. al-Mundhir al-Ḥizāmī (d. 236/850–51), was a traditionist. Cf. al-Ṭabarī, I, 967; Ibn al-Nadīm, I, 244, 246; Ibn ʿAbd Rabbihi, III, 190, 210.

People say that Solomon asked his Lord to bestow on him sovereignty such as should not belong to any after him. They do claim that that period was twenty years."[436] Muḥammad b. ʿAlī said: "I don't know what tales are current with the people, but my father told me on the authority of his father on the authority of ʿAlī on the authority of the Prophet, who said: "God will not prolong the life of a king in a community (*ummah*)—in the event that he has been preceded by a prophet—for a period longer than the life of that prophet." [1740]

In this year al-Walīd b. Yazīd b. ʿAbd al-Malik b. Marwān[437] became caliph after the death of Hishām b. ʿAbd al-Malik. According to Hishām b. Muḥammad al-Kalbī: Al-Walīd became caliph on a Saturday in Rabīʿ II, 125[438] [February 1–March 2, 743]. According to Muḥammad b. ʿUmar (al-Wāqidī): Al-Walīd b. Yazīd b. ʿAbd al-Malik acceded to the caliphate on Wednesday, the sixth of Rabīʿ II, 125 [Wednesday, February 6, 743]. ʿAlī b. Muḥammad (al-Madāʾinī) concurred with Muḥammad b. ʿUmar in this dating.

---

435. Cf. n. 370.
436. An allusion to Qurʾān 38, v. 5.
437. Cf. the Umayyad genealogical table.
438. The possible Saturdays were February 2, 9, 16, or 23, 743.

The Caliphate of al-Walīd b. Yazīd b. ʿAbd al-Malik b. Marwān

The Events of the Year 125 (cont'd)

(November 4, 742–October 24, 743)

Some of the Reasons Why al-Walīd Acceded to the Caliphate

I have already mentioned why al-Walīd's father, Yazīd b. ʿAbd al-Malik b. Marwān, nominated al-Walīd to succeed to the caliphate after his (Yazīd's) brother, Hishām b. ʿAbd al-Malik. On the day when al-Walīd's father, Yazīd, appointed him (to succeed after Hishām), al-Walīd was eleven years old and Yazīd did not die until his son al-Walīd reached the age of fifteen. Later on, Yazīd regretted having nominated his brother Hishām as caliph. When [1741] he looked at his son al-Walīd, Yazīd would say: "It is God who stands between me and the one who put Hishām between me and you."[439] When Yazīd b. ʿAbd al-Malik died, his son al-Walīd was

439. For the early life of al-Walīd II, cf. Gabrieli, "Al-Walīd"; Derenk, *Leben*, 27–38. Al-Walīd's father, Yazīd, had been persuaded in 101 (719) by Maslamah b. ʿAbd al-Malik to nominate Hishām as caliph and that Yazid's own son, al-Walīd, should be second successor. Yazīd may well have regretted this decision, but, as his exclamation here suggests, he regarded the arrangement as a solemn obligation before God which he could not change. Therefore Hishām had duly succeeded to the caliphate in 105 (724) and al-Walīd had to wait another nineteen years for his turn.

fifteen years old and Hishām became caliph. Hishām was generous, respectful, and kind toward al-Walīd and their relationship continued in that style until al-Walīd b. Yazīd began to show signs of wanton behavior and to drink wine.[440]

According to Aḥmad b. Zuhayr—ʿAlī b. Muḥammad (al-Madā'inī)—Juwayriyah b. Asmā', Isḥāq b. Ayyūb, ʿĀmir b. al-Aswad,[441] and others: It was ʿAbd al-Ṣamad b. ʿAbd al-ʿAlā al-Shabbānī,[442] the brother of ʿAbdallāh b. ʿAbd al-ʿAlā,[443] who incited al-Walīd to act in this way. ʿAbd al-Ṣamad was the tutor of al-Walīd. Al-Walīd also acquired drinking companions. Hishām wanted to keep them away from al-Walīd, so he put him in charge of the pilgrimage in 116 [January 8–13, 735].[444] Al-Walīd took with him some dogs[445] in boxes, one of which, according to ʿAlī b. Muḥammad (al-Madā'inī)—his *shaykh*s whose names I have given—fell from the camel. In the box was a dog. People trained whips on the man who had hired out the camel and they beat him hard. Al-Walīd also took with him a domed canopy,[446] which had been made to the exact size of the Kaʿbah so that he could place it over the Kaʿbah. He also took wine with him. He wanted to erect the domed canopy over the Kaʿbah and to sit in it.[447] His compan-

440. For al-Walīd's relationship with Hishām, cf. al-Iṣfahānī, *Aghānī*, VI, 102–03, 107–08; Ibn ʿAbd Rabbihi, II, 117, 282, 285; al-Balādhurī, *Ansāb* (Derenk), 6–9.

441. ʿĀmir b. Ḥafṣ, also known as Suḥaym b. Ḥafṣ (d. 190/806), was a prolific writer. Many fragments of his work are preserved in Ibn Qutaybah, *Maʿārif*. According to Ibn Durayd, he was the mawlā of the Banū al-ʿUjayf. Cf. *Ishtiqāq*, 235. Cf. also Sezgin, II, 266–67; Rosenthal, 381.

442. Scabrous stories were rife about this man. Cf. al-Iṣfahānī, *Aghānī*, II, 78; VI, 102, 104–05. His *nisbah*, which appears in the text as al-Shaybānī, is corrected by the editor to al-Shabbānī (*Add.*, p. DCCXI). The Cairo edition (209) has al-Shabbānī. bānī. Al-Balādhurī calls him ʿAbd al-Ṣamad b. ʿAbd al-ʿAlā, al-Shāʿir ("the poet"). Cf. *Ansāb* (Derenk), 6.

443. ʿAbdallāh b. ʿAbd al-ʿAlā al-Shabbānī, the poet. Cf. al-Ṭabarī, I, 2064; al-Iṣfahānī, *Aghānī*, XII, 111; XVI, 157.

444. The pilgrimage proper begins on the eighth of Dhū al-Ḥijjah and ends on the thirteenth of Dhū al-Ḥijjah. In 116 A.H. these days correspond to January 8–13, 735. For corroboration of the year 116 (735), cf. Ibn Khayyāṭ, 377; al-Iṣfahānī, *Aghānī*, II, 78; *Fragmenta*, 113; Ibn al-Athīr, V, 198; al-Balādhurī, *Ansāb* (Derenk), 7.

445. Presumably for the hunt. The dog was ritually unclean. Cf. Smith, *Dogs*, p. xxix–xxx.

446. *Qubbah*. Cf. Ibn Aʿtham, VIII, 137; al-Yaʿqūbī, *Historiae*, II, 400.

447. Ibn al-Athīr (loc. cit.) and *Fragmenta* (loc. cit.) have "to drink wine in it."

ions frightened him off the idea and said: "We don't feel safe, either on your behalf or our own,[448] from what the people might do." So al-Walīd did not move the canopy [on to the Kaʿbah]. Even so, the people saw him behaving in a contemptuous and flippant way toward religion, and Hishām came to hear about it. Hishām wanted to depose him (as his heir) and to have the oath of allegiance given to his son Maslamah b. Hishām. Hishām tried to [1742] persuade al-Walīd to annul the oath of allegiance sworn to him and to give it instead to Maslamah, but al-Walīd refused. Hishām then said to al-Walīd: "Give Maslamah the oath of allegiance (to succeed) after yourself," but this too al-Walīd refused to do. Thereafter Hishām changed his attitude toward al-Walīd and did him mischief. He took steps in secret to have the oath of allegiance given to his son, and a number of people complied with Hishām's request. Amongst those who did so were his maternal uncles, Muḥammad and Ibrāhīm, the sons of Hishām b. Ismāʿīl al-Makhzūmī, and the sons of al-Qaʿqāʿ b. Khulayd al-ʿAbsī,[449] as well as others among Hishām's close followers.

Al-Walīd persisted in his wine-drinking and his pursuit of pleasure and he exceeded all due bounds. Hishām said to him: "Fie on you, Walīd! By God, I do not know whether you are for Islam or not. You commit every reprehensible action without feeling any shame or bothering to conceal it." So al-Walīd wrote Hishām the following poem:

O you who ask about our religion,
    we follow the religion of Abū Shākir.
We drink it (the wine) both pure and mixed,
    sometimes warmed and sometimes cooled.[450]

Hishām was furious with his son Maslamah, whose *kunyah* was Abū Shākir,[451] and he said to him: "Al-Walīd is making use of

---

448. Literally, "We do not feel safe for you or for us who are with you from the people."

449. For the history of this family, who were involved in several Umayyad succession disputes, cf. Crone, 105–06.

450. The meter is *sarīʿ*. For these verses, cf. al-Iṣfahānī, *Aghānī*, VI, 102; *Fragmenta*, 114; Ibn al-Athīr, V, 198; Gabrieli, "al-Walīd," 46; al-Balādhurī, *Ansāb* (Derenk), 7.

451. Maslamah had become friendly with al-Walīd and had joined in some of al-Walīd's hedonistic activities. Cf. al-Balādhurī, loc. cit. Al-Walīd's response involv-

you to mock me. To think I was rearing you for the caliphate! Behave in a civilized way and attend the collective prayer." Hishām put Maslamah in charge of the pilgrimage in 119 [December, 737].[452] Maslamah devoted himself to acts of religious devotion and behaved in a steady and gentle manner. He distributed money in Mecca and Medina, and a mawlā belonging to the Medinans recited the following lines:

O you who ask about our religion,
 we follow the religion of Abū Shākir.
The one who generously donates hairless horses[453] with their
 halters
 and who is neither a free-thinker[454] nor an unbeliever.

The poet was referring obliquely to al-Walīd.

The mother of Maslamah b. Hishām was Umm Ḥakīm,[455] the daughter of Yaḥyā b. al-Ḥakam b. Abī al-ʿĀṣ.[456] Al-Kumayt[457] recited as follows:

Verily the stakes (of the tent) of the caliphate will be
 transferred
 after al-Walīd to the son of Umm Ḥakīm.

[1743] Khālid b. ʿAbdallāh al-Qasrī said: "I want nothing to do with a caliph whose *kunyah* is Abū Shākir." Maslamah b. Hishām was

---

ing Maslamah is therefore particularly offensive to Hishām. For al-Walīd's affection and kind treatment toward his friend Maslamah, cf. al-Iṣfahānī, *Aghānī*, VI, 103–04; Ibn ʿAbd Rabbihi, II, 286.

452. For Maslamah's leading the pilgrimage, cf. Ibn Khayyāṭ, 377.

453. *Al-jurda* ("horses endowed with fine hairs"). Cf. Freytag, *Lexicon*, 77. *Jurd* is the reading followed by *Fragmenta*, 114; al-Balādhurī, *Ansāb* (Derenk), 7; and Ibn al-Athīr, V, 198. Al-Iṣfahānī has *al-buzla* (camels that have attained their full strength). Cf. *Aghānī* VI, 102; Lane, I, 200.

454. *Zindiq* is a difficult term to translate accurately since it is often used as a general term of abuse, as well as to denote Manichaeans and those of other "heretical" beliefs.

455. Umm Ḥakīm was famous for her beauty as her mother Zaynab bint ʿAbd al-Raḥmān had been before her. Umm Ḥakīm was very fond of wine, a characteristic of hers that is recorded in verse by al-Iṣfahānī, *Aghānī*, XV, 48.

456. The uncle of the Umayyad caliph ʿAbd al-Malik and governor of Palestine. Cf. Crone, 125.

457. Al-Kumayt b. Zayd al-Asadī (d. 126/743 or 127/744). Other verses of his are quoted in al-Ṭabarī, II, 1574–75. Cf. *EI*², "Kumayt b. Zayd" (J. Horovitz/ C. Pellat); Sezgin, II, 347–49; al-Iṣfahānī, *Aghānī*, XVII, 40; XV, 113. The meter is *kāmil*.

furious with Khālid, and so when Asad b. ʿAbdallāh,[458] the brother of Khālid b. ʿAbdallāh, died, Abū Shākir (Maslamah) wrote to Khālid b. ʿAbdallāh, sending a poem in which Nawfal[459] lampooned Khālid and his brother Asad:[460]

May a Lord who has given the people respite from Asad
liberate them from Khālid by destroying him too!
As for his father, he was of impure lineage,
a low-born slave who was himself begotten of slaves with stunted limbs.[461]

Maslamah sent a scroll by postal courier to Khālid. Khālid thought that it contained a message of condolence on the death of his brother. He broke the seal but found in the scroll nothing but the lampooning verses. Then he said: "Never have I seen condolences like those I have received today."[462]

Hishām used to criticize and denigrate al-Walīd. He frequently scoffed at al-Walīd and his friends and often pointed out his faults. When al-Walīd realized what Hishām's attitude was he went away, accompanied by some of his retinue and his mawlās, and lived in al-Azraq between the territory of the Balqayn[463] and the Fazārah[464] at a watering-place called al-Aghdaf.[465] Al-Walīd

---

458. Cf. n. 1116.

459. The text has Nawfal. This is later emended to Yaḥyā b. Nawfal; cf. *Add.*, p. DCCXI. The poet's *nisbah* was al-Ḥimyarī. Cf. al-Iṣfahānī, *Aghānī*, II, 149; III, 138; XIV, 57.

460. The repetition of the phrase "when he (Asad) died" has been omitted in the translation.

461. *Li-aʿbudin qufudi. Qufud* is used here instead of *qufd*, the plural of *aqfad*. Cf. *Gloss.*, p. CDXXX. *ʿAbdun aqfadu:* "a slave having rigid and contracted arms and legs, with short fingers and toes." Cf. *Lisān*, III, 135. The meter of these lines is *munsariḥ*.

462. For a discussion of this incident, cf. Gabrieli, *Califfato*, 22–23, n. 3. These verses in a longer form are given in Ibn al-Athīr, V, 162. Cf. also al-Balādhurī, *Ansāb* (Derenk), 8.

463. Balqayn is a contraction of the name Banū al-Qayn. The Balqayn were a subgroup of the Quḍāʿah. Cf. al-Yaʿqūbī, *Les Pays*, 175; Ibn al-Kalbī, II, 455; *EI*², "Al-Ḳayn" (W. M. Watt).

464. The Fazārah were a subgroup of the Dhubyān. Cf. Ibn al-Kalbī, II, 246.

465. On the topographical problems presented by this passage, cf. Gabrieli, "al-Walīd," 6, n. 4. Gabrieli translates the Arabic *fa-nazala bi-al-Azraq bayna arḍi Balqayn wa-Fazārah ʿalā māʾin yuqālu lahu al-Aghdaf* as "e ando a stabilirsi . . . ad al-Azraq, tra la terra dei Balqayn e dei Fazarah, sul fiumicello al-Aghdaf." The problem which Gabrieli sets out clearly is that elsewhere al-Azraq and al-Aghdaf

left behind at al-Ruṣāfah his scribe ʿIyāḍ b. Muslim, the mawlā of ʿAbd al-Malik b. Marwān, and he said to ʿIyāḍ: "Write to me about whatever is going on where you are." Al-Walīd took with him ʿAbd al-Ṣamad b. ʿAbd al-ʿAlā. They were drinking one day, and
[1744] when the wine began to have an effect on them al-Walīd said to ʿAbd al-Ṣamad: "Abū Wahb, recite some verses". So ʿAbd al-Ṣamad recited the following:[466]

Did you not see how the star, the moment that it ceased to shine,[467]
went hurrying back to its mansion?
In confusion it strayed from its proper path,
and having arrived at its place of setting,[468] it sought its place of rising.
I said, having marvelled at its activity
and with burgeoning hope as it appeared,
"Perhaps the reign of al-Walīd has drawn near,
now that the time has become auspicious.
We have been hoping that he would rule,
just as the owner of barren land hopes that it will become verdant.
We have made the firmest plans[469] for him
with all our hearts, since he is a worthy repository for them."[470]

The poem was recited (in other places) and Hishām came to hear

---

are shown to be in two distinctly separate localities. Al-Azraq is a citadel in the Wādī Sirḥān, 27 km from Quṣayr ʿAmrah. Cf. Dussaud, 21, 81, 136, 175; Creswell, I, 405–06. Al-Aghdaf has been identified as Qaṣr al-Ṭūbah, 61 km south of al-Azraq. Cf. Derenk, 121; Gabrieli, loc. cit. The account of al-Balādhurī is clear: "He (al-Walīd) settled in al-Azraq." *Ansāb* (Derenk), 10.

466. This episode and the verses that follow are recounted by al-Iṣfahānī, *Aghānī*, VI, 104–05. Cf. also *Fragmenta*, 116; al-Balādhurī, *Ansāb* (Derenk), 11.

467. *Shuyyiʿā*. Al-Iṣfahānī, *Aghānī*, VI, 105 has *sabʿā*.

468. *Al-Ghawr*. This term also denotes the low-lying area of Jordan where al-Walīd liked to spend his time.

469. *Muḥkamāti al-umūri*. The variant reading in the apparatus and in *Fragmenta*, 116 also makes good sense: *muḥkamāti al-ʿuhūdī*, "the firmest oaths."

470. The meter is *mutaqārib*. The tenor of these lines indicates that they probably date from the time when al-Walīd still enjoyed Hishām's favor to the full, a theory corroborated by their immediate sequel. This was probably the time, too, that al-Farazdaq wrote his panegyric to al-Walīd as crown prince. Cf. Hell, 37–65.

of it. He stopped the regular allowance he paid to al-Walīd and he wrote to him as follows: "I have heard that you have taken ʿAbd al-Ṣamad as friend, confidant, and drinking companion. As far as I am concerned, that just confirms what I have already heard about you. Moreover, I do not find you blameless in any wickedness (that has been done). Send ʿAbd al-Ṣamad away in disgrace."[471] Al-Walīd therefore sent ʿAbd al-Ṣamad away, and he recited the following verses about him:

They have accused Abū Wahb of a great sin—
no indeed, of one far greater than great!
I testify that they have lied against him,
with the testimony of one knowledgeable and with long experience of them.[472]

Al-Walīd wrote to Hishām telling him that he had sent ʿAbd al-Ṣamad away, and he apologized for what Hishām had heard about his drinking companion.[473] He then asked Hishām if he would permit Ibn Suhayl to join him. Ibn Suhayl was a Yamanī who had [1745]
governed Damascus on more than one occasion,[474] and he was among al-Walīd's close circle of friends. Hishām, however, flogged Ibn Suhayl and sent him away. Hishām then seized ʿIyāḍ b. Muslim, al-Walīd's scribe, as he had heard that ʿIyāḍ was sending information to al-Walīd. He gave him a severe flogging and made him wear coarse cloth. When al-Walīd heard about this he exploded: "Who can trust anybody? What's the point of doing good to others? My father preferred this accursed cross-eyed man to the members of his own family and he made him his heir. Now you see how he treats me. As soon as he finds out that I have become attached to someone, he trifles with him. He wrote to me asking me to send ʿAbd al-Ṣamad away, so I sent him away. Then I

471. Al-Balādhurī is more explicit: "Bring ʿAbd al-Ṣamad to me with my messenger." Cf. *Ansāb* (Derenk), 11.

472. The meter is *wāfir*. Cf. al-Iṣfahānī, *Aghānī*, VI, 105; *Fragmenta*, 116; al-Balādhurī, *Ansāb* (Derenk), 11.

473. *Munādamatihi* ("the person(s) with whom he drank"). The subsequent fate of ʿAbd al-Ṣamad is recorded in al-Balādhurī, *Ansāb* (Derenk), 11 and *Fragmenta*, 116–17. Hishām sent him and his brother to Yūsuf b. ʿUmar, who walled them up in a room where they died of thirst.

474. Al-Balādhurī adds that he may have been head of the *shurṭah* in Damascus. Cf. *Ansāb* (Derenk), 12.

wrote to him asking him to allow Ibn Suhayl to come and join me. So he beat Ibn Suhayl and sent him away, although he knew how highly I thought of him.[475] He found out how attached ʿIyāḍ b. Muslim is to me and that he is under my protection. He knew that I have a high regard for him and that he is my scribe. So he beat him and imprisoned him, just to harm me. O God, protect me from him!"[476] Then al-Walīd recited as follows:

It is I who[477] warn the man who would constantly bestow favor
on people of dubious character,[478] not having experienced their faithlessness.
If you treat them with honor, you will find them insolently ungrateful;[479]
if you treat them with contempt, you will find them tractable.
How can you exalt yourself above us when we are the very source of your prosperity?
Just you wait until[480] fortune veers in our favor.
Look around, and if the only likeness you can find
for him is that of a dog,[481] then try that![482]
[1746] His master fattens him up for the hunt
until he has grown strong,[483] after his formerly emaciated state,
And thereupon the dog attacks him—and although that assault fails to harm him,
if he were able to devour him, he would do so.[484]

---

475. *Ra'yī fīhī* ("my (good) opinion about him"). Cf. *Gloss.*, p. CCLV.
476. For Hishām's treatment of ʿIyāḍ b. Muslim, cf. al-Iṣfahānī, *Aghānī*, VI, 105; al-Balādhurī, *Ansāb* (Derenk), 12.
477. Literally, "I am the warner who."
478. *Al-maqārīf.* Cf. *Gloss.*, p. CDXX.
479. *Buṭur:* plural of *baṭūr.* Cf. *Gloss.*, p. CXXXVI.
480. Literally, "You will find out when."
481. Cf. n. 350.
482. The text has *fa-uḍrubhu.* This is emended to *fa-aḍribhu* by Gabrieli, "Al-Walīd," 54.
483. *Nawā.* Al-Iṣfahānī has *istawā;* cf. *Aghānī*, V, 105.
484. The meter is *basīṭ.* There is a strong possibility that some of the last few lines (1746, ll.1–4) are out of order here. The version of al-Balādhurī is more coherent, incorporating parts of al-Ṭabarī's version: *baynā yusamminuhā li-al-*

Al-Walīd wrote the following letter to Hishām:[485]

I have heard what cuts the Commander of the Faithful has made in my income and how he has ruined my friends, my women, and my family. I had never thought that God would thus test the Commander of the Faithful nor that he (Hishām) would thus defame me. Even if Ibn Suhayl did behave in that way,[486] it would be like the ass presuming to think it is as good as the wolf.[487] My kind actions toward Ibn Suhayl, my favorable treatment of him, and my letter to the Commander of the Faithful about him do not deserve the extreme measures taken by the Commander of the Faithful in breaking off relations with me. But if this has come about because of something specific in the mind of the Commander of the Faithful against me, (let him remember that) the succession which God decreed for me, the span of life which He ordained for me, and the substance which He allotted to me are matters which nobody apart from God can ever diminish by one jot from their appointed term; nor can anyone change their allotted times in any way. For the irreversible decree of God (*qadar*) runs according to His predetermined decisions, irrespective of the wishes of men.[488] There is no way to delay Him when He hastens and there is no hastening of His allotted span.[489] In such a situation, the sins that men under God commit are against themselves and because of them they [1747] deserve punishment. The Commander of the Faithful is the person in his community best fitted to perceive this and

---

ṣaydi ṣāḥibuhu ʿadā ʿalayhi falaw yastaṭīʿuhu aklā ("while his master is fattening him up for the hunt, he attacks him and, if he could, he would eat [him]"). Cf. *Ansāb* (Derenk), 13.

485. For other versions of this letter, cf. al-Iṣfahānī, *Aghānī*, VI, 106–07; al-Balādhurī, *Ansāb* (Derenk), 13–14. For a detailed analysis of the various textual and translation problems connected with this letter and Hishām's reply, cf. Appendix 1.

486. "Even if Ibn Suhayl were as the Commander of the Faithful made him out to be"; al-Iṣfahānī, *Aghānī*, loc. cit.

487. "It would be enough for the ass (i.e., Ibn Suhayl) merely to approach the wolf (Hishām)" (in order to be devoured); al-Iṣfahānī, *Aghānī*, loc. cit.

488. Literally, "whether people like it or dislike it."

489. Literally, "there is no delaying of His hastening and no hastening of His allotted span."

should be the one most mindful of it. May God be the One who directs the Commander of the Faithful to good judgments in his conduct of affairs!

Hishām inquired of Abū Zubayr: "Nasṭās,[490] do you think that the people will be satisfied with al-Walīd if anything happens to me?" Nasṭās said: "Rather, may God prolong your life, O Commander of the Faithful!" Hishām retorted: "Fie on you! Death is an inevitable fact. So do you think that the people will be satisfied with al-Walīd?" Nasṭās said: "O Commander of the Faithful, an oath of allegiance to al-Walīd is already obligatory for the people." Thereupon Hishām replied: "If the people are satisfied with al-Walīd, I can only think that the popular dictum 'anyone who is caliph for three days will not enter the fire' is false."

Hishām then wrote to al-Walīd as follows:[491]

The Commander of the Faithful has understood what you have written about the cuts he has imposed on you and about other matters. The Commander of the Faithful asks pardon from God for the allowance he used to give you. The Commander of the Faithful is more afraid for his own soul because of the wrong he has done against himself in giving you the allowance he gave you than because he has made the cuts he has made and ruined those of your companions whom he has ruined. This is for two reasons. The first is that the Commander of the Faithful gave you preferential treatment in the allowance he bestowed on you, even though he knew what your attitude toward it was and that you spent it in an inappropriate way.[492] The second reason is that he made much of your friends and gave them lavish allowances (too). They do not have to put up with the kind of setbacks that the Mus-
[1748] lims undergo every year when the campaigns are curtailed. Your friends remain in your company and you drag them off

490. Naṣṭās was the freedman of Ṣafwān b. Umayyah; the name is obviously an arabicized form of the Greek name Anastasios. Cf. al-Iṣfahānī, *Aghānī*, VI, 103.

491. For other versions of Hishām's letter, cf. al-Iṣfahānī, *Aghānī*, VI, 107–08; al-Balādhurī, *Ansāb* (Derenk), 14–15. For a discussion of textual and translation problems in this letter, cf. Appendix 1.

492. Al-Balādhurī has: "even though he knew the places where you put it and that you were spending it on the path of disobedience." Cf. *Ansāb* (Derenk), 14.

with you in your folly. The Commander of the Faithful feels that it is more fitting for him to impose cuts on you and to give you only a bare minimum rather than to exceed the proper limits with you in this matter. But God has supported the Commander of the Faithful in the cuts that he has imposed on you, which he has made in the hope of His forgiveness for what he dreads may result from his previous actions in this matter.[493]

As for Ibn Suhayl, by my life, if he enjoyed the special position he had with you, and he was worthy of your affection,[494] God would not have made him as he is. Is Ibn Suhayl—for goodness' sake![495]—anything more than a singer and dancer, whose foolishness knows no bounds? Moreover, Ibn Suhayl is no worse than any other of the characters whom you choose as your companions in those activities which, out of nobility, the Commander of the Faithful refrains from mentioning but for which you, by God's life! would be worthy of censure. If you think that the Commander of the Faithful is eager to make trouble for you, then that would release you from any family obligation[496] because of the evil inclinations of the Commander of the Faithful in that matter. As for that which you said God has ordained for you, it was God who gave the Commander of the Faithful precedence in that respect and He chose him for it, and verily God attains His purpose.[497] The Commander of the Faithful has come to the firm conviction[498] that it is not for his own profit that he possesses what God in His goodness has given

493. I.e., Hishām fears God's anger for his former generosity toward al-Walīd and his friends.

494. Literally, "and he was worthy that you should be pleased about him or displeased."

495. It is difficult to find an appropriate translation for *lillāhi abūka,* an expression that denotes wonder and praise. Cf. Lane, I, 11.

496. The text has *bi-ghayri illin* ("without a compact"). The Cairo edition (VII, 214) has *bi-ghayri ālin* ("without family [obligation]"). This latter reading has been used in the translation.

497. Qur'ān 65, v. 3.

498. The text has *wa-huwa 'alā al-yaqīni min rabbihi* . . . ("he is sure from his Lord . . ."), as does al-Balādhurī, *Ansāb* (Derenk), 15. Al-Iṣfahānī's version (loc. cit.) makes better sense: *wa-huwa 'alā al-yaqīni min ra'yihi* ("he is firm in his opinion").

him—for the attainment of either evil or good—but that it is only a trust to him from God and that it is inevitable that he must (eventually) relinquish it. God is too merciful and compassionate to His servants to entrust command over them to one of them—no matter who—that is not pleasing to Him. Indeed, the Commander of the Faithful, because of his high
[1749] regard for his Lord, is extremely hopeful that He will give him the task of delivering that office to one who is acceptable to Him and to them. Indeed, God's goodness to the Commander of the Faithful far exceeds his ability to describe it or to render Him sufficient thanks, except by God's own help. If He has decreed an imminent death for the Commander of the Faithful, there is in that place to which he is ultimately traveling, if God wills and by the goodness of God, a replacement for this earthly life. By my life, the content of your letter to the Commander of the Faithful is fully in accord with your foolishness and stupidity. So restrain yourself from committing excesses and be moderate in your actions. To God belong chastisements and mighty power. He strikes therewith those of His servants whom He wishes,[499] and He inclines his ear to those of His servants whom He wishes. The Commander of the Faithful implores God for protection and for right direction toward those things that are dearest and most pleasing to Him.

Al-Walīd wrote the following reply to Hishām:

I have seen you sparing no effort to erect a barrier between you and me;
(whereas) if you possessed a grain of intelligence,[500] you would demolish what you have built.
You sow a crop of hatred against those still alive;
woe to them, when you die, from the evil harvest you have garnered!
I can imagine them saying at best, "If only we were"
but by then "if only we were" will be of no avail.

---

499. There is an echo here of Qur'ān 7, v. 156: *'adhābī uṣību bihi man ashā'u* ("I smite with My punishment whom I will").

You have spurned the hand of one who offers kindness. If you had taken it, [1750]
the Compassionate One, the possessor of grace and beneficence, would have rewarded you for it.[501]

Al-Walīd continued to live in that desert until Hishām died. On the morning of the day that al-Walīd became caliph[502] he sent for Abū al-Zubayr al-Mundhir b. Abī ʿAmr. The latter came to al-Walīd, who said to him: "Abū Zubayr! As far back as I can remember I have never spent a longer night than last night. During the night I was assailed with anxieties and I kept thinking about things connected with the rule of that man (meaning Hishām). He has evil designs on me.[503] Come riding with us and let's get some air." So they went riding. After going two *mīls*,[504] al-Walīd stopped at a sandy hill and began complaining about Hishām. Then suddenly he saw a cloud of dust and he exclaimed: "These are messengers from Hishām. Let us pray to God that they bring good news." Then two men on post-horses hove into sight; one of them was a mawlā of Abū Muḥammad al-Sufyānī and the other was Jardabah. When they came nearer they went toward al-Walīd, dismounted, ran up to him, and greeted him as caliph. Al-Walīd was struck dumb with amazement. Jardabah began to repeat his salutation to him as caliph, so al-Walīd said: "Steady on! Are you telling me that Hishām is dead?" Jardabah said: "Yes." So al-Walīd asked: "Who sent your letter?" Jardabah replied: "Your mawlā, Sālim b. ʿAbd al-Raḥmān, the master of the chancellery." Al-Walīd read the letter and the two men turned to leave. Then

---

500. *Fa-law kunta dhā irbin*. Al-Iṣfahānī (loc. cit.) has *fa-law kunta dhā hazmin* ("if you had any determination/judgment"). *Fragmenta*, 117, has . . . *dhā ʿaqlin* ("if you had any intelligence").

501. For these verses, cf. al-Iṣfahānī, *Aghānī*, VI, 104; *Fragmenta*, 117–18; al-Balādhurī, *Ansāb* (Derenk), 15 (only part of the verses); Ibn al-Athīr, V, 199; Gabrieli, "al-Walīd," 60–61. The meter is *ṭawīl*. In the *Aghānī* the verses occur in a different context, namely, when Hishām is attempting to depose al-Walīd and make his own son his heir.

502. For similar accounts of the way in which al-Walīd heard of Hishām's death, cf. al-Balādhurī, *Ansāb*, (Derenk), 20–21; al-Iṣfahānī, *Aghānī*, VI, 108; Ibn Aʿtham, VIII, 139.

503. *Qad awlaʿa bī*: i.e., Hishām wishes al-Walīd dead.

504. Two *mīls*: approximately 4 km. Cf. Hinz, 63.

al-Walīd called back the mawlā of Abū Muḥammad al-Sufyānī and asked him about his secretary, ʿIyāḍ b. Muslim. The mawlā said: "O Commander of the Faithful, he stayed in prison until
[1751] God's decree struck Hishām. When Hishām reached a point where he was no longer expected to recover, ʿIyāḍ sent a message to the storekeepers asking them to keep hold of what they had in their possession and saying that on no account should anyone remove anything.[505] Hishām recovered consciousness and asked for something, but they refused to let him have it. Then Hishām said: 'So it seems that we have been storekeepers for al-Walīd!' and he died shortly afterwards. ʿIyāḍ came out of prison, sealed the doors of the storehouses, and gave orders concerning Hishām. Hishām was taken from his bed, but people could not find a container in which to warm the water to wash him and they actually had to ask to borrow one. Nor could they procure a shroud from the storehouses. So Ghālib, the mawlā of Hishām, found him a shroud."

Al-Walīd wrote to al-ʿAbbās b. al-Walīd b. ʿAbd al-Malik b. Marwān,[506] telling him to go to al-Ruṣāfah to estimate what possessions and how many sons Hishām had there and to arrest his agents and dependents, except for Maslamah b. Hishām. In the case of Maslamah, al-Walīd wrote to al-ʿAbbās saying that he should not interfere with him nor should anyone enter his house, for Maslamah had often begged his father to show leniency in regard to al-Walīd and had made Hishām refrain from taking steps against him. So al-ʿAbbās went to al-Ruṣāfah and carried out the written instructions that al-Walīd had given him. Then he wrote to al-Walīd informing him that he had arrested Hishām's sons and dependents and that he had counted Hishām's possessions. Al-Walīd responded as follows:[507]

Would that Hishām were alive to see
his capacious milking pail topped up!

---

505. In an earlier version of this story (cf. p. 72) the closing of the treasury occurred after the death of Hishām, not before.

506. Cf. the Umayyad genealogical table.

507. For some of these lines, cf. al-Balādhurī, *Ansāb* (Derenk), 22. The meter is *sarīʿ*.

Al-Walīd recited:[508]

Would that Hishām had lived to see [1752]
his capacious corn-measure sealed up.
We have meted out to him the same measure that he meted out (to us before),
and we have not deprived him of a single ounce of it.[509]
It was not out of innovation that we did so,
but the Distinguishing Book[510] fully permitted it to us.

Al-Walīd appointed agents, and (letters giving him) the oath of allegiance reached him from far-flung areas. The agents wrote to him and delegations came to him. Marwān b. Muḥammad wrote to him as follows:[511]

> May God's blessing[512] be on the Commander of the Faithful in the command of His servants and the inheritance of His lands which He has bestowed on him! It was because Hishām was overwhelmed by the submerging flood[513] brought on by the intoxication of power that he was induced to attempt to diminish those rights of the Commander of the Faithful which God had magnified. He sought to achieve something that was too difficult for him. People of unsound opinions and beliefs responded to him in that, but they also found[514] what he desired too difficult. It was then that he buckled under the full weight of the decrees of God.

---

508. For these verses (with minor variants), cf. al-Iṣfahānī, *Aghānī*, VI, 109; *Fragmenta*, 121, Ibn al-Athīr, V, 200; Gabrieli, "al-Walīd," 49–50. The meter is *sarī'*.

509. Cf. Qur'ān 4, v. 44; 11, vv. 85–86.

510. *Al-furqān:* "the Criterion of right and wrong." Cf. Qur'ān 2, v. 53. Al-Balādhurī, *Ansāb* (Derenk), 22, and *Fragmenta*, 121, have "*al-Qur'ān.*"

511. Marwān b. Muḥammad was the cousin of al-Walīd's father and later was to become the last Umayyad caliph. He had served on the frontier in Armenia. For a good summary of his career, cf. Schönig, 7. Cf. also n. 4.

512. For other versions of this letter, cf. al-Balādhurī, *Ansāb* (Derenk), 35–36; *Fragmenta*, 124–25.

513. Cf. Qur'ān 23, v. 56: *fa-dharhum fī ghamratihim* ("therefore leave them in [the submerging flood of] their ignorance"). Cf. also Qur'ān 23, v. 65; 51, v. 11.

514. *Fa-wajadū* ("they found"). The apparatus has a variant, *fa-wajada* ("he found"), which is adopted also by the Cairo edition (VII, 216). This makes better sense.

The Commander of the Faithful (i.e., al-Walīd) was in a place of God's protection until the time when He girded him with the noblest belt of the caliphate. He has assumed responsibility for matters which God has judged him competent to decide, and he stands confirmed in absolute control of the charge which has been laid upon him. Previous revelations[515] have foretold the appointed span of his rule. God has singled him out from His creatures to rule, for He sees their circumstances. God has invested him with the caliphal ornament hanging around his neck and has bestowed on him the reins of the caliphate and the torque[516] of authority. Praise be
[1753] to God Who has chosen the Commander of the Faithful for His caliphate and to maintain the firm foundations of His religion![517] He has preserved him from the evil designs of the wicked;[518] and He has elevated him and has brought them low. Anyone who persists in such base actions[519] destroys his soul and angers his Lord, but anyone whom repentance directs to the true course, abstaining from what is wrong and turning to what is right, will find God ever disposed to forgive and be merciful.

I should like to inform the Commander of the Faithful, may God's beneficence be upon him, that when I heard about his accession to God's caliphate I mounted my pulpit, holding two swords in readiness against any mischief-makers. I announced to the people in front of me the favor that God had conferred on them in appointing the Commander of the Faithful. At this they rejoiced and said: "No other caliphal accession has filled us with greater hope or made us more joyful than the accession of the Commander of the Faithful." I had already stretched out my hand to give the oath of allegiance to you. Now I renewed it and confirmed it with weighty convenants, repeated pledges, and strong oaths.

---

515. *Al-zubur.*
516. *ʿIṣam* is the plural of *ʿuṣmah* ("collar").
517. *Wathāʾiqi ʿurā dīnihi.*
518. Cf. Qurʾān 12, v. 76; 21, v. 58; 86, v. 16.
519. *Al-khasīsah min al-umūri.* Al-Balādhurī has *al-khaṭīʾah* ("crime, sin"): *Ansāb* (Derenk), 35.

Thereafter, all of them gave excellent and obedient responses.

O Commander of the Faithful, reward them for their obedience from the wealth of God which He has given you, for you are the most generous and open-handed of men! They have been waiting for you, hoping that you would reveal your bounty toward them because of the close ties of kinship that they claim with you. Show more generosity toward them than your predecessors did, so that your preference for them over your other subjects may thus be made manifest.[520] Were it not for the efforts I am making to guard the frontier where I now am, I fear that my strong yearning for the Commander of [1754] the Faithful would lead me to appoint a deputy against his orders and to come in person to see the Commander of the Faithful face to face, for there is no pleasure, however great it might be, which would equal that for me. If the Commander of the Faithful thinks it appropriate to allow me to travel to him so that I may speak of matters which I do not want to put in writing, then let him do so.

When al-Walīd came to power he made provision for the cripples and blind amongst the people of Syria. He gave them clothing and ordered that each of them should have a servant. He made available perfume and clothing among those with large families to support[521] and he increased what Hishām had given them. He augmented the stipend for everyone by ten dirhams and then, after that increase of ten, he made a further increase of ten for the Syrians in particular.[522] He doubled the allowances of those of his family who came asking for his help. When al-Walīd had been heir-apparent, he used to give food to those who came to him on their way back from the summer campaign. At a staging-post called Zīzā'[523] he would also feed for a period of three days people

520. *Wa-zidhum ziyādatan yufḍalu bihā man kāna qablaka ḥattā yaẓhara faḍluka 'alayhim 'alā ra'iyyatika.* Here the Cairo edition (217) adds a *wa*: *ḥattā yaẓhara faḍluka 'alayhim wa-'alā ra'iyyatika* ("so that your favor to them and your subjects may be manifest").

521. Cf. Ibn A'tham, VIII, 139.

522. Cf. Wellhausen, 353.

523. Zīzā' was a large village, one of the stages on the *ḥajj* route. It was in the Balqā' province. Cf. Le Strange, *Palestine*, 554.

returning from the pilgrimage. He would give fodder to their riding animals and would refuse nothing that was asked of him. People used to say to him: "If you (just) say 'Let me see,' it is a promise with which the suppliant will be satisfied."[524] Al-Walīd replied: "I do not train my tongue to say anything that I am not accustomed to doing."

Al-Walīd recited the following:[525]

I guarantee to you, if no obstacles hinder me,
 that the cloud of affliction will be lifted from you.
Soon both augmentation and increase,
 as well as gifts, will be bestowed on you by me.
[1755] Sacred (to me) is your register in which
 each month scribes write down and seal your grants.

In this year al-Walīd b. Yazīd had the oath of allegiance given to his two sons, al-Ḥakam and ʿUthmān, so that they should succeed him, and he made them both his heirs, one after the other, putting al-Ḥakam before ʿUthmān. Al-Walīd wrote letters on this matter to the garrison cities, and one of the people to whom he wrote about this was Yūsuf b. ʿUmar, who was at that time al-Walīd's agent in Iraq. Yūsuf b. ʿUmar wrote to Naṣr b. Sayyār about this and the text of the letter to him was as follows:

> In the name of God, the Merciful, the Compassionate. From Yūsuf b. ʿUmar to Naṣr b. Sayyār. And now to our subject. I have sent ʿAqqāl b. Shabbah al-Tamīmī and ʿAbd al-Malik al-Qaynī to bring you a copy of the letter from the Commander of the Faithful in which he wrote informing those under my authority that he has appointed his sons, al-Ḥakam and ʿUthmān, as his heirs after him.[526] I have given orders to ʿAqqāl and ʿAbd al-Malik to expatiate on this matter with you. When they reach you, gather the people together to hear the reading of the letter from the Commander of the Faithful. Give orders that people should be brought together

---

524. *Inna fī qawlīka anẓuru ʿidatan mā yuqīmu ʿalayhā al-ṭālibu.* The translation is only tentative.

525. The meter is *ṭawīl.* For these verses, cf. also al-Balādhurī, *Ansāb* (Derenk), 26; al-Iṣfahānī, *Aghānī*, VI, 111; Ibn al-Athīr, V, 201.

526. The word order in the Arabic is very unwieldy and has been changed around in the translation.

for it and perform with them what the Commander of the Faithful has written. When you have finished, have the letter read out and allow those who want to speak to do so. Then have the people give the oath of allegiance to the two sons of al-Walīd in God's name and blessing. Exact oaths from them according to what I have copied for you at the end of this letter of mine, (which is taken) from what the Commander of the Faithful wrote to us in his letter. Explain it and have the [1756] oath of allegiance given on that basis. We ask God to bless the Commander of the Faithful and his subjects in what He has decreed for them through the words of the Commander of the Faithful. We ask God to set al-Ḥakam and ʿUthmān on the right path and to bless them and us through them. Greetings to you.

Al-Naḍr[527] wrote on a Thursday, in the middle of Shaʿbān 125 [Thursday, June 13, 742]:

In the name of God, the Merciful, the Compassionate, give the oath of allegiance to the servant of God, al-Walīd, the Commander of the Faithful, and to al-Ḥakam, the son of the Commander of the Faithful, if he outlives him, and to ʿUthmān, the son of the Commander of the Faithful, if he outlives al-Ḥakam, to heed and to obey. And if anything should happen to either of them, the Commander of the Faithful will appoint as his successor someone from amongst his sons or subjects, giving precedence to whom he wishes and holding back whom he wishes. In this matter the oath and covenant of God are binding upon you.

A poet recited the following lines about this matter:[528]

We have high expectations of ʿUthmān, after al-Walīd,
    or of al-Ḥakam, and then we hope for Saʿīd,
Just as when Yazīd was in power
    he used to have hopes for al-Walīd.[529]

---

527. The identity of this person is not clear. He may be al-Naḍr b. Shumayl, who is mentioned in the company of Hishām. Cf. Ibn ʿAbd Rabbihi, III, 17, 19.

528. For these verses, cf. *Fragmenta*, 131. The meter is *mutaqārib*.

529. *Nuʾammilu ʿUthmāna baʿda al-Walīdi liʾl-ʿahdi fīnā wa-narjū Yazīdan* ("We are hoping for ʿUthmān after al-Walīd to rule among us and we hope for

But the caliphate became too remote (from us),
so we hope that it will return to what it was before,
And if it does return, then satisfy the
near relative with it,[530] so that the distant one will despair of it.

According to Aḥmad (b. Zuhayr)—ʿAlī (al-Madāʾinī)—his *shaykh*s whom I have already mentioned: ʿAqqāl b. Shabbah and ʿAbd al-Malik b. Nuʿaym came to see Naṣr and they brought the letter, which read as follows:[531]

Now to our subject. Verily God, may His names be blessed, His praise be made glorious and all reference to Him be exalt-
[1757] ed, made Islam the religion of His choice and He created Islam as the best thing for the chosen of His creatures.[532] Then He chose messengers from amongst angels and men.[533] He sent them forth with His message (Islam) and gave them orders concerning it. And between them and the nations which succeeded each other and throughout the centuries which elapsed in turn (there was conflict), but they would (still) summon men to what is better[534] and call them to a straight path. This continued until the grace of God culminated in His calling of Muḥammad, may the blessings of God

---

Yazīd"). For the second hemistich, the version in *Fragmenta*, 131, makes better sense in the context: *aw Ḥakaman thumma narjū Saʿīdan* ("or Ḥakam, then we hope for Saʿīd"). Al-Walīd had fifteen sons, one of whom was Saʿīd. Cf. the discussion of al-Walīd's family, listing primary sources, in H. ʿAṭwān, *Al-Walīd b. Yazīd: ʿarḍun wa-naqdun* (Beirut, 1981), 90–91. The Cairo edition (VII, 219) has *nubāʾī* for *nuʾammilu*.

530. *Fa-awṣī al-qarība ʿanhā* ("bequeath it to the near relative[?]"). The Cairo edition (VII, 219) has *fa-arḍī al-qarība ʿanhā*. With *awṣā*, the normal preposition would be *bi*. The version in the Cairo edition based on one manuscript reading is better grammatically and has been preferred here.

531. For a full discussion of the background and significance of this letter, cf. Crone and Hinds, *God's Caliph*, 116–18. They provide an annotated translation of the letter, 118–26. A longer discussion of this letter is to be found in Appendix 2.

532. *Wa-jaʿalahu khayra khiyaratihi*. The apparatus (BM and O) has *dīn* for *khayr*, as does the Cairo edition, 219. Crone and Hinds, 118, prefer this reading: "he has made it the religion of the chosen ones of His creation."

533. Cf. Qurʾān 35, v. 1.

534. The syntax of this passage is faulty and it is clear that some words have been omitted. The missing words must refer to the succession of prophets whose message was ignored by their own people and on whom God inflicted His punishments. The words in brackets in the translation are purely hypothetical.

be upon him, to prophethood, at a time when knowledge had passed beyond recall,[535] when blindness afflicted the people, when disunity was rife with men following their own personal inclinations,[536] when faction had made people take divergent paths and when the signs of the truth had become obliterated. (It was at such a time that) God made the right way clear by means of Muḥammad; by him He dispelled the darkness[537] and by him He brought deliverance from error and destruction. By him He made religion flourish[538] and He caused him to be a blessing for His creatures.[539] By him He set the seal on His revelation. In Muḥammad, God accumulated the bounties which He had bestowed on the prophets who had preceded him. He made him follow in their footsteps, reaffirming and embracing all that He had revealed through them, summoning to it and commanding by it.

In due course there emerged those of His community who responded to Muḥammad's call and adopted the religion which God had graciously bestowed on them. They were able to confirm the truth of the message preached by earlier prophets of God which their own people had rejected as false[540] and to accept the good counsels of those prophets which (once) they used to spurn. So they defended their sacred things which once they had violated and exalted that which they used to belittle. There was no member of the community of Muḥammad who, having been made to listen to anyone denying any of God's prophets through the message which God had entrusted to him, speaking disparagingly about him or harming him by treating him contemptuously or giving him the lie, denying what God had revealed through [1758]
him, did not consider it to be licit to shed his blood and to

535. Literally, "had become effaced."
536. *Tashtitin min al-hawā:* Literally, "a state of disunion from (following) divergent inclinations."
537. Literally, "blindness."
538. *Wa-abhaja bihi al-dīna.* Crone and Hinds read *anhaja* ("He elucidated the religion through him"). Cf. *God's Caliph,* 119. Their reading follows Ṣafwat, *Rasā'il,* II, 448.
539. *Raḥmatan li'l-ʿālamīn.* Cf. Qur'ān 21, v. 107. Cf. also Qur'ān 3, v. 8; 11, v. 28; 44, v. 5.
540. Literally, "in that in which their people used to call them liars."

break the bonds that existed between them, even if he were his father, son or fellow tribesman.

Then God appointed His caliphs to follow in the path of Muḥammad's prophetic ministry, after He had taken His prophet unto Himself, and (after) He had sealed His revelation by Muḥammad, in order that His rule should be accomplished, His *sunnah* and His penalties established, and His precepts and laws adopted. This was done so that, by His caliphs, God might confirm Islam, by them He might consolidate its sway,[541] by them He might strengthen its ties,[542] by them He might safeguard its sanctities,[543] (and) by them He might administer justice amongst His servants and might maintain the common weal in His lands. For God, most blessed and glorious, says: "And if God had not repelled some men by others the earth would have been corrupted. But God is a Lord of Kindness to (His) creatures."[544]

The caliphs of God succeeded each other as sovereigns over that which God had made them inherit from His prophets and that which He had entrusted to them. No one contests the right of the caliphs without God striking him down; no one abandons their commonality[545] without God destroying him; no one treats their authority lightly and challenges the decree of God vested in them without God granting them mastery and power over such a person and making an example of him and a warning to others. Thus does God deal with those who forsake the obedience to which God has called them and which He has commanded to be adopted and observed and by which the heavens and the earth are sustained. God, may He be blessed and glorified, said: "Then turned He to the heaven when it was smoke, and said unto it and unto
[1759] the earth: Come both of you, willingly or loth." They said: "We come, obedient."[546] God, may the utterance of His

541. The text has *tashyīdan.* The apparatus has *tashdīdan,* which is better.
542. Literally, "the strengthening of His rope."
543. *Daf'an bi-him 'an ḥarīmihi:* literally, "fending (people) off from its (Islām's) or His (God's) forbidden things."
544. Cf. Qur'ān 2, v. 251.
545. *Jamā'ah.*
546. Cf. Qur'ān 41, v. 11.

name be glorified, also said: "And when thy Lord said unto the angels: 'Lo! I am about to place a viceroy in the earth,' they said: 'Wilt Thou place therein one who will do harm therein and will shed blood, while we, we hymn Thy praise and sanctify Thee?' He said: 'Surely I know that which ye know not.' "[547]

So it is by the caliphate that God preserves those of His servants on earth whom it is His will to preserve[548] and those whom He has appointed to inhabit the earth. It is in showing obedience to those whom God has appointed to rule on earth that there lies happiness for those whom God inspires thereto and who are made to understand it.[549] For God, may He be praised and glorified, knows that there is no stability or well-being for anything save through that same obedience, by which God preserves His due, by which He carries out His command, by which He repulses those who rebel against Him, safeguarding those things that are sacred to Him and protecting His inviolable precepts. He who accepts his portion of that obedience becomes the friend of God; he is obedient to His command, he obtains right guidance from Him, and he is singled out for God's blessing both in this life and in the life to come. But he who abandons that obedience, turns his face against it and opposes God thereby, squanders his allotted portion, disobeys his Lord, and loses for himself the things of this life and the next. His lot is cast with those overcome by wretchedness, possessed by sinful actions[550] which drag those in their thrall to drink in the foulest of waterholes and which betray them to the most dreadful of ends,[551] so that God afflicts them (even) in this world with humiliation and retribution and reduces them to a state of

547. Cf. Qur'ān 2, v. 30.

548. Literally, "God has preserved those of His servants on earth whom He has preserved."

549. The text has *su'ida man ulhimahā wa-nuṣirahā* ("those who are inspired thereto and who are assisted therein attain a state of felicity"). Dr. M. F. Al-Shayyal suggested the reading *wa-buṣṣirahā,* which has been followed here. Both *ulhimahā* and *buṣṣirahā* are passive since the action comes from God.

550. *Al-umūru al-ghāwiyatu:* Literally, "deviating matters."

551. *Ilā sharri al-maṣāri'i* ("the most dreadful places of slaughter").

dreadful punishment and intense sorrow (in the next world).[552]

Next to the proclamation of God's oneness, by which He distinguishes between His servants, obedience is the very pinnacle of this matter; obedience is its uppermost peak, its most prominent aspect, its guide, its foundation, its protection and its mainstay. It is by obedience that the successful receive their stations from God and are entitled to their reward from Him; whereas it is disobedience[553] that causes others (the unfortunate) to be assailed and struck down by
[1760] His retribution and that necessitates His (just) displeasure and chastisement, because they have abandoned obedience, lost it, turned their back on it and given it away. God destroys those who go astray, who are inordinately proud, who are blind, who exceed proper limits and depart from the paths of piety and fear of God. So hold fast to obedience in God in those matters which may befall you, come to you, or happen to you. Be the faithful advocate of obedience, hold firmly to it, hasten toward it, take honest action to attain it, and seek diligently to approach nearer God by it. For you have seen the workings of God's judgment on behalf of those who practice obedience, by His exalting them and making their argument prevail and by His rejecting as false those who oppose them, who attack them, who compete with them, or who want to extinguish God's light which shines upon them. You have been warned, moreover, what those who are disobedient can expect in the way of reproof and straitening until their situation is reduced to sheer destruction, abasement, humiliation, and perdition. For anyone who possesses judgment and accepts sound advice, there is in that a clear warning[554] from

552. *Fīmā ʿindahum.* Crone and Hinds, op. cit., 121, have the reading *fīmā aʿadda lahum* "(grief) which He has prepared for them," following Ṣafwat, *Rasāʾil,* II, 450 n.

553. *Wa-al-tabaddulu bi-hā* ("giving it away in exchange for it [i.e., disobedience]"). Variants mentioned in the apparatus add *li-al-maʿṣiyati* or *bi-al-maʿṣiyati.* Crone and Hinds (loc. cit.) read *tabadhdhul* ("carelessness").

554. *Wa-fī dhālika li-man kāna raʾyun wa-mawʿiẓatun ʿibratun.* Crone and Hinds translate this as "In that there is a warning and a lesson for the perceptive person" (op. cit., 122). The problem here is the *wa* between *raʾyun* and *mawʿiẓatun* (or *aw* in the variant reading). The text as it stands should take *raʾyun wa-mawʿiẓatun* together.

which he may derive benefit[555] and from which he may attain a state of felicity, and by which he may know the blessing of God's decree to those who are deserving of it.[556]

Moreover, God—to whom belongs praise and who dispenses favor and beneficence—has rightly guided the community to the best of outcomes,[557] making its condition healthy, by preventing the shedding of its blood, by consolidating the bonds of its fellowship, by making all its tongues agree, by establishing its pillars in good order, and by promoting the weal of its common people. The special repository of blessing bestowed on the community in this world, next to His caliphate which He established for them as a foundation and as a support for ruling them, is the covenant which God directed His caliphs to confirm and oversee for the Muslims in matters of moment; so that, whenever something befalls their caliphs, it might be an assurance of refuge, a shelter in [1761] times of calamity, a means of repairing disorder and of reconciling mutually hostile men, a way of consolidating the boundaries of Islam and of frustrating that which the Devil's followers desire from his enticements and to which he incites them, which is the destruction of this religion, the division of the unity of its people, and the sowing of dissension where He has united them through His religion. God's sole judgement for the evildoers in this matter is to afflict them[558] and to frustrate their desires. They will find that God's ordinance for His followers is to safeguard the conduct of their affairs[559] and that He has driven away from them anyone who wishes to make mischief or practice dishonesty in those affairs, or who wishes to weaken what God has made fast or who wishes to rely on what God has shunned.

555. Literally, "from whose clarity he may derive benefit."

556. *Bi-hā*. It is not clear to which of the feminine antecedents this may refer. It is probably the blessing.

557. The text has *'āfiyatan*. The Cairo edition (VII, 221), which prefers the variant reading *'āqibatan*, has been followed here. Cf. also Crone and Hinds, loc. cit.

558. Literally, "God will show the evildoers in this matter only that which will harm them. . . ."

559. Literally, "they will find God has made firm, by that which He has decreed for His followers thereby, the knots (*'uqad*) of their affairs."

It is by these (blessings)[560] that God has consummated—both for His caliphs and for His party which fears Him and whom He has entrusted with obedience to Him—the best of those things to which He has accustomed them; and He has enabled them to attain their purpose by what He has afforded them of His might, ennobling power, and ability to exalt and strengthen.[561] The authority embodied in this covenant[562] is integral to the completeness of Islam; it is a fraction[563] of the perfect bounties by which God has made the Muslims indebted to Him; it is an earnest of what God has in store, through this covenant, for those whom He has willed to execute it and those whom He has decreed should pronounce it.[564] He has made this covenant efficacious for those whom He has appointed to this office so as to be for Him the most excellent of treasures and the best reminder for Muslims of the benefits which He bestows on them and the protection which He affords them and of His strength on which they rely and His refuge to which they resort, a refuge which God himself has made for them, as a means of protection. For by it He defends them from every danger, by it He unites them against every faction, by it He lays low the hypocrites, and by
[1762] it He preserves them from every division or schism.

So praise God, your Lord, who has been merciful to you, and who has applied in your affairs what He has shown you of this covenant—a covenant that He has made for you as an abode, a place of shelter[565] in which you may find rest, (a tree) in whose branches you may find shade, an instrument by which He has directed you to the right path wherever you

560. *Bi-hā*. It is not clear to what the *hā* refers. Rather than referring to obedience or the caliphate, it probably refers to God's benevolent actions toward those who follow Him.

561. Literally, "God has perfected . . . the best of that to which He has accustomed them and enabled them to attain from His reinforcing, honoring, exalting, and empowering."

562. *Fa-amru hādhā al-ʿahdi*. *Amr* can also mean "matter." Cf. Crone and Hinds, op. cit., 123.

563. The words *it is a fraction* have been added for stylistic reasons.

564. Literally, "and is part of that which God has made therein (in the covenant? Islam?) for the one by whose hands He has accomplished it and on whose tongue He has decreed it."

565. *Muʿawwalan:* literally, "a place in which one may place confidence."

may turn your heads,[566] point your faces or convene[567] in your activities in this world and the next. In this there is a rich store of blessing; in this there is a great favor[568] from God who lavishly bestows (His) well-being. This is recognized by men of understanding and goodwill who think carefully about the consequences of their actions and who know the light that illumines the paths of right guidance. For it is proper that you should thank God for the way in which He has preserved your religion and your state of unity, (since) you are able to realize how greatly He deserves such thanks and praise for what He has determined for you by His religion. So let the position that religion has in your heart and its excellent status within your souls match God's great favor toward you in this matter, if God wills. There is no power but in God.

Moreover, ever since God appointed the Commander of the Faithful as His caliph, he (the Commander of the Faithful) has been more concerned and preoccupied with this covenant than with anything else, because he knows its crucial role in the affairs of the Muslims and because he knows those things which God has revealed to them in it for which they should be thankful. The caliph is gracious to them in his decrees. Of his own volition, he expends all his energies in this matter, both for his own good and for that of the people. He entreats his Lord and Master, in whose hand is authority and who possesses knowledge of what is hidden, to pass judgment therein on behalf of himself and his people, for He is all-powerful. In this matter the caliph asks God to help him to do what is most just, for himself in particular and for the [1763]
Muslims in general.

So the Commander of the Faithful has thought it appropriate to bequeath to you a double covenant (of succession) that thereby you, like your predecessors before you, might be freed from care and blessed with abundant hope and peace of

---

566. Literally, "necks."

567. Literally, "the meeting of your forelocks (*nawāṣīkum*) in the matter of your religion and this world."

568. Cf. Qur'ān 8, v. 17.

mind, and with mutual hostilities allayed. Thus you will realize to the full the importance of this matter which God has ordained for His people as a means of protection, salvation, well-being and life, while for every hypocrite and transgressor who wishes to destroy this religion and corrupt its people it is a means of abasement, destruction, and straitening. Therefore the Commander of the Faithful has appointed as his successor in that office his son al-Ḥakam and thereafter ʿUthmān, another son of the Commander of the Faithful. It is the hope of the Commander of the Faithful that the two of them are of those whom God created and fashioned for that office and in whom He perfected the ideal qualities of those whom He would wish to appoint to it, namely good judgment, sound religion, abundant manliness, and a knowledge of the proper management of affairs. In this the Commander of the Faithful has spared no effort both in his own interest and in yours.

Therefore give the oath of allegiance to al-Ḥakam, the son of the Commander of the Faithful, in the name of God and with His blessing, and after al-Ḥakam give the oath to his brother to heed and to obey. Expect as a reward for that the best of what God has already showered on you, repeatedly given you, accustomed you to, and taught you about through similar instances in the past when He bestowed widespread prosperity, general good, and great bounty, the hope,[569] security, well-being, safety, and protection of which you have achieved. This is the matter that you thought to be slow in coming and that you sought to hasten. You praised God for
[1764] having achieved it and for ordaining it for you. You gave hearty thanks for it and you saw it as your good fortune. You will compete with each other and do your utmost to fulfill God's due which is incumbent on you, for you have already received from God's blessings, goodness, and generous portion all that you could (legitimately) want, and your enthusi-

569. Crone and Hinds read *rakhāʾihi* ("ease") for *rajāʾihi* (op. cit., 125). This makes better sense than the version in the Leiden text, which has been translated here.

asm for it matches what He has conferred on you and what He has done for you therein.

Moreover, if anything should happen to one of his two heirs, the Commander of the Faithful is entirely within his rights to fill his position and to put in his place whomsoever he wishes to put there, whether from his community or from his sons, and to give such a person precedence over the survivor of the two sons, if he so wishes, or to put him after that son. Be sure you understand that. We ask God—there is no God but He—Knower of the Invisible and the Visible,[570] the Merciful, the Compassionate, to bless the Commander of the Faithful and you in what He has determined and decreed through the words of the caliph. We ask Him to ensure that the outcome of His covenant is soundness, happiness, and joy, for the entire matter is in His hand; He alone has power over it. No one makes requests outside its remit. May the peace and the mercy of God be upon you.

Samāl[571] wrote this letter on Tuesday, eight days before the end of Rajab 125 [Tuesday, May 21, 743(?)].[572]

In this year al-Walīd appointed Naṣr b. Sayyār as governor of the whole of Khurāsān and put him in sole charge of it.

In this year Yūsuf b. 'Umar came to al-Walīd and he bought off Naṣr and his agents from al-Walīd, who gave him back the governorship of Khurāsān.

In this year Yūsuf b. 'Umar wrote to Naṣr b. Sayyar ordering [1765]
him to come to him and to bring with him what he could in the way of tribute and money.[573]

570. Cf. Qur'ān 6, v. 74.

571. This name is odd and the person has not been identified.

572. The last day of Rajab in that year [i.e., Wednesday, the thirtieth of Rajab 125] corresponds to May 29, 743; eight days before corresponds to the twenty-second of Rajab (Tuesday, May 21, 743).

573. This is a rather obscure passage and the sequence of events is not clear. The following anecdotes have to do with Naṣr being first confirmed in his office by al-Walīd and then, after Yūsuf's machinations, dismissed. Cf. Wellhausen, 482–83.

What Transpired between Yūsuf and Naṣr in the Matter [of Tribute]

According to ʿAlī (al-Madāʾinī)—his *shaykhs*: Yūsuf b. ʿUmar wrote to Naṣr on that matter and ordered him to come to him with all his dependents. When Yūsuf's letter reached Naṣr, he raised tribute from the people of Khurāsān and his agents.[574] He made ready every slave, female and male, and every spirited horse in Khurāsān, and he bought a thousand slaves, equipped them with weapons, and mounted them on horses.[575]

Some reports said: Naṣr made ready five hundred maidservants, and he gave orders that gold and silver ewers and statues of gazelles, lions' heads, ibexes, and other things should be made. When Naṣr had finished all these preparations, al-Walīd wrote to him urging him to hurry, so Naṣr sent the presents and the first of them reached Bayhaq.[576] Then al-Walīd wrote to him ordering him to send him guitars and lutes, and one of their poets recited the following lines:

Rejoice, you who are God's entrusted one,
    rejoice in the good news,
In camels laden with wealth
    like granaries
And mules carrying wine,
    their bags bulging like mandolins,
And the coquetry of Berber women
    as they play the bass[577] and high[578] strings (of the lute)
With now the beating of a tambourine
    and now the piping of flutes
Such is your portion in this world
    and in Paradise delight itself will be yours.[579]

---

574. *Qasama ʿalā ahli Khurāsān al-hadāyā.* The context that follows, where Naṣr is busy collecting valuable items to take to Yūsuf, makes it clear that this sentence does not mean that Naṣr distributed presents to the people of Khurāsān and his officials, as Muir suggests (*Caliphate,* 415–16). For the use of the term *hadāyā* as tribute, cf. Løkkegaard, 144.

575. Cf. Ibn al-Athīr, V, 202.

576. Cf. n. 334.

577. *Al-bamm.*

578. *Al-zīr.*

579. Cf. Qurʾān 43, v. 70.

In Hishām's time, al-Azraq b. Qurra al-Mismāʿī came from al-Tirmidh[580] to Naṣr and he said to Naṣr: "I dreamed I saw al-Walīd b. Yazīd when he was heir-apparent, fleeing, as it were, from Hishām. I saw him on a couch, drinking honey, and he gave me some of it to drink." Then Naṣr gave al-Azraq four thousand dīnārs and a set of clothes and he dispatched him to al-Walīd with a letter.[581] Al-Azraq came to al-Walīd and gave him the money and the set of clothes. Al-Walīd, pleased with this, gave al-Azraq presents and also rewarded Naṣr well. Then al-Azraq departed; he heard about Hishām's death on his way back to Naṣr before Naṣr had any idea of what he had been doing. When al-Azraq reached Naṣr, he told him what had happened. On becoming caliph, Walīd wrote to al-Azraq and to Naṣr and gave orders to his messenger that he should go first to al-Azraq and give him his letter. The messenger reached al-Azraq at night and gave him his letter as well as Naṣr's letter, but al-Azraq did not read his own letter. (Instead) he brought the two letters to Naṣr. Walīd's letter to Naṣr instructed him to acquire guitars, mandolins, and gold and silver ewers for him, to collect from Khurāsān as many female cymbal players, falcons, and spirited horses as he possibly could, and to dispatch all this personally with prominent people from Khurāsān. [1766]

A man from the Banū Bāhilah said: A number of astrologers kept warning Naṣr that a time of trial (*fitnah*) was imminent, so Naṣr sent for Ṣadaqah b. Waththāb, who was in Balkh and was an astrologer in his service. Yūsuf kept asking Naṣr to come and see [1767]
him and Naṣr continually hesitated to do so. Then Yūsuf sent a messenger with instructions that he should keep on pressing Naṣr to come, and that if he did not do so Yūsuf would proclaim publicly[582] that Naṣr had been dismissed from his office. When the messenger reached Naṣr, Naṣr gave him presents and bought him off.[583] Then Naṣr made for his citadel, which nowadays is the *dār al-imārah*, and he was on his way there when trouble

580. The most important town of the Ṣaghāniyān district at the place where the Zamīl and Oxus rivers join. Cf. Le Strange, *Lands*, 440–41; Bosworth, "Chaghāniyān," 1–2.

581. Literally, "he sent him to al-Walīd and Naṣr wrote to him."

582. Literally, "or he would proclaim publicly."

583. Literally, "satisfied him."

broke out. So Naṣr went to his citadel in Mājān.[584] He appointed ʿIṣmah b. ʿAbdallāh al-Asadī as his deputy to govern Khurāsān. He put al-Muhallab b. Iyās al-ʿAdawī in charge of the *kharāj* and he made Mūsā b. Warqā' al-Nājī governor of al-Shāsh. He made Ḥassān al-Asadī, who was from Ṣaghāniyān,[585] governor of Samarqand, and he put Muqātil b. ʿAlī al-Sughdī in charge of Āmul.[586] Naṣr gave orders to these men that if they heard that he had left Marw, they were to gather[587] the Turks together and to raid[588] the land across the Oxus. In that way, he could join them after leaving Marw, using that fighting as an excuse. Then one day, as Naṣr was on his way to Iraq, a mawlā from the Banū Layth came to him by night (with the news of al-Walīd's death).[589] In the morning the people were called to prayer, and Naṣr sent for al-Walīd's messengers. After praising and glorifying God, Naṣr said: "You know where I was going and you have seen what tribute I have sent. Now somebody comes to me at night and tells me that al-Walīd has been killed, unrest has broken out in Syria, Manṣūr b. Jumhūr has gone to Iraq, and Yūsuf b. ʿUmar has fled.[590] You know the state of the country we live in and how numerous our
[1768] enemies are!" Then Naṣr called for the leader (of the messengers) and made him swear that the news he had brought was the truth. The man swore that it was so. Then Salm[591] b. Aḥwaz said: "May God keep the *amīr* on the right path! If I had taken an oath I would have told the truth. This is a trick of the Quraysh who

584. Mājān was a village in the Marw area. Cf. Yāqūt, IV, 378. Mājān became a flourishing suburb of Marw under Abū Muslim. Cf. Ibn Ḥawqal, 420–21; Le Strange, *Lands*, 398–99.

585. Ṣaghāniyān is probably to be identified as the modern town of Sar-i Asyā on the upper course of the Ṣaghāniyān River. Ṣaghāniyān was also the name of a district that lay to the west of the Wakhsh River and that was bounded on the south by the Oxus. Cf. Le Strange, *Lands*, 439–40.

586. Amul lay on the left bank of the Oxus, about 120 miles to the northeast of Marw. To distinguish it from Āmul in Ṭabaristān, it was later called Amū or Amūyah. Cf. Le Strange, *Lands*, 403–04; Yāqūt, I, 365; *EI*², s.v. (M. Streck).

587. *Amarahum . . . an yastaḥlibū*. Ibn al-Athīr, V, 202, has *yastajlibū*. For *yastaḥlibū* ("urge to assemble"), cf. *Gloss.*, p. CC. For *yastajlibū* ("to summon"), cf. *Gloss.*, p. CLXIV. Both verbs make good sense in the context.

588. For *yughīru*, Ibn al-Athīr (V, 202) has *yaʿburū* ("that they should cross").

589. The addition in parentheses is from Ibn al-Athīr, V, 202.

590. This isolated snippet about al-Walīd's murder and the events that ensued is placed too early in al-Ṭabarī's narrative. These events are discussed in detail later, under the year 126 (744). Cf. Wellhausen, 482–83.

591. He is called Sālim by Ibn al-Athīr (V, 202).

want to cast aspersions on your obedience. So clear off and don't speak calumny against us." He (the messenger)[592] said: "Salm, you are a man who is knowledgeable about military matters. You are, moreover, obedient to the Umayyads. But as for this kind of matter, your opinion on it is (as valueless as) the opinion of a slave girl with her front teeth broken!" Then Naṣr said: "Since (the time of) Ibn Khāzim,[593] I have encountered no difficult situation where my judgment was not superior (to that of others)."[594] The people said: "We know that and we think your opinion is correct."

In this year al-Walīd b. Yazīd sent his maternal uncle Yūsuf b. Muḥammad b. Yūsuf al-Thaqafī to be governor of Medina, Mecca, and al-Ṭā'if, having handed over to his custody Ibrāhīm and Muḥammad, the two sons of Hishām b. Ismā'īl al-Makhzūmī, who were tied up tightly in their cloaks.[595] Yūsuf arrived in Medina with them on Saturday, twelve days before the end of Sha'bān 125 [Saturday, June 14, 743] and paraded them before the people of Medina. Then al-Walīd wrote to him ordering him to send them to Yūsuf b. 'Umar, who was at that time his agent in Iraq. When Ibrāhīm and Muḥammad came to Yūsuf, he tortured them to death. They had been accused before al-Walīd of having embezzled large sums of money.

In this year Yūsuf b. Muḥammad dismissed Sa'd b. Ibrāhīm from the post of *qāḍī* of Medina and appointed to it Yaḥyā b. Sa'īd al-Anṣārī.

In this year al-Walīd b. Yazīd sent his brother al-Ghamr b. [1769]
Yazīd b. 'Abd al-Malik to carry out raids. Al-Walīd put al-Aswad b. Bilāl al-Muḥāribī[596] in charge of his naval forces and ordered him to go to Cyprus and to give the population the choice of going

---

592. The speaker is probably the messenger.

593. The allusion here is unclear (Ibn al-Athīr omits this saying of Naṣr's) but according to the index (321), the Ibn Khāzim in question is 'Abdallāh b. Khāzim al-Sulamī (d. 73/692–93), a governor of Khurāsān around whom legends developed. Cf. Wellhausen, 416–21; *EI*², s.v. (H. A. R. Gibb).

594. *Lam ashhad . . . amran mufẓi'an ilā kuntu al-mufri'a fī-al-rā'yi.* The Cairo edition (VII, 226) has *al-mufẓi'a* for *al-mufri'a.* The Leiden text has been preferred in the translation. For a definition of *mufri'*, cf. *Lisān*, II, 1082.

595. They had now to pay the penalty for having sided with the caliph Hishām when he tried to have allegiance sworn to Maslamah instead of al-Walīd. Cf. al-Ṭabarī, II, 1742; al-Ya'qūbī, *Historiae*, II, 397.

596. Al-Muḥādhī in Ibn al-Athīr, V, 206.

either to Syria or to Byzantium. One group of them opted for asylum in Muslim territory, so al-Aswad took them to Syria. Others of them chose to go to Byzantium and they went in that direction.[597]

In this year Sulaymān b. Kathīr, Mālik b. al-Haytham, Lāhiz b. Qurayẓ, and Qaḥṭabah b. Shabīb arrived in Mecca.[598]

According to some biographers, they met Muḥammad b. ʿAlī[599] and they told him about Abū Muslim and what they had seen of him. Muḥammad asked them: "Is Abū Muslim a free-born man or a slave?" They replied: "ʿĪsā[600] alleges that he is a slave but Abū Muslim himself says that he is free-born." Muḥammad said: "Buy him and manumit him." Then they gave Muḥammad b. ʿAlī two hundred thousand dirhams and clothes worth thirty thousand dirhams. Muḥammad said to them: "I do not think that you will ever meet me again after this year. Should anything happen to me, your master is Ibrāhīm b. Muḥammad. I trust him and I enjoin you to treat him well just as I have enjoined him to treat you well."[601] Then they left Muḥammad b. ʿAlī and he died on the first night of Dhū al-Qaʿdah [Monday, July 25, 743] at the age of 63.[602] Between his death and the death of his father, ʿAlī, was seven years.

According to Aḥmad b. Thābit—his informants—Isḥāq b. ʿĪsā—Abū Maʿshar: In this year Yūsuf b. Muḥammad b. Yūsuf al-Thaqafī led the pilgrimage.

[1770] In this year Yaḥyā b. Zayd b. ʿAlī was killed in Khurāsān.

The Killing of Yaḥyā b. Zayd b. ʿAlī

We have already mentioned how Yaḥyā b. Zayd b. ʿAlī came to be in Khurāsān and the reason for his being there.[603] We will now

---

597. Cf. Ibn al-Athīr, V, 206. For the early history of the Muslims in Cyprus, cf. *EI*², "Ḳubrus" (A. H. de Groot).

598. Cf. the preceding account given by al-Ṭabarī (II, 1726–27). The ʿAbbāsid *nuqabāʾ* were on the pilgrimage. Cf. also al-Yaʿqūbī, *Historiae*, II, 397.

599. Cf. n. 370.

600. I.e., ʿĪsā b. Maʿqil al-ʿIjlī.

601. Cf. al-Dīnawarī, 340.

602. The death of Muḥammad b. ʿAlī is reported in the sources as having occurred in either 124 or 125 A.H. Ibn al-Athīr says that Muḥammad was seventy-three when he died (V, 206).

603. Cf. al-Ṭabarī, II, 1714.

give an account of why he was killed, since that occurred in this year.[604]

According to Hishām b. Muḥammad al-Kalbī—Abū Mikhnaf: Yaḥyā b. Zayd b. ʿAlī stayed with al-Ḥarīsh[605] b. ʿAmr b. Dāwūd in Balkh until Hishām b. ʿAbd al-Malik died and al-Walīd b. Yazīd b. ʿAbd al-Malik became caliph. Yūsuf b. ʿUmar wrote to Naṣr b. Sayyār telling him that Yaḥyā b. Zayd had left Iraq and letting him know where he was staying. Finally, Yūsuf told Naṣr that Yaḥyā was at the house of al-Ḥarīsh and he instructed Naṣr to send his men for Yaḥyā and to take him by force. So Naṣr b. Sayyār sent word to ʿAqīl b. Maʿqil al-ʿIjlī ordering him to seize al-Ḥarīsh and not to let him go until al-Ḥarīsh gave up the ghost or until he brought Yaḥyā b. Zayd to him. Accordingly, ʿAqīl sent for al-Ḥarīsh and questioned him about Yaḥyā. Al-Ḥarīsh said: "I know nothing about him." Then ʿAqīl gave him six hundred lashes. Al-Ḥarīsh said to him: "By God, if he were under my very feet I would not lift them from him so that you could take him." When Quraysh b. al-Ḥarīsh heard of this he went to ʿAqīl and [1771]
said: "Don't kill my father. I will show you where Yaḥyā is." ʿAqīl sent someone with Quraysh, who showed him where Yaḥyā was. He found Yaḥyā in a (concealed) room inside a house and seized him, together with Yazīd b. ʿUmar,[606] and al-Faḍl, the mawlā of ʿAbd al-Qays who had come with Yaḥyā from al-Kūfah. ʿAqīl brought Yaḥyā to Naṣr b. Sayyār, who put him in prison and wrote to Yūsuf b. ʿUmar informing him of what he had done. Yūsuf wrote on this matter to al-Walīd b. Yazīd, who then wrote to Naṣr b. Sayyār ordering him to grant Yaḥyā safe-conduct and to set him and his associates free. Naṣr b. Sayyār summoned Yaḥyā and he ordered him to fear God, warned him against making discord, and commanded him to go to al-Walīd b. Yazīd. Naṣr ordered that Yaḥyā should have two thousand dirhams and two

---

604. For other accounts of the death of Yaḥyā b. Zayd, cf. Ibn Aʿtham, VIII, 126–36; al-Yaʿqūbī, *Historiae*, II, 397–98; al-Balādhurī, *Ansāb* (ed. Maḥmūdī), 260–65; al-Masʿūdī, *Murūj*, VI, 2–4.

605. This name is uncertain. The apparatus also has al-Jarīsh, while Ibn al-Athīr gives al-Ḥuraysh (V, 203). According to al-Balādhurī, al-Ḥarīsh was from the Rabīʿah (*Ansāb*, 261).

606. Yazīd b. ʿUmar had looked after Yaḥyā for six months in Sarakhs. Cf. al-Balādhurī, *Ansāb*, 260.

mules,[607] and Yaḥyā and his associates departed. Yaḥyā got as far as Sarakhs[608] and then he stayed there. In charge of Sarakhs was ʿAbdallāh b. Qays b. ʿUbbād. Naṣr b. Sayyār wrote to him requesting that he should send Yaḥyā away from Sarakhs. Naṣr also wrote to al-Ḥasan b. Zayd al-Tamīmī, who was the leader of the Banū Tamīm and who was in charge of Ṭūs,[609] saying: "Keep your eyes open for Yaḥyā b. Zayd, and if he passes your way don't let him stay in Ṭūs but send him away from there." Naṣr further ordered both ʿAbdallāh and al-Ḥasan that if Yaḥyā passed them they should make sure that they handed him over[610] to ʿAmr b. Zurārah in Abrashahr.[611] Accordingly, ʿAbdallāh b. Qays sent Yaḥyā out of Sarakhs. Yaḥyā then passed al-Ḥasan b. Zayd, who ordered him to be on his way and put him in the care of Sirḥān b.
[1772] Farrukh b. Mujāhid b. Balʿāʾ al-ʿAnbarī Abū al-Faḍl, who had charge of a group of armed guards.

Sirḥān said: When I went in to see Yaḥyā, he spoke disparagingly about Naṣr b. Sayyār and about what Naṣr had given him.[612] Then he mentioned the Commander of the Faithful, al-Walīd b. Yazīd, and spoke ill of him.[613] He said that he went around with his associates and that he only did so because he was afraid that he would be poisoned or suffocated. He made a veiled reference to Yūsuf (b. ʿUmar) and said that he was frightened of him. He confessed that he had also wanted to criticize Yūsuf, but had refrained from doing so. I said to Yaḥyā: "Say what you like, may God have mercy on you, for you need fear no spying on my part. Indeed, Yūsuf has behaved toward you in a way that should

---

607. Al-Balādhurī has: "Two thousand dirhams and a pair of sandals." Cf. *Ansāb*, 261.

608. Sarakhs in Khurāsān lay on the road from Ṭūs to Marw. It was on the great postal route. Cf. Le Strange, *Lands*, 395–96; *Ḥudūd*, 104; al-Yaʿqūbī, *Les Pays*, 85–86; Ibn Rustah, 200–01.

609. Ṭūs: a city in Khurāsān, due east of Nīshāpūr. Cf. Le Strange, *Lands*, 388–89; Ibn Ḥawqal, 419; al-Yaʿqūbī, *Les Pays*, 83–84.

610. Literally, "they should not leave him until they had given him to ʿAmr."

611. The text has "Abarshahr." This is corrected later to "Abrashahr." Cf. *Introd.*, p. DCCXI. Abrashahr was one of the names of Nīshāpūr in the early Islamic period. This is the name given on Umayyad and ʿAbbāsid dirhams. Cf. Le Strange, *Lands*, 383; al-Yaʿqūbī, *Les Pays*, 417.

612. Literally, "he mentioned Naṣr b. Sayyār and what he gave him and there he was as if belittling him."

613. The text has *fa-athnā ʿalayhi*. This phrase is ambiguous since *athnā* can mean both to speak well or ill of someone, although the former is more common.

invite comment from you." Then Yaḥyā replied: "What a surprising remark from someone who appoints guards or commands guards!"[614] In saying that, he was trying to elicit information(?).[615] By God, if I had wanted to send men after him, he would have been brought (to me) in fetters. Then I said to him: "No, by God, those guards are not meant for you. This is a practice which is always followed in this area because the treasury is here."[616] I then apologized to him for accompanying him and I went with him for over a *farsakh* until we chanced upon ʿAmr b. Zurārah.[617] ʿAmr ordered one thousand dirhams for him and gave him an escort as far as Bayhaq. Yaḥyā was afraid that Yūsuf might act treacherously toward him and having left Bayhaq, which is on the border of Khurāsān and Qūmis,[618] he then returned to ʿAmr b. Zurārah with seventy men.[619] Some merchants passed Yaḥyā (on the road) and he took their riding beasts, saying: "We must pay for them."[620] Then ʿAmr b. Zurārah wrote to Naṣr b. Sayyār, who [1773]
in turn wrote to ʿAbdallāh b. Qays and al-Ḥasan b. Zayd requesting them forthwith to go to join ʿAmr b. Zurārah, who was in authority over them, and instructing them to provoke a fight with

614. *Alladhī yuqīmu al-aḥrāsa aw amara al-aḥrāsa.* The speaker obviously cannot remember the exact wording he used and therefore gives two versions.

615. The text has *yatafassaḥa* ("to speak eloquently"). The Cairo edition (229) also has this reading. Later, the editor emends this to *yatafaḥḥasa* ("to seek information"). Cf. *Introd.*, p. DCCXI.

616. Literally, "No, by God, this has not been done because of you, but this is a thing that is always done in this area because of the position of the treasury."

617. Literally, "I went with him . . . and we came with him until we chanced upon ʿAmr . . ." A *farsakh* consists of three *mīls*, i.e., about six km. Cf. Hinz, 62.

618. The province of Qūmis lay between the two provinces of the Jibāl to the west and Khurāsān to the east. Its major city was Damghān. Cf. Le Strange, *Lands*, 364–68.

619. The sequence of events is very confused here and the text corrupt: "He advanced (*aqbala*) from Bayhaq, which is the furthest point of the territory of Khurāsān and the nearest of Qūmis, and he advanced (*aqbala*) with seventy men toward ʿAmr b. Zurārah." The account of al-Balādhurī is much clearer: "When he left Bayhaq he was afraid that he would fall into the hands of Yūsuf and that he would cause him mischief, and Bayhaq is the border of the province of Khurāsān . . . so he (Yaḥyā) returned to ʿAmr b. Zurārah." Cf. *Ansāb*, 261–62. It would appear that Yaḥyā felt panic and *returned* to Abrashahr (Nīshāpūr) where ʿAmr was and asked permission to stay there a little while before going to Balkh. Cf. *Ansāb*, 262. This is also the version given by Ibn al-Athīr, V, 203.

620. *Qāla ʿalaynā athmānuhā.* This action in acquiring more riding animals was clearly viewed as irregular by ʿAmr and was used as the pretext to attack Yaḥyā.

Yaḥyā b. Zayd. So they went and joined ʿAmr b. Zurārah, and those assembled numbered ten thousand men. Yaḥyā b. Zayd took the field against them, having with him only seventy men. (Yet) Yaḥyā routed them, killing ʿAmr b. Zurārah and striking down numerous horses. Then Yaḥyā advanced as far as Herat. In charge of Herat was Mughallis b. Ziyād al-ʿĀmirī. Neither Yaḥyā nor Mughallis made a hostile move toward the other. Then Yaḥyā b. Zayd passed through Herat. Naṣr b. Sayyār sent Salm b. Aḥwaz in search of Yaḥyā b. Zayd, but when Salm reached Herat, Yaḥyā b. Zayd had already left the city. Salm then went in pursuit of Yaḥyā and caught up with him at a village in the area of al-Jūzajān,[621] which was under the charge of Ḥammād b. ʿAmr al-Sughdī.

Yaḥyā b. Zayd was joined by a man of the Banū Ḥanīfah called Abū al-ʿAjlān. This man was killed that day with Yaḥyā. Yaḥyā was also joined by al-Ḥasḥās al-Azdī. Later on, Naṣr cut off his hand and his foot. Salm b. Aḥwaz put Sawrah b. Muḥammad b. ʿAzīz al-Kindī on his right side and Ḥammād b. ʿAmr al-Sughdī on his left. Then he launched into a fierce battle against Yaḥyā. Some accounts said that a man from the Banū ʿAnazah[622] whose
[1774] name was ʿĪsā, the mawlā of ʿĪsā b. Sulaymān al-ʿAnazī, shot an arrow at Yaḥyā and hit him in the forehead.[623] Muḥammad was present on that day.[624] Salm had ordered him to prepare his men for battle, but Muḥammad pretended to be ill, so it was Sawrah b. Muḥammad b. ʿAzīz al-Kindī who made them ready. They fought and were killed to the last man. Sawrah passed Yaḥyā b. Zayd and took away his head. Al-ʿAnazī had seized his spoils and his shirt, but then Sawrah took Yaḥyā's head away from him by force.

According to Hishām (b. Muḥammad al-Kalbī)—Mūsā b. Ḥabīb: When Yaḥyā b. Zayd was killed and al-Walīd b. Yazīd received news of it, al-Walīd wrote to Yūsuf b. ʿUmar as follows: "When this letter of mine reaches you, look for the calf[625] of Iraq,

---

621. The village was called Arghūnah. Cf. Ibn Aʿtham, VIII, 134. Al-Masʿūdī has Arʿawanah. Cf. *Murūj*, VI, 2.

622. For the Banū ʿAnazah, cf. *EI*², s.v. (E. Gräf).

623. Cf. al-Balādhurī, *Ansāb*, 262.

624. Presumably the Muḥammad in question is Muḥammad b. ʿAzīz al-Kindī, the father of Sawrah. This, at any rate, is the tentative opinion of the editor. Cf. al-Ṭabarī, II, 1774, note b.

625. *ʿIjl.* Cf. Qurʾān 20, v. 88; 7, v. 148. These details about burning the "calf of

burn him, then scatter him as dust in the river."[626] Yūsuf gave orders to Khirāsh b. Ḥawshab and he brought Yaḥyā down from the gibbet,[627] burned his body, then crushed it, put it in a date basket, placed it in a boat, and then scattered Yaḥyā's remains in the Euphrates.

In this year the agents of the garrison cities were the same as in the preceding year and we have already mentioned them.

Iraq" are also mentioned in some sources in connection with Zayd. Cf. al-Balādhurī, *Ansāb*, 257; al-Iṣfahānī, *Maqātil*, 143–44.

626. *Fī al-yammi*. Cf. Qur'ān 20, v. 39.

627. Literally, "from his tree."

[1775]

The Events of the Year 126

(October 25, 743–October 12, 744)

One of the important events taking place during this year was the killing of al-Walīd b. Yazīd by Yazīd b. al-Walīd,[628] who was known as the Inadequate (*al-Nāqiṣ*).[629]

The Reason for Yazīd's Killing of al-Walīd and the Manner of His Killing

We have already given some account of al-Walīd b. Yazīd, mentioning his immorality, his wantonness, and his flippant and frivolous attitude toward religion before he became caliph. When his accession came and the caliphate passed to him, he only persisted

628. Cf. the Umayyad genealogical table.

629. Although, as will be discussed later, Yazīd b. al-Walīd was given the pejorative title *al-Nāqiṣ* because he cut back (*naqaṣa*) on the people's pensions, there is also a suggestion here of incompleteness and of physical inadequacy as well. The term *al-Nāqiṣ* has therefore been translated as "inadequate" rather than as "curtailer" in an attempt to render the double entendre. On the reasons for Yazīd's receiving this nickname, cf. Ibn 'Abd Rabbihi, I, 17; al-Mas'ūdī, *Murūj*, VI, 19–20.

all the more in his pursuit of idle sport and pleasures, hunting, drinking wine, and keeping company with libertines. I have left to one side the accounts which deal with all this as I would hate to make my book any longer by mentioning them. These aspects of al-Walīd's behavior troubled his subjects and his soldiery deeply and they hated what he was doing. One of the worst offences he committed against himself, and which finally led to his death, was the way in which he aroused disaffection against himself amongst the sons of his two uncles, Hishām and al-Walīd, who were the sons of ʿAbd al-Malik b. Marwān,[630] as well as amongst the Yamāniyyah who formed the major part of the Syrian *jund.*

Part of the Account of al-Walīd's Causing Disaffection among the Sons of His Two Uncles, Hishām and al-Walīd [1776]

According to Aḥmad b. Zuhayr—ʿAlī (al-Madāʾinī)—al-Minhāl b. ʿAbd al-Malik: Al-Walīd loved idle sport, hunting, and pleasures. When he became caliph he began to dislike places where there were people. This continued to be the case until he was killed.[631] He kept on moving about and going out hunting, and he distressed the people and his soldiers. He (particularly) upset the sons of Hishām, for he sentenced Sulaymān b. Hishām[632] to one hundred lashes, shaving his head and beard and banishing him to ʿAmmān, where he put him in prison; there Sulaymān remained until al-Walīd was killed.

Al-Walīd took a slave-girl belonging to the family of al-Walīd (b. ʿAbd al-Malik). ʿUmar b. al-Walīd spoke to al-Walīd about this matter but al-Walīd said: "I will not give her back." So ʿUmar

630. Cf. the Umayyad genealogical table.

631. After he became caliph, al-Walīd never once entered a Syrian city until his death. Cf. *Fragmenta,* 130–31.

632. According to *Fragmenta,* 130, al-Walīd could not forget that Sulaymān b. Hishām had been against him when Hishām was caliph. Sulaymān had advised his father to depose al-Walīd as his heir. Cf. also al-Balādhurī, *Ansāb* (Derenk), 45. The text has *wa-ishtadda ʿalā Banī Hishāmi ḍaraba Sulaymāna.* The Cairo edition, 231, punctuates this passage differently and adds *fa*: *wa-ishtadda ʿalā Banī Hishāmi; fa-ḍaraba Sulaymān.* This alternative has been followed in the translation. Al-Balādhurī has a clearer version: *wa-ishtadda ʿalā Banī Hishāmi ḥattā ḍaraba Sulaymāna.* Cf. *Ansāb* (Derenk), 46.

said: "In that case, there will be much neighing of horses around your troops."[633]

He (al-Walīd) imprisoned Yazīd b. Hishām al-Afqam[634] and wanted the oath of allegiance to be given to his two sons, al-Ḥakam and ʿUthmān.[635] Al-Walīd consulted Saʿīd b. Bayhas b. Suḥayb on this, who said: "Don't do it; for they are young boys who have not yet reached puberty. Have the oath of allegiance given to ʿAtīq b. ʿAbd al-ʿAzīz b. al-Walīd b. ʿAbd al-Malik." Al-Walīd was furious and put Saʿīd in prison, where he died. Al-Walīd wanted Khālid b. ʿAbdallāh[636] to give the oath of allegiance to his two sons but Khālid refused. Some of Khālid's family said to him: "The Commander of the Faithful wanted you to give the oath of allegiance to his two sons yet you refused to do so!" Khālid retorted: "Fie on you! How can I give the oath of allegiance to those behind whom I cannot say my prayers or whose testimony (*shahādah*) I cannot accept?"[637] They replied: "What about al-Walīd? You know all about his wantonness and depravity, yet you still accept his testimony!" Khālid replied: "Al-Walīd's activities
[1777] are hearsay. I cannot be sure about them. It is only vulgar tittle-tattle." But al-Walīd was furious with Khālid.

ʿAmr b. Saʿīd al-Thaqafī said: "Yūsuf b. ʿUmar sent me to al-Walīd. When I went in to see him, al-Walīd greeted me: 'Well, how do you find the libertine?' meaning by that himself. Then he went on: 'Beware lest anyone should hear you saying such a thing.' I rejoined: 'I would divorce Ḥabībah, the daughter of ʿAbd al-Raḥmān b. Jubayr, rather than allow my ear to hear such things as long as you live.'" Then al-Walīd laughed.

Al-Walīd deeply distressed the people (by his behavior), and the sons of Hishām and of al-Walīd (b. ʿAbd al-Malik) charged him with being an unbeliever and with having debauched the mothers of his father's sons. They also alleged that al-Walīd had taken one hundred collars(?) and had written on each of them the name of one of the Umayyads whom he intended to kill thereby.[638] His

633. Cf. *Fragmenta,* 131.

634. Al-Afqam was the *laqab* of Yazīd b. Hishām. Cf. al-Iṣfahānī, *Aghānī,* VI, 140; Ibn ʿAbd Rabbihi, II, 291; al-Balādhurī, *Ansāb* (Derenk), 46.

635. Cf. the genealogical table of the Umayyads.

636. Al-Qasrī.

637. They were minors. For a similar account, cf. *Fragmenta,* 131; al-Balādhurī, *Ansāb* (Derenk), 46.

638. Cf. al-Balādhurī, *Ansāb* (Derenk), 45; *Fragmenta,* 130. The text has *wa-*

detractors also accused him of being a free-thinker.[639] The most vociferous of the critics of al-Walīd was Yazīd b. al-Walīd b. ʿAbd al-Malik. The people were well-disposed to listen to him because he performed public acts of asceticism and would adopt a humble stance, merely saying: "We cannot afford to be satisfied with al-Walīd." (This continued) until he induced the people to assassinate al-Walīd.

According to Aḥmad b. Zuhayr—ʿAlī (al-Madāʾinī)—Yazīd b. Maṣād al-Kalbī—ʿAmr b. Sharāḥil: Hishām b. ʿAbd al-Malik sent us to Dahlak[640] where we remained until Hishām's death and the accession of al-Walīd. Then our case was brought up, but al-Walīd refused to do anything and said: "By God, Hishām never did anything that is more deserving of forgiveness by me than his killing and banishment of the Qadariyyah".[641] Al-Ḥajjāj b. Bishr b. Fayrūz al-Daylamī was in charge of us and he used to say: "Al-Walīd will survive for only eighteen months before he is killed [1778]
and his killing will bring about the destruction of the rest of his family."

A group of the Quḍāʿah, and especially of al-Yamāniyyah from Damascus, resolved to kill al-Walīd. Then Ḥurayth, Shabīb b. Abī Mālik al-Ghassānī, Manṣūr b. Jumhūr, Yaʿqūb b. ʿAbd al-Raḥmān, Ḥibāl b. ʿAmr, who was Manṣūr's cousin, Ḥumayd b. Naṣr al-Lakhmī, al-Aṣbagh b. Dhuʾālah, Ṭufayl b. Ḥārithah, and al-Sarī b. Ziyād b. ʿIlāqah came to Khālid b. ʿAbdallāh, and asked him to join in their enterprise.[642] Khālid did not agree to it.[643] Then they

---

kataba ʿalā kulli jāmiʿatin isma rajulin. The meaning of *jāmiʿah* as a collar or manacles joining the hands to the neck is well attested. Cf. *Lisān,* II, 501 and Kazimirski, I, 328. Presumably, if such collars were made of metal (or even leather) they could be both written on and tightened so as to strangle the wearer. However, this is only a tentative translation. It may be that *jāmiʿah* could be translated more blandly as "document," but the lengthy entries in the standard dictionaries give no support for this interpretation. Moreover, there might then be a problem with the phrase *"li-yaqtula bihā."* Al-Balādhurī, however, omits *bihā* (*Ansāb,* 45).

639. *Al-zandaqah.*

640. The term *Dahlak* refers to a group of islands off the west coast of the Red Sea opposite Eritrea. Dahlak al-Kabīr was used as a place to which the Umayyad caliphs sent opponents, such as the Qadariyyah. Cf. *EI²*, s.v. (S. H. Longrigg).

641. Cf. Hishām's treatment of Ghaylān.

642. For a recent discussion of the elements that comprised the opposition to al-Walīd II, cf. Hawting, 93. Al-Walīd's father, Yazid, had espoused anti-"southern" (Kalbī and Yemeni) policies, and al-Walīd had already in his short rule confirmed Yūsuf b. ʿUmar (a Qaysī) in the key post of governor of Iraq.

643. Literally, "he did not answer them."

asked him to keep quiet about their plans and Khālid said: "I will not mention any of your names." But when al-Walīd wanted to go on the pilgrimage, Khālid was afraid that the conspirators would assassinate him en route. Khālid therefore went to al-Walīd and said: "O Commander of the Faithful, put off going on the pilgrimage this year." When al-Walīd asked him why, Khālid would not tell him. So al-Walīd ordered that Khālid should be cast into prison and that whatever Iraqi revenues Khālid had should be taken from him.[644]

According to ʿAlī (al-Madāʾinī)—al-Ḥakam b. al-Nuʿmān: Al-Walīd resolved to dismiss Yūsuf (b. ʿUmar) and to appoint as governor ʿAbd al-Malik b. Muḥammad b. al-Ḥajjāj. So he wrote to Yūsuf as follows:

> You have written to the Commander of the Faithful explaining how Ibn al-Naṣrāniyyah (i.e., Khālid b. ʿAbdallāh al-Qasrī) has allowed the country to go to rack and ruin, and you go on to say that it was for that reason that you delivered such small revenues to Hishām.[645] It was only to be expected that you would have made the land prosper to such an extent that you restored it to its former state. So come to the Com-
> [1779] mander of the Faithful and confirm his high expectations of you by what you bring him to show how you have made the land prosper. (Do this so that) the Commander of the Faithful may be assured of your superiority over other men, because of the close kinship that God has made between you and the Commander of the Faithful—for you are his maternal uncle and the person most entitled to give generously to him—and because you know that the Commander of the Faithful has given instructions that the stipends of the Syrians and of others should be increased. (You know, too,) what he has given the members of his family—to the detriment of the treasuries—because of the churlish treatment which they endured for so long at the hands of Hishām.[646]

644. Al-Balādhurī adds after the same account: "He (al-Walīd) gave him (Khālid) to Yūsuf b. ʿUmar, who tortured him to death." Cf. *Ansāb* (Derenk), 47. Cf. also *Fragmenta*, 132.

645. Literally, "you brought to Hishām what you brought."

646. Cf. Wellhausen, 357. This letter is a transparently desperate ploy on the part of al-Walīd to raise money and was to culminate in al-Walīd's selling Khālid al-Qasrī to Yūsuf b. ʿUmar.

Yūsuf accordingly set out, having appointed as his deputy his cousin Yūsuf b. Muḥammad and taking with him unprecedented quantities of money, goods, and drinking vessels from Iraq. When he arrived, Khālid b. ʿAbdallāh was in prison. Ḥassān al-Nabaṭī met Yūsuf at night and told him that al-Walīd was determined to appoint ʿAbd al-Malik b. Muḥammad b. al-Ḥajjāj as governor and that Yūsuf would have to ingratiate himself with al-Walīd's ministers.[647] Yūsuf said: "I don't have any spare cash." Ḥassān replied: "I have five hundred thousand dirhams. If you want them, you can have them, and you can return them if you like, should things go well for you." Yūsuf said: "You know more than I do about these men and their standing with the caliph, so distribute the money amongst them to the best of your knowledge." Ḥassān acted accordingly and when Yūsuf arrived,[648] the people treated them respectfully. Then Ḥassān said to Yūsuf: "Don't go in to see al-Walīd in the morning but go to him in the evening. Write a letter to yourself from your deputy saying, 'I have written to tell you that your only hope lies in the palace.' Go in to see al-Walīd, having the letter hidden on you and wearing a sad expression. Read the letter to him and order Abān b. ʿAbd al-Raḥmān al- [1780] Numayrī to buy Khālid from al-Walīd for forty million dirhams." Yūsuf acted accordingly and al-Walīd said to him: "Return to your post." Then Abān said to al-Walīd: "If you give me Khālid, I will give you forty million dirhams." Al-Walīd replied: "Who will act as your guarantor?" Abān said: "Yūsuf." So al-Walīd asked Yūsuf: "Will you act as his guarantor?" Yūsuf replied: "No! On the contrary, give him to me and I will extract fifty million dirhams from him."[649] So al-Walīd gave Khālid to Yūsuf, who took him away on a litter without a seat below to sit on.[650]

Muḥammad b. Muḥammad b. al-Qāsim said: I took pity on Khālid and I put some tasty things we had with us, including some dried dates and other things, in a napkin. I was riding a

---

647. Literally, "it was inevitable that he would have to settle the matter of his ministers." Ibn al-Athīr has: "he advised him to take bribes to his ministers" (V, 212).

648. At the court.

649. Ibn al-Athīr's account is much more straightforward. Yūsuf bought Khālid from al-Walīd for fifty million dirhams and al-Walīd gave him to Yūsuf (V, 212). Cf. also al-Dīnawarī, 347–48.

650. *Wiṭā'*: "what is placed or spread beneath one, to sit or lie upon." Cf. Lane, I, 2949.

lively she-camel and I hurried up to Khālid without Yūsuf noticing,[651] and threw the napkin into his litter. Then Khālid said to me: "These are goods from 'Umān," referring to the fact that my brother al-Fayḍ[652] was in charge of 'Umān and that he had sent me a large sum of money. So I said to myself: "Here is this man in this (miserable) state and he still won't drop this matter." Then Yūsuf noticed me and said to me: "What did you say to Ibn al-Naṣrāniyyah?" (i.e., Khālid). I replied: "I asked him if he needed anything." Yūsuf said: "You did well. He is a prisoner." [Muḥammad continued:] If Yūsuf had been aware of what I had thrown to Khālid, some harm would have befallen me at his hands. Yūsuf arrived in al-Kūfah and killed Khālid under torture.

According to al-Haytham b. 'Adī: Al-Walīd b. Yazīd recited a poem in which he reproached the Yamāniyyah for failing to come to the help of Khālid b. 'Abdallāh. According to Aḥmad b. Zuhayr—'Alī b. Muḥammad (al-Madā'inī)—Muḥammad b. Sa'īd
[1781] al-'Āmirī, from the Banū 'Āmir of Kalb:[653] This poem was recited by one of the Yamanī poets who put it into the mouth of al-Walīd in order to rouse the Yamāniyyah against him:[654]

Have your emotions not been stirred to recall your union (with your beloved),
and a knot which once was tied and then was loosed?
Yes, indeed! So let your tears flow freely,
like water gushing continuously from clouds.[655]
Remember no more the people of Su'dā,[656]
for we are the greatest in numbers and wealth.[657]

---

651. *Fa-taghaffaltu Yūsufa.* Literally, "I watched for Yūsuf to be unmindful."

652. Al-Fayḍ b. Muḥammad b. al-Qāsim al-Thaqafī. He was from Yūsuf's family. Cf. Ibn Khayyāṭ, 553. Presumably the money was tainted in some way.

653. The text has 'Āmir Kalb. This should probably read "'Āmir b. Kilāb" or "'Āmir b. Ka'b." Cf. *EI*², "'Āmir b. Ṣa'ṣa'a" (W. Caskel); Ibn al-Kalbī, II, 160.

654. The order of the lines or half-lines of this poetry, as presented by al-Ṭabarī, is rather unsatisfactory. A number of them seem to be in the wrong place. Cf. Ibn al-Athīr, V, 212–13; al-Balādhurī, *Ansāb* (Derenk), 48; *Fragmenta,* 132–33; al-Dīnawarī, 347. The meter is *wāfir.* Only the most important textual differences have been noted here. Al-Dīnawarī's version is the most at variance with the others.

655. *Ka-mā'i al-muzni yansajilu insijālā.* Al-Dīnawarī, 347, has *ka-mā'i al-gharbi yanhamilu inhimālā.*

656. For the Banū Su'dā, cf. Ibn al-Kalbī, II, 515.

657. This hemistich seems to be in the wrong place.

We are kings who rule men by force,
inflicting on them humiliation and punishment.[658]
We have trampled on the Ash'arīs with the might of Qays,[659]
and what a trampling for you! Its like will not recur.
Behold Khālid a prisoner in our midst![660]
Had they been true men they would have protected him,
Their lord and master in days of yore.
We have made shame dog him like a shadow.
Had they been tribes who wielded any power,
We would not have showered benefits (on them) in vain.
Nor would they have left him dispossessed and in captivity,
with only our heavy chains to talk to.[661]

Al-Madā'inī reported: "struggling with our chains."

As for the tribes of Kindah and Sakūn,[662] they have never risen up again,[663]
nor have their horses been relieved of their saddles.
Through them we have inflicted every sort of ignominy on mankind,
and devastated both the plains and the mountains.
But battles have brought them low,
and torn them up and driven them away,
So they remain forever subservient to us; [1782]
We inflict humiliation and degradation upon them.[664]
And so the next morning I was ruling the people,
with a crown on my head which will not be removed.

'Imrān b. Halbā' al-Kalbī gave the poet the following reply:[665]

---

658. Al-Dīnawarī has an extra line here.

659. *Bi-'izzi Qaysin.* Al-Dīnawarī has *bi-kulli arḍin.* For the Ash'arīs (al-Ash'ariyyūn), cf. Ibn al-Kalbī, II, 200.

660. *Fīnā. Fragmenta,* 132 and *Ansāb,* 48 have *amsā asīran* (a *ḥāl* clause). Ibn al-Athīr has *asīrun,* which is also possible grammatically as the *khabar.*

661. *Yu'āliju min salāsilinā.* This is the version preferred by Ibn al-Athīr (V, 212); al-Balādhurī, *Ansāb* (Derenk), 48; *Fragmenta,* 133. Al-Dīnawarī, 348, has *nuḥammiluhu salāsilanā.*

662. The Sakūn were a branch of the Kindah. Cf. Ibn al-Kalbī, II, 503.

663. The text has *fa-mā istiqālū.* Ibn al-Athīr, V, 212, has *fa-mā istaqāmū,* which makes better sense. Al-Dīnawarī, 348, has *qad ista'ādhū.*

664. The second hemistich is almost a repetition of 1781, line 6.

665. This reply is not in the other sources.

Rein in your riding she-camel, O Ḥalāl,
and cut the cord of the one who has already severed union.
Has it not grieved you that he who has opposed
the chieftains of Yaman should be held in high esteem?
We have given long days
to the tribes of Nizār[666] on the Day of al-Marj[667]
And through us the crowned one of the Quraysh became king,[668]
and the good fortune of those who had perished perished with them.
When[ever] you confront the Sakūn and the Kalb
and the ʿAbs,[669] you may be sure that your sovereignty is at an end.
For unless a man is found to be just,
his own words will compass his downfall.
Prepare, O people of Ḥimyar,[670] whenever the call to arms is raised,
Indian swords and blood-spilling[671] spears,
And every[672] youthful horse with high short ribs
and endowed with two flanks, lean in belly and tall as mountains[673]
Will leave behind on every battlefield a dead warrior,
a man who had grown tired of the call[674] (to battle), surrounded by birds.
If you reviled us for the deeds we have done,
you would be saying a dreadful thing.

---

666. I.e., Muḍar and Rabīʿah.

667. This is probably a reference to the battle of Marj Rāhiṭ near Damascus in 64 (684), at which the Qudaʿah led by the Kalb tribe defeated a confederation of Qays tribes and ensured that the caliphate would remain in the Marwānid line. For a discussion of the tribal implications of this battle, cf. Crone, 35; Wellhausen, 171–83; Rotter, 126–51; Dixon, 83–120.

668. I.e., the Umayyad caliph, Marwān I.

669. For the Banū ʿAbs, cf. Ibn al-Kalbī, II, 135; cf. *EI*², "Ghaṭafān" (J. Fück).

670. For the Banū Ḥimyar, cf. Ibn al-Kalbī, II, 324.

671. *Al-nihālā:* literally, "(blood) drinking."

672. The text has *wukulla.* This is emended to *wakullu.* Cf. *Emend.*, p. DCCXI.

673. The text has *al-ḥibālā.* The Cairo edition (236) has *al-jibālā,* which has been preferred in the translation.

674. *Qad madhila al-suʾālā.* This is instead of *min al-suʾāli* (lit., "who has become weary of asking"). Cf. *Gloss.*, p. DCLXXXIII.

As for the brothers of al-Ashʿath,[675] they were killed,
but they were neither trampled on nor humiliated.
As for the sons of al-Muhallab,[676] we have joined battle
against them, but you have fought none of them.
And the men of Judhām,[677] together with those of Lakhm,[678] [1783]
have set themselves against their brothers,
killing and scattering them.
We fled, refusing to help you against them,
but those who have assisted you have committed a grave error.
So if you do return, you should know that we have swords
which are sharp and which we polish continually.
We will mourn[679] Khālid by using your Indian swords,
nor will his great deeds be lost [from memory].
Has not Khālid been the rain sought by orphans
when they came to you and you gave them nothing?[680]
Khālid used to provide shrouds for the dead of Nizār,
and enrich the quick (of Nizār) with land and wealth.
If those who had done him wrong had been
in the courts of his own people, they would have been severely punished.
You will encounter, if you remain alive, clearly marked horses,
stern of expression, which are never without[681] their trappings.

According to Aḥmad b. Zuhayr—ʿAlī b. Muḥammad (al-Madā'inī): The people's rage against al-Walīd only increased when

675. This is probably a reference to the rebellion of Ibn al-Ashʿath in 80–82 (699–702). Cf. *EI*², s.v. (Veccia Vaglieri); Hawting, 67–71; Dixon, 151–68; Crone, 110–11; Wellhausen, 232–48.

676. For the rebellion of Yazīd b. al-Muhallab in 102 (720), cf. Wellhausen, 312–18; Shaban, *'Abbāsid Revolution*, 93–95; Hawting, 73–76; al-Ṭabarī, II, 1402–05.

677. For the Banū Judhām, cf. *EI*², "D̲judhām" (C. E. Bosworth). In the Umayyad period, they were close supporters of the Banū Marwān. The text has *Judhāmun.* This is corrected to *Judhāmu.* Cf. *Emend.*, p. DCCXII.

678. For the Banū Lakhm, cf. *EI*², s.v. (H. Lammens-I. Shahid). They were closely linked in Umayyad times with the Judhām.

679. The Leiden text has *satabkī.* The Cairo edition (VII, 236) has *sanabkī* ("we will mourn"), as does the emended version. Cf. *Emend.*, p. DCCXII.

680. Literally, "while you were leanness for them."

681. The text has *lā yuzāyalna.* This is later emended to *lā yuzāyilna.* Cf. *Emend.*, p. DCCXII.

this poem was recited. Then Ibn Bīḍ[682] declaimed the following lines:[683]

You have loaded the cloud of affliction with further affliction, after
you asserted that the cloud of affliction would be lifted from us.
Would that Hishām were still alive ruling over us,
and that we still had our hopes and aspirations intact!

Hishām had appointed al-Walīd b. al-Qaʿqāʿ[684] as agent of Qinnasrīn[685] and ʿAbd al-Malik b. al-Qaʿqāʿ in charge of Ḥimṣ. Al-Walīd b. al-Qaʿqāʿ had given Ibn Hubayrah one hundred lashes.[686] When al-Walīd became caliph, the Banū al-Qaʿqāʿ[687] fled from him and sought refuge at the grave of Yazīd b. ʿAbd al-Malik.[688] Al-Walīd sent people to seize them. He then handed them over to Yazīd b. ʿUmar b. Hubayrah,[689] who was in charge of Qinnasrīn. Ibn Hubayrah tortured them, and al-Walīd b. al-Qaʿqāʿ, ʿAbd al-Malik b. al-Qaʿqāʿ and two other men from the Qaʿqāʿ family died under torture.

[1784] The sons of al-Walīd (b. ʿAbd al-Malik) and of Hishām, as well as the family of al-Qaʿqāʿ and the Yamāniyyah, conceived a deep

682. Ibn al-Athīr has Hamzah b. Bīḍ (V, 213). *Fragmenta*, 133, and al-Balādhurī, *Ansāb* (Derenk), 48, give the poet the *nisbah* al-Ḥanafī. Cf. also Ibn ʿAbd Rabbihi, I, 289; al-Iṣfahānī, *Aghānī*, XII, 42–43.

683. The meter is *ṭawīl*. Ibn al-Athīr has more lines of poetry, also by Ibn Bīḍ, at this point (loc. cit.). These are also in *Fragmenta*, 133.

684. Al-Walīd b. al-Qaʿqāʿ had served in Armenia under Maslamah and in Khurāsān under Junayd. Cf. al-Balādhurī, *Futūḥ*, 206; al-Ṭabarī, II, 1529, 1550. He was appointed *ʿāmil* of Qinnasrīn by Hishām in 119 (737). Cf. al-Ṭabarī, II, 1593. For the history of this family, cf. Crone, 105.

685. For this well-known city of northern Syria, cf. Le Strange, *Palestine*, 353–57; *EI²*, s.v. (N. Elisséeff).

686. ʿUmar b. Hubayrah al-Fazārī had been made governor of al-Jazīrah under ʿUmar II in 100 (718–19). Cf. al-Ṭabarī, II, 1349; Wellhausen, 319–22, 326–28, 453–55. For the one hundred lashes, cf. also *Fragmenta*, 122.

687. The Banū al-Qaʿqāʿ had supported Hishām in his unsuccessful attempts to have al-Walīd ousted as his heir apparent. Cf. al-Ṭabarī, II, 1742.

688. The Umayyad caliph, Yazīd II, who ruled 101–05 (720–24). Cf. the Umayyad genealogical table. *Fragmenta*, 122 has the Banū al-Qaʿqāʿ fleeing to the grave of Marwān.

689. Yazīd b. ʿUmar b. Hubayrah later joined up with Marwān II. Cf. Ibn Khayyāṭ, 564. He was killed by the ʿAbbāsids in 132 (749–50). Cf. al-Ṭabarī, II, 1913; III, 61; Crone, 107.

hatred for the caliph al-Walīd because of his treatment of Khālid b. ʿAbdallāh. Accordingly, the Yamāniyyah went to Yazīd b. al-Walīd and tried to persuade him to have the oath of allegiance given to him. Yazīd consulted ʿAmr[690] b. Yazīd al-Ḥakamī, who said: "The people will not give the oath of allegiance to you over this matter. Consult your brother al-ʿAbbās b. al-Walīd, for he is the head of the Banū Marwān.[691] If al-ʿAbbās gives you the oath of allegiance, no one else will oppose you. If al-ʿAbbās refuses, then the people will be more likely to obey him. If you insist on sticking to your opinion, then proclaim publicly that al-ʿAbbās has given the oath of allegiance to you." At that time Syria was plague-ridden and the conspirators went out into the desert country. Yazīd b. al-Walīd was encamped in the desert and al-ʿAbbās was at al-Qasṭal.[692] There was a distance of a few *mīl*s between the two of them.[693]

According to Aḥmad b. Zuhayr—ʿAlī (al-Madāʾinī): Yazīd came to his brother al-ʿAbbās and told him what had been happening.[694] Yazīd asked his advice and spoke abusively of al-Walīd. Then al-ʿAbbās said to him: "Go easy, Yazīd. By breaking God's oath you corrupt both true religion and this life on earth." Yazīd returned home and worked secretly among the people, who clandestinely gave him the oath of allegiance. Yazīd also issued secret instructions to al-Aḥnaf al-Kalbī, Yazīd b. ʿAnbasah al-Saksakī, and a group of notables and chiefs who were in his confidence, and they privately canvassed people to join the cause. Then Yazīd paid another visit to his brother al-ʿAbbās, accompanied by their mawlā, Qaṭan.[695] Yazīd sought his brother's advice on this whole matter and told him that people were coming to him and trying to persuade him to accept their oath of allegiance. Al-ʿAbbās chided

690. The text has ʿAmr. Ibn al-Athīr has ʿUmar. For his biography, cf. Crone, 156.

691. Cf. the Umayyad genealogical table.

692. Al-Qasṭal was a place near al-Balqāʾ in the area of Damascus, on the road to Medina. Cf. Yāqūt, IV, 95; Derenk, 121; Dussaud, 80, 85; Gaube, 67–73, 76–78, 85–86.

693. For these events, cf. *Fragmenta*, 133–34; al-Balādhurī, *Ansāb* (Derenk), 48–49; Ibn al-Athīr, V, 213.

694. Cf. Ibn Khayyāṭ, 381.

695. According to al-Jahshiyārī, Qaṭan was in charge of *al-khātam al-kabīr* (*Wuzarāʾ*, 44).

him and said: "If you resort to this kind of behavior again, I will certainly tie you up tightly and take you to the Commander of the Faithful," so Yazīd and Qaṭan went away. Then al-ʿAbbās sent word to Qaṭan, saying: "Look here, Qaṭan! Do you think that Yazīd is in earnest?" Qaṭan said: "To tell the truth, I don't think
[1785] he is. But he can no longer endure[696] what he has heard of al-Walīd's treatment of the sons of Hishām and the sons of al-Walīd (b. ʿAbd al-Malik) and of the caliph's flippant and contemptuous attitude toward religion." Al-ʿAbbās replied: "By God, I myself think that he is the ill-starred one[697] of the Banū Marwān. Were it not for the fact that I am afraid that al-Walīd would act hastily and unfairly toward us, I would truss up Yazīd hand and foot[698] and take him to al-Walīd. So dissuade him from what he plans to do. He listens to you." Then Yazīd said to Qaṭan: "What did al-ʿAbbās say to you when he saw you?" So Qaṭan told Yazīd what al-ʿAbbās had said and Yazīd said: "No, by God, I won't hold back!"[699] When Muʿāwiyah b. ʿAmr b. ʿUtbah heard about the people's activities, he went to al-Walīd and said: "O Commander of the Faithful, you coax forth my tongue when we have a friendly conversation, but I hold it back out of reverence for you. I hear what you do not hear and I fear things which do not worry you.[700] Shall I speak honestly or remain silent out of obedience?" Al-Walīd said: "Everything is acceptable from you. God has hidden knowledge about us; it is our destiny to reach him. If the Banū Marwān knew that they are kindling a fire on red-hot stones which they are casting into their own bellies, they would not act in this way. Let us go back[701] (to what we were talking about) and we will hear what you have to say." Marwān b. Muḥammad heard

---

696. *Mā qad ḍāqa bihi dharʿan.*

697. *Ashaʾma sakhlatin* ("the most inauspicious lamb"). It is tempting to use the English idiom "black sheep" here, but such an idiom does not take account of the nuance of ill luck in Arabic. Men who are *sukhkhāl* are weak and commit foul deeds (*ardhal*): cf. *Lisān*, II, 114. *Fragmenta*, 134 has *ashamma* ("disdainful"). Ibn al-Athīr, V, 213 has *ashaʾma mawlūdin* ("the most inauspicious offspring").

698. Literally, "I would tie Yazīd up tightly."

699. Cf. al-Balādhurī, *Ansāb* (Derenk), 49; *Fragmenta*, 134.

700. Literally, "I fear that against which I see you feeling secure."

701. The text has *naʿūdhu* as does *Fragmenta*, 134. The apparatus has one suitable variant, *naʿūdu*, which is adopted by the Cairo edition (238), and which makes better sense. Al-Balādhurī also has *naʿūdu*. Cf. *Ansāb* (Derenk), 50.

in Armenia that Yazīd was fomenting discord amongst the people and inciting them to depose al-Walīd. So Marwān wrote to Sa'īd b. 'Abd al-Malik b. Marwān,[702] who was a God-fearing man,[703] ordering him to forbid the people to take such action and to restrain them, and saying:[704]

> Verily God has created for the benefit of all the members of a family pillars on which they may lean and by which they may guard themselves against dangers. By the grace of your Lord, you are one of the pillars of [the members of] your family. I have heard that a group of fools in your household have set in motion a certain matter.[705] If they achieve their aim in this matter, having agreed to abrogate their oath of allegiance, they will open a door which God will not shut for them until much blood of theirs has been shed. I myself am fully occupied on the most perilous of the Muslim frontiers. If I could get hold of these people, I would put their wrongdoing to rights with my own hand and with my own words. I would, moreover, fear God[706] if I did not act in this way[707] because I know what mischief is caused to religion and to this earthly life as a consequence of schism. (I know too) that the strength of a group will only ever be destroyed if they fall into disagreement amongst themselves and that if their words become confused their enemy will seek to overcome them. You are closer to these people than I am. Use deceit to find out what they are plotting and pretend to be on their side. When you find out anything about their conspiracy, [1786]

702. Cf. Ibn 'Abd Rabbihi, II, 192, 292, 298; al-Balādhurī, *Futūḥ*, 332. He was made governor of Palestine. Cf. al-Ṭabarī, II, 1831.

703. The text has *wa-kāna Sa'īdu yatāllahu.* The editor says that he has put this only as a tentative reading but that it was known that Sa'īd had a pious reputation. Cf. al-Ṭabarī, II, 1174. The editor's reading is supported by al-Balādhurī, who has *wa-kāna Sa'īdu muta'allihan.* Cf. *Ansāb* (Derenk), 50. The Leiden text does not have the *hamzah*: it should read *yata'allahu,* as the Cairo edition (238) has it.

704. For another version of Marwān's letter, cf. al-Balādhurī, *Ansāb* (Derenk), 50.

705. *Qad istannū amran.* Cf. *Gloss.*, p. CCXCVIII. Al-Balādhurī has *qad assasū amran.* Cf. *Ansāb* (Derenk), 50.

706. I.e., God's wrath.

707. Literally, "in neglecting that."

threaten that you will reveal their secrets. Grip them by your words and make them afraid of the consequences (of their acts). Perhaps God will restore to them what they have lost of their religion and their senses, for in the course of their striving, the general good is blighted[708] and the state is destroyed. So act quickly in this matter, whilst the cord of friendship is still tied fast, whilst the people are quiet and the frontiers are still protected. For (in the course of time) communal unity turns to disunity, prosperity is ousted by poverty,[709] and the numbers (of men) diminish. For the people of this world,
[1787] these are (only) vicissitudes which come and go in the fluctuation between waxing and waning.[710] We, the people of this family, have received a prolonged series of blessings and this has caused distress[711] to all nations, to those who are hostile to such blessings and who envy those that possess them. It was because of the envy of Iblīs that Adam was driven out of Paradise. This group (of conspirators) have pinned their hopes on strife, but perhaps it is their souls which will perish without their achieving what they anticipated. Every family has ill-fated individuals because of whom God removes His favor. May God protect you from being one such person. Keep me informed of what they are up to. May God preserve your religion for you, may He deliver you from what He has made you enter into, and may He cause your reason to overcome your natural inclinations!

Saʿīd took this matter seriously and he sent Marwān's letter to al-ʿAbbās. Al-ʿAbbās summoned Yazīd and he reproached and threatened him. Yazīd warned al-ʿAbbās, saying: "I am afraid, brother, that one of those enemies of ours who envy us this prosperity wants to stir up trouble between us." Then Yazīd swore an

---

708. Literally, "there is a changing of favors (from God)." Cf. Qur'ān 8, v. 55.

709. Here al-Balādhurī's version of the letter ends.

710. *Wa-duwalu al-layālī mukhalifatun ʿalā ahli al-dunyā wa-al-taqallubu maʿa al-ziyādati wa-al-nuqṣāni:* literally, "The turnings of the nights are varied on the people of this world and (there is) fluctuation between increasing and decreasing." Cf. Qur'ān 3, v. 140.

711. The text has *qad yuʿnā bihā.* The Cairo edition (238) has *qad yaʿībuhā* ("have castigated them").

oath to al-ʿAbbās that he had not done anything wrong, and his brother believed him.

According to Aḥmad—ʿAlī (al-Madāʾinī)—Ibn Bishr b. al-Walīd b. ʿAbd al-Malik: My father Bishr b. al-Walīd[712] went in to see my uncle al-ʿAbbās and spoke to him on the matter of deposing al-Walīd and giving the oath of allegiance to Yazīd. Al-ʿAbbās was against the idea and my father argued the opposing point of view with him. I rejoiced and told myself: "Here is my father daring to speak to my uncle and to dispute what he says with him." I could see where my father was correct in what he said, but the truth (really) lay with what my uncle said.[713] Al-ʿAbbās sighed: "O Banū Marwān! I do believe that God has permitted your destruc- [1788]
tion." He then recited the following verses:[714]

I beseech God to protect you from temptations
that loom as high as mountains, and then violently erupt.
Verily God's creatures have grown tired of your policies,
so hold fast to the pillar of religion, and keep a tight rein on yourselves.
Do not offer yourselves as prey to men who are wolves,
for wolves devour meat whenever they are offered it.
And do not rip open your bellies with your own hands,
for by then neither sorrow nor alarm will bring you relief.

After Yazīd had made his arrangements and while he was still living in the desert, he went toward Damascus until he reached a distance of four nights from Damascus; he was in disguise, accompanied by seven people, riding asses. They then stopped at Jarūd,[715] which was a day's journey from Damascus. Yazīd threw himself down and went to sleep. The people with him said to a mawlā of ʿAbbād b. Ziyād: "If you have any food, we will buy it." The mawlā replied: "I won't sell you anything, but you may have

---

712. Cf. the Umayyad genealogical table. Bishr and al-ʿAbbās were brothers.

713. This is presumably what is meant here. The text has *wa-kuntu arā anna al-ṣawāba fīmā yaqūlu abī wa-kāna al-sawabu fīmā yaqūlu ʿammī.* Alternatively, Ibn Bishr could mean that he saw the right in both viewpoints.

714. Cf. al-Balādhurī, *Ansāb* (Derenk), 51; al-Iṣfahānī, *Aghānī,* VI, 137; Ibn al-Athīr, V, 214. The meter is *basīṭ.*

715. A village of Maʿlūlā. Cf. Yāqūt, II, 65; Le Strange, *Palestine,* 463.

hospitality and food enough from me." So he brought them hens, young chickens, honey, clarified butter, and curds, which they ate. Then Yazīd set off again and entered Damascus at night. Most of the people of Damascus had already given the oath of allegiance secretly to Yazīd, as had the people of al-Mizzah,[716] apart from Muʿāwiyah b. Maṣād al-Kalbī, who was their leader.
[1789] Accordingly, Yazīd marched off immediately to the house of Muʿāwiyah b. Maṣād, accompanied by a small group of his followers. Al-Mizzah was a *mīl* or more away from Damascus. (On their way) they met with heavy rain. When they arrived at the house of Muʿāwiyah b. Maṣād, they knocked on his door and somebody opened it for them. Yazīd went in and Muʿāwiyah said to him: "Mind the carpet, for God's sake." Yazīd replied: "Indeed, I do have mud on my feet and I don't want to ruin your carpet." Muʿāwiyah said: "What you want us to do is worse" (than ruining the carpet). Then Yazīd talked to him and Muʿāwiyah gave him the oath of allegiance. Some reports said that his name was Hishām b. Maṣād.

Thereafter, Yazīd returned to Damascus, taking the canal road and riding on a black ass.[717] He then lodged in the house of Thābit b. Sulaymān b. Saʿd al-Khushanī.[718] Al-Walīd b. Rawḥ departed, having sworn that he would enter Damascus only if he were armed. So he girded himself with his weapons and covered them with his clothes. He took the Nayrāb[719] road, riding a piebald horse, and rode until he had caught up with Yazīd. In charge of Damascus (at this time) was ʿAbd al-Malik b. Muḥammad b. al-Ḥajjāj b. Yūsuf.[720] Since he was afraid of the plague, he left Damascus and took up residence in Qaṭāna,[721] having appointed his son as his deputy in Damascus while Abū al-ʿĀj Ka-

---

716. Al-Mizzah was a large village in the upper part of the Ghūṭah of Damascus. Cf. Yāqūt, IV, 522; Le Strange, *Palestine*, 508. The area was well-known for its Qadarī sympathies. Cf. *Fragmenta*, 135; al-Balādhurī, *Ansāb* (Derenk), 51.

717. Perhaps this is a hint at a messianic status. Cf. Hawting, 93.

718. The text has al-Khushanī. *Fragmenta*, 135, has al-Khushaynī. Al-Iṣfahānī has al-Ḥasanī; cf. *Aghānī*, VI, 137.

719. Al-Nayrab was a village near Damascus, famous for its gardens. Cf. Yāqūt, IV, 855; Le Strange, *Palestine*, 515.

720. Cf. al-Ṭabarī, II, 1778–79.

721. Qaṭanā was one of the villages in the area. Cf. Yāqūt, IV, 137; Le Strange, *Palestine*, 483.

thīr b. ʿAbdallāh al-Sulamī[722] was in charge of his *shurṭah*. Then Yazīd decided to come out into the open. The governor was told that Yazīd was raising a rebellion, but he did not believe it. Yazīd sent for his followers between the dusk prayer and the late night prayer on a Thursday night in 126 [October 25, 743–October 12, 744].[723] They hid themselves at the Farādīs Gate[724] until the [1790] muezzins had made the dusk call to prayer. Then the rebels went into the mosque and performed the prayer. Now there were at the mosque guards who had the task of dispersing the people from the mosque at night. So after the people had prayed, the guards shouted to them to leave. Yazīd's followers lingered behind and began leaving by the *maqṣūrah* door[725] and going back in again by another door. This continued until there was no one left in the mosque but the guards and Yazīd's followers, who then seized the guards. Yazīd b. ʿAnbasah went to Yazīd b. al-Walīd, told him what had happened, took his hand, and said: "Rise, O Commander of the Faithful and rejoice in God's help and succour!" Yazīd arose and said: "O God, if it is pleasing to you, then assist me to perform this task and reveal to me the right way in it. If it is not pleasing to you, then relieve me of the task by my death."[726]

Yazīd went forth with twelve men. On reaching the donkey market, they met forty of their companions. When they came to the grain market, they were joined by some two hundred of their supporters.[727] Then they proceeded to the mosque. They went inside, made for the *maqṣūrah* door and knocked on it, saying: "We are messengers from al-Walīd." A servant opened the door to them. They seized him, went inside, and captured Abū al-ʿĀj, who

722. He had been governor of al-Baṣrah from 120 to 122 (737–40). Cf. al-Ṭabarī, II, 1667.

723. This rather unsatisfactory date is repeated in the other sources. Only al-Iṣfahānī is more precise. He gives a Friday in the following year, Jumādā II, 127 [March 10–April 7, 745]. Cf. *Aghānī*, VI, 138.

724. There was a quarter of the city of Damascus called Farādīs, after which the city gate was named. Cf. Le Strange, *Palestine*, 439; Yāqūt, III, 862.

725. For the probable location of the *maqṣūrah* door of the mosque, cf. Creswell, I, 172, fig. 89.

726. Cf. *Fragmenta*, 135–36; al-Balādhurī, *Ansāb* (Derenk), 51–52; al-Iṣfahānī, *Aghānī*, VI, 137–38; Ibn al-Athīr, V, 214.

727. Al-Balādhurī writes that they were about two hundred and sixty men. Cf. *Ansāb* (Derenk), 52. Cf. also *Fragmenta*, 136.

was drunk. They also seized the treasurers of the *bayt al-māl*[728] and the postmaster. Then Yazīd sent men to all the people whom he feared and they were arrested. Yazīd immediately sent people to Muḥammad b. ʿUbaydah, the mawlā of Saʿīd b. al-ʿĀṣ, who was in charge of Baʿlabakk,[729] and he was arrested. Yazīd also dispatched men at once to ʿAbd al-Malik b. Muḥammad b. al-Ḥajjāj,
[1791] and he too was seized. Then Yazīd sent to al-Thaniyyah[730] to his followers requesting them to join him. Yazīd ordered the gatekeepers[731] (of the city): "In the morning, open the gate only to those who give you our password," and they left the gates chained up. There were many weapons inside the mosque which Sulaymān b. Hishām had brought from the Jazīrah. The treasurers had not managed to appropriate them, so Yazīd's followers took them, and acquired a large number of them. In the morning Ibn ʿIṣām and the people of al-Mizzah came, and by the middle of the day the people had given the oath of allegiance to Yazīd, who recited the following lines:[732]

When they are made to dismount from their horses to stab
each other, they stride
toward death in the manner of refractory camels.

Yazīd's followers were amazed and said: "Look at this man! Before dawn he was glorifying God and now he is reciting poetry!"

According to Aḥmad b. Zuhayr—ʿAlī (al-Madāʾinī)—ʿAmr b. Marwān al-Kalbī—Razīn b. Mājid: In the morning we went with ʿAbd al-Raḥmān b. Maṣād—we numbered around fifteen hundred

---

728. The *bayt al-māl* was situated inside the Great Mosque of Damascus, on the northwest side of the courtyard. Cf. the description given by al-Muqaddasī and quoted by Le Strange, *Palestine*, 227.

729. Baʿlabakk (Heliopolis) was part of the *jund* of Damascus in Umayyad times. Cf. Yaʿqūbī, *Les Pays*, 172–73; Yāqūt, I, 672, 675; Le Strange, *Palestine*, 295–98; *EI*², s.v. (J. Sourdel-Thomine).

730. This is a reference to Thaniyyat al-ʿUqāb (the Eagle's Gorge), which was a pass situated to the north of Damascus. Cf. Yāqūt, I, 936; III, 691; Le Strange, *Palestine*, 383, 545.

731. It is not quite clear whether this is a reference to the doors of the mosque or the gates of the city. *Fragmenta*, 137, specifies that it was the gates of the city; this seems more probable.

732. The meter is *ṭawīl*. For these verses, cf. al-Balādhurī, *Ansāb* (Derenk), 53; al-Iṣfahānī, *Aghānī*, VI, 128; *Framenta*, 137. The Cairo edition of al-Ṭabarī, 241, notes that this is from the *dīwān* of al-Nābighah.

men—as far as the Jābiyah Gate.[733] We found it to be locked, and there was a messenger of al-Walīd. He said: "Why these (warlike) preparations and equipment? Indeed, by God, I shall certainly inform the Commander of the Faithful," so a man from al-Mizzah killed him. Then we entered Damascus by the Jabīyah Gate. We went first into the Kalbiyyīn alley, but it was too narrow for us (because of our large numbers). So some of us took the route through the grain market. Then we assembled at the door of the mosque and we went in to see Yazīd. Before the last of our [1792]
number had finished greeting Yazīd, the Sakāsik[734] arrived, numbering around three hundred men. They had entered the city from the Sharqī Gate and when they reached the mosque they came in by the Daraj door.[735] Thereafter Ya'qūb b. 'Umayr b. Hānī al-'Absī[736] arrived with the people of Dārayyā.[737] They entered Damascus through the Bāb al-Ṣaghīr.[738] Then 'Īsā b. Shabīb al-Taghlibī[739] came with the people of Dūma and Ḥarastā,[740] and they came in through the Tūmā Gate.[741] Ḥumayd b. Ḥabīb al-Lakhmī brought the people of Dayr al-Murrān,[742] al-Arzah, and Saṭrā,[743] entering Damascus by the Farādīs Gate. Al-Naḍr b.

733. The Bāb al-Jābiyah was at the western end of the "Street called Straight." Jābiyah was a suburb of the city. Cf. Le Strange, *Palestine*, 231.

734. The Sakāsik were a branch of the Kindah. They had fought for the Umayyads at Marj Rāhit in 64 (683). Cf. Ibn al-Kalbī, II, 503.

735. The Daraj door is not identifiable but in this same context al-Balādhurī calls it Bāb Jayrūn. Cf. *Ansāb* (Derenk), 53. This was the eastern door of the mosque. Cf. Le Strange, *Palestine*, 260.

736. There is some doubt about this man's *nisbah*. In the text it is al-'Absī but in the apparatus the variant al-'Ansī is given. Ya'qūb's father, 'Umayr, was used by al-Ḥajjāj to control the Kurds and was later made deputy governor of al-Kūfah. Cf. Ibn Khayyāṭ, 385; Crone, 140. Al-Balādhurī gives him no *nisbah* (loc. cit.). Ibn al-Athīr, V, 215, has al-'Absī.

737. Dārayyā was a village in the Damascus area. Cf. Yāqūt, II, 536; Le Strange, *Palestine*, 436.

738. The Bāb al-Ṣaghīr was situated at the southwestern angle of the Damascus city wall. Cf. Le Strange, *Palestine*, 231.

739. Cf. Crone, 160–61.

740. Ḥarastā was a farmstead in the Damascus area. Cf. Le Strange, *Palestine*, 237; Yāqūt, II, 241.

741. The Bāb Tūmā was a city gate of Damascus facing northeast. Cf. Le Strange, *Palestine*, 254.

742. Dayr al-Murrān was a monastery near Damascus. Cf. Yāqūt, I, 696; IV, 480.

743. Saṭrā was a village of the Damascus area. Cf. Le Strange, *Palestine*, 532; Yāqūt, III, 90.

ʿUmar al-Jarashī came with the people of Jarash,[744] al-Ḥadīthah,[745] and Dayr Zakkā,[746] entering by the Sharqī Gate. Ribʿī b. Hāshim al-Ḥārithī arrived with a group of the Banū ʿUthrah[747] and Salāmān,[748] and they came in by the Tūmā Gate. The Banū Juhaynah[749] and those affiliated to them came with Ṭalḥah b. Saʿīd,[750] and one of their poets recited the following verses:[751]

Their supporters flocked to them at daybreak,
among them the Sakāsik, the courageous tent-dwellers.
The Kalb brought them horses, and furnished them[752]
with bright white swords and with their torsos and forearms.
[1793] Honor them as the bulwarks of a tradition (*sunnah*),[753]
for it was they who protected their honor against every unbeliever.
And Shaʿbān[754] and al-Azd joined them with spears extended,
and ʿAbs and Lakhm acted as protectors and defenders,
As did Ghassān[755] and the two tribes of Qays and Taghlib,[756]
whilst every weak-kneed laggard declined the challenge.
So as soon as morning broke upon them, they were kings of powerful authority,

---

744. Jarash (the ancient Gerasa) was a town in Transjordan to the southeast of the Jabal ʿAjlūn. Cf. Yāqūt, II, 61; *EI²*, s.v. (D. Sourdel).

745. Al-Ḥadīthah was a village in the Ghūṭah of Damascus. It was also called Ḥadīthat Jarash. Cf. Yāqūt, II, 225; Le Strange, *Palestine*, 445.

746. Dayr Zakkā was also a village in the Ghūṭah. Cf. Yāqūt, II, 665; Le Strange, *Palestine*, 435.

747. For the Banū ʿUthrah, cf. Ibn al-Kalbī, II, 565–66. The tribe were within the sphere of the Ghassānids, and well before the coming of Islam had gone to Syria and become Christians.

748. The Banū Salāmān were a subgroup of the Banū ʿUthrah who settled in Syria. Cf. Ibn al-Kalbī, II, 414.

749. For the Banū Juhaynah, cf. n. 227.

750. This may be the same person who had earlier been deputy governor of al-Baṣrah. Cf. Ibn Khayyāṭ, 414, and the discussion in Crone, 139.

751. The meter is *ṭawīl*. For these verses, cf. also al-Balādhurī, *Ansāb* (Derenk), 54. The textual differences are only minor.

752. Literally, "brought them horses and supplies."

753. Literally, "honor them as the firm supporters of a tradition."

754. For the Banū Shaʿbān, a branch of the Ḥimyar, cf. Ibn al-Kalbī, II, 521.

755. For the Banū Ghassān, cf. *EI²*, s.v. (I. Shahid).

756. For the Banū Taghlib, an important tribe of the Rabīʿah, cf. Ibn al-Kalbī, II, 541–42. The Taghlib were allowed to remain Christians during the Umayyad period without having the status of the *ahl al-dhimmah*.

and firm was their hold over every disobedient, insolent rebel.

According to Aḥmad b. Zuhayr—'Alī b. Muḥammad (al-Madā'inī)—'Amr b. Marwān al-Kalbī—Qusaym b. Ya'qūb and Razīn b. Mājid and others: Yazīd b. al-Walīd sent 'Abd al-Raḥmān b. Maṣād with two hundred or so horsemen to Qaṭanā[757] to seize 'Abd al-Malik b. Muḥammad b. al-Ḥajjāj b. Yūsuf, who had entrenched himself in his castle. 'Abd al-Raḥmān gave him safe-conduct and 'Abd al-Malik came out to him. We then entered the castle and there we discovered two saddlebags, each containing thirty thousand dīnārs. When we reached al-Mizzah, I said to 'Abd al-Raḥmān b. Maṣād: "Take one or both of these saddlebags home with you. You will never get anything like them from Yazīd!" 'Abd al-Raḥmān replied: "(If I did that) I would be the first to [1794]
commit treachery. No, the Arabs shall not say that I was the first person to act treacherously in this affair." Then he took the money to Yazīd b. al-Walīd.

Yazīd b. al-Walīd sent word to 'Abd al-'Azīz b. al-Ḥajjāj b. 'Abd al-Malik and gave him orders that he should station himself at the Jābiyah Gate.[758] Then Yazīd said: "Let anyone who has a stipend come and get it. Anyone who has no stipend may have a subsidy of one thousand dirhams." Next, Yazīd instructed the sons of al-Walīd b. 'Abd al-Malik—he had thirteen of them with him: "Disperse yourselves among the people so that they can see you, and whip up enthusiasm in them." He then said to al-Walīd b. Rawḥ b. al-Walīd: "Bring al-Rāhib down,"[759] and al-Walīd did so.

According to Aḥmad (b. Zuhayr)—'Alī (al-Madā'inī)—'Amr b. Marwān al-Kalbī—Dukayn b. al-Shammakh al-Kalbī and Abū 'Ilāqah b. Ṣāliḥ al-Salāmānī: Yazīd b. al-Walīd issued the following proclamation: "Anyone who joins up to fight against the libertine (al-Walīd) will have one thousand dirhams." Even so, fewer than one thousand men gathered to Yazīd. Then he caused the

757. The text has Qaṭan. Earlier, al-Ṭabarī reported that 'Abd al-Malik had fled the plague and taken up residence in Qaṭanā. Cf. II, 1789.

758. Literally, "he ordered him and he stood at the Jābiyah Gate."

759. *Anzil al-rāhiba fa-fa'ala* ("bring the monk down, so he did (?)"). This isolated snippet is not explained nor is there information in any of the other sources.

760. For a long biography of Manṣūr b. Jumhūr al-Kalbī, cf. Crone, 158–59.

following proclamation to be made: "Anyone who joins up to fight the libertine will have fifteen hundred dirhams", and on that day fifteen hundred joined up. Yazīd put Manṣūr b. Jumhūr[760] in charge of one contingent, Ya'qūb b. 'Abd al-Raḥmān b. Sulaym al-Kalbī in charge of another, Harim b. 'Abdallāh b. Daḥyah[761] over
[1795] another, and Ḥumayd b. Ḥabīb al-Lakhmī over another. In overall charge of these men, Yazīd appointed 'Abd al-'Azīz b. al-Ḥajjāj b. 'Abd al-Malik, who set out and made camp at al-Ḥīrah.

According to Aḥmad b. Zuhayr—'Alī (al-Madā'inī)—'Amr b. Marwān al-Kalbī—Ya'qūb b. Ibrāhīm b. al-Walīd: When Yazīd b. al-Walīd rose up in rebellion, a mawlā of al-Walīd got on his horse and went off at once to al-Walīd. His horse died when he reached his destination. The mawlā told al-Walīd what had happened, whereupon al-Walīd gave him one hundred lashes and threw him into prison. Then al-Walīd summoned Abū Muḥammad b. 'Abdallāh b. Yazīd b. Mu'āwiyah, gave him money, and sent him to Damascus. Abū Muḥammad departed and on reaching Dhanabah,[762] he made a halt. Yazīd b. al-Walīd sent 'Abd al-Raḥmān b. Maṣād to him. Then Abū Muḥammad made his peace with him and gave the oath of allegiance to him. News of this reached al-Walīd when he was at al-Aghdaf,[763] which is in the 'Ammān area. Bayhas b. Zumayl al-Kilābī said—or, according to another report, the speaker was Yazīd b. Khālid b. Yazīd b. Mu'āwiyah—"O Commander of the Faithful, go and establish yourself in Ḥimṣ, as it is well-fortified. Send troops against Yazīd so that he may be killed or imprisoned." However, 'Abdallāh b. 'Anbasah b. Sa'īd b. al-'Āṣ said: "It is not fitting for a caliph to leave his camp[764] and his women before he has fought and (thus) shown himself to be without blame. It is God who strengthens and succors the Commander of the Faithful." Yazīd b. Khālid said: "What should the caliph have to fear for his women when it

---

761. The editor gives two vocalizations: Daḥyah and Diḥyah. The latter has been preferred because of the known form of the name Diḥyah b. Khalīfah, who was one of the Prophet's Companions. Cf. Ibn al-Kalbī, II, 232; Crone, 156–57.

762. Dhanabah was one of the districts of Damascus. Cf. Yāqūt, II, 724; Le Strange, *Palestine*, 437.

763. For al-Aghdaf, cf. n. 465. Al-Balādhurī has al-Azraq; cf. *Ansāb* (Derenk), 55.

764. It would be more appropriate in this context to translate *'askar* as "camp" rather than "troops." Al-Balādhurī has "his camp, his treasures, and his women." Cf. *Ansāb* (Derenk), 56. Cf. also a similar version in *Fragmenta*, 139.

is only 'Abd al-'Azīz b. al-Ḥajjāj b. 'Abd al-Malik[765] who would head the opposing forces? (After all,) he is their paternal cousin." Al-Walīd, (however,) took the advice of Ibn 'Anbasah. Then al-Abrash Sa'īd b. al-Walīd al-Kalbī said to al-Walīd: "O Commander of the Faithful, Tadmur[766] is well fortified and my people there will defend you." Al-Walīd replied: "I don't think it is wise for us to go to Tadmur,[767] since the people there are the Banū 'Āmir who are the ones who have rebelled against me. But suggest another fortified place to me." Al-Abrash said: "I think you should stay in al-Qaryah."[768] Al-Walīd replied: "I don't like it." Al-Abrash said: "Then there is al-Hazīm."[769] Al-Walīd said: "I hate its name." So al-Abrash said: "Then there is al-Bakhrā',[770] the citadel of al-Nu'mān b. Bashīr." Whereupon al-Walīd exclaimed: "Fie on you. How ugly are the names of your watering places!" Then al-Walīd set out with two hundred men on the Samāwah[771] road and he left the cultivated land behind him. Al-Walīd recited the following verses:[772] [1796]

If you do not mingle good with evil, you will not find
   a faithful adviser nor anyone to help you when need
   overtakes you.
Whenever they intend to commit one of their sinful actions,
   I will bare my head and uncover my face.

---

765. Literally, "it is only 'Abd al-'Aziz b. al-Ḥajjāj b. 'Abd al-Malik coming to them."

766. Viz., Palmyra. Cf. *EI*[1], "Palmyra" (F. Buhl); Yāqūt, I, 828.

767. Al-Balādhurī and *Fragmenta* add: "and its name is its name" (loc. cit.). *Tadmuru* means "you perish."

768. Al-Qaryah. This is vocalized by Guidi in the indices to the *Aghānī*, 761, as al-Qurayyah. Probably this is a place-name too. Perhaps it is a reference to the village at Palmyra or to the well-known place al-Qaryatayn.

769. Hazīm was due south of Palmyra. Cf. Dussaud, 79. *Hazīm* can mean "a voice like thunder." Cf. *Lisān*, III, 805.

770. Al-Bakhrā': the feminine of *abkhar* ("to have a stinking mouth"). Al-Bakhrā' has been sited variously in eastern Syria (Huart, I, 276); near al-Qaryatayn between Damascus and Palmyra (von Kremer, I, 152); and 25 km south of Palmyra (Derenk, 46). Derenk's location is probably the correct one. Al-Nu'man b. Bashīr was a Companion of the Prophet, after whom the town of Ma'arrat al-Nu'mān was named. Cf. Le Strange, *Palestine*, 495–97.

771. Al-Samāwah was the name of the desert between al-Kūfah and Syria. Cf. Yāqūt, III, 131; Le Strange, *Palestine*, 530.

772. These verses are also to be found in al-Balādhurī, *Ansāb*, loc. cit.; al-Iṣfahānī, *Aghānī*, VI, 111. The meter is *ṭawīl*.

Al-Walīd passed by the well country[773] of al-Ḍaḥḥāk[774] b. Qays al-Fihrī, where he came across some of his[775] sons and grandsons, who numbered forty men, and they went with him. They said to al-Walīd: "We are unarmed. What about ordering some arms for us?" but he did not give them a single sword or spear. Then Bayhas b. Zumayl said to al-Walīd: "Since you have refused to go to Ḥims or Tadmur, what about this fortress, al-Bakhrā'? It is well fortified and was built by the Persians. Stay here." Al-Walīd
[1797] replied: "I am afraid of the plague." Whereupon Bayhas replied: "What is in store for you is worse than the plague." Then al-Walīd settled at the fortress of al-Bakhrā'.

Yazīd b. al-Walīd summoned the people to fight with ʿAbd al-ʿAzīz against al-Walīd, and he issued a proclamation that anyone who went with ʿAbd al-ʿAzīz would receive two thousand dirhams. Then two thousand men joined up and Yazīd gave them two thousand dirhams each, saying to them: "Your destination is Dhanabah".[776] But (only) twelve hundred men reached Dhanabah. Then Yazīd said to them: "You must now go to the stronghold of the sons of ʿAbd al-ʿAzīz b. al-Walīd[777] in the desert." But only eight hundred men reached it. ʿAbd al-ʿAzīz[778] moved on and met up with al-Walīd's baggage train, which they seized. They then camped near al-Walīd.

An envoy from al-ʿAbbās b. al-Walīd reached al-Walīd with a message from al-ʿAbbās to the effect that he was coming to join him. Then al-Walīd said: "Bring out a couch." A couch was brought out and he sat down on it, saying: "So men dare to attack me, when I attack the lion and strangle the serpent?"[779] and al-Walīd and his followers awaited the arrival of al-ʿAbbās.

---

773. *Fa-marra bi-shabakati Ḍaḥḥāk.*

774. Ḍaḥḥāk b. Qays al-Fihrī was a very influential leader of the Qays in Muʿāwiyah's time, first as his *ṣāḥib al-shurṭah* and then as governor of Damascus. He was killed at Marj Rāhit in 64 (684). For an account of his career, cf. *EI*², s.v. (A. Dietrich).

775. Ibn al-Athīr makes it clear that "his" sons and grandsons is a reference to al-Ḍaḥḥāk (V, 216).

776. Al-Iṣfahānī has D.nyah for this place name. Cf. *Aghānī*, VI, 138.

777. The sons of ʿAbd al-ʿAzīz b. al-Walīd b. ʿAbd al-Malik. Cf. the Umayyad genealogical table.

778. It is not clear from the text who is meant here. Presumably it is the leader, ʿAbd al-ʿAzīz, who had been sent out against al-Walīd by Yazīd.

779. The text has *a-ʿalayya tawaththaba al-rijālu wa-anā athibu ʿalā al-asadi?*

Then ʿAbd al-ʿAzīz launched the attack against al-Walīd and his followers.[780] In charge of his right flank was ʿAmr b. Ḥuwayy al-Saksakī[781] whilst Manṣūr b. Jumhūr headed the vanguard.[782] In charge of the infantry was ʿUmārah b. Abī Kulthūm al-Azdī.[783] ʿAbd al-ʿAzīz called for a black mule of his to be brought and he mounted it. ʿAbd al-ʿAzīz sent Ziyād b. Ḥusayn al-Kalbī to speak to al-Walīd and his followers and to summon them to the Book of God and the *sunnah* of His Prophet, but Qaṭarī,[784] the mawlā of al-Walīd, killed Ziyād. Then Yazīd's men withdrew, ʿAbd al-ʿAzīz dismounted, and his followers fled. A number of soldiers of ʿAbd [1798] al-ʿAzīz had been killed and their heads had been taken to al-Walīd, who was at the gate of the citadel of al-Bakhrāʾ, having displayed the flag of Marwān b. al-Ḥakam which Marwān had raised at al-Jābiyah.[785] ʿUthmān al-Khashabī[786] was amongst the followers of al-Walīd b. Yazīd who were killed; he had been slain by Junaḥ b. Nuʿaym al-Kalbī. ʿUthmān was one of the sons of the Khashabiyyah[787] who had been with al-Mukhtār.

When ʿAbd al-ʿAzīz heard that al-ʿAbbās b. al-Walīd was com-

The version in al-Balādhurī is more satisfactory, replacing *tawaththaba* with *yatawaththabu*. Cf. *Ansāb* (Derenk), 57. Cf. also *Fragmenta*, 140.

780. Literally, "'Abd al-ʿAzīz fought them."

781. ʿAmr b. Huwayy al-Saksakī was a descendant of a *sharīf* of Damascus who fought for Muʿāwiyah at Ṣiffīn.

782. Cf. Ibn Khayyāṭ, 222. Oddly enough, ʿAmr b. Ḥuwayy himself is listed as being amongst those men on whom Yazīd showered honors, having suppressed their rebellion. Cf. al-Ṭabarī, II, 1831; Crone, 155.

783. This is the form of the name given by al-Ṭabarī. Al-Balādhurī and *Fragmenta* have ʿUmārah b. Kulthūm al-Azdī (loc. cit.). He was a close associate of Khālid al-Qasrī and was executed by Marwān II. Cf. Crone, 163.

784. Al-Balādhurī also has Qaṭarī (loc. cit.). A variant in the apparatus (from MS. B) has Qaṭan. Qaṭan was certainly a mawlā, too, but he was the mawlā of Yazīd and his brother, al-ʿAbbās. Cf. al-Ṭabarī, II, 145.

785. Before the battle of Marj Rāhit in 64 (684), the aged Marwān b. al-Ḥakam (Marwān II) had pitched camp at al-Jābiyah. Cf. *EI*¹, s.v. (H. Lammens). Al-Balādhurī and *Fragmenta* have: "which he had raised at al-Jābiyah to fight al-Ḍaḥḥāk b. Qays." (loc. cit.).

786. Al-Iṣfahānī has Yazīd b. ʿUthmān al-Khashabī (loc. cit.).

787. *Khashabiyyah* ("men armed with clubs") was originally an abusive name for the mawlās who were armed with clubs and formed the main body of al-Mukhtār's supporters. Cf. al-Ṭabarī, II, 684; *EI*², "Khashabiyya" (C. van Arendonk). For a recent account of the revolt of al-Mukhtār, which centered on al-Kūfah between 65 and 68 (685–687), cf. Hawting, 51–53.

ing, he despatched Manṣūr b. Jumhūr with some cavalry and said: "You will meet al-ʿAbbās and his sons at al-Shiʿb.[788] Seize them." So Manṣūr left with some cavalry, and when they came to al-Shiʿb they saw al-ʿAbbās with thirty of his sons. Manṣūr's men said to al-ʿAbbās: "Join ʿAbd al-ʿAzīz," whereupon al-ʿAbbās hurled insults at them. Then Manṣūr said to al-ʿAbbās: "By God, if you advance any further, I will surely penetrate your stronghold, by which I mean your breastplate."[789] According to Nūḥ b. ʿAmr b. Ḥuwayy al-Saksakī: It was Yaʿqūb b. ʿAbd al-Raḥmān b. Sulaym al-Kalbī who met al-ʿAbbās b. al-Walīd. Yaʿqūb asked al-ʿAbbās to join forces with ʿAbd al-ʿAzīz but al-ʿAbbās refused to do so.

Then Yaʿqūb said: "O son of Qusṭanīn,[790] if you refuse, I shall strike you on the head."[791] Al-ʿAbbās looked at Harim b. ʿAbdallāh b. Diḥyah and said: "Who is this?" Harim replied: "It is Yaʿqūb b. ʿAbd al-Raḥmān b. Sulaym." Then al-ʿAbbās said: "In-
[1799] deed, by God, how horrified his father would be to see his son in this position." Then Yaʿqūb brought al-ʿAbbās to the camp of ʿAbd al-ʿAzīz.[792] Al-ʿAbbās did not have his followers with him, as he had gone ahead of them with his sons, so he said: "We belong to God!" Al-ʿAbbās was brought before ʿAbd al-ʿAzīz, who adjured him: "Give the oath of allegiance to your brother Yazīd b. al-Walīd." This al-ʿAbbās did. Then he stood up and the rebels raised a flag, saying: "This is the flag of al-ʿAbbās b. al-Walīd, who has given the oath of allegiance to the Commander of the Faithful, Yazīd b. al-Walīd." Thereupon al-ʿAbbās said: "We belong to God! This is one the wiles of the Devil. The house of Marwān is destroyed!"

Thereafter, people defected from al-Walīd's army[793] and came to join al-ʿAbbās and ʿAbd al-ʿAzīz. Al-Walīd came forth, wearing two coats of mail, and his two horses, al-Sindī and al-Zā'id,[794]

---

788. Al-Shiʿb ("the Pass").

789. Literally, "your stronghold, meaning your breastplate."

790. He was called son of Constantine because his mother was a Christian. Cf. *Gloss.*, p. DCCXII. *Fragmenta,* 141, has Qusṭanīn.

791. Literally, "I will strike that in which your (two) eyes are."

792. Al-Balādhurī adds: "He (al-ʿAbbās) was like a prisoner amongst them." Cf. *Ansāb* (Derenk), 58. Cf. also *Fragmenta,* 141.

793. Literally, "defected from al-Walīd."

794. For these two horses, cf. Masʿūdī, VI, 13, 16. The horse called al-Zā'id had belonged to Hishām. *Fragmenta* has al-Sandarī for al-Sindī (loc. cit.).

were brought to him. Then he launched himself fiercely into the fray.[795] Somebody shouted to the rebels: "Kill the enemy of God in the way Lot's family were killed. Throw stones at him." When al-Walīd heard that, he went into the citadel and locked the door and ʿAbd al-ʿAzīz and his followers surrounded the citadel. Then al-Walīd went up to the door and said: "Is there anyone amongst you who is an honorable man of noble descent and who has a proper sense of shame, to whom I can speak?" Yazīd b. ʿAnbasah al-Saksakī said to him: "Speak with me." Al-Walīd asked him who he was and he replied: "I am Yazīd b. ʿAnbasah." Then al-Walīd exclaimed: "O brother of the Sakāsik! Did I not increase your stipends? Did I not remove onerous taxes from you? Did I not make gifts to your poor and give servants to your cripples?" Yazīd b. ʿAnbasah replied: "We don't have any personal grudge against you. We are against you because you have violated the sacred ordinances of God, because you have drunk wine, because [1800] you have debauched the mothers of your father's sons, and because you have held God's command in contempt."[796] Al-Walīd replied: "That's enough from you, brother of the Sakāsik! By my life, you have said too much and gone too far. God's dispensation to me leaves scope for what you have mentioned."[797] With that he went into the room, sat down, took a copy of the Qur'ān, and said: "This is a day like the day ʿUthmān was killed,"[798] and he began to recite. Then the rebels began to scale the wall. The first person over the top was Yazīd b. ʿAnbasah al-Saksakī. He climbed down and went up to al-Walīd, whose sword was at his side. Then Yazīd said to him: "Take off your sword." Al-Walīd replied: "If I had wanted my sword, the situation between you and me would have been different from this." Then Yazīd took al-Walīd's hand, wanting to take him into custody and to have consultations about

795. Literally, "then he fought them a fierce fight."

796. Al-Balādhurī adds to this catalog of sins the allegation that al-Walīd was a homosexual (loc. cit.).

797. *Wa-inna fīmā uḥilla lī la-saʿatan ʿammā dhakarta* ("In what has been allowed to me there is scope for what you have mentioned"). Cf. the same wording in al-Iṣfahānī, *Aghānī*, VI, 139. Al-Balādhurī (loc. cit.) has *wa-inna fīmā aḥalla Allāhu la-mandūḥatun ʿammā dhakarta* ("verily in what God has decreed as permissible there is ample scope for what you have mentioned").

798. The third caliph of Islam, ʿUthmān, had been killed while reading the Qur'ān.

what should be done with him.[799] At that point ten men came down from the wall;[800] amongst them were Mansūr b. Jumhūr, Ḥibāl b. 'Amr al-Kalbī, 'Abd al-Raḥmān b. 'Ajlān, who was the mawlā of Yazīd b. 'Abd al-Malik, Ḥumayd b. Naṣr al-Lakhmī, al-Sarī b. Ziyād b. Abī Kabshah, and 'Abd al-Salām al-Lakhmī. 'Abd al-Salām struck al-Walīd on the head and al-Sarī hit him in the face; then five of them seized him to take him outside. A woman who was with al-Walīd in the room screamed, so they let go of al-Walīd and did not take him out. Then Abū 'Ilāqah al-Quḍā'ī cut off al-Walīd's head. He took some gut and sewed up the wound on al-Walīd's face. Thereupon Rawḥ b. Muqbil took al-Walīd's head to Yazīd (b. al-Walīd) and said: "Rejoice, O Commander of the Faithful. The libertine, al-Walīd, has been slain and those who were with him and with al-'Abbās have been taken prisoner!"
[1801] Yazīd was eating his lunch and both he and his companions prostrated themselves (in thanks to God).[801] Then Yazīd b. 'Anbasah al-Saksakī stood up, took the hand of Yazīd (b. al-Walīd)[802] and said: "O Commander of the Faithful, arise and rejoice in God's victory." Yazīd removed his hand from the hand of Ibn 'Anbasah and said: "O God, if this is pleasing to you, then direct me to the right way." Yazīd asked Yazīd b. 'Anbasah: "Did al-Walīd speak to you?" Ibn 'Anbasah said: "Yes, al-Walīd spoke to me from behind the door. He said: 'Is there anyone of noble descent among you to whom I may speak?' So it was I who spoke to him and I upbraided him. Then al-Walīd replied: 'That's enough from you. By my life, you have gone too far and said too much. The disunity amongst you will never be healed,[803] and dissension amongst you will never be put right and your tongues will never agree.'"

---

799. Al-Balādhurī has: "to have consultations with Yazīd b. al-Walīd about him" (loc. cit.).

800. The account in the *Aghānī* is clearer and has been followed here: *fa-nazala min al-ḥā'iṭi 'asharatun fīhim* (loc. cit.). The text in al-Ṭabarī states that there were ten men and then enumerates only six of them.

801. Ibn A'tham has: "he (Yazīd) and those with him prostrated themselves out of joy before Almighty God, just as Abū al-'Abbās al-Saffāḥ prostrated himself when Marwān b. Muḥammad died" (VIII, 140–41).

802. In view of the fact that the narrative involves two people called Yazīd, the aim here has been to clarify which Yazīd is performing which action.

803. Cf. al-Balādhurī, loc. cit. This might be an optative, which may use the present tense: "may the disunity amongst you never be healed . . ."

According to Aḥmad (b. Zuhayr)—'Alī (al-Madā'inī)—'Amr b. Marwān al-Kalbī—Nūḥ b. 'Amr b. Huwayy al-Saksakī: We went out to fight against al-Walīd on nights when there was no moon; (it was so dark that) I could not see the stones at all, let alone distinguish between black stones and white.[804] Al-Walīd b. Khālid, the nephew of al-Abrash al-Kalbī, was on the left flank of al-Walīd's forces with the Banū 'Āmir. There were also men of the Banū 'Āmir on the right flank (of the forces) of 'Abd al-'Azīz, so the men on al-Walīd's left flank would not fight those on the right flank of 'Abd al-'Azīz, and they defected en masse to 'Abd al-'Azīz b. al-Ḥajjāj. Nūḥ b. 'Amr said: "I saw the servants and dependents of al-Walīd b. Yazīd, on the day he was killed, seizing hold of the rebels' hands and showing them where al-Walīd was."[805]

According to Aḥmad (b. Zuhayr)—'Alī (al-Madā'inī)—'Amr b. Marwān al-Kalbī—al-Muthannā b. Mu'āwiyah: Al-Walīd came and camped at al-Lu'lu'ah.[806] He ordered his son, al-Ḥakam, and [1802]
al-Mu'ammal b. al-'Abbās to apportion a stipend of sixty dīnārs to anyone who would join them. So I went with my paternal cousin, Sulaymān b. Muḥammad b. 'Abdallāh, to al-Walīd's camp. Al-Mu'ammal allowed me to approach him[807] and he said: "I will take you in to see the Commander of the Faithful and I will speak to him about his assigning you one hundred dīnārs." (The narrative of al-Muthannā continues). Then al-Walīd left al-Lu'lu'ah and camped at al-Mulaykah,[808] where a messenger from 'Amr b. Qays[809] came to him from Ḥimṣ to tell him that 'Amr had sent

---

804. This is only a tentative translation.

805. Cf. al-Balādhurī, *Ansāb* (Derenk), 59; *Fragmenta*, 142.

806. Lu'lu'ah is a quarter of Damascus outside the Bāb al-Jābiyah. Cf. Le Strange, *Palestine*, 494; Yāqūt, IV, 371.

807. Literally, "let me come near and brought me close."

808. This form is uncertain and the place itself has not been identified. The name could also be al-Malīkah.

809. Qays b. Thawr al-Sakūnī was a *sharīf* from Ḥimṣ in the entourage of Mu'āwiyah. His son, 'Amr b. Qays, had fought with Maslamah in 98 (716–17). Cf. al-Ṭabarī, II, 1317; Crone, 99.

810. Al-Walīd was well known to have been a lover of fine clothes. He preferred colored garments, especially of yellow. Cf. al-Iṣfahānī, *Aghānī*, II, 65. For a detailed discussion of this topic, cf. R. Hillenbrand, "*La Dolce Vita* in early Islamic Syria," 12, 27. The Umayyad caliphs and their courtiers used clothing of luxury fabrics. Sulaymān and his retinue wore exclusively garments of *washī* (variegated silk). Cf. *EI*², "Libās" (Y. K. Stillman).

him five hundred horsemen under the leadership of ʿAbd al-Raḥmān b. Abī al-Janūb al-Bahrānī. Then al-Walīd summoned al-Ḍaḥḥāk b. Ayman from the Banū ʿAwf b. Kalb and ordered him to go to Ibn Abī al-Janūb, who (by this time) had reached al-Ghuwayr, and to tell him to come in all haste to al-Walīd at al-Mulaykah. The following morning al-Walīd ordered the company to break camp. He himself left (as well), riding on a chestnut horse. He was wearing a silk gown and silk turban. Around his waist he wore a thin roll of cloth and over his shoulders he had draped a yellow shawl over his sword.[810] En route the sons of Sulaym b. Kaysān joined him with sixteen horsemen. When al-Walīd had gone a little further, the Banū al-Nuʿmān b. Bashīr met him with more horsemen. Then al-Walīd (b. Yazīd) was joined by al-Walīd, the nephew of al-Abrash, with the Banū ʿĀmir of Kalb. Al-Walīd took the nephew of al-Abrash along with him and gave him clothes. Al-Walīd continued along the road and then he turned off at a hill[811] called al-Mushbihah,[812] where Ibn Abī al-Janūb met up with him, accompanied by the men from Ḥimṣ. Then al-Walīd arrived at al-Bakhrāʾ. It was then that the troops clamored and said: "We have no fodder for our riding animals." So al-Walīd gave orders that it should be announced publicly that the Commander of the Faithful had bought the standing corn
[1803] from the village. The soldiers said: "What can we do with green corn? It will make our animals ill." The soldiers only wanted dirhams.

Al-Muthannā said: I came to al-Walīd and I went in to see him, entering at the back of the tent. He asked for a meal, and when the food had been put in front of him, a messenger who was called ʿAmr b. Murrah came to him from Umm Kulthūm, the daughter of ʿAbdallāh b. Yazīd b. ʿAbd al-Malik. The messenger told al-Walīd that ʿAbd al-ʿAzīz b. al-Ḥajjāj had camped at al-Luʾluʾah, but al-Walīd paid no attention to him. Then Khālid b. ʿUthmān al-Mikhrāsh,[813] who was his chief of police, brought al-Walīd a man

---

811. *Talʿah* ("high land"). The word can also mean "stream".

812. This is tentative vocalization. The text has *al-M.sh.b.hah*. There is a variant reading, *al-M.s.b.h.h.*

813. For a history of this man's family, cf. Crone, 93–94. According to Ibn al-Kalbī, he had been head of police for Hishām as well (II, 343).

from the Banū Ḥārithah b. Janāb,[814] who said to al-Walīd: "I was in Damascus with ʿAbd al-ʿAzīz and I have come to tell you what I know. Here are fifteen hundred dirhams which I have brought with me." At this point he untied a purse from his waist and showed it (to al-Walīd). (He went on:) "ʿAbd al-ʿAzīz has encamped at al-Luʾluʾah and he will be coming to you from there tomorrow morning." Al-Walīd vouchsafed him no reply. Instead, he turned to a man who was beside him and began a conversation with him which I could not hear. I asked one of the people who were standing between al-Walīd and me what al-Walīd was saying. That person informed me: "Al-Walīd was asking the man about the canal which he had dug in Jordan and inquired how much more there was to do."[815] Then ʿAbd al-ʿAzīz approached from al-Luʾluʾah. Having arrived in al-Mulaykah he took possession of it. He dispatched Manṣūr b. Jumhūr, who took Sharqī al-Qurā, a high hill in a desert area[816] on the road from Nihyā[817] to al-Bakhrāʾ.

Al-ʿAbbās b. al-Walīd was making preparations with about one hundred and fifty of his mawlās and sons. He then sent a man from the Banū Nājiyah,[818] who was called Ḥubaysh,[819] to al- [1804]
Walīd to ask him to decide whether al-ʿAbbās should come and join him or march against Yazīd b. al-Walīd. Al-Walīd had his suspicions about al-ʿAbbās, so he sent word ordering him to come and join him. Manṣūr b. Jumhūr intercepted al-Walīd's messenger and asked him what his mission was, and the messenger told him. Then Manṣūr said to the messenger: "Tell al-ʿAbbās: By God, if you leave your present position[820] before sunrise, I will certainly kill you and your men! In the morning let him go wher-

---

814. The Banū Ḥārithah b. Janāb were a branch of the Banū ʿAbdallāh b. Kinānah from the Banū Kalb. Cf. Ibn al-Kalbī, II, 316.

815. Cf. Braslavski, "Hat Welīd II den Jordan ablenken wollen?", 97–100.

816. *Fī arḍin malsāʾa. Malsāʾu:* a desert in which there are no herbage, trees, or wild animals. Cf. Lane, I, 2736.

817. For a tentative siting of Nihyā (southwest of Palmyra) cf. Dussaud's map (op. cit., 79).

818. For the Banū Nājiyah, cf. Ibn al-Kalbī, II, 442.

819. The vocalization comes from the Cairo edition, 248.

820. The text has *zaḥalta* ("if you withdraw"), which is a conjecture on the part of the editor. The Cairo edition (249) has *raḥalta* ("if you march"), which also makes good sense.

ever he wants." Al-ʿAbbās continued to make his preparations.[821] In the morning we heard the soldiers of ʿAbd al-ʿAzīz, who had reached al-Bakhrāʾ, uttering the *takbīr*.[822] Then Khālid b. ʿUthmān al-Mikhrāsh came out and deployed al-Walīd's men in battle order; but there was no fighting between them until after sunrise. The soldiers of Yazīd b. al-Walīd carried a notice board[823] attached to a spear on which was written: "We summon you to the Book of God and the *sunnah* of His prophet, and (we request) that the matter should be determined by consultation" (*shūrā*).[824] Then they began to fight and ʿUthmān al-Khashabī was killed. About sixty of al-Walīd's men were also killed. Manṣūr b. Jumhūr advanced on the Nihyā road and approached al-Walīd's troops from behind. Manṣūr went toward al-Walīd, who was in his tent at a time when there was nobody to stop Manṣūr attacking al-Walīd.[825] When I saw Manṣūr, ʿĀṣim b. Hubayrah al-Muʿāfirī, the deputy of al-Mikhrāsh, and I came out. The soldiers of ʿAbd al-ʿAzīz withdrew as did those of Manṣūr. Sumayy b. al-Mughīrah was struck down and killed. Then Manṣūr turned to join ʿAbd al-ʿAzīz.

[1805] Al-Abrash was on a horse of his called al-Adīm, and was wearing a hat with two straps which he had tied securely under his beard.[826] He began shouting to his nephew: "You son of a stinking woman![827] Hoist your flag!" His nephew replied: "I can't find

821. I.e., he did not move until after sunrise.

822. The *takbīr* is the pronouncement of the statement *Allāhu akbaru*.

823. *Kitāb* has been translated here as "notice-board," since the object involved must have been large enough to have been seen aloft on a spear.

824. The appeal to a *shūrā* ("consultation") had often been made by opponents of the Umayyads, such as Ibn al-Zubayr and al-Ḥārith b. Surayj. For an analysis of the call for a *shūrā* by Yazīd b. al-Walīd, cf. Hawting, 94–95. Yazīd justified the use of force against al-Walīd II because the latter had used force to resist the call (ibid.).

825. Literally, "he was in his tent, there being nobody between him and Manṣūr."

826. *ʿAlayhi qalansuwatun dhātu ʿuthnayni qad shaddahā taḥta liḥyatihi*. The *qalansuwah* could designate a close-fitting cap or hood. It was under the ʿAbbāsids that the use of the tall, conical, Persian hat, the *qalansuwah ṭawīlah*, became widespread. Cf. *EI*², "Libās" (Y. K. Stillman).

827. *Lakhnāʾ*. Cf. *Gloss.*, p. CDLXVII. According to the definition given by Ibn Qutaybah, *lakhnāʾ* is used to designate someone with stinking breath. Cf. Ibn Qutaybah, *Kitāb al-ʿArab* in M. Kurd ʿAlī, *Rasāʾil al-Bulaghāʾ* (Cairo, 1953), 352. This is the prime meaning given in *Lisān*, III, 356. It does, however, indicate that *lakhnāʾ* may also mean a woman who has not been circumcised.

a way forward. These men are from the Banū ʿĀmir."[828] Then al-ʿAbbās b. al-Walīd arrived, but the men of ʿAbd al-ʿAzīz blocked his path. A mawlā of Sulaymān b. ʿAbdallāh b. Diḥyah who was called al-Turkī launched an attack on al-Ḥārith b. al-ʿAbbās b. al-Walīd and thrust at him with a blow which knocked him from his horse.[829] Al-ʿAbbās struck out in the direction of ʿAbd al-ʿAzīz. Al-Walīd's men were confused[830] and retreated in disarray.

Then al-Walīd b. Yazīd sent al-Walīd b. Khālid to ʿAbd al-ʿAzīz b. al-Ḥajjāj to tell him that al-Walīd would give him fifty thousand dīnārs, that he would appoint him to the governorship of Ḥimṣ for his lifetime, and that he would protect him in every difficult situation (that might arise), provided he went away and stopped fighting. ʿAbd al-ʿAziz rejected this offer[831] and would not agree to any of these terms.[832] Al-Walīd (b. Yazīd) prevailed upon al-Walīd b. Khālid to go back to ʿAbd al-ʿAzīz and make him the same offer again. Al-Walīd b. Khālid did so, but ʿAbd al-ʿAzīz remained obdurate. Then al-Walīd (b. Khālid) moved a short distance off, turned his horse around, approached ʿAbd al-ʿAzīz once more, and addressed him as follows: "Will you put five thousand dīnārs at my disposal and do likewise for al-Abrash, seeing that I have an exclusive status with my people? Then I will come in with you and join your enterprise." ʿAbd al-ʿAzīz replied: "On condition that you attack al-Walīd's soldiers at once." Accordingly, al-Walīd b. Khālid did so. Now in charge of the right flank of [1806]
the caliph al-Walīd's army was Muʿāwiyah b. Abī Sufyān b. Yazīd b. Khālid.[833] He said to ʿAbd al-ʿAzīz:[834] "Will you give me twenty thousand dīnārs, the governorship of Jordan, and a share of the command if I join up with you?" ʿAbd al-ʿAzīz answered: "On condition that you attack al-Walīd's army immediately." This

828. Cf. *Fragmenta*, 143; al-Balādhurī, *Ansāb* (Derenk), 60.

829. The text has *ardāhu*. The Cairo edition, 249, has *adhrāhu*, as does a variant MS. reading.

830. *Fa-usqiṭa fī aydī aṣḥābi al-Walīdi.* Cf. *Fragmenta* and *Ansāb*, which have *suqiṭa* (loc. cit.). According to Lane, *suqiṭa* is better. The phrase denotes repentance or perplexity or error. Cf. Qur'ān 7, v. 148; Lane, I, 1380. Thus the translation could also be: "al-Walīd's men repented (of what they had done)" or "al-Walīd's men realized they had committed an error." With the close relationship between the men on both sides, any of these translations make sense.

831. Literally, "he did not agree to it/answer him."

832. Literally, "he did not agree with him in anything."

833. Cf. Ibn Khayyāṭ, 547; Crone, 154.

834. Literally, "it was said to him."

Muʿāwiyah did and al-Walīd's army fled; al-Walīd himself arose and went into al-Bakhrā'.

ʿAbd al-ʿAzīz came forward and stood by the gate which was barred by a chain. Then one man after another began entering (the citadel) under the chain. Thereupon ʿAbd al-Salām b. Bukayr b. Shammākh al-Lakhmī came up to ʿAbd al-ʿAzīz and said to him: "Al-Walīd is saying that he will come out on your authority." So ʿAbd al-ʿAzīz said: "Let him come out." But no sooner had he turned around than people upbraided him: "What are you doing, letting him come out? Leave him there and let the people deal with him for you." So ʿAbd al-ʿAzīz called back ʿAbd al-Salām and said: "There is no need for me to do what has been suggested to me." [Al-Muthannā's narrative continues]: At this juncture I saw a tall young man on a horse approaching the wall of the citadel. Then he climbed over it and went inside the citadel. I myself entered the citadel and I saw al-Walīd standing there. He was wearing a shirt shot through with silver[835] and trousers of variegated cloth,[836] and his sword was in a scabbard; the people were shouting abuse at him. Then Bishr b. Shaybān, the mawlā of Kinānah b. ʿUmayr, who was the man who had climbed over the wall to get inside, went toward al-Walīd. Al-Walīd moved toward the door—I think he wanted to go to ʿAbd al-ʿAzīz—and ʿAbd al-Salām was on his right and the messenger from ʿAmr b. Qays was on his left. Then Bishr hit al-Walīd on the head; the other men struck him repeatedly with their swords and he fell dead. ʿAbd al-Salām threw himself on to al-Walīd and cut off his head. Yazīd b. al-Walīd had put a price of one hundred thousand dirhams on al-
[1807] Walīd's head. Then Abū al-Asad, the mawlā of Khālid b. ʿAbdallāh al-Qasrī, came up and ripped off a handful of al-Walīd's skin and he took it to Yazīd b. Khālid b. ʿAbdallāh, who was being held prisoner in al-Walīd's camp. The people plundered al-Walīd's camp and stores. Then Yazīd al-ʿUlaymī Abū al-Baṭrīq b. Yazīd, whose daughter was married to al-Ḥakam b. al-Walīd, came to me and said: "Protect my daughter's belongings for me," for every-

835. As well as the basic meaning of "reeds," *qaṣab* is "anything made of silver and of other material, resembling (in form) the kind of round and hollow bone thus called" and "fine, thin, delicate or soft garments." Cf. Lane, I, 2529–30.

836. *Washī*. For al-Walīd's taste for fine clothes, cf. n. 810.

body was appropriating whatever they could lay their hands on.[837]

According to Aḥmad (b. Zuhayr)—ʿAlī (al-Madāʾinī)—ʿAmr b. Marwān al-Kalbī: After al-Walīd was killed,[838] his left hand was cut off. It was bundled off to Yazīd b. al-Walīd and it arrived before al-Walīd's head. The hand arrived on the Thursday night and the head was brought the next day. After the prayer, Yazīd displayed the head prominently to the people. The people of Damascus had been in a state of agitation about ʿAbd al-ʿAzīz, but when al-Walīd's head was brought to them they quietened down and their behavior was restrained.

When Yazīd ordered that al-Walīd's head should be displayed, Yazīd b. Farwah, the mawlā of the Banū Marwān,[839] remonstrated with him: "Only the heads of rebels are displayed publicly. This is your paternal cousin and a caliph. I am afraid that if you exhibit his head, the people's hearts will soften toward him and the members of his family will be angry about what has happened to him." Yazīd replied: "By God, I certainly will exhibit it!" and he stuck al-Walīd's head on a spear. Then he said to Ibn Farwah: "Off you go with it. Take it around the city of Damascus and go into his father's house[840] with it." Ibn Farwah did as he was told and was greeted with an uproar from the citizens and al-Walīd's family. Then he brought the head back to Yazīd who said: "Take it to your house."[841] The head remained with Ibn Farwah for nearly a month until Yazīd told him to hand it over to al-Walīd's brother Sulaymān. Now Sulaymān, al-Walīd's brother, [1808]
was one of the people who had acted against his brother. Ibn Farwah washed the head, put it in a basket, and took it to Sulaymān. When Sulaymān saw it he said: "A curse on him! I testify that he was a wine-bibber, wanton and licentious, and that he tried to corrupt me."[842] So Ibn Farwah left the house. Directly

837. *Fa-mā waṣala aḥadun ilā shayʾin zaʿama annahu lahu.* This sentence seems a little odd. It has been translated tentatively as if it read *fa-mā waṣala . . . illā zaʿama* ("nobody came to anything except that he claimed that it was his").

838. Cf. al-Balādhurī, *Ansāb* (Derenk), 60–61; *Fragmenta,* 143–44.

839. Ibn al-Athīr has the Banū Murrah (V, 217).

840. *Fragmenta,* 144, has *dāra ibnihi* ("the house of his son").

841. Literally, "the people of the house."

842. *La-qad arādanī ʿalā nafsī al-fāsiqa.* Even seduction may be suggested here.

afterwards he met a slave girl of al-Walīd[843] to whom he said: "Alas! How violently Sulaymān abused al-Walīd! He alleged that al-Walīd had tried to corrupt him." The woman retorted: "By God, that wicked blackguard was lying! Al-Walīd did not do that. If he had wanted to corrupt Sulaymān, he would have done so and Sulaymān would not have been able to prevent him from doing so."

According to Aḥmad (b. Zuhayr)—'Alī (al-Madā'inī)—'Amr b. Marwān al-Kalbī—Yazīd b. Maṣād: Yazīd b. al-Walīd sent me to Abū Muḥammad al-Sufyānī.[844] Al-Walīd had sent him off as governor of Damascus when he had heard the news of Yazīd's rebellion. When Abū Muḥammad reached Dhanabah, Yazīd received the news about him and he sent me to Abū Muḥammad. When I reached Abū Muḥammad, he made his peace (with our party) and gave the oath of allegiance to Yazīd. We did not even have time to move on before someone appeared in the distance, coming from the direction of the desert. I sent people to him and he was brought to me. The man turned out to be Abū Kāmil al-Ghuzayyil[845] the singer, riding on a she-mule called Maryam[846] which belonged to al-Walīd. He told us that al-Walīd had been killed. Then I sped off to Yazīd, but he had heard the news before I reached him.[847]

According to Aḥmad (b. Zuhayr)—'Alī (al-Madā'inī)—'Amr b.
[1809] Marwān al-Kalbī—Dukayn b. Shammākh al-Kalbī al-'Āmirī: I saw Bishr b. Halbā' al-'Āmirī on the day al-Walīd was killed. He struck the gate of al-Bakhrā' with his sword and said:[848]

We shall weep for Khālid with Indian swords,
and may his good deeds not go for nought.

According to Aḥmad (b. Zuhayr)—'Alī (al-Madā'inī)—Abū

---

843. Literally, "a female mawlā of al-Walīd met him."

844. Abū Muḥammad (b. Yazīd) al-Sufyānī is to be identified as Ziyād b. 'Abdallāh b. Yazīd b. Mu'āwiyah, who was related to al-Walīd through al-Walīd's grandmother. Cf. Wellhausen, 362.

845. Abū Kāmil (or Kumayl) Ghuzayyil al-Dimashqī. Cf. Ibn 'Abd Rabbihi, III, 207.

846. Even al-Walīd's choice of name for his she-mule, Maryam, is shown to be irreverent. Al-Balādhurī omits this name. Cf. *Ansāb* (Derenk), 63.

847. Literally, "I found the news had reached him before I reached him."

848. For these lines, cf. al-Ṭabarī, II, 1783. The meter is *wāfir*.

ʿĀṣim al-Ziyādī: Ten men claimed that they had killed al-Walīd. (Abū ʿĀṣim continued): "I saw Wajh al-Fals holding a piece of skin from al-Walīd's head in his hand and he said: "I killed al-Walīd and I took this piece of his skin. Then somebody came and cut off al-Walīd's head and this piece of skin remained in my hand." The real name (*ism*) of Wajh al-Fals ("Farthing-face") was ʿAbd al-Raḥmān.

Al-Ḥakam b. al-Nuʿmān, the mawlā of al-Walīd b. ʿAbd al-Malik, said: Manṣūr b. Jumhūr, accompanied by ten men, amongst whom was Rawḥ b. Muqbil, brought al-Walīd's head to Yazīd. Then Rawḥ said: "Rejoice, O Commander of the Faithful, that the libertine has been killed and al-ʿAbbās has been taken prisoner." Amongst those who brought the head were ʿAbd al-Raḥmān Wajh al-Fals and Bishr, the mawlā of the Kinānah[849] of Kalb. Yazīd gave each of them ten thousand dirhams. On the day al-Walīd was killed, he said, while he was fighting the rebels: "Anyone who brings a head will have five hundred dirhams." When a number of people brought heads, al-Walīd said: "Write their names down."[850] Then a mawlā of his who was one of the people who had brought a head, said: "O Commander of the Faithful, today is not a day on which to use credit!"[851]

The singers Mālik b. Abī al-Samḥ[852] and ʿUmar al-Wādī[853] were with al-Walīd. When his men forsook him and he was sur- [1810]
rounded, Mālik said to ʿUmar: "Let's leave."[854] ʿUmar replied: "That would be disloyal; besides, we won't be touched, since we are not fighting men." Mālik said: "Come off it! By God, if the rebels are victorious against us, you and I will be the first to be

849. The Kinānah (b. ʿAwf) were a branch of the Kalb. Cf. Ibn al-Kalbī, II, 371.

850. In exactly the same context, al-Balādhurī (loc. cit.) tells this story about Yazīd, not al-Walīd. In view of al-Walīd's well-known attitude toward money and his lack of ready cash earlier to pay his troops (cf. al-Ṭabarī, II, 1803), the anecdote is more likely to refer to al-Walīd. Al-Iṣfahānī also attributes this story to al-Walīd. Cf. *Aghānī*, VI, 139.

851. *Laysa hādhā bi-yawmin yuʿmalu fīhi bi-nasīʾatin*. Cf. *Gloss.*, p. DXI. Al-Iṣfahānī has *laysa hādhā . . . yawman yuʿāmilu fīhi bi-al-nasīʾati* (loc. cit.).

852. For Mālik b. Abī al-Samḥ al-Ṭāʾī, cf. Ibn ʿAbd Rabbihi, III, 198, 207.

853. The text has ʿAmr al-Wādī. The name is given in other sources as ʿUmar al-Wādī b. Dāwūd b. Zādhān. Cf. Ibn ʿAbd Rabbihi, III, 207; al-Iṣfahānī, *Aghānī*, VI, 64–65, 109–10, 139–44. The form ʿUmar has been used in the translation.

854. Literally, "go with us."

killed. Al-Walīd's head will be put between our heads and the people will be told: 'Look who was with him even in this (abject) state.' There will be no worse criticism of him than that."[855] So the two of them fled.

According to Abū Ma'shar—Aḥmad b. Thābit—his informant(s)—Isḥāq b. 'Īsā: Al-Walīd b. Yazīd was killed on a Thursday, two nights before the end of Jumādā II, 126 [Thursday, April 15, 744]. Hishām b. Muḥammad, Muḥammad b. 'Umar al-Wāqidī, and 'Alī b. Muḥammad al-Madā'inī give the same date. Historians disagree, however, as to the length of al-Walīd's caliphate.[856] According to Abū Ma'shar—Aḥmad b. Thābit—his informants—Isḥāq b. 'Īsā:[857] Al-Walīd's caliphate lasted one year and three months. Hishām b. Muḥammad (al-Kalbī) said: Al-Walīd's caliphate lasted one year, two months and twenty-two days.

Historians also disagree about al-Walīd's age on the day he was killed. Hishām b. Muḥammad al-Kalbī said that al-Walīd was killed when he was thirty-eight years old. Muḥammad b. 'Umar (al-Wāqidī) said he was killed when he was thirty-six. Some other historians said he was killed when he was forty-two; others said it was when he was forty-one, others said forty-five, and yet others forty-six.[858]

Al-Walīd's patronymic was Abū al-'Abbās. His mother was Umm al-Ḥajjāj,[859] the daughter of Muḥammad b. Yūsuf al-Tha-
[1811] qafī. Al-Walīd was a man of great strength and he had prehensile toes.[860] He used to take an iron ploughshare with a rope in it, have the rope tied to his foot, and then jump on his horse and pull the ploughshare along. He could ride without holding onto his horse, and he was a poet, much addicted to wine-drinking.

According to Aḥmad (b. Zuhayr)—'Alī (al-Madā'inī)—Ibn Abī al-Zinād[861]—his father: (Abū al-Zinād's narrative begins): Once I

---

855. Literally, "they will not censure him for anything worse than this."

856. Literally, "they disagreed on the amount of time in which he was caliph."

857. This chain of transmitters has been arranged in the usual way, although it is somewhat different from usual in the text.

858. For other sources on the date of al-Walīd's death and the length of his life and his caliphate, cf. al-Balādhurī, *Ansāb* (Derenk), 66–67; *Fragmenta,* 145; al-Ya'qūbī, *Historiae,* II, 400; Ibn Khayyāṭ, II, 380; Hamzah, 129; Ibn Qutaybah, 186; Ibn A'tham, VIII, 140.

859. Al-Walīd's mother's name was Zaynab. Cf. 'Aṭwān, 61.

860. Literally, "long toes." Cf. Ibn A'tham, VIII, 137.

861. Literally, "Ibn Abī al-Zinād, who said, 'My father said.'" For Abū al-Zinād,

was with Hishām when al-Zuhrī[862] was present. They referred to al-Walīd, criticizing him and finding serious fault with him. However, I myself took no part in what they were saying. Then al-Walīd asked permission to enter; this was granted to him. I saw anger on his face. He sat for a little while and then he got up. Later, when Hishām died, somebody wrote a letter against me and I was taken to al-Walīd. He greeted me, saying "How are you, Ibn Dhakwān?" and asked kindly about me. Then he said: "Do you remember the day when that squint-eyed man (Hishām) had that libertine[863] al-Zuhrī with him and they were pulling me to pieces?" I said: "I remember that, but I took no part in what they were saying." Al-Walīd replied: "That's true. Did you see the slave who was standing behind Hishām?" I said: "Yes." Al-Walīd said: "It was he who passed on to me what they said. By God, I swear if that libertine—meaning al-Zuhrī—had lived, I would have killed him." I replied: "I saw from your face that you were angry when you came in." Then al-Walīd said: "Ibn Dhakwān, that squint-eyed man has made me waste the best years of my life."[864] I said: "No, rather may God prolong your life for you, O Commander of the Faithful, and may He allow the community to enjoy your continuing presence!" Then al-Walīd called for supper and we ate it. When it was time for the evening prayer, we performed it and we conversed until the hour for the late night prayer. After we had prayed, al-Walīd sat down and asked for something to drink and they brought in a covered vessel. Three slave girls came and they lined up between him and me.[865] Then

---

the important jurist and traditionist, cf. al-Iṣfahānī, *Aghānī,* VI, 106; Ibn 'Abd Rabbihi, III, 287. His names were Abū al-Zinād 'Alī b. Dhakwān al-Qurashī. He had been secretary to 'Umar II; cf. Wellhausen, 270, 347. He died in 131 (748); cf. Sezgin, I, 405.

862. For Abū Bakr Muḥammad b. Muslim al-Zuhrī (d. 124/742) the famous traditionist and historian, cf. Sezgin, I, 28; Duri, 95–121. He was on very good terms with Hishām, who made him his son's tutor. Cf. Duri, 118.

863. *Al-fāsiq.*

864. Literally, "that squint-eyed man has taken away my life."

865. The text has *ṣaffaqna bayna yadayhi baynī wa-baynahu. Ṣaffaqa* can mean to transfer wine from one vessel to another in order for it to become clear, i.e., to decant the wine (Cf. Lane, I, 1700). Thus a literal translation would be "they decanted (the wine) in front of him between me and him." The wording *baynī wa-baynahu* is rather odd; it is unlikely that the girls divided the wine between al-Walīd and Abū al-Zinād. *Fragmenta,* 129, has *fa-ṣuffifna baynī wa-baynahu* ("they were positioned between me and him"). The version of al-Iṣfahānī

[1812] al-Walīd began to drink, they went away[866] and we chatted. When al-Walīd asked for another drink, the slave girls did as they had done before.[867] Al-Walīd went on talking and asking for more to drink, and the slave girls continued bringing him wine until dawn. I counted that he had drunk seventy cups.

In this year Khālid b. ʿAbdallāh al-Qasrī was killed.

The Killing of Khālid al-Qasrī and the Reason for It

We have already given an account of how Hishām dismissed Khālid from his post as governor of ʿIrāq and Khurāsān[868] and of how Hishām had appointed Yūsuf b. ʿUmar as governor of ʿIrāq. As already mentioned, Khālid had worked in that post for Hishām for fifteen years, apart from a few months, since as already said he became governor of ʿIrāq for Hishām in 105 [June 10, 723–May 28, 724] and was dismissed from the post on Jumādā I, 120 [April 26, 738–May 25, 738]. When Hishām dismissed Khālid, Yūsuf came to Wāsiṭ[869] to get Khālid, seized him, and imprisoned him there. Then Yūsuf b. ʿUmar went to al-Ḥīrah and Khālid remained imprisoned in al-Ḥīrah for a full eighteen months, with his brother Ismāʿīl b. ʿAbdallāh, his son Yazīd b. Khālid, and his nephew al-Mundhir b. Asad b. ʿAbdallāh. Yūsuf begged Hishām for permis-

---

(*Aghānī*, VI, 106) is the most straightforward: *fa-qumna baynī wa-baynahu* ("they stood between me and him"). Later the editor emends the reading to *ṣafafna* (his vocalization). Cf. *Add.*, p. DCCXII. The Cairo edition (253) has *ṣufifna*, which is more satisfactory. It is always conceivable that *ṣaffaqna*, the original reading of the editor, was correct, especially in view of the sentence that follows: "He asked for drink and they did as they had done at first." The tentative translation provided here omits the phrase *bayna yadayhi* and thus follows the *Fragmenta* and the *Aghānī*.

866. The text has *dhahabna*. The Cairo edition (loc. cit.) has *dhahabnā* ("we went away").

867. Literally, "continued doing like that."

868. Literally, "from his post and his governorship." For a parallel account, cf. Ibn al-Athīr, V, 207–10.

869. Wāsiṭ, in Iraq, had been founded by al-Ḥajjāj b. Yūsuf in 83 (702) or 84 (703). He had built a large prison there, which is presumably where Khālid al-Qasrī was put by Yūsuf b. ʿUmar. For a long discussion of the exact site of medieval Wāsiṭ, cf. *EI*[1], s.v. (M. Streck). Cf. also Yāqūt, IV, 881–88; Le Strange, *Lands*, 39–40. The city was called Wāsiṭ because it lay equidistant from al-Kūfah, al-Baṣrah, and Ahwāz.

sion to be allowed a free hand with Khālid and to torture him, but (at first) Hishām would not allow Yūsuf to do that. Then, after Yūsuf had asked repeatedly and had made excuses to him for a shortfall in the *kharāj* and for loss of revenue, Hishām did on one occasion give Yūsuf permission.[870] But he sent a guard to witness the torture and he swore that if Khālid met his end while he was in Yūsuf's hands, then he (Hishām) would certainly kill Yūsuf. So Yūsuf summoned Khālid and he sat on a bench (*dukkān*) in al- [1813]
Ḥīrah,[871] with the people all assembled. Yūsuf was free with his tongue[872] against Khālid, but Khālid did not utter a single word until Yūsuf abused him by calling him Ibn Kāhin, meaning Shiqq b. Sa'b al-Kāhin.[873] Thereupon Khalid retorted: "You fool! You revile me by questioning my noble birth, but your father, O Ibn al-Sabbā', was only a wine-merchant," meaning that he sold wine. At this, Yūsuf sent Khālid back to his prison. Then in Shawwāl 121 [September 10, 739–October 8, 739] Hishām wrote to Yūsuf ordering him to release Khālid, and Khālid settled in the citadel of Ismā'īl b. 'Abdallāh in Dūrān behind the Kūfah bridge. Yazīd b. Khālid set out by himself, going through the territory of the Banū Ṭayy[874] as far as Damascus. Then Khālid set out, accompanied by Ismā'īl and al-Walīd, after 'Abd al-Raḥmān b. 'Anbasah b. Sa'īd b. al-'Āṣ had equipped them (for the journey). Khālid sent the heavy baggage to the citadel of the Banū Muqātil,[875] but Yūsuf had sent

870. Cf. al-Jahshiyārī, 41.

871. *Fa-jalasa 'alā dukkānin fī-al-Ḥīrah. Dukkān:* "a kind of wide bench, of stone or brick, etc., generally built against a wall, upon which one sits." Cf. Lane, I, 900. A shop (also *dukkān*) in the market was a booth with a raised platform (*maṣṭabah*). Cf. J. M. Rogers, *The Spread of Islam*, 66. For a detailed discussion of *maṣṭabah* and *dukkān*, cf. Sadan, 123–24.

872. *Wa-basaṭa 'alayhi.* As well as verbal attacks, this phrase could also mean that Yūsuf stretched out his hand against Khālid.

873. For an account of the attempts made by Abū 'Ubaydah and others to denigrate the genealogy of Khālid b. 'Abdallāh, cf. Goldziher, I, 188–89. Khālid traced his origins back to the South Arabian tribe of the Bājilah and he counted amongst his ancestors the famous soothsayer Shiqq. Cf. al-Iṣfahānī, *Aghānī*, XIX, 57–58. Shiqq was allegedly only half a man (one arm and one leg, hence *shiqq*). Cf. the biography of Khālid given by Ibn Khallikān, II, 313; al-Dīnawarī, 344. According to al-Dīnawarī, Khālid's response to Yūsuf was: "Your father and grandfather were only shopkeepers in al-Ṭā'if" (ibid.).

874. For this important North Arabian tribe, cf. Ibn al-Kalbī, II, 555.

875. This citadel was at 'Ayn al-Tamr on the route from al-Ḥīrah to Syria and was named after Muqātil b. Ḥassān. Cf. Yāqūt, IV, 121, 137; Ibn al-Kalbī, II, 431.

cavalry (after them) and they seized Khālid's provisions, heavy baggage and camels as well as his mawlās who were looking after Khālid's possessions. Yūsuf confiscated and sold[876] what he took from them and sent some of the mawlās back into slavery. So when Khālid arrived at the citadel of the Banū Muqātil, all the (movable) possessions which he and his sons owned had been taken. After moving on to Hīt,[877] they made for al-Qaryah,[878] which is situated opposite the gate of al-Ruṣāfah, where Khālid remained for the remainder of Shawwāl and during the months of Dhū al-Qa'dah, Dhū al-Ḥijjah, al-Muḥarram, and Ṣafar [October 9, 739–February 3, 740]. (During this time) Hishām would not allow them to come in and see him. Al-Abrash was in correspondence with Khālid (during this period, which was the time that) Zayd b. 'Alī rose in rebellion and was killed.

According to al-Haytham b. 'Adī—his relaters: Yūsuf wrote to
[1814] Hishām as follows: "The members of this family, the Hāshimites, had been dying of hunger, to the point that every one of them was preoccupied solely with finding food for their dependents. Then, when Khālid became governor of Iraq, he gave them money, by means of which they so recovered their strength that they began to cherish aspirations to the caliphate. Zayd rose in rebellion only on Khālid's advice. That is proved by the fact that Khālid stayed at al-Qaryah, which is on the route to Iraq, so that he could get news from there." Hishām remained silent until he had finished reading the letter. Then Hishām said to al-Ḥakam b. Ḥazn al-Qaynī, who was in charge of the delegation (from Yūsuf), and whom Yūsuf had ordered to confirm what was written in it—he had in fact done so—"You are lying and so is the person who sent you. Whatever suspicions we may have had about Khālid, we have never doubted his obedience." Then Hishām ordered that the messenger's throat should be cut.[879] When Khālid heard

876. *Fa-ḍaraba wa bā'a*. Presumably this is the meaning of *ḍaraba* in this context. Certainly if the mawlās were beaten, the text would have to read *ḍarabahum*.

877. Hīt, a town in Iraq, lay on the right bank of the Euphrates, at the spot where caravans trading between Iraq and Syria crossed the river. Cf. *EI*², s.v. (M. Streck); Le Strange, *Lands*, 64–65.

878. The phrasing of the Arabic here seems to indicate that al-Qaryah is a place name rather than "the village": *thumma taḥammalū ilā al-qaryati wa-hiya*. Ibn al-Athīr has *al-qaryati allatī* ("the village which . . ." (V, 207).

879. Literally, "he gave orders concerning him and his throat was cut."

about that, he went to Damascus where he stayed until the (time for) the summer expedition arrived. Then he left with the expedition, accompanied by Yazīd and Hishām, his two sons.[880]

The person in charge of Damascus at that time was Kulthūm b. ʿIyāḍ al-Qasrī,[881] who was ill-disposed[882] toward Khālid. When the expedition was well on the way to Byzantine territory,[883] fires began to break out every night in the houses of Damascus. A man from Iraq called Abū al-ʿUmarras and some companions of his started the fire, and while it raged they would plunder and steal.[884] Ismāʿīl b. ʿAbdallāh and al-Mundhir b. Asad b. ʿAbdallāh and the two sons of Khālid, Saʿīd and Muḥammad, were on the coast because there had been bad news from Byzantium.[885] At this juncture, Kulthūm wrote to Hishām mentioning the fire and saying that there had never been such a fire before and that it was the work of the mawlās of Khālid, who wanted to attack the treasury (*bayt al-māl*). Hishām wrote back ordering Kulthūm to [1815] imprison Khālid's family, both young and old, as well as their mawlās and womenfolk. So Kulthūm seized Ismāʿīl, al-Mundhir, Muḥammad, and Saʿīd from where they were stationed on the coast, and they were brought back in manacles, together with those mawlās whom they had with them. Kulthūm imprisoned Umm Jarīr, Khālid's daughter, al-Rāʾiqah,[886] and all the women and young boys.

Then Abū al-ʿUmarras was overpowered and he and his associates were seized. Al-Walīd b. ʿAbd al-Raḥmān, the superintendent

---

880. Literally, "the two sons of Khālid b. ʿAbdallāh." According to al-Dīnawarī (345), Khālid asked Hishām's permission to raid in the direction of Ṭarsūs.

881. Cf. al-Ṭabarī, II, 1716. Kulthūm was sent as governor of Ifrīqiyah in 123 (740–41) and died in 124 (741–42). Cf. n. 306.

882. *Wa-kāna mutaḥāmilan*. Cf. *Gloss.*, pp. CCIII–CCIV.

883. *Fa-lammā adrabū*. Cf. Lane, I, 866.

884. Cf. al-Dīnawarī, 345; Ibn al-Athīr, V, 208.

885. *Li-ḥadathin kāna min al-Rūmī* ("because of bad news which was from Byzantium[?]"). If, as al-Dīnawarī says, Khālid was at Ṭarsūs, he was at the most important of the frontier fortresses, since it guarded the Cilician Gates. Cf. Le Strange, *Lands*, 132. Ṭarsūs is on the coast, as al-Ṭabarī says. Alternatively, *ḥadath* might be a reference to the Darb al-Ḥadath, the northeastern pass through the Taurus guarded by the fortress of Ḥadath. Cf. Le Strange, *Lands*, 121–22. This is improbable, given the statement that Khālid was on the coast. According to al-Balādhurī, as cited by Le Strange, the Darb al-Ḥadath ("the road of bad news") was given the name Darb al-Salāmah ("the road of safety") after the fortress was captured by the Muslims (loc. cit.).

886. Cf. al-Ṭabarī, II, 1739.

of the *kharāj* in Damascus, wrote to Hishām telling him that Abū al-ʿUmarras and his associates had been taken, giving their names one by one and detailing their tribes and garrison towns. Al-Walīd b. ʿAbd al-Raḥmān did not, however, include amongst them a single one of Khālid's mawlās. Then Hishām wrote to Kulthūm upbraiding and reproaching him, and ordering him to release all the people he had imprisoned. Kulthūm let them all go, but he appropriated the mawlās for himself in the hope that Khālid would speak to him about them when the latter returned from the summer campaign. When the soldiers returned from the frontier,[887] Khālid received word that his family had been imprisoned; but he did not hear that they had been set free again. Yazīd b. Khālid secreted himself in a crowd of men until he reached Ḥimṣ, whilst Khālid came and stayed in his house in Damascus. When people came to Khālid the following morning, he sent for his two daughters, Zaynab and ʿĀtikah, and said: "I am growing old and I would like you to look after me." His daughters were very happy to do that. Then his brother Ismāʿīl and his sons, Yazīd and Saʿīd, came in to see him. Khālid gave permission (to other people to come in), and his daughters stood up intending to withdraw.[888] So Khālid said: "Why should they withdraw when Hi-
[1816] shām drives them to prison day after day?" Then the people came in and Ismāʿīl and Khālid's two sons stood in front of his two daughters concealing them.

Khālid said: "I went out raiding in God's cause, hearing and obeying. Then people machinated behind my back and my women and the women of my family were seized and put in prison with criminals as is the practice with unbelievers. What was to stop a group of you standing up and saying: 'Why have the women of this man who hears and obeys been imprisoned?' Were you afraid that you would all be killed? May God inspire fear in you!" Then Khālid added: "As for the position between me and Hishām, (it is this): If he does not lay off me, I will certainly summon (people to follow) the one who is ʿIrāqī in passion, Syrian in family, and Ḥijāzī in origin (meaning Muḥammad b. ʿAlī b.

887. Literally, "when the people came and they went away from the frontier."
888. *Fa-qāmat ibnatāhu li-yatanaḥḥayā.* Ibn al-Athīr (V, 208) has *fa-qāma banātuhu yaḥtajibna* ("his daughters stood up to veil themselves").

ʿAbdallāh b. ʿAbbās).[889] You have my permission to go and tell Hishām that." When Hishām heard what Khālid had said he declared: "Abū al-Haytham[890] has lost his reason."[891]

According to Abū Zayd—Aḥmad b. Muʿāwiyah—Abū al-Khaṭṭāb: Khālid said: "By God, if the lord of al-Ruṣāfah—meaning Hishām—does wrong,[892] we will certainly raise in support of us the Syrian, the Ḥijāzī, the ʿIrāqī (i.e. Muḥammad b. ʿAlī) and if he makes the slightest noise,[893] it (i.e., al-Ruṣāfah) will collapse on all sides." When Hishām heard what Khālid had said he wrote to him as follows: "You talk raving nonsense.[894] Are you threatening me with the insignificant, vile tribe of Bajīlah?"

(The narrative of Abū al-Khaṭṭāb continues.) By God, no one, apart from a man of the Banū ʿAbs, supported him either in deed or word. The man from the Banū ʿAbs recited the following:[895]

Verily, the sea of generosity has become calm, [1817]
a captive of the Banū Thaqīf,[896] bound in chains,
But even though you have imprisoned al-Qasrī, you will not have imprisoned his reputation,
nor will you have imprisoned his beneficence amongst the tribes.

Khālid and Yazīd and other members of Khālid's family remained in Damascus, while Yūsuf (b. ʿUmar) kept plying Hishām with requests for Hishām to send him Yazīd. Then Hishām wrote to Kulthūm b. ʿIyāḍ ordering him to seize Yazīd and to send him to Yūsuf. Accordingly, Kulthūm sent cavalry to take Yazīd, who was in his house. Yazīd attacked the cavalry, who fell back from him, and then Yazīd himself escaped on horseback. Then the

---

889. The imām of the Shīʿīs. Cf. al-Ṭabarī, II, 1769. Al-Dīnawarī, 345, has Ibrāhīm b. Muḥammad b. ʿAlī b. ʿAbdallāh b. ʿAbbās.

890. The *kunyah* of Khālid al-Qasrī. Cf. Ibn Khallikān, II, 308.

891. Cf. Ibn al-Athīr (loc. cit.); al-Dīnawarī (loc. cit.).

892. *La'in sāʾa.* A variant reading has *lā'in shāʾa* ("if he wishes"). It might have been more usual to expect *la'in asāʾa.*

893. Literally, "if he snorts a snort."

894. *Innaka hadhdhāʾatun hudharatun.* Cf. *Gloss.*, p. DXL.

895. The meter is *ṭawīl.* The poet is named by Ibn Khallikān as Abū al-Shaghb al-ʿAbsī. Ibn Khallikān also quotes the verses (loc. cit.). Al-Dīnawarī, 347, has similar, although not always identical, lines, which he attributes to al-Ashʿath b. al-Qīnī.

896. Cf. Ibn al-Kalbī, II, 553.

cavalry returned to Kulthūm and told him what had happened. The day after Yazīd had left, Kulthūm sent cavalry to take Khālid. Khālid called for his clothes and he put them on. His women[897] all began to wail, so one of the cavalrymen said (to Khālid): "Why don't you tell these women to shut up?" Khālid replied: "Why should I? Were it not for my obedience (to the caliph), the slave of the Banū Qasr would learn that he can't treat me in this way. So tell him what I said and if he is a true Arab, as he claims to be, just let him come and seek his fortune from me."[898] Then Khālid left with the cavalry and he was incarcerated in the prison at Damascus. Ismā'īl immediately left for al-Ruṣāfah to see Hishām. Ismā'īl went in to see Abū al-Zubayr,[899] his chamberlain (*ḥājib*), and told him that Khālid had been imprisoned. Then Abū al-Zubayr went in to Hishām and informed him. Hishām wrote to Kulthūm[900] reproaching him, saying: "You have released those whom I ordered you to imprison, and you have imprisoned those whom I did not order you to imprison," and ordering Kulthūm to release Khālid. This Kulthūm did.

[1818] Whenever Hishām wanted anything done, he would order al-Abrash (to deal with it). Accordingly, Hishām wrote through al-Abrash to Khālid. Al-Abrash wrote as follows: "The Commander of the Faithful has heard that 'Abd al-Raḥmān b. Thuwayb al-Dinnī, of the Banū Dinnah of Sa'd, the brothers of 'Uthrah b. Sa'd,[901] stood up before you and said: 'O Khālid, I love you because you have ten special qualities. Truly, God is noble and so

---

897. Literally, "the women."

898. *La-yaṭlub jaddahu minnī:* there are a number of problems with the word *jaddahu* (thus vocalized by the editor). Firstly, it is not clear whether Khālid is speaking about Yūsuf, Hishām, or Kulthūm. Secondly, *jadd* may mean "fortune" or "grandfather." Thirdly, there is a variant reading, *ḥadd* ("prescribed punishment, extremity"). A possible solution is as follows. Although most evidence points to Kulthūm's not being a relation of Khālid's (he would appear to have been a Qaysī; cf. Crone, 128, and *EI*², s.v. [R. Basset]), there was obviously at least one strand of tradition that said he was (cf. al-Dīnawarī, 345, who claims that Kulthūm was a paternal cousin of Khālid's). Thus, it may be that here too Khālid is making a furiously ironic allusion to the fact that his relative is the one who is arresting him.

899. Abū al-Zubayr Nasṭās. Cf. al-Ṭabarī, II, 1749.

900. Cf. n. 306.

901. Al-Dīnawarī (346) has al-Kalbī. For this rather complicated genealogy, cf. Ibn al-Kalbī, II, 242.

are you. God is generous and so are you. God is merciful and so are you. God is forbearing and so are you.' And so ('Abd al-Raḥmān continued in this way) until he had enumerated ten qualities.[902] Now the Commander of the Faithful swears by God that if that incident is authenticated to his own satisfaction, the shedding of your blood will be licit. So write and tell me about the matter properly, so that I may inform the Commander of the Faithful about it." Then Khālid wrote the following reply: "That assembly had too many people present for it to be possible that unjust or wicked persons could falsify the truth of what was said. 'Abd al-Raḥmān b. Thuwayb stood before[903] me and said: 'O Khālid, I love you because you have ten special qualities. Truly, God is noble; He loves every noble person and He (therefore) loves you and I love you because God loves you. . .' and 'Abd al-Raḥmān continued in this way until he had enumerated ten qualities. But worse than that was (your condoning) the way in which Ibn Shaqqī al-Ḥimyarī stood up before the Commander of the Faithful and said: 'O Commander of the Faithful, which do you prize more highly: your deputy (*khalīfah*) among your people, or your messenger?' So the Commander of the Faithful replied: 'My deputy among my people.'[904] Then Ibn Shaqqī[905] said: 'You are the deputy of God and Muḥammad is His messenger. By my life, if a man of the Banū Bajīlah[906] goes astray, it is certainly a more paltry matter both to the common people and to the court [1819]
that if the Commander of the Faithful (himself) goes astray.'" Al-Abrash read out Khālid's letter to Hishām, who said: "Abū al-Haytham has become senile."[907]

Khālid remained in Damascus during the (remainder of the time) that Hishām was caliph, until Hishām died. After Hishām's

---

902. Al-Dīnawarī lists all ten qualities (loc. cit.).

903. *Fa-amma* ("he turned"). The Cairo edition (257) has *fa-qāma,* which is the emended version of the Leiden edition. Cf. *Emend.*, p. DCCXII.

904. According to al-Dīnawarī, Hishām was angry because 'Abd al-Raḥmān had attributed to Khālid merits that no single caliph had possessed (loc. cit.).

905. Cf. Ibn al-Athīr, V, 209. Al-Dīnawarī calls him 'Abdallāh b. Ṣayfī (loc. cit.).

906. Khālid's own tribe. He means himself here.

907. Al-Dīnawarī's account is less elliptical. In it Khālid upbraids Hishām for his harsh treatment of 'Abd al-Raḥmān, whilst in the face of the blasphemous remarks of 'Abdallāh b. Ṣayfī (called Ibn Shaqqī by al-Ṭabarī), Hishām did nothing at all to refute them (loc. cit.).

death, al-Walīd became caliph and the leaders of the *junds*, including Khālid, came to see him, but al-Walīd would not allow a single one of them in to see him. Khālid complained (that he was unwell)[908] and sought permission (to go home). This was granted to him, and accordingly he went back to Damascus where he remained for some months. Then al-Walīd wrote to Khālid as follows: "The Commander of the Faithful is apprised of the matter of the fifty million (dirhams). Didn't you know?[909] So come to the Commander of the Faithful with his envoy. He has ordered him to give you enough time to make your preparations." Then Khālid sent for a number of his close advisers, amongst whom was ʿUmārah b. Abī Kulthūm al-Azdī, and Khālid read out the letter to them and said: "Advise me on what I should do." They replied: "Al-Walīd is not to be trusted in regard to you. We think that you should go into Damascus, seize the treasuries, and summon people to follow whomsoever you wish. The majority of the people are for you, and nobody will raise a dissenting voice against you." Khālid said: "What action other than that (could I take)?" They replied: "Seize the treasuries and stay put until your position has become secure." Khālid then asked: "What else could I do?" His advisers replied: "You could hide."

Then Khālid declared: "As regards your suggestion that I should summon people to follow whomsoever I wish, I would hate to have discord and disagreement on my hands. As for your suggestion that I should make my position secure, you do not feel that I am safe against al-Walīd when I have done nothing wrong, so how can you hope that he will keep faith with me when I have seized the treasuries? As for hiding, by God, I have never covered my head in fear of anyone, and now that I have reached the age I am now, I won't do so either. On the contrary, I will go (to al-Walīd) and I will ask God for help." Then Khālid departed and came to al-Walīd, but al-Walīd did not summon him or speak to
[1820] him and Khālid remained in his own house with his mawlās and his servants until the time that the head of Yaḥyā b. Zayd was

908. *Wa-ishtakā*. Later on in this narrative Khālid says that he is unable to walk and that he has to be carried. It may be that this was the result of the earlier torture he had undergone at the hands of Yūsuf b. ʿUmar.

909. *A-lam taʿlam?* Ibn al-Athīr has *allatī taʿlamu* ("which you know about") (V, 209).

brought from Khurāsān. Then the people were assembled in a portico (*riwāq*) and al-Walīd sat down (with them). The chamberlain came and stood (by Khālid) and Khālid said to him: "You can see the state I am in. I can't walk. I can only be carried in my chair." The chamberlain replied: "Nobody who is being carried can go in to see al-Walīd," and he gave permission for three other people to go in. Then he said: "Stand up, Khālid!" to which Khālid replied: "I have already told you what a state I am in." So the chamberlain allowed another one or two people to enter. Then he repeated "Stand up, Khālid!" to which Khālid again replied: "I have already told you what a state I am in." This continued until the chamberlain had allowed ten people in. Then, after saying once more: "Stand up, Khālid," he gave permission for everyone to go in[910] and gave instructions that Khālid should be admitted in his chair. So Khālid was taken in to see al-Walīd, who was sitting on his couch. The tables were set; the people were in front of him in two rows. Shabbah b. ʿAqqāl or ʿAqqāl b. Shabbah was speaking and the head of Yaḥyā b. Zayd had been raised aloft. Khālid was taken to one of the two rows and when the speaker had finished his speech al-Walīd stood up. The people were sent away and Khālid was taken back to his family. When he had taken off his clothes, al-Walīd's messenger came to him and took him back again. When Khālid reached the door of the tent he stopped. Then the messenger of al-Walīd came out to him and said: "The Commander of the Faithful asks you: 'Where is Yazīd b. Khālid?'" Khālid replied: "Yazīd became the object of Hishām's anger.[911] Hishām sent people to look for him and Yazīd fled from him. We used to see Yazīd in the company of the Commander of the Faithful until God made him caliph. Then when Yazīd did not appear we thought that he was in his home territory of al-Sharāh[912] or thereabouts." The messenger came back to him again and said: "No: you have left Yazīd behind to stir up trouble." Then Khālid said to the messenger: "The Commander of the Faithful knows that we are a family of obedience—I, my father,

---

910. Literally, "Then he said, 'Stand up, Khālid!' and allowed all the people to go in."

911. Literally, "a claw struck him from Hishām." Cf. *Gloss.*, p. CCCXLVI.

912. In the Damascus province. Cf. Le Strange, *Palestine*, 32–33.

and my grandfather before me." Then Khālid interpolated (to the
[1821] narrator): "I could tell by the speed of the messenger's return that al-Walīd was near enough to hear what I was saying." Then the messenger came back and said: "The Commander of the Faithful says to you: 'Either you bring Yazīd or I will surely kill you.'"[913] At that Khālid raised his voice and said: "Say to him: 'So that's what you have been wanting all along, is it? By God, even if Yazīd were under my very feet I would not lift them up for you, so do whatever you want.'" Then al-Walīd ordered Ghaylān,[914] the chief of his guards, to beat Khālid, saying: "Let me hear his voice." So Ghaylān took Khālid to his house and tortured him with chains but Khālid did not open his mouth. Then Ghaylān went back to al-Walīd and said: "By God, I won't torture anyone who never speaks or cries out!" Al-Walīd said: "Lay off him and imprison him at your place." So he kept Khālid in prison until Yūsuf b. 'Umar brought money from Iraq.[915] Then al-Walīd and his associates deliberated the matter amongst themselves and al-Walīd held an assembly with the people at which Yūsuf was present. He[916] spoke to Abān b. 'Abd al-Raḥmān al-Numayrī about Khālid and said: "I will buy him for fifty million (dirhams)." Then al-Walīd sent word to Khālid saying: "Yūsuf will buy you for fifty million. If you can guarantee (to give me) that amount, (well and good). Otherwise I will hand you over to Yūsuf." Khālid replied: "(True) Arabs cannot be sold. By God, if you asked me to guarantee this"—and he picked up some wood from the ground—"I would not do it. So think again." Accordingly, al-Walīd handed Khālid over to Yūsuf, who stripped him of his clothes, threw a woolen cloak over him, bundled him into another, and took him away in a litter without a seat. Khālid's companion on the road was Abū Quḥāfah al-Murrī, the nephew of al-Walīd b. Talīd, who had been Hishām's governor in al-Mawṣil.[917]

Yūsuf took Khālid away and he camped at al-Muḥdathah, about

913. The text has *la-urhiqanna.* The Cairo edition (259) has *la-uzhiqanna* ("I will surely kill"). The latter version has been followed.

914. Al-Dīnawarī (347) calls him Sa'īd b. Ghaylān.

915. Cf. al-Ṭabarī, II, 1779–80.

916. It is not clear whether this refers to Yūsuf or al-Walīd.

917. According to al-Dīnawarī (348) Yūsuf took Khālid to Wasīṭ.

a day's journey from al-Walīd's camp. Then Yūsuf called Khālid and referred to his mother (in a scandalous context). Khālid replied: "Why are you talking about mothers? May God curse you! [1822] By God, I will never speak a word to you again." Then Yūsuf lashed Khālid and tortured him severely but Khālid did not utter a single word. Then Yūsuf proceeded on his journey with Khālid. After some distance, Zayd b. Tamīm al-Qaynī sent a mawlā of his called Sālim al-Naffāṭ[918] to give Khālid a drink of *sawīq*[919] made from pomegranate seeds. When Yūsuf heard about this, he sentenced Zayd to five hundred lashes and Sālim to one thousand lashes. Then Yūsuf reached al-Ḥīrah and he summoned Khālid, together with Ibrāhīm and Muḥammad, the sons of Hishām (b. Ismāʿīl al-Makhzūmī). Yūsuf had Khālid flogged but Khālid did not tell him anything. Ibrāhīm b. Hishām bore up under torture but Muḥammad b. Hishām was broken. After Khālid had remained under torture for one day, Yūsuf placed the spiked rack[920] on his chest and killed him that night. Khālid was buried in the cloak which he had been wearing in the area of al-Ḥīrah in al-Muḥarram 126 (October 25–November 24, 743) according to the report given by al-Haytham b. ʿAdī. Then ʿĀmir b. Sahlah al-Ashʿarī came and killed[921] his horse at Khālid's grave and Yūsuf gave him seven hundred lashes.

According to Abū Zayd—Abū Nuʿaym—an (unnamed) man: I was present when Yūsuf brought Khālid. Yūsuf called for some wood, which was placed on Khālid's feet, and then people stood on him until his feet were broken. But by God, he did not cry out or allow any expression[922] to cross his face. Then they stood on his legs until they were broken, then on his thighs, on his loins, and on his chest until he died. But by God, he did not (once) cry out or allow any expression to cross his face.

---

918. The naphtha thrower.

919. *Sawīq:* a soup or paste made from flour and water to which honey, oil or pomegranate syrup is added. Cf. *Lisān*, II, 243; *EI*¹ s.v. (J. Ruska).

920. *Al-muḍarrasah.* Cf. al-Dīnawarī, 348; Ibn al-Athīr, V, 210. Here Ibn al-Athīr quotes from al-Farazdaq's verses against Khālid al-Qasrī.

921. *Fa-ʿaqara farsahu:* "he hamstrung/killed his horse." A pre-Islamic practice. Cf. the tradition quoted by Lane: *lā ʿaqra fī al-Islāmi* ("there will be no slaughtering (at the grave) in Islam"). Cf. Lane, I, 2108.

922. Literally, "frown."

When al-Walīd b. Yazīd was killed, Khalaf b. Khalīfah[923] recited the following:[924]

The Kalb and the forefathers of Madhḥij[925] have silenced
[1823] a soul tormented with thirst[926] which clamored sleeplessly the whole night long.
In avenging Khālid, they have left[927] the Commander of the Faithful
prostrate upon his nose, though not in the act of worship.
So if you have snapped the cord of a necklace of ours,
we have in retaliation rent the cords of many necklaces of yours.
And if you have diverted our attention from dispensing largesse,
we have in turn diverted al-Walīd's attention from the singing of maidens.
And if al-Qasrī has embarked on a journey of no return,
(Remember that) Abū al-ʿAbbās also is no longer to be seen.

Ḥassān b. Jaʿdah al-Jaʿfarī[928] gave the lie to Khalaf b. Khalīfah in these verses of his:[929]

Surely a man who claims that he himself killed al-Walīd and not
the caliph's uncles, has a soul brimful of lies.
He is naught but a man whose hour of death is nigh,

---

923. Khalaf b. Khalīfah, the mawlā of Qays b. Thaʿlabah. Cf. Ibn ʿAbd Rabbihi, II, 301.

924. Cf. Ibn ʿAbd Rabbihi, loc. cit. The meter is *ṭawīl.*

925. For the Banū Madhḥij, cf. Ibn al-Kalbī, II, 381.

926. *Ṣadan.* Cf. Lane, I, 1671. The translation here is based on the basic meaning of *ṣadiyā* ("to thirst vehemently"). Others will argue that what is meant here is the bird (often an owl) that cries in the head of the slain when his blood has not been avenged by retaliation. Cf. ibid. The translation here, "tormented with thirst," is based on an oral explanation of the term *ṣadan* given in 1970 by Professor A. F. L. Beeston, who convincingly related the term to the Ugaritic practice of placing water in the grave so that the soul of the deceased should not thirst in eternity.

927. *Tarakna* ("they have left"). Ibn ʿAbd Rabbihi (loc. cit.) has *taraknā* ("we have left").

928. Cf. al-Ṭabarī, II, 1378.

929. The meter is *basīṭ.*

one against whom the Banū Marwān have marched
alongside the Arabs.

Abū Miḥjan, Khālid's mawlā, recited the following:[930]

Ask al-Walīd, ask his troops,
when in the morning our hailstorm rained down on him,
Did a single soul from the Muḍar come to shield him,
when the horses were charging under the dust cloud of death? [1824]
The man who in his folly lampoons us in verse we will cut to pieces
with shining white swords; indeed, we use them to lampoon and smite (our foes).

Naṣr b. Sa'īd al-Anṣārī recited the following:[931]

Convey to Yazīd[932] of the Banū Kurz a stark message,[933]
that from afar my thirst for vengeance has been slaked and that I am no longer after revenge.[934]
You have cut down the limbs of a slave (*qinnawr*)[935] in rage
with a sharp, well-worn Indian sword.
In the evening, the wives of a slave have suffered mutilation
because of the downfall of the slave, the son of a slave,
And the dogs of Damascus continued to grip him with their teeth,
as if his limbs were the limbs of a pig.
They left only fragments of him at the place where he died,
the debris of a decaying corpse dragged over the tent ropes.
You made your sword the judge when you were not satisfied
with their judgment,

---

930. This meter is also *basīṭ*.
931. Again, the meter is *basīṭ*.
932. Yazīd, Khālid's son. Kurz was an ancestor of Khālid al-Qasrī. Cf. Ibn Khallikān, II, 309; Goldziher, I, 188–89.
933. *Mughalghalatan*.
934. The text has *qinnawr*. This is later changed tentatively to *qinnūr*. Cf. *Emend.*, p. DCCXII. The original version seems to accord better with the form in *Lisān*, III, 179, where the vocalization is *qinnawr* and the word is defined as *al-'abd* ("slave"). This is also the view expressed by the editor. Cf. *Gloss.*, p. CDX-CDXXIII. The Cairo edition (261) has *qannūr*.
935. The double force of *al-'abdi qinnawrin* has not been rendered in English.

for only the sword passes judgment without seeking justification.
So do not accept from Khālid, if you are far-sighted,
anything except every great and famous deed.
[1825] You have set fire to the kingdom of the Nizār and then terrified them
with galloping horses which bear haughty warriors.
There were none among the family of a slave, nor
among their offspring,[936] equal to the moon in the sky, suffused with light.

In this year the oath of allegiance was given to Yazīd b. al-Walīd b. ʿAbd al-Malik, who was called Yazīd the "Inadequate"[937] (*al-Nāqiṣ*). Yazīd was given the title of the "Inadequate" only because he cut back the increase of ten dirhams in the people's stipends which al-Walīd b. Yazīd had decreed for them. After al-Walīd was killed, Yazīd revoked their increase and restored their stipends to what they had been in the time of Hishām b. ʿAbd al-Malik. It was said that the first person to call Yazīd by this name was Marwān b. Muḥammad.[938]

According to Aḥmad b. Zuhayr—ʿAlī b. Muḥammad (al-Madāʾinī): Marwān b. Muḥammad reproached Yazīd b. al-Walīd and called him al-Nāqiṣ b. al-Walīd. So he dubbed him the "Inadequate" and that is why the people called him that.

---

936. Literally, "nor did they beget."
937. Cf. n. 629.
938. Cf. Ibn al-Athīr, V, 220.

The Caliphate of Yazīd b. al-Walīd

The Events of the Year 126 (cont'd)

(October 25, 743–October 12, 744)

In this year the unity of the Banū Marwān was disturbed and discord prevailed.

The Discords That Occurred

One such source of discord was the uprising of Sulaymān b. Hishām b. ʿAbd al-Malik in ʿAmmān after the killing of al-Walīd b. Yazīd. According to Aḥmad b. Zuhayr—ʿAlī b. Muḥammad (al-Madāʾinī): When al-Walīd was killed, Sulaymān b. Hishām came out of prison—he had been imprisoned in ʿAmmān[939]—took what revenues there were in ʿAmmān, and made for Damascus, where he began cursing al-Walīd and upbraiding him for being an unbeliever.

In this year the people of Ḥimṣ attacked the dependents of [1826] al-ʿAbbās b. al-Walīd. They destroyed his house and declared publicly that they were seeking vengeance for the blood of al-Walīd b. Yazīd.

939. Cf. al-Ṭabarī, II, 1776. For Sulaymān's activities after his release from prison, cf. also Ibn al-Athīr, V, 220; *Fragmenta*, 146.

The Uprising in Ḥimṣ

According to Aḥmad (b. Zuhayr)—ʿAlī (al-Madāʾinī): Marwān b. ʿAbdallāh b. ʿAbd al-Malik was al-Walīd's governor in Ḥimṣ. He was one of the most prominent members of the Banū Marwān as far as nobility, generosity, intellect, and good looks were concerned. When al-Walīd was killed and the news of his murder reached the people of Ḥimṣ, they closed the town gates and they long continued to lament and mourn for al-Walīd. The people asked how al-Walīd had come to be killed and one of the people who had come to them (to tell them the news) said: We continued to maintain law and order among the people, and to keep them under control, until al-ʿAbbās b. al-Walīd arrived and defected to the side of ʿAbd al-ʿAzīz b. al-Ḥajjāj. Then the people of Ḥimṣ rose up and wrecked and looted the house of al-ʿAbbās; they carried off his women and took away his sons, whom they cast into prison. They began searching for al-ʿAbbās, but he escaped to Yazīd b. al-Walīd. Then the people wrote to the *jund*s, summoning them to seek vengeance for al-Walīd's blood, and the *jund*s responded. The people of Ḥimṣ who were in the *jund*s wrote to the effect that they would not give the oath of obedience to Yazīd, that if al-Walīd's two heirs[940] were still alive they would give the oath of allegiance to them and that otherwise they would give it to the best person they knew, on the condition that he give them stipends each Muḥarram and that he make provision that their children should inherit them.[941] They chose Muʿāwiyah b. Yazīd b. Huṣayn[942] as their leader. He wrote a letter to Marwān b. ʿAbdallāh b. ʿAbd al-Malik, who was in the *amīr*'s residence in Ḥimṣ. When Marwān had read the letter he said: "This is a letter that was written with God's approval,"[943] and he agreed to do what they wanted. When Yazīd b. al-Walīd heard about the people of Ḥimṣ he sent envoys to them, amongst whom was Yaʿqūb b. Hānīʾ, and he wrote a letter to them saying that he was not calling them to accept himself but that he was summoning them to the

---

940. The two sons mentioned in al-Walīd's succession letter, i.e., al-Ḥakam and ʿUthmān.

941. Literally, "he would give (stipends) to them for the children."

942. Muʿāwiyah b. Yazīd b. Ḥuṣayn b. Numayr al-Sakūnī. Cf. Crone, 97.

943. This translation is only tentative.

shūrā. ʿAmr b. Qays al-Sakūnī[944] replied: "We are content with our heir-apparent" (*walī ʿahd*), meaning the son of al-Walīd b. Yazīd. At that Yaʿqūb b. ʿUmayr[945] took hold of ʿAmr's beard and berated him: "You decrepit old man! Your judgment is unsound and you have lost your reason. Even if the person you mean[946] were an orphan in your care, it would not be lawful for you to give him his money, so how could it be otherwise in the case (not just of money, but) of the *ummah* itself?"[947] Then the people of Ḥimṣ attacked the envoys of Yazīd b. al-Walīd and drove them out. In charge of Ḥimṣ was Muʿāwiyah b. Yazīd b. Ḥuṣayn. Marwān b. ʿAbdallāh had no authority over them. Al-Simṭ b. Thābit[948] was with the people of Ḥimṣ, too, but relations between him and Muʿāwiyah b. Yazīd were strained. Abū Muḥammad al-Sufyānī,[949] who was also with the rebels, declared to them: "If I went to Damascus and showed only myself to the people there, they would not oppose me." [1827]

Then Yazīd b. al-Walīd dispatched Masrūr b. al-Walīd and al-Walīd b. Rawḥ with a large number of troops, most of whom were from the Banū ʿĀmir of Kalb, and they camped at Ḥuwwārayn.[950] Thereafter, Sulaymān b. Hishām came to Yazīd. Sulaymān was well received by Yazīd, and Yazīd married Sulaymān's sister, Umm Hishām, the daughter of Hishām b. ʿAbd al-Malik. Yazīd also returned to Sulaymān those of his family's possessions that al-Walīd had seized. Then Yazīd sent Sulaymān b. Hishām to Masrūr b. al-Walīd and al-Walīd b. Rawḥ, ordering them to heed and obey him. Then the people of Ḥimṣ arrived and camped at a village belonging to Khālid b. Yazīd b. Muʿāwiyah.

According to Aḥmad (b. Zuhayr)—ʿAlī (al-Madāʾinī)—ʿAmr b.

944. For his biography, cf. Crone, 99.

945. The name is written thus in the text. On the preceding page, however, Yaʿqūb b. Hānīʾ was mentioned in the delegation sent to Ḥimṣ by Yazīd. There is probably a scribal error here and the name should be Yaʿqūb b. Hānīʾ.

946. One of the two sons of al-Walīd, who were still minors.

947. Literally, "how is the case of the *ummah!*"

948. Al-Simṭ b. Thābit b. Yazīd b. Shuraḥbīl b. al-Simṭ. For his later career, cf. al-Yaʿqūbī, *Historiae*, II, 404, 495. For the history of his family, cf. Crone, 101–02.

949. Abū Muḥammad Muḥammad b. ʿAbdāllah b. Yazīd b. Muʿāwiyah al-Sufyānī, an Umayyad. For a discussion of this name, cf. *Fragmenta*, 138, and the editor's note C. Cf. also Wellhausen, 362, 365–66.

950. Of the places that bear this name in Syria, the most likely here is a fortress near Ḥimṣ. Cf. Yāqūt, II, 355; Le Strange, *Palestine*, 465; Dussaud, 79.

Marwān al-Kalbī—ʿAmr b. Muḥammad and Yaḥyā b. ʿAbd al-Raḥmān al-Bahrānī: Marwān b. ʿAbdallāh stood up and addressed them: "You who are gathered here! You have risen up in rebellion
[1828] to wage war against your enemy and to avenge the blood of your caliph and you have taken a path of rebellion for which I hope that God will reward you and give you a good recompense. People have shown their readiness to fight you and have revealed aggressive intentions toward you. If you foil their attempts, the rest will follow of itself and you will be nearer to your objectives and (your enemies) will be easier for you (to deal with). I do not think it is advisable for you to go to Damascus with this army at your back."[951] Then al-Simṭ said: "By God, this is an enemy who is right on your doorstep and who wants to disrupt your unity. And he has Qadarī inclinations." Thereupon the soldiers attacked and killed Marwān b. ʿAbdallāh and his son, and exhibited their heads[952] to the people. By making these remarks, however, al-Simṭ had only wanted to disagree with Muʿāwiyah b. Yazīd.

When Marwān b. ʿAbdallāh was killed, the people of Ḥimṣ appointed as their governor Abū Muḥammad al-Sufyānī. They further sent word to Sulaymān b. Hishām, saying: "We are coming to you, so remain where you are," so he stayed put. Then the people of Ḥimṣ bypassed Sulaymān's troops on their left and advanced toward Damascus. Sulaymān got wind of where they were going, so he departed in haste and met up with them at al-Sulaymāniyyah, which was an estate belonging to Sulaymān b. ʿAbd al-Malik (and was located) behind ʿAdhrā',[953] fourteen miles from Damascus.

According to ʿAlī (al-Madā'inī)—ʿAmr b. Marwān b. Bashshār and al-Walīd b. ʿAlī: When Yazīd heard about what the people of Ḥimṣ had been up to, he summoned ʿAbd al-ʿAzīz b. al-Ḥajjāj and sent him off with three thousand men, ordering him to make himself master of the ʿUqāb pass.[954] Yazīd also sent for Hishām b.

951. Literally, "and to leave this army behind you." Ibn al-Athīr has: "if you are victorious over them what follows them will be easier for you" (V, 221).

952. There is no dual in the Leiden text here, but the Cairo edition (VII, 264) corrects it without comment.

953. ʿAdhrā' was a well-known village of the Ghūṭah district around Damascus. Cf. Yāqūt, III, 625; Le Strange, *Palestine*, 383.

954. This is presumably a reference to the Eagle's Gorge which lay near ʿAdhrā'. Cf. Le Strange, loc. cit.

Maṣād and dispatched him with fifteen hundred men, ordering him to seize the mountain road at al-Salāmah[955] and instructing the forces to provide each other with mutual support.

According to ʿAmr b. Marwān—Yazīd b. Maṣād: I was with Sulaymān's troops. When we came upon the people of Ḥimṣ, they had camped at al-Sulaymāniyyah. They had positioned themselves with the olive grove on their right, the mountain to the north of them, and the wells behind them. So there was only one way of approaching them. They had camped there at the begin- [1829]
ning of the night and had rested their riding animals, whereas we had spent the whole night traveling until we had come upon them. When the sun was high and the heat had become intense and our animals were exhausted and our armor weighed heavily on us, I went up to Masrūr b. al-Walīd and said to him, within earshot of Sulaymān: "O Abū Saʿīd, I swear to you by God that the *amīr* (of Ḥimṣ) is sending his *jund* forward to fight (us) at this very moment." Then Sulaymān rode up and said: "Young man, be steadfast. By God, I will not dismount until God has decreed His will for me and them (the people of Ḥimṣ)."[956] Then Sulaymān moved forward (into the fray); in charge of his right flank was al-Ṭufayl b. Ḥārithah al-Kalbī and in command of his left was al-Ṭufayl b. Zurārah al-Ḥabashī.[957] The people of Ḥimṣ launched an attack on us and our right and left flanks withdrew a distance of more than two bowshots, whilst Sulaymān maintained his position in the center. Then Sulaymān's men attacked the army of Ḥimṣ, pushing them back to their original position. Thereafter there were repeated attacks from both sides. Around two hundred of the men of Ḥimṣ were killed, including Ḥarb b. ʿAbdallāh b. Yazīd b. Muʿāwiyah, and about fifty of Sulaymān's followers lost their lives. Abū al-Halbāʾ al-Bahrānī, who was a prominent horseman from Ḥimṣ, sallied forth and issued a challenge to single combat, so Ḥayyah b. Salāmah al-Kalbī came out against him. Abū al-Halbāʾ struck Ḥayyah a blow which unseated him from his horse. Then Abū Jaʿdah, a mawlā of Quraysh from Damascus,

955. The text has al-Salāmah. Ibn al-Athīr has al-Salāmiyyah (V, 221). Certainly al-Salāmiyyah (unlike al-Salāmah) can be located in the area between Ḥamāh and Ḥimṣ. Cf. Le Strange, *Palestine*, 528; Dussaud, 79.

956. Literally, "until God has decreed what He decrees between me and them."

957. For these two men called Ṭufayl, cf. Crone, 162.

attacked Abū al-Halbā' and killed him. Next, Thubayt b. Yazīd al-Bahrānī sallied forth and issued a challenge to single combat, whereupon Īrāk al-Sughdī, who was a descendant of the kings of Sughd and was attached to Sulaymān b. Hishām, came out against him. Now Thubayt was short and Īrāk was massive. When Thubayt saw Īrāk advancing toward him he retreated, so Īrāk stood and shot an arrow at him which pinned his leg muscle
[1830] to his saddle cloth. While they were thus engaged, ʿAbd al-ʿAzīz approached from the ʿUqāb pass and he attacked the men of Ḥimṣ with such vigor that he broke through their lines killing (some of them) and then reached us.

According to ʿAlī (al-Madā'inī)—ʿAmr b. Marwān—Sulaymān b. Ziyād al-Ghassānī:[958] I was with ʿAbd al-ʿAzīz b. al-Ḥajjāj. When he caught sight of the troops of Ḥimṣ, he said to his followers: "Your destination is that hill which is in the center of their troops. By God, any of you who falls behind will be beheaded by me personally." Then, ordering his personal standard-bearer to advance, he launched into the fray and we went with him. We killed everyone in our way until we reached the hill. ʿAbd al-ʿAzīz had split up the troops of Ḥimṣ who were in disarray. Then Yazīd b. Khālid b. ʿAbdallāh al-Qasrī shouted: "Fear God, fear God when dealing with your own people!"[959] and thus he restrained them, for his heart misgave him at what Sulaymān and ʿAbd al-ʿAzīz had done. Hostilities almost broke out between Sulaymān, supported by the Dhakwāniyyah,[960] and the Banū ʿĀmir from Kalb. The Dhakwāniyyah were stopped from attacking the Banū ʿĀmir on being assured that the latter would give the oath of allegiance to Yazīd b. al-Walīd. Then Sulaymān b. Hishām sent men to Abū Muḥammad al-Sufyānī and Yazīd b. Khālid b. Yazīd b. Muʿāwiyah, and they were seized. As they were being taken past al-Ṭufayl b. Ḥārithah, they shouted out to him: "We beseech you, uncle,[961] by God and kinship, (help us)." So al-Ṭufayl went with them to

958. The Cairo edition (265) puts in Aḥmad (b. Zuhayr) at the beginning of this chain of transmitters.

959. *Allāha Allāha fī qawmika.*

960. The Dhakwāniyyah were the armed retinue of Sulaymān b. Hishām, numbering several thousand men. Cf. Crone, 53, 241, n. 393.

961. Their maternal uncle.

Sulaymān, but he imprisoned them both. The Banū 'Āmir were afraid that he would kill the two of them, so a group of the Banū 'Āmir came and remained with the two captives in the tent. Then Sulaymān sent them on to Yazīd b. al-Walīd, who imprisoned them in the Green Palace[962] with al-Walīd's two sons. Yazīd also imprisoned with them Yazīd b. 'Uthmān b. Muḥammad b. Abī Sufyān, the maternal uncle of 'Uthmān b. al-Walīd. Then Sulaymān and 'Abd al-'Azīz went toward Damascus and lodged at 'Adhrā'. The people of Damascus reached agreement and gave the oath of allegiance to Yazīd b. al-Walīd. Then the people went (back) to Damascus and Ḥimṣ. Yazīd allotted them stipends and gave presents to their leaders, amongst whom were Mu'āwiyah b. Yazīd b. al-Ḥusayn, al-Simṭ b. Thābit, 'Amr b. Qays, Ibn Ḥuwayy, and al-Ṣaqr b. Ṣafwān. Yazīd appointed Mu'āwiyah b. Yazīd b. Ḥuṣayn, [1831]
who was from Ḥimṣ, as governor. The remainder (of the rebels) stayed in Damascus and then left to join the people of Jordan and Palestine. Three hundred of the inhabitants of Ḥimṣ had been killed that day.[963]

In this year the inhabitants of Palestine and Jordan rose up and killed their governor.[964]

The Rebellion of the People of Palestine and Jordan and the Treatment They Received from Yazīd b. al-Walīd

According to Aḥmad (b. Zuhayr)—'Alī b. Muḥammad (al-Madā'inī)—'Amr b. Marwān al-Kalbī—Rajā' b. Rawḥ b. Salāmah b. Rawḥ b. Zinbā':[965] Sa'īd b. 'Abd al-Malik, a man of good character, was al-Walīd's governor in Palestine. Yazīd b. Sulaymān (b. 'Abd al-Malik) was the chief of his father's sons.[966] They had been

962. *Al-Khaḍrā'*: the palace built at Damascus by Mu'āwiyah, the first Umayyad caliph. It is perhaps significant that the audience hall at al-Ruṣāfah and the palace at Wāsiṭ also had green domes. Cf. the discussion in Grabar, *Al-Mushatta*, 106.

963. For an analysis of the revolt of the men of Ḥimṣ, cf. Shaban, *Islamic History*, I, 157; Wellhausen, 365–66.

964. Cf. Ibn al-Athīr, V, 222–23.

965. For the history of this family, cf. Crone, 99–101.

966. Literally, "the sons of Sulaymān b. 'Abd al-Malik." For Yazīd b. Sulaymān, cf. the Umayyad genealogical table.

living in Palestine, and the people there liked them because of the protection that they extended to them. When al-Walīd was killed, the leader of the people in Palestine at that time, Saʿīd b. Rawḥ b. Zinbāʿ, wrote to Yazīd b. Sulaymān, saying: "The caliph has been killed. Come to us and we will appoint you to rule over us." Then Saʿīd (b. Rawḥ) gathered his people to him and wrote to Saʿīd b. ʿAbd al-Malik, who was at that time camped at al-Sabaʿ,[967] saying: "Leave us. The situation here has become very troubled and we have chosen as our ruler a man under whose government we can be content." Accordingly, Saʿīd b. ʿAbd al-Malik went away to Yazīd b. al-Walīd. Then Yazīd b. Sulaymān summoned the people of Palestine to fight against Yazīd b. al-Walīd. The people of Jordan heard about their activities and so they appointed Muḥammad b. ʿAbd al-Malik to rule over them, whilst it was Saʿīd b. Rawḥ and Ḍibʿān b. Rawḥ[968] who were in command of the people of Palestine. When Yazīd (b. al-Walīd) heard about the doings of the people of Jordan and Palestine, he sent Sulaymān b. Hishām against them, accompanied by the men of Damascus and the men of Ḥimṣ who had been with al-Sufyānī. According to ʿAlī (al-
[1832] Madāʾinī)—ʿAmr b. Marwān—Muḥammad b. Rashīd al-Khuzāʿī: The men of Damascus numbered eighty-four thousand even before Sulaymān b. Hishām went out to join them.[969]

According to Muḥammad b. Rāshid: Sulaymān b. Hishām[970] kept on sending me to Ḍibʿān and Saʿīd, the two sons of Rawḥ, and to al-Ḥakam and Rāshid, the two sons of Jirʾ of the Balqayn, and I would make them promises and raise their hopes (of what they would receive) if they gave the oath of allegiance to Yazīd b. al-Walīd. Accordingly, they agreed to do so. According to ʿUthmān b. Dāwūd al-Khawlānī: Yazīd b. al-Walīd sent me, together with Ḥudhayfah b. Saʿīd, to Muḥammad b. ʿAbd al-Malik and Yazīd b. Sulaymān to call on them to submit to him and to make them promises and raise their hopes. So we began with the men of

---

967. Two places called al-Sabaʿ (Le Strange has al-Sabʿ) were located in the province of Filasṭīn. The more likely one here is the district that lies between Jerusalem and al-Karak. Cf. Le Strange, *Palestine*, 523.

968. Ḍibʿān is the vocalization given by the editor. *Fragmenta*, 152, has Ḍabʿān.

969. Literally, "the men of Damascus were eighty-four thousand, and Sulaymān b. Hishām went to them."

970. Cf. n. 368.

Jordan and Muḥammad b. ʿAbd al-Malik. A group of them had gathered to him and I addressed him. Then one of them said: "May God show the *amīr* the right way! Accept what this young man says."[971] Then the prayer began,[972] and I spoke privately with him and said: "I have been sent by Yazīd with a message for you.[973] By God, all the flags I have left behind me are hoisted over the heads of your own people. Every dirham that has left the treasury is in their hands and they (all) have some kind of grievance against you."[974] Muḥammad said: "Are you sure about that?" I said: "Yes." Then I went away, came to Ḍibʿān b. Rawḥ, and said the same things to him. I also said to him: "Yazīd will make you governor of Palestine for as long as he remains in power." So Dibʿān agreed to what I had proposed and I left. Before the following day the people of Palestine had decamped.

According to Aḥmad (b. Zuhayr)—ʿAlī (al-Madāʾinī)—ʿAmr b. Marwan al-Kalbī—Muḥammad b. Saʿīd b. Ḥassān al-Urdunnī: I was a scout for Yazīd b. al-Walīd in Jordan. When the situation had settled down in his favor, he made me superintendent of the *kharāj* in Jordan. When the people rebelled against Yazīd b. al-Walīd, I went to Sulaymān b. Hishām and I asked him to detail some cavalry to accompany me in making a raid on Ṭabariy- [1833]

---

971. The text has *aqbil hādhā al-fatā uqīmat al-ṣalātu.* This would appear to be faulty. At minimum the insertion of *wa* or *fa* before *uqīmat* is necessary. Thus a literal translation would be: "'Accept this young man' and then the prayer began." The Cairo edition (VII, 267) has a longer, quite different reading here: *uqtul hādhā al-Qadariyya al-khabītha fa-kaffahum ʿannī al-Ḥakam b. Jirʾ al-Qīnī,* which the editor says is a variant reading, although the Leiden edition gives no variants at all. Ibn al-Athīr glosses over this problem by omitting it (V, 222). In this very unsatisfactory situation, the former solution with the addition of *wa* has been adopted. It accords better with the following details of a private conversation between the messenger and Muḥammad b. ʿAbd al-Malik.

972. Cf. n. 148.

973. Literally, "I am Yazīd's messenger to you."

974. The meaning of this is rather obscure. A literal translation of the text would be: "By God, I have not left behind me any flag except that it is raised over the head of a man of your family and there is no *dirham* which leaves the treasury except in the hand of a man from amongst them." The Arabic then continues: *wa-huwa yaḥmilu laka kadhā wa-kadhā.* Presumably what the messenger is suggesting here is that there are troops mobilized and paid from the family of Muḥammad b. ʿAbd al-Malik already on the side of Yazīd b. al-Walīd and that Muḥammad would do well to submit at once. The precise meaning of *yaḥmilu* is not clear, but *ḥamala* may mean "to be angry, to have a grievance" (cf. Lane, I, 647) and has tentatively been translated thus in this sentence.

yah.[975] But Sulaymān refused to send anyone with me. Then I went to Yazīd b. al-Walīd and told him what had happened. Yazīd wrote a letter over his own signature to Sulaymān, ordering him to let me take with me whatever I wanted. Then I took the letter to Sulaymān, and he sent Muslim b. Dhakwān[976] and five thousand men with me. I left with them at night and made them camp at al-Baṭīḥah. Then they dispersed into the villages. I went with a group of them to Ṭabariyyah and they wrote letters contacting their own groups. The people of Ṭabariyyah said: "Why should we stand by when troops are searching our houses and oppressing our people?" Then they went to the residence of Yazīd b. Sulaymān and Muḥammad b. ʿAbd al-Malik, plundered their belongings, seized their riding-animals and weapons, and returned to their own villages and houses.

When the people of Palestine and Jordan had dispersed, Sulaymān went to al-Ṣannabrah,[977] where the people of Jordan gathered to him and gave the oath of allegiance to Yazīd b. al-Walīd. Then on the Friday Sulaymān sent people toward Ṭabariyyah; he himself crossed the lake by boat and traveled alongside his men[978] (who were on the road) until he reached Ṭabariyyah. Then he led the people in the Friday prayer, made the oath of allegiance (to Yazīd b. al-Walīd) with the people who were there, and returned to his camp. According to Aḥmad (b. Zuhayr)—ʿAlī (al-Madāʾinī)—ʿAmr b. Marwān al-Kalbī—ʿUthmān b. Dāwūd: When Sulaymān camped at al-Ṣannabrah, he sent me to Yazīd b. al-Walīd, instructing me to transmit the following message to Yazīd: "You know how churlish the people of Palestine are, but God has (so far) taken it upon Himself to defend you from them. I have resolved to appoint Ibn Surāqah as governor of Palestine and al-Aswad b. Bilāl al-Muḥāribī as governor of Jordan." So I went to

975. Ṭabariyyah (Tiberias), the capital of the province of Jordan. Cf. Le Strange, *Palestine*, 334–51.

976. The commander of the Dhakwāniyyah, a freedman of Yazīd b. al-Walīd. Cf. Crone, 241, n. 394.

977. This place is vocalized in the text as al-Ṣinnabrah. According to Le Strange, basing his reading on Yāqūt, III, 419, it should be al-Ṣannabrah. This was a place in the province of Jordan, three miles from Ṭabariyyah (*Palestine*, 531).

978. The text has *wajjaha Sulaymānu ilā . . . fa-jaʿala yusāyiruhum*. There would appear to be an implied object ("them," "the people") with *wajjaha*. Otherwise, *tawajjaha* would be more usual.

Yazīd and I told him what Sulaymān had instructed me to tell him. Yazīd said: "Tell me what you said to Ḍibʿān b. Rawḥ," so I told him. Then he said: "And what did Ḍibʿān do?" I replied: "Before morning, he decamped with the people of Palestine and Ibn Jirw and the people of Jordan did likewise." Then Yazīd said: "No one keeps his promises better than we do. Go back and tell Sulaymān not to leave until he has gone to al-Ramlah and make the people there give the oath of allegiance (to me). I have already [1834] appointed Ibrāhīm b. al-Walīd as governor of Jordan, Ḍibʿān b. Rawḥ as governor of Palestine, Masrūr b. al-Walīd over Qinnasrīn, and Ibn al-Ḥusayn over Ḥimṣ."

After the murder of al-Walīd, Yazīd b. al-Walīd delivered a sermon. After giving praise and thanks to God and praying for His prophet Muḥammad he went on:[979]

> O people! By God, I did not rise up in rebellion out of overweening insolence and pride[980] nor out of a craving (to possess the things of) this world nor out of a desire for kingship. Nor do I have an inflated opinion of myself. Indeed, without the mercy of my Lord, I would be lost. On the contrary, I have rebelled out of righteous anger for God's cause, His prophet, and His religion, and I came to summon people to God, His book, and the *sunnah* of His prophet. (And this was at a time) when the signposts indicating the right path had been destroyed,[981] the light of pious folk had been extinguished, and there had appeared that stiff-necked tyrant who declared licit every forbidden thing and who was responsible for one innovation (*bidʿah*) after another. Nor, moreover, by God, did he confirm the truth of the Book or believe in the Day of Reckoning, although in the matter of noble descent he was my (paternal) cousin and was my equal as regards lineage. When I saw (all) this, I sought God's favor in my dealings with him

979. For other versions of this famous *khuṭbah*, cf. *Fragmenta*, 150–51; Ibn al-Ṭiqṭaqah, 130–31; Ibn Khayyāṭ, 382–83; Ibn ʿAbd Rabbihi, II, 144; al-Jāḥiẓ, *al-Bayān*, II, 141–42. Only significant differences are noted below. For a recent discussion of this *khuṭbah*, cf. Hawting, 95.

980. *Baṭaran*. Cf. Qur'ān 28, v. 58.

981. *Hudimat*. Ibn ʿAbd Rabbihi (loc. cit.) and Ibn Khayyāṭ (loc. cit.) have *durisat* ("had been effaced").

(al-Walīd) and I implored Him not to let me yield to self-interest in this matter. I summoned to that cause those under my command who answered my call and I strove therein until God, by His own power and might and not through mine, granted His servants and lands surcease from him (al-Walīd).

O people, I give you my pledge that I will not place stone upon stone nor brick upon brick,[982] I will not dig any river, I will not accumulate wealth or give it to any wife or child. (I swear too) that I will not transfer wealth from one town to another until I have made good the loss to that town and [1835] repaired adequately the fortune of its people.[983] If there is any surplus, I will take it[984] to the next town and to those who are in greatest need of it.[985] I will not detain you for long periods at the frontiers, thereby sorely testing you and your families. I will not close my door against you so that the strong amongst you will devour the weak, nor will I place on those of you who pay the poll-tax (burdens) which will drive you from your lands and decimate your progeny.[986] With me in charge you will receive your stipends every year and your rations every month, so much so that there will be an abundance of sustenance for (all) Muslims, be they far distant or near at hand. If I keep my word to you, then it is your duty to heed, to obey, and to provide help generously. But if I do not keep faith with you, it is up to you to depose me, with the proviso that you should (first) ask me to repent and if I do so you should accept such repentance from me. If you know of anyone of proven probity who of his own accord will give you

---

982. These are attacks on the building activities of his predecessor, al-Walīd.

983. *Ḥattā asudda . . . khasāsata ahlihi bi-mā yuʿnīhum.* This is later amended to *yughnīhum* ("until I have restored the fortune of its people by that which satisfies them"). Cf. *Emend.*, p. DCCXIII. The Cairo edition (269) has *bi-mā yuʿīnuhum* ("by that which keeps them").

984. *Fa-in faḍala faḍlatun naqaltuhu.* The Cairo edition (269) corrects *faḍlatun* to *faḍlun.*

985. *Naqaltuhu ilā al-baladi yalīhi mimman huwa aḥwaju ilayhi.* The version of Ibn ʿAbd Rabbihi (loc. cit.) makes better sense: *ilā al-baladi alladhi yalīhi wa-man huwa aḥwaju ilayhi.* This is the version adopted in the translation.

986. Literally: "will drive *them* from *their* lands and decimate *their* progeny."

what I would give you, and you want to give the oath of allegiance to him, then I would be the first to give him my allegiance and submit to him.

O people! Obedience to a (created) human being should not involve disobedience to the Creator nor should you keep faith (with a human ruler) by breaking a covenant (with God). Obedience consists solely in obedience to God. So obey him (the caliph), in (your) obedience to God, as long as he (the caliph) obeys (God). But if he (the caliph) disobeys God and summons (you) to disobey God too, then he deserves to be disobeyed and killed. This is what I have to say and may God forgive me and you.

Then Yazīd b. al-Walīd called on the people to renew their oath of allegiance to him. The first person to do so was Yazīd b. Hishām, whose *laqab* was al-Afqam. Then Qays b. Hānī' al-ʿAbsī gave him the oath of allegiance and declared: "O Commander of the Faithful, fear God and continue to conduct yourself as you are doing now, for no member of your family has behaved as (well as) you have. If people affirm that ʿUmar b. ʿAbd al-ʿAzīz[987] (did so), (the difference is that) you obtained the caliphate by upright means,[988] whereas ʿUmar took it in a wicked way." When Marwān b. Muḥammad heard what Qays had said, he exclaimed: [1836]
"What's wrong with him? May God strike dead him who defamed us all and ʿUmar as well." (Later) when Marwān became caliph he sent somebody and said: "When you go into the mosque at Damascus, look for Qays b. Hānī'—he has been praying there for a long time—and kill him." So the man went away, entered the Damascus mosque, caught sight of Qays saying his prayers, and killed him.

In this year Yazīd b. al-Walīd dismissed Yūsuf b. ʿUmar from the governorship of Iraq and appointed Manṣūr b. Jumhūr to it.

---

987. *Fragmenta,* 151, gives an alternative *laqab,* al-Ashdaq ("having a wide mouth") for Yazīd b. Hishām. The Umayyad ʿUmar II, 99–101 (717–20) is traditionally characterized as the only pious caliph of the dynasty and the only legitimate caliph in a line of "kings." Cf. Hawting, 15.

988. The text has *bi-ḥablin ṣāliḥin. Fragmenta* has *bi-sababin ṣāliḥin* (loc. cit.).

The Dismissal of Yūsuf b. ʿUmar and the Appointment of Manṣūr b. Jumhūr (as Governor of Iraq)

When Yazīd b. al-Walīd had secured for himself the obedience of the Syrians, it was reported that he invited ʿAbd al-ʿAzīz b. Hārūn b. ʿAbdallāh b. Daḥyah b. Khalīfah al-Kalbī to be governor of Iraq. ʿAbd al-ʿAzīz said to Yazīd: "If I had a *jund,* I would accept." So Yazīd dropped the idea of choosing him[989] and appointed Manṣūr b. Jumhūr to the post.

According to Abū Mikhnaf—Hishām b. Muḥammad (al-Kalbī): Al-Walīd b. Yazīd b. ʿAbd al-Malik was killed on a Wednesday, two nights before the end of Jumādā II, 126 [Wednesday, April 15, 744], and the people gave the oath of allegiance to Yazīd b. al-Walīd b. ʿAbd al-Malik in Damascus. On the day that al-Walīd b. Yazīd was killed, Mansūr b. Jumhūr, who was the seventh (son) of seven,[990] left al-Bakhrāʾ for Iraq. When Yūsuf b. ʿUmar heard that Manṣūr was coming, he fled.[991] Manṣūr b. Jumhūr arrived in al-Ḥīrah early in Rajab [mid-April, 744].[992] He seized the treasuries and distributed the stipends to those entitled to them and (did
[1837] likewise with) the rations. Manṣūr appointed Ḥurayth b. Abī al-Jahm[993] as governor of Wāsiṭ, having gone by night to the previous governor, Muḥammad b. Nubātah,[994] imprisoning him and putting him in fetters. Manṣūr also appointed Jarīr b. Yazīd (b. Yazīd) b. Jarīr[995] as governor of al-Baṣrah. After that, Manṣūr remained there, appointing governors and receiving the oath of allegiance to Yazīd b. al-Walīd from the people in the various regions of Iraq. He stayed there for the remainder of Rajab and

989. Literally, "left him."

990. *Wa-huwa sābiʿu sābiʿatin.* On the significance of the number seven in the Islamic world, cf. F. C. Endres and A. M. Schimmel, *Das Mysterium der Zahl,* 162–66.

991. Cf. *Fragmenta,* 151; Ibn Khayyāṭ, 348; Ibn al-Athīr, V, 223.

992. Rajab 126 began on Sunday, April 19, 744.

993. Ḥurayth b. Abī al-Jahm al-Kalbī was from the subtribe of ʿĀmir. Cf. Crone, 157.

994. Muḥammad b. Nubātah al-Kilābī. For a biography of his family, cf. Crone, 152.

995. The name appears in the text as Jarīr b. Yazīd b. Yazīd b. Jarīr. This must be a mistake. One Yazīd has therefore been omitted.

during Sha'bān and Ramaḍān [April–mid-July, 744] and left a few days before the end of Ramaḍān.

According to reports other than that of Abū Mikhnaf: Manṣūr b. Jumhūr was a rough Bedouin. He was a supporter of Ghaylān and was not a man of religion. He joined Yazīd's cause only because of his Ghaylānī beliefs and out of zeal to avenge the killing of Khālid. That was also why he was present at the murder of al-Walīd. When Yazīd appointed Manṣūr as governor of Iraq, he said to him: "I have appointed you as governor of Iraq. Go there and fear God! (You should) know that I killed al-Walīd only because of his depravity and tyranny.[996] It is not fitting that you should behave in the manner that caused us to kill al-Walīd."

Then Yazīd b. Ḥajarah al-Ghassānī came in to see Yazīd b. al-Walīd. Yazīd b. Ḥajarah was a pious and virtuous man who was influential amongst the Syrians and who had fought against al-Walīd for religious reasons. He said (to Yazīd b. al-Walīd): "O Commander of the Faithful, have you appointed Manṣūr as governor of Iraq?" The caliph answered: "Yes, I have done so, because of his achievements and the valuable assistance (he gave me)." Yazīd b. Ḥajarah said: "O Commander of the Faithful, there is no one there like Manṣūr in his rough Bedouin ways and his coarseness in matters of religion." The caliph replied: "If I do not appoint Manṣūr, who has given such valuable assistance (to me), whom should I appoint?" Yazīd b. Ḥajarah said: "You should appoint someone who is God-fearing and upright, who hesitates before (judging) doubtful legal matters,[997] and who is well acquainted with the precepts and punishments (of Islam). Why is it that I don't see any of the Qays, either in attendance on you or standing at your door?" Yazīd b. al-Walīd replied: "If it were not for the fact that I want nothing to do with bloodshed I would have dealt quickly with the Qays. By God, they are strong only when Islam is weak."

When Yūsuf b. 'Umar received the news that al-Walīd had been killed, he began to seek out those of the Yamāniyyah who were in his entourage and to throw them into prison. Then he began to

---

996. Literally, "because of what he manifested in the way of tyranny."
997. *Wa-al-wuqūfi 'inda al-shubhāti.* This translation is only tentative.

speak privately to a succession of men from the Muḍariyyah and
[1838] to say to them: "What would you do if a covenant were broken or a compact were dissolved?" Each man would say in reply: "I am a Syrian. I give the oath of allegiance to the person to whom the Syrians give allegiance and I do as they do." Yūsuf did not care for their attitude, so he released those of the Yamāniyyah who were in prison. He sent word to al-Ḥajjāj b. 'Abdallāh al-Baṣrī and Manṣūr b. Naṣīr, who were aware of the situation between Yūsuf and the Syrians, and he ordered them to keep him informed by letter of what was going on. Yūsuf also posted lookouts on the road to Syria and remained in al-Ḥīrah, a prey to fear. Manṣūr approached (al-Ḥīrah) and when he was at al-Jum'[998] he wrote the following letter to Sulaymān b. Sulaym b. Kaysān:[999]

> Now for the substance of my letter. Verily, God does not change the condition of a folk until they (first) change that which is in their hearts; and if God wills a misfortune for a folk there is none than can repel it. Truly, al-Walīd b. Yazīd exchanged the blessing of God for unbelief. He shed blood, so God shed his blood and hastened his progress toward the Fire (of hell). God (then) appointed to His caliphate one who was better than al-Walīd, one who follows the right path more closely—Yazīd b. al-Walīd—and the people have already given him the oath of allegiance. Yazīd has appointed al-Ḥārith b. al-'Abbās b. al-Walīd as governor of Iraq. Al-'Abbās has sent me to seize Yūsuf and his agents and he is camped at al-Abyaḍ,[1000] which is a two days' journey behind me. So seize Yūsuf and his agents. Do not let a single one of them escape you and I will imprison them on your behalf. But beware if you oppose (this), for that would bring down upon you and your family a fate that you would be powerless to resist. So make up your mind or leave.

Other reports said that when Manṣūr was at 'Ayn al-Tamr[1001]

---

998. Al-Jum' was a castle in the Petra area, in the Jabal al-Sharāh. Cf. Yāqūt, II, 118; Le Strange, *Palestine*, 466.

999. The leader of the Syrian troops at al-Ḥīrah. Cf. Wellhausen, 368.

1000. For Qaṣr al-Abyaḍ, cf. Dussaud, 79.

1001. 'Ayn al-Tamr is a small town between Anbār and al-Kūfah eighty miles west of Karbalā'. Cf. *EI*², s.v. (S. A. El-Ali).

he wrote to those Syrian commanders who were in al-Ḥīrah informing them that al-Walīd had been killed and ordering them to seize Yūsuf and his agents. Manṣūr sent all the letters to Sulaymān b. Sulaym b. Kaysān and ordered him to distribute them to the commanders. Sulaymān took them and went in to see Yūsuf. When Sulaymān had read out to Yūsuf the letter from Manṣūr, Yūsuf was at his wit's end (as to what he should do next).[1002]

According to Ḥurayth b. Abī al-Jahm: I was staying in Wāsiṭ [1839] when the letter from Manṣūr b. Jumhūr came to me out of the blue telling me to seize Yūsuf's agents, for it was I who carried out his orders in Wāsiṭ. So I assembled my mawlās and my men and we rode, forming a group of around thirty armed men, as far as the city (of Wāsiṭ).[1003] (At once) the gatekeepers said: "Who are you?" I answered: "I am Ḥurayth b. Abī al-Jahm." Then they replied: "We swear by God that it must be an important matter if it brings Ḥurayth here." When they had opened the gate, we went inside and seized the governor, who submitted to us. The following morning we received the oath of allegiance from the people in the name of Yazīd b. al-Walīd.

According to 'Umar b. Shajarah: When 'Amr b. Muḥammad b. al-Qāsim[1004] was governor of Sind, he seized Muḥammad b. Ghazzān—or 'Izzān—al-Kalbī, and beat him. He then sent him to Yūsuf, who (also) beat him and demanded a large sum of money from him which he was to pay in installments every Friday. (Yūsuf ordered that) if Muḥammad did not do so, he would be given twenty-five lashes. (Eventually) Muḥammad's hand and some of his fingers became shriveled.[1005] When Manṣūr b. Jumhūr became governor of lraq, he appointed Muḥammad b. Ghazzān as governor of Sind and Sijistān. When Muḥammad arrived in Sijistān he took the oath of allegiance on behalf of Yazīd (from the people there). Then he advanced to Sind, where he seized 'Amr b. Muḥammad, trussed him up in fetters, and ap-

---

1002. Cf. Ibn al-Athīr, V, 223.

1003. Presumably this story only makes sense if Ḥurayth was outside the city of Wāsiṭ when he received Manṣūr's letter.

1004. 'Amr b. Muḥammad b. al-Qāsim had been appointed governor of Sind by Yūsuf b. 'Umar in 122 (739–40). Cf. Ibn Khayyāṭ, 369.

1005. The clear inference is that Muḥammad did not keep up with the payments.

pointed guards to keep watch over him. After that, as Muḥammad was rising to perform the prayer, ʿAmr seized a sword from the guards and fell on it when it was drawn so that it went right into his belly. People began shouting and Ibn Ghazzān came out and said: "What made you do what you have done?" ʿAmr replied: "I was afraid of being tortured." Ibn Ghazzān said: "I was not going to go to the extremes to which you have gone yourself." ʿAmr survived for three days and then he died. Ibn Ghazzān received the oath of allegiance on behalf of Yazīd (from the people there).

When Sulaymān b. Sulaym b. Kaysān al-Kalbī had read the letter of Manṣūr b. Jumhūr to Yūsuf b. ʿUmar, Yūsuf said to him: "What do you think I should do?" Sulaymān replied: "You do not have an *imām* on whose side you can fight. The Syrians will not fight beside you against al-Ḥārith b. al-ʿAbbās and I do not think
[1840] you are safe from Manṣūr b. Jumhūr if he takes the field against you. Your only sensible course of action is to return to your own country, Syria." Yūsuf said: "That is my view too, but how can I manage it?" Sulaymān said: "Make a public profession of obedience to Yazīd and pray for him in your sermon. Then when Manṣūr comes, I will send you off with people I can trust." When Manṣūr had camped in a place from which his men could reach the town the following morning, Yūsuf made his way to the house of Sulaymān b. Sulaym, where he remained for three days. Then Sulaymān sent men with Yūsuf to accompany him on the road to al-Samāwah until he reached al-Balqāʾ.[1006]

It is said that Sulaymān advised (Yūsuf): "You should hide and leave Manṣūr to take over the job."[1007] Yūsuf replied: "With whom (can I hide)?" Sulaymān said: "With me. I will put you in a safe place." Then Sulaymān went to ʿAmr b. Muḥammad b. Saʿīd b. al-ʿĀṣ, told him what the situation was, and asked him to grant asylum to Yūsuf. Sulaymān said to ʿAmr: "You are a man of the Quraysh and your maternal uncles are from the Bakr b. Wāʾil." So ʿAmr gave Yūsuf a place to hide.

ʿAmr said: "I have never seen a man so overweeningly proud

1006. Al-Balqāʾ is one of the districts of the province of Damascus. Its major town was ʿAmmān. Cf. Le Strange, *Palestine*, 34–35. For more details of its limits, cf. *EI*², s.v. (J. Sourdel-Thomine).

1007. Literally, "leave Manṣur and the governorship/job."

and yet so thoroughly scared as he was. I brought him a valuable slave girl and I said (to myself:) "She will warm him up and calm him down." But, by God, he did not go near her nor did he even look at her. Then one day he sent for me and I went in to see him. He said to me: "You have done very well and you have behaved admirably. But I still need one thing." I said to him: "Tell me what it is." Yūsuf said: "Get me out of al-Kūfah and back to Syria." I said I would do so. Manṣūr b. Jumhūr reached us the next morning. He referred to al-Walīd and fulminated against him; he mentioned Yazīd b. al-Walīd and praised him;[1008] he touched on Yūsuf and his tyranny. Then the preachers stood up and poured censure on al-Walīd and Yūsuf. I went to Yūsuf and I told him what these people had been saying. Whenever I mentioned one of the people who had spoken disparagingly of him he would interrupt: "It is my duty to God to give him one hundred lashes—or two or three hundred." I was amazed that he still wanted to be governor and that he was still threatening people. Sulaymān b. Sulaym left Yūsuf (for a while) and then he sent him to Syria, where he hid, before moving to al-Balqā'.[1009]

According to ʿAlī b. Muḥammad (al-Madā'inī): Yūsuf b. ʿUmar
sent a man from the Banū Kilāb with five hundred men and he [1841]
said to them: "If Yazīd b. al-Walīd comes your way, do not on any account allow him to pass." Then Manṣūr b. Jumhūr approached them with thirty men and they did not engage him in battle. He relieved them of their weapons and made them accompany him to al-Kūfah. The only people who left al-Kūfah with Yūsuf b. ʿUmar were Sufyān b. Salāmah b. Sulaym b. Kaysān, Ghassān b. Qiʿās al-ʿUdhrī, and some sixty of Yūsuf's own children, both male and female. Manṣūr entered al-Kūfah early in Rajab,[1010] took possession of the treasuries, distributed the stipends and rations, and released those agents and tax officials who were in Yūsuf's prisons. It was when Yūsuf reached al-Balqā' that Yazīd b. al-Walīd received word of his activities.

According to Aḥmad b. Zuhayr—ʿAbd al-Wahhāb b. Ibrāhīm b.

1008. The text has *fa-qarraḍahu*. This is emended by the Cairo edition (273) to *fa-qarraẓahu* ("he eulogized him"). Both versions are acceptable.

1009. Cf. Ibn al-Athīr, V, 224.

1010. Rajab 126 began on April 19, 744.

Yazīd b. Huraym—Abū Hāshim Mukhallad b. Muḥammad b. Ṣāliḥ, the mawlā of ʿUthmān b. ʿAffān—Muḥammad b. Saʿīd al-Kalbī, who was one of the commanders of Yazīd b. al-Walīd: When Yazīd received word that Yūsuf was with his family at al-Balqāʾ, he sent Muḥammad b. Saʿīd to search for Yūsuf b. ʿUmar. [Muḥammad's narrative continues:] So I set off with fifty or more horsemen and surrounded Yūsuf's house at al-Balqāʾ. We carried out a thorough search (of the house) but we could not find anything, (for) Yūsuf had put on women's clothes and was sitting with his wives and daughters. Then Muḥammad searched among the women and found him in their midst. He brought Yūsuf out in fetters and threw him into prison with the two young sons of al-Walīd. Yūsuf remained in prison for the whole period of Yazīd's caliphate and for two months and ten days of Ibrāhīm's rule. Then, when Marwān came to Syria and approached Damascus, he gave Yazīd[1011] b. Khālid the task of killing them. So Yazīd dispatched a mawlā of Khālid's, whose patronymic was Abū al-Asad,
[1842] with a number of other henchmen of his.[1012] Abū al-Asad went into the prison and battered in the heads of the two young boys with clubs and then he brought out Yūsuf b. ʿUmar and executed him.

Other reports said that when Yazīd b. al-Walīd heard that Yūsuf had reached al-Balqāʾ, he sent out fifty horsemen. Thereupon a man from the Banū Numayr[1013] came to Yūsuf and said: "By God, cousin, you are a dead man. So do as I say and put up a fight. Leave it to me and I will snatch you out of the clutches of these men." Yūsuf said: "No." So the Numayrī said: "Let me kill you then, and don't let these Yamāniyyah kill you and thus arouse our intense wrath at your murder." Yūsuf replied: "I don't have the option of either of the suggestions you have made to me." The man said: "You know best." Then they brought Yūsuf to Yazīd, who said: "What has brought you here?" Yūsuf said: "Manṣūr b. Jumhūr came to take over as governor, so I left him and the job." Yazīd replied: "No! It was you that hated (the idea of) governing

---

1011. Yazīd was the most suitable person to avenge the death of his father by killing Yūsuf.

1012. Ibn al-Athīr suppresses the details of the way in which the two sons of al-Walīd and Yūsuf met their end (V, 224).

1013. Cf. Ibn al-Kalbī, II, 450.

for me," and he then ordered that Yūsuf should be thrown into prison.

Other reports said that Yazīd summoned Muslim b. Dhakwān and Muḥammad b. Saʿīd b. Muṭarrif al-Kalbī, and he said to them: "Word has come to me that the libertine Yūsuf b. ʿUmar has reached al-Balqā'. Go and bring him to me." So they searched for him but they could not find him. Then they frightened a son of Yūsuf's into saying: "I will show you where he is," and he told them that Yūsuf had gone to an estate of his, thirty *mīl*s away. The two men took with them fifty men from the *jund* at al-Balqā' and they found Yūsuf sitting there. When he realized that they had found him, he ran away, leaving his sandals behind. The two men searched for him and they found him with some women who had thrown a silk drape over him and were sitting on the hem of it, with their heads bared. The men dragged him away by his foot while Yūsuf started imploring Muḥammad b. Saʿīd to use his good offices with the Kalb and (in return) he would pay (him) ten thousand dīnārs and the blood-money of both Kulthūm b. ʿUmayr and Hāni' b. Bishr. When Muslim and Muḥammad came to see Yazīd (with Yūsuf), an agent of Sulaymān's, who was taking his turn at guard duty, came up to Yūsuf. He grabbed Yūsuf's beard, tugged at it, and pulled some of it out; Yūsuf's stature was of the shortest, just as his beard was of the longest.[1014] Then Muslim and Muḥammad took Yūsuf in to see Yazīd, whereupon Yūsuf grabbed hold of his own beard, which at that time reached below [1843]
his navel, and said: "By God, O Commander of the Faithful, he has pulled out my beard and he has not left me a single hair of it." Then Yazīd gave orders concerning Yūsuf and he was imprisoned in the Green Palace. (Later) Muḥammad b. Rashīd went in to see Yūsuf and he asked him: "Are you not afraid that one of the people whom you have wronged will bear down on you and throw stones at you?" Yūsuf replied: "No, by God, I hadn't thought of that. I beseech you, by God, to speak to the Commander of the Faithful about moving me to a different place from this, even if it

---

1014. Literally, "he was one of the largest of men as regards beard and one of the shortest as regards stature." Cf. the marked hostility shown toward Yūsuf by Wellhausen, who calls him in the same paragraph both a goblin and a toad (op. cit., 368).

is more cramped than this one." Muḥammad b. Rashīd said: "I told Yazīd (what Yūsuf had said) and Yazīd replied: "This is just one sign of Yūsuf's foolishness. I imprisoned Yūsuf only in order to send him to Iraq, so that he should be presented to the people and so that the injustices that he has perpetrated should be put right by his own money and by his own blood."

When Yazīd b. al-Walīd had killed al-Walīd b. Yazīd and sent Manṣūr b. Jumhūr to Iraq, Yazīd b. al-Walīd wrote a letter to the people of Iraq in which he outlined the evil deeds of al-Walīd. According to Aḥmad b. Zuhayr—ʿAlī b. Muḥammad (al-Madā'inī): Some of the contents of the letter were as follows:[1015]

> God has chosen Islam as a religion; He has looked with favor upon it and has purified it. He has prescribed laws in it whereby He has laid down (what good men should do) and prohibited (men) from committing those acts that He has forbidden, so as to test the obedience or disobedience of His servants. In Islam, God has perfected every embodiment of good and the greatest of His bountiful gifts. Moreover, He took on the responsibility for it, preserving it and keeping charge of those of its people who observe its ordinances, protecting them and making known to them the excellence of Islam. Whenever God gives the blessing of the caliphate to anyone who submits to the divine command and acts according to it, and then somebody else competes with God's caliph through the medium of a covenant, or tries to give away what God has bestowed on him (the caliph) or breaks a compact, that person's perfidy is always brought to naught and his machinations are foiled[1016] until such time as God has

---

1015. This letter has recently been translated by Crone and Hinds, *God's Caliph*, 126–28. They draw attention to the version of the letter found in al-Balādhurī, *Ansāb* (MS.), fols. 170a–b, where the date of the letter is given as 28 Rajab 126/May 15, 744 and the scribe is named as Thābit b. Sulaymān b. Sa'īd (i.e., Sa'd). Crone and Hinds follow the text of al-Ṭabarī and point out only the significant variants found in al-Balādhurī's version.

1016. Literally, "God does not give the blessing of the caliphate to anyone who accepts the command of God and comes to Him, then someone (else) competes with him (the caliph) with a covenant or tries to give away what God has bestowed on him (the caliph) or a violator violates (a compact) except that that person's perfidy is most feeble and his deceit is most worthless." In 1.17, the reading *aw bi-ḥulūli ṣarfi* has been changed to *aw yuḥāwilu ṣarfa mā*, following the Cairo edition (VII, 275). This is based on a variant in the apparatus.

finished giving His gifts to the caliph, and bestowed on him His reward and the recompense which He has kept in store for him, whilst He makes his enemy lose his way totally and frustrates all his efforts.

The caliphs of God succeeded each other as guardians of His religion, passing judgement therein by His ordinance and [1844] following therein His book. Because of that they had an abundance of blessings (heaped) upon them as a result of God's friendship and His assistance;[1017] and God was pleased with His caliphs in that office[1018] until the time when Hishām died. Then the command passed to the enemy of God, al-Walīd, the violator of sacred things such as no Muslim would ever approach and toward which (even) an infidel would not venture, but rather avoid going near their like.[1019] When (the news of) that behavior of his spread abroad and became publicly known, when the affliction he caused worsened, blood was shed because of him, possessions were unlawfully seized, and acts of profligacy were committed which God will condone only for a little while in those who commit them, I went to al-Walīd, expecting that he would return (to the right path), whilst excusing myself in the sight of God and the Muslims,[1020] repudiating al-Walīd's activities and the flagrant way in which he had disobeyed God, and seeking from God the fulfillment of what I purposed; namely,[1021] to restore the pillars of religion and to adopt for His people that which is pleasing to Him.

1017. Literally, "because of that, they had from His friendship and help that which completed the blessings upon them."

1018. *Al-amru.* Crone and Hinds have "office" (loc. cit.).

1019. *Tukarruman ʿan.* This presumably applies to both the Muslim and non-Muslim.

1020. *Sirtu ilayhi maʿa intiẓāri murājaʿatihi wa iʿdhārin ilā Allāhi wa-ilā al-Muslimīna munkiran li-ʿamalihi. . .* Crone and Hinds have: "I went to him with the expectation that he would mend his ways and apologize to God and to the Muslims, disavowing his behavior. . . ." (loc. cit.). An alternative translation could read: "I went to him with the expectation that he would return (to the right path) and *excusing myself* to God and the Muslims, rejecting his activities." The interpretation here is based on the premise that Yazīd, not al-Walīd, is apologizing to God and the Muslims and that he (Yazīd) is dissociating himself with al-Walīd's profligate activities.

1021. Literally, "the fulfillment of that which I purposed consisting of the restoring. . . ."

Then I came across a *jund* whose breasts seethed with wrath at the enemy of God because of the way they had seen him behaving—for truly, whenever the enemy of God encountered one of the ordinances of Islām he wanted to change it and to act in respect of it in a manner that was contrary to God's revelation. (All) that (conduct) on his part was known to all and comprehensive in scope;[1022] it was in full view (of everyone), for God had drawn no veil over it, nor was anybody in any doubt about it. Then I mentioned to the *jund* what I abominated and feared, which was the corruption of both religion and worldly affairs. So I roused them to restore and defend their religion. They vacillated in this, fearing that they would only be saving themselves by the action they would be taking. Then I summoned them to put the matter right and they hastened to answer my call. God sent a group of them, men who were pious and pleasing (to Him), to inform the rest[1023] and I sent ʿAbd al-ʿAzīz b. al-Ḥajjāj b. ʿAbd al-Malik to be in charge of them. He met the enemy of God near a village called al-Bakhrāʾ. They called upon al-Walīd to agree that the matter should be referred to a *shūrā* in which the Muslims should decide for themselves whom they would agree to appoint to rule (over them). The enemy of God would not agree to that and opted only to sink deeper into error. He was the first to launch an attack on them in ignorance of
[1845] God, but he found God a mighty judge and His grip agonizingly painful. God killed al-Walīd because of his evildoing and He killed a group of his followers—they did not number as many as ten—who were companions of his and

---

1022. *Shāmilan.* Crone and Hinds have "generally" (loc. cit.).

1023. The text has *fa-ibtaʿatha Allāhu minhum baʿthan yukhbiruhum man/min awlā al-dīni wa-al-riḍā.* This is very unsatisfactory. It is possible to render it as "God sent a group of them to inform them (the others), those (*man*) possessed of religion and what is pleasing to God," with *man awlā al-dīni wa-al-riḍā* in apposition to *baʿthan.* This is certainly the inference of the punctuation of the Cairo edition (VII, 276). Alternatively, if *min* is read instead of *man,* a possible translation would be: "God sent a group of them to inform them (the others), (a group) consisting of those possessed of religion and what is pleasing." Crone and Hinds emend *yukhbiruhum* to *bi-khayrihim,* which makes good sense (loc. cit.). Their translation thus reads: "God sent a deputation made up of the best of those possessed of religion and what is pleasing."

came from the depraved inner circle of his intimates. The remainder of al-Walīd's associates agreed to follow the right path to which they had been summoned. Thus God extinguished his fire and granted His servants relief from him. A curse on him and those who follow in his way!

I wanted to tell you (all) this and to notify you quickly about it so that you might give praise and thanks to God, for you have today reached the best possible situation for yourself (in view of the fact that) your governors are the best people from amongst you and justice has opened wide its arms to you and you will not be ruled in any other way than this. On that account, therefore, praise your Lord all the more and follow[1024] Manṣūr b. Jumhūr, for I have selected him for you on the basis that God's covenant and compact and the culmination of what has been promised and laid down for any of His creatures are binding upon you. So heed and obey me and those whom I shall appoint to succeed me and on whom the community has agreed. I have a similar duty toward you. I shall certainly deal with you according to the ordinance of God and the *sunnah* of His prophet, and I shall follow in the path of the best of your predecessors. We ask God, our Lord and our Guardian, to favor us most generously with His assistance and the best of His decree.

In this year Naṣr b. Sayyār refused to give up his post to the agent of Manṣūr b. Jumhūr after Yazīd b. al-Walīd had appointed Manṣūr to govern Khurāsān together with Iraq. According to Abū Ja'far al-Ṭabarī himself: I have already given some account of Naṣr. (I mentioned) what happened about the letter of Yūsuf b. 'Umar to Naṣr in which he instructed Naṣr to bring him the tribute for al-Walīd b. Yazīd and to go in person from Khurāsān to Iraq; and (I mentioned) how Naṣr traveled slowly and how he then received the news of al-Walīd's murder.

According to 'Alī b. Muḥammad (al-Madā'inī)—al-Bāhilī: Bishr b. Nāfi', the mawlā of Sālim al-Laythī who was in charge of coinage in Iraq, came to Naṣr. Bishr said: "When Manṣūr b. Jumhūr [1846]

1024. The text has *tābi'ū*. Crone and Hinds follow al-Balādhurī, who has *bayi'ū* (loc. cit.).

came as *amīr* of Iraq, Yūsuf b. ʿUmar fled. Manṣūr sent his brother Manẓūr b. Jumhūr[1025] as governor of al-Rayy[1026] and I accompanied him there. Then I said (to myself): "I will go to Naṣr and tell him (what is going on)." When I reached Nīshāpūr,[1027] Ḥumayd, Naṣr's mawlā, threw me into prison and said: "You will not get out of here until you tell me (why you are here)." So I told him and I made him swear by God's oath and covenant that he would not tell anyone until I had reached Naṣr and informed him, so Ḥumayd did that. Then we all went to Naṣr, who was in his citadel in Mājān. We asked permission to go in and see him, but a eunuch of his said that Naṣr was asleep. We pressed him further and he went off and told Naṣr. Naṣr came out and grabbed my hand and took me inside. He did not say anything to me until we were inside the room. Then he asked me (why I had come) and I told him. Naṣr said to Ḥumayd, his mawlā: "Take him away and give him a present." Then Yūnus b. ʿAbd Rabbihi[1028] and ʿUbaydallāh b. Bassām came to me and I told them (the news). Salm b. Aḥwaz (also) came to me and I told him.

(Bishr's narrative continues.) Al-Walīd b. Yūsuf was with Naṣr. When Naṣr heard the news, Naṣr kept al-Walīd with him. Al-Walīd sent people to me and when I had told them the news[1029] they called me a liar. So I said (to Naṣr): "You should get these men to confirm (what they say)." After three days had passed

1025. Manẓūr b. Jumhūr was later murdered in India by Rifāʿah b. Thābit al-Judhāmī. Rifāʿah was seized by Manṣūr b. Jumhūr and walled up alive in a pillar. Cf. al-Ṭabarī, II, 1895; al-Yaʿqūbī, *Historiae,* II, 407; Crone, 159.

1026. Al-Rayy was an important city of the province of Jibāl, which stood near the site of modern Tehran. Cf. Le Strange, *Lands,* 214–17; al-Yaʿqūbī, *Les Pays,* 79–80; Schwarz, 446–48, 740–83.

1027. Nīshāpūr was one of the four great cities of Khurāsān. Cf. Le Strange, *Lands,* 382–88; Barthold, *Historical Geography,* 95–102.

1028. For a discussion of Naṣr's relationship with Yūnus b. ʿAbd Rabbihi, another of his mawlās, cf. Crone, 53.

1029. This is rather an obscure narrative, which seems to be in no other source. A literal translation would be: "he made him stay (*aqarrahu*) when the news reached him; then he sent (people) to me, and when I told them, they called me a liar, so I said: 'Seek confirmation (*istawthiq*) from these people.'" A possible sequence of events here is that Naṣr kept Yūsuf's son with him. Al-Walīd b. Yūsuf sent some of his associates to Bishr. They tried to refute the news that Bishr told them—namely that al-Walīd was dead and Yūsuf b. ʿUmar had fled. Bishr then told Naṣr to make the others confirm the truth of what they had said. The emended version of this passage in the Cairo edition (VII, 277) is of no use.

Naṣr posted eighty men to guard me. The news was slower to arrive than I had expected. Then on the ninth night, which was the night of Nawrūz,[1030] the news reached them, confirming what I had already told them. Naṣr publicly sent me most of the tribute (intended for al-Walīd)[1031] and he ordered that I should be given a horse with its saddle and bridle. He (also) gave me a Chinese saddle and he said to me: "Stay on so that I can give you a full hundred thousand (dirhams)."

When Naṣr was sure that al-Walīd had been killed, he gave back that tribute (intended for al-Walīd), freed the slaves, divided up the pick of the slave girls amongst his sons and his close associates, distributed those vases amongst the common people,[1032] and sent out governors, ordering them to act honorably. (Bishr's narrative continues.) The Banū Azd in Khurāsān caused turmoil by spreading false rumors[1033] that Manẓūr b. Jumhūr was coming [1847] there. Then Naṣr preached a sermon in which he said: "If a suspect *amīr* comes to us, we will cut off his hands and his feet." After that, Naṣr revealed the man's name, calling him ʿAbdallāh, the deserted one, the mutilated one.[1034]

Naṣr appointed (governors) over the Banū Rabīʿah and the Yamāniyyah. Naṣr made Yaʿqūb b. Yaḥyā b. Ḥuḍayn governor of upper Ṭukhāristān and appointed Masʿadah b. ʿAbdallāh al-Yashkirī to rule over Khwārazm.[1035] Khalaf recited the following verses about Masʿadah:[1036]

When I am close to Kardar I say to my companions,

1030. Nawrūz is the first day of the Persian solar year, which now occurs at the vernal equinox. It was also in earlier times deemed to be at the midsummer solstice. For a discussion of the history of the dating of Nawrūz, cf. *EI*[1], s.v. (R. Levy).

1031. *Al-hadāyā.* Cf. n. 574.

1032. *Ibid.*

1033. *Wa-arjafat al-Azdu. Arjafa,* "to cause agitation in others by spreading false rumors." Cf. Lane, I, 1042.

1034. *Thumma bāḥa bihi baʿdu fa-kāna yaqūlu ʿAbda Allāhi al-makhdhūla al mabtūra* ("then he revealed it after that and he would say ʿAbdallāh, the deserted one, the mutilated one"). These imprecations were no doubt intended as a warning to anyone who wanted to take Khurāsān from Naṣr. The Cairo edition (VII, 278) has *al-mathbūr* ("overcome") for *al-mabtūr.*

1035. Khwārazm was the province lying along the lower course of the Oxus. Cf. *EI*[2], s.v. (C. E. Bosworth).

1036. The meter is *ṭawīl.*

"Truly Mas'adah al-Bakrī is the reviving rain supplicated
by widows."

Then Naṣr appointed Abān b. al-Ḥakam al-Zahrānī (in place of Mas'adah) and he appointed al-Mughīrah b. Shu'bah al-Jahḍamī as governor of Quhistān.[1037] Naṣr ordered his governors to behave uprightly. He summoned the people to give the oath of allegiance, which they did. In this connection a poet recited (the following lines):[1038]

I declare to Naṣr, having pledged allegiance to him
against most of the (Banū) Bakr and their allies,
My hand is surety for you against the Bakr of Iraq,
against their leader and the son of the most distinguished one amongst them.
I (You)[1039] have given assurance to the Muslims,
to the people of the (Muslim) lands near and far
(That) whenever we exceed[1040] your desire,
Swift, light-footed camels will make their way to you.
You have called upon the troops to give allegiance (to you),
and you were absolutely in the right to do so.[1041]
You have safeguarded Khurāsān for the Muslims
when the earth was about to convulse.
And when the Muslims were restored to mutual harmony,
you lavished money on those who composed their differences.
You have granted[1042] protection and security to the people of the towns
and to those settled on their borders;

1037. A number of areas were called Quhistān ("the mountain country"). The district meant here is Quhistān-i Khurāsān, the mountainous region that stretches south from Nīshāpūr to Sīstān. Cf. Le Strange, *Lands*, 352–63; *EI*[2], s.v. (J. H. Kramers).

1038. The meter is *mutaqārib*.

1039. The text has *akhadhtu*. It would make better sense if it is read as *akhadhta*.

1040. The text has *idhā lā tujību ilā mā turīdu*. This is later emended to *idhā mā nuzīdu*. Cf. *Emend.*, p. DCCXIII.

1041. This hemistich seems to be in the wrong place. An alternative translation might be "and you treated all of them with absolute justice."

1042. This line seems also to be in the wrong place and it is difficult to determine the subject of *ajāra*.

And to the soldiers in both east and west you have become
a milch-camel, its udders overflowing with milk for them.
We will remain in that situation[1043] [1848]
until the paths to be followed become clear to the pathfinders,
And until the Quraysh have revealed that which
is hidden in the depths of their hearts.
I have sworn that it is better for the
grazing-camels who make journeys to be stripped of their wool,[1044]
And added to what is paid by those of the Quraysh who live in the valleys,[1045]
first those of noble birth and then the base-born.[1046]
If he who becomes powerful robs the weak,
we will beat their horses on their manes.
We have found fodder, no matter what its source,
which the horses feed on once it has been heated up for them.
As long as they have a share in it, their
flanks will become heavy (with fat), when formerly they were lean.
We continue as before to maintain our support for
the Quraysh, and we are content with their allies;
We shall be satisfied to have your power as a place of refuge for them,
for your power is their bulwark.
Perhaps the Quraysh, when they vie amongst themselves,
will hit some[1047] of their targets,
And they will overwhelm the plotters in Iraq
who have up-ended the bucket from the east by its hooks.

1043. This line also does not fit here. The meaning seems to be "we will remain loyal to you."

1044. The text has *li'l-ghazwi*. This is emended by the editor to *lal'urwu*. Cf. *Emend.*, p. DCCXIII. The Cairo edition (VII, 279) follows this correction.

1045. Literally, "the Quraysh of the valleys."

1046. Literally, "their low-ranking men after their high-born ones."

1047. The text has a lacuna here: *tuqarṭisu . . . fī ahdāfihā*. The Cairo edition (VII, 279) has *tuqarṭisu fī ba'ḍi ahdāfihā*.

Indeed, we are like lions,[1048] and lions are endowed with
manes above their shoulders.
If they scatter in fright, fearing destruction,
(they will find that) the vicissitudes of time are yet closer
to them (in destruction).
For your sake we have remained steadfast (in battle)[1049]
when their ranks crumbled and collapsed.[1050]
We have found you to be benevolent and kind to us,
showing us the tender loving kindness of a mother.
Our allegiance to you was not a passing whim
to be rescinded at the earliest opportunity,
Like a young girl who rushed to meet her (intended) husband,
before her fingers had been dyed
And who was unveiled by the bridegroom before the marriage
contract had been drawn up,
and who therefore encountered him with aversion.

[1849] Naṣr had appointed ʿAbd al-Malik b. ʿAbdallāh al-Sulamī as governor of Khwārazm. ʿAbd al-Malik used to preach to the people there and in his sermon he would say: "I am neither a rough Bedouin nor a Fazārī[1051] who follows the ways of the Nabateans.[1052] Circumstances have favored me and I have taken full advantage of them. Verily, by God, I shall certainly use the sword where appropriate and the whip where appropriate, and I shall throw open the prison (to be used). You will assuredly find me extremely harsh in crushing any dissension. Either you will go undeviatingly along the same road as me, galloping like a young camel on the widest of paths, or I shall certainly strike you in the way a lynx-eyed man strikes water birds,[1053] striking them first on one side and then on the other."

1048. The translation is only tentative. The Cairo edition (loc. cit.) has *wa-bi-al-usdi minnā* ("and with lions of ours").

1049. Literally, "by you our feet have remained firm."

1050. Literally, "when their banks collapse."

1051. For the Banū Fazārah, a North Arabian tribe, cf. *EI*², s.v. (W. M. Watt).

1052. For the pre-Islamic Aramaic-speaking Arab people, the Nabataeans (*al-Anbāṭ*), cf. *EI*¹, s.v. (E. Honigmann). During the Islamic period the term *Nabataean* in the mouth of Arabs was one of abuse. Cf. the long discussion in Goldziher, I, 145.

1053. *Al-qāriba* "water birds." Cf. *Gloss.*, p. CDXIX.

(One day) a man of the Balqayn turned up in Khurāsān at the behest of Manṣūr b. Jumhūr. A mawlā of Naṣr's called Ḥumayd, who was in charge of coinage[1054] in Nīshāpūr, seized him, beat him, and broke his nose. The man complained to Naṣr, who ordered twenty thousand (dirhams) to be given to him and presented him with a set of clothes. Naṣr said: "The person who broke your nose is a mawlā of mine. He is not a social equal, so that I may take retaliation from him on your behalf. So don't complain any more."[1055] Then ʿIṣmah b. ʿAbdallāh al-Asadī said: "Brother from the Balqayn, broadcast what manner of man it is that you have come to see. We have lined up the Qays for the Rabīʿah, and the Tamīm for the Azd. Only the Kinānah do not have anyone to equal them!" Naṣr retorted: "Whenever I have put a matter right you ruin it."

According to Abū Zayd ʿUmar b. Shabbah—Aḥmad b. Muʿāwiyah—Abū al-Khaṭṭāb: Qudāmah b. Muṣʿab al-ʿAbdī and a man from the Banū Kindah came to Naṣr b. Sayyār on behalf of Manṣūr b. Jumhūr. Naṣr said: "Is the Commander of the Faithful (really) dead?" They said: "Yes." Then Naṣr asked: "And Manṣūr b. Jumhūr has been made governor of Iraq and Yūsuf b. ʿUmar has relinquished control of Iraq?"[1056] The two men confirmed that this was so. Then Naṣr said: "We have no faith in what you lot have said."[1057] Thereupon Naṣr imprisoned both the men but he allowed them ample living space. Naṣr (then) dispatched a man who, when he got to al-Kūfah, saw Manṣūr preaching. Then Naṣr released the two men and said to Qudāmah: "Has a man from the Banū Kalb been appointed as governor over you?" Qudāmah re- [1850]
plied: "Yes. We are only from the Qays and the Yamāniyyah." So Naṣr said: "Why isn't one of you appointed as governor (of Iraq)?" Qudāmah said: "Because it is with us as the poet said:

If ever we fear any tyranny from a ruler,
we call on Abū Ghassān and he comes to the rescue with his troops.

1054. *Sikak.* This is rather ambiguous, since it can mean either the engraved pieces of metal used for stamping coins or streets.

1055. Literally, "so do not say anything but good."

1056. Literally, "has fled from the throne of Iraq."

1057. *Innanā bi-jumhūrikum min al-kāfirīna.*

Naṣr laughed and attached Qudāmah to his retinue.

When Manṣūr b. Jumhūr reached Iraq, he either appointed 'Ubaydallāh b. al-'Abbās as governor of al-Kūfah, or he found him already ensconced as governor there and confirmed him in the post.[1058] Manṣūr put Thumāmah b. Ḥawshab in charge of his *shurṭah*. Later on he dismissed him and appointed al-Ḥajjāj b. Arṭāh al-Nakha'ī.[1059]

In this year Marwān b. Muḥammad wrote to al-Ghamr b. Yazīd, the brother of al-Walīd b. Yazīd, ordering him to avenge the blood of his brother al-Walīd.

The Text of Marwān's Letter to al-Ghamr

According to Aḥmad (b. Zuhayr)—'Alī (b. Muḥammad al-Madā'inī): Marwān wrote to al-Ghamr b. Yazīd as follows:

> Now to the point. Truly this caliphate is from God and follows the paths laid down by the prophethood[1060] of His messengers and the establishment of the precepts of His religion. God has blessed the caliphs by that with which He has invested them, honoring them (thereby) and honoring those who honor them. May destruction fall on anyone who vies with His caliphs and who seeks to follow a path different from theirs! The caliphs have continued to be trustees of what God has set apart for them in the caliphate, with one after another of them appearing[1061] to conduct its affairs justly, with the help of those Muslims who support it.
>
> Of (all) God's creatures, the Syrians were the most obedient to Him, the most zealous to defend His sacred ordinances, the most faithful in keeping His covenant,[1062] and the most severe in destroying anyone who deviated from, opposed, obliterated, and strayed from the truth. God's bounty flowed copiously upon them, Islam flourished through them, and

1058. On 'Ubaydallāh cf. Crone, 152.

1059. Cf. his biography in Crone, 157. He later became the *kātib* to the 'Abbāsid caliph, al-Manṣūr. Cf. al-Ṭabarī, III, 276, 322.

1060. Literally, "on the basis of the paths of prophethood."

1061. Literally, "one riser after (another) riser performs."

1062. The text has "a covenant."

polytheism and its followers were brought low by them. But (recently) they have violated God's command and tried to violate His covenants. For that reason there came forward someone to fan the flames (of *fitnah*),[1063] even though men's hearts had turned away from him.[1064] Those who (now) seek [1851] (vengeance for) the blood of the caliph[1065] are the (true) leaders of the Banū Umayyah, for his (al-Walīd's) blood will not have been shed in vain, even though discord has been stilled by them (the rebels) and public affairs have been restored to good order.[1066] For there is no opposing what God has willed.

You have written (telling me) about your situation and your opinion on what they have done. I will remain silent until I think the moment is right for a rebellion,[1067] and then I will attack in vengeance, and I will avenge God's religion which has been persecuted and His precepts which have been abandoned as if they were of no value.[1068] I have a group of men whose hearts God has made obedient to me; they are people who are daring enough for what I have in mind for them to do. There are (also) other people like them, whose hearts are full to overflowing and look only to find an opportunity (for revenge). Retribution has its auspicious moment and appointed time from God.[1069] I would not be worthy of

---

1063. *Man ash'ala ḍirāmaha.* The reference is presumably to *fitnah* ("discord"), which, however, has not been explicitly mentioned, and to Yazīd's rebellion.

1064. *Wa-in kānat al-qulūbu 'anhu nāfiratun* ("although hearts had turned away from him"). This is rather obscure. It is more probable that the people would have turned away from al-Walīd, whose behavior had alienated them, than from Yazīd, who stepped forward to oppose him. However, it may simply mean that Yazīd was not in the public eye until he rebelled. Alternatively, *'anhu* could refer to God.

1065. I.e., al-Walīd.

1066. Another possible translation of this might be: "Those demanding the blood of the caliph (i.e., al-Walīd's murderers) are the leaders of the Banū Umayyah. But [instead of 'for' (*fa-inna*)] his blood will not have been shed in vain, even though discord has been stilled by them and public affairs have been restored to good order."

1067. *Ghiyaran.* Cf. *Gloss.*, p. CCCXCIV.

1068. The text has *antaqimu li-dīni Allāhi al-matbūlī wa-farā'iḍihi al-matrūkati majjānatan.* The Cairo edition (VII, 281) has "I am exacting vengeance for God's religion, whose precepts have been cast aside (*al-manbūthati*), and which has been abandoned as valueless (*majjānatan*)." *Majjān* is not usually feminine.

1069. Literally, "vengeance has its turning which comes from God and an appointed time."

the name[1070] of Muḥammad or Marwān if, when I saw a rebellion, I did not exert myself to the utmost against the Qadariyyah and if I did not strike them with my sword, wounding and stabbing them, with God's decree ordaining what He wills therein and visiting His punishment on those whom He chooses to punish.[1071] I am remaining silent only because of what I am expecting to come from you, so do not be too feeble to exact blood vengeance for your brother, for truly God is your protection and your sufficiency and God's will and help are sufficient.

According to Aḥmad (b. Zuhayr)—ʿAlī b. Muḥammad (al-Madāʾinī)—ʿAmr b. Marwān al-Kalbī—Muslim b. Dhakwān: Yazīd b. al-Walīd spoke to al-ʿAbbās b. al-Walīd about Ṭufayl b. Ḥārithah al-Kalbī, saying that Ṭufayl had incurred a bloodwit and had asked al-ʿAbbās if he would write to Marwān b. Muḥammad interceding for Ṭufayl with him, so that Marwān would allow Ṭufayl to ask his kinsfolk for it. (It so happened that) Marwān b. Muḥammad used to prevent people from drawing from the stipend fund for that purpose.[1072] Now al-ʿAbbās agreed to do as Yazīd asked and he deposited the letter with the postal service. The letter of al-ʿAbbās with its full contents reached the most far-flung areas (of the empire). Then Yazīd (also) wrote to Marwān, saying that he had made a transaction to buy[1073] an estate for eighteen thousand dīnārs from Abū ʿUbaydah b. al-Walīd and that he needed (an extra) four thousand dīnārs.

[1852] According to Muslim b. Dhakwān: Yazīd called me and said: "Go with Ṭufayl taking these letters with you and discuss this matter with him." So we went off, without al-ʿAbbās knowing that I had gone, and when we reached Khilāṭ[1074] we met ʿAmr b.

1070. Literally, "I would not resemble Muḥammad or Marwān." Muḥammad was his father and Marwān his grandfather.

1071. Here, the Cairo edition (VII, 282) adds *bī* after *qaḍāʾu Allāhi* and *bihim* after *yarmī:* "whatever God's decree ordains therein for me or whatever punishment He inflicts on those whom He chooses to punish."

1072. Literally, "prevent people from asking for any of that with the stipend."

1073. *Ishtarā.* Presumably the transaction had not yet been completed, as Yazīd needed four thousand more dīnārs.

1074. Khilāṭ (Akhlāṭ) is a town at the northwestern corner of Lake Van (in modern Turkey). Cf. *EI*², "Akhlāṭ" (V. Minorsky).

Ḥārithah al-Kalbī. He asked us how we were and we told him, whereupon he said: "You are lying! There is something going on between you two and Marwān." We said: "What could that be?" Then when I wanted to leave, 'Amr took me aside and said to me: "Do the people of al-Mizzah number one thousand?" I said: "More (than that)." Then 'Amr said: "How far is it between al-Mizzah and Damascus?" I replied: "Within hailing distance." He then inquired: "At what do you estimate the numbers of the Banū 'Āmir to be" (meaning the Banū 'Āmir of Kalb)? I said: "Twenty thousand men." Then 'Amr moved his finger (to indicate that I should leave) and turned his face away.

(Muslim's narrative continues:) When I heard that, I wanted (to see) Marwān, and I wrote him the following letter purporting to come from Yazīd: "Now to the point of my letter. I have sent Ibn Dhakwān, my mawlā, to you, on a matter that he will mention to you and put before you. So say what you like to him, for he is one of the best of my associates and the most trustworthy of my mawlās. He will be a trusty person and a reliable confidant, if God wills." Then we came to Marwān and Ṭufayl gave the letter from al-'Abbās to the chamberlain. Ṭufayl told the chamberlain that he had with him the letter from Yazīd b. al-Walīd and he read it (out). The chamberlain came out and said: "Do you have any letter other than this one with you? Did he entrust you with any message?" Ṭufayl replied:[1075] "No, but I do have Muslim b. Dhakwān with me." Then the chamberlain went in and told Marwān. He emerged (again) and said: "Order the mawlā of al-'Abbās to go away."

(Muslim's narrative continued:) So I went away, and when the time came for the dusk prayer I made my way to the *maqṣūrah*. When Marwān (had) performed the prayer, I left to say the prayer a second time, for I did not put any value on Marwān's prayer. When I straightened up in the prayer a eunuch came up to me, and after he had scrutinized me he made off. I shortened my prayer and caught up with him. He took me in to see Marwān, who was in one of the women's rooms. I greeted him and sat down. Then Marwān inquired: "Who are you?" I replied: "Muslim b. Dhakwān, the mawlā of Yazīd." Marwān said: "Are you a [1853]

1075. Reading *qāla* for *qultu*.

manumitted mawlā or a voluntarily commended (*tibā'ah*) mawlā?"[1076] I replied: "A manumitted one". Marwān said: "That is better. There is merit in both kinds. Now tell me whatever you want." Then I said: "It is up to the *amīr* to guarantee my personal safety no matter what I say, whether I agree with him or disagree," and he granted my request. Then I praised God and prayed for His prophet. I described how God had graciously bestowed the caliphate on the Banū Marwān and how the common people had been satisfied with them. (I then mentioned) how al-Walīd had broken covenants and corrupted the people's hearts and how the common folk poured censure upon him. I told Marwān everything about al-Walīd and when I had finished, Marwān began to speak. By God, he did not give praise to God nor did he recite the *shahādah*. He merely said: "I have heard what you have said. You have done well and your words have struck home. The judgment of Yazīd is best. I call God to witness that I have given the oath of allegiance to Yazīd (al-Walīd), freely expending my efforts and my money in this matter and only desiring thereby my due from God. By God, I could not have asked for more from al-Walīd. Indeed, he honored kinship and delegated authority to us and let us share in his rule,[1077] but I testify that he did not believe in the Day of Reckoning." Then Marwān asked me how Yazīd was and I magnified and exaggerated the situation. Marwān said: "Hide your business here. I have satisfied your friend's need, have discharged for him the matter of his bloodwit, and have ordered that he be given one thousand dirhams." I stayed on for a few days, and then one day Marwān summoned me at noon and instructed me: "Go to your friend and say to him: 'May God direct you on the right path! Go ahead as God has commanded, for you are in God's sight.'" Then Marwān wrote an answer to my letter and he said to me: "If you can travel without stopping or fly, then fly, for there will be a rebellion in the Jazīrah within six or seven days, and I am afraid that it will be a protracted affair[1078] and you will

1076. Clientage was known as *walā'*. It arose either on *'itāqah* (manumission) or *tibā'ah* (voluntary commendation). Cf. Crone, 49, 236–37.

1077. *Laqad waṣala wa-fawwaḍa wa-ashraka fī mulkihi.* The translation is tentative, taking *waṣala* to mean "to keep close family ties," *fawwaḍa* as "to delegate," and *ashraka* as "to give a share."

1078. Literally, "a rebel will rebel in the Jazīrah within six or seven days and I am afraid that their affair will become protracted."

not be able to get through." I asked Marwān: "What does the *amīr* know about this?" Marwān laughed and said: "I satisfy all those with deviant views so that they will tell me their secret intentions."[1079] I said to myself: "I am one of those people"; then I remarked (to Marwān): "If you have done that, God will set you aright. Indeed, the following story was told about Khālid b. Yazīd b. Mu'āwiyah, who said: 'I obtained this information (in the fol- [1854]
lowing way). I went along with the people in their erroneous ideas and shared their sentiments with them until they divulged to me what they were thinking and passed on to me their innermost thoughts.'"

(Muslim's narrative continues:) Then I took my leave of Marwān and departed. When I got as far as Āmid,[1080] I met a succession of postal couriers (who reported) al-Walīd's murder and that 'Abd al-Malik b. Marwān had attacked al-Walīd's agent in the Jazīrah and driven him out of the area, and that he had placed scouts on the road. Then I left the postal couriers, hired a riding-animal and a guide, and came back to Yazīd b. al-Walīd.

In this year Yazīd b. al-Walīd dismissed Manṣūr b. Jumhūr from (his post as governor of) Iraq, appointing in his place 'Abdallāh b. 'Umar b. 'Abd al-'Azīz b. Marwān.

The Dismissal of Manṣūr b. Jumhūr from the Post of Governor of Iraq

It is reported that Yazīd b. al-Walīd said to 'Abdallāh b. 'Umar b. 'Abd al-'Azīz:[1081] "The people of Iraq have shown themselves to be well disposed to your father. So go there. I have appointed you governor of Iraq."

According to Abū 'Ubaydah: 'Abdallāh b. 'Umar was a pious man who was in bad health.[1082] When he came to Iraq he personally sent out messengers and letters to the Syrian commanders

1079. Literally, "there are no people of erroneous opinions (*ahli hawā*) except that I give them satisfaction until they have told me their secret intentions."

1080. The well-known city of the province of Diyār Bakr, now known in modern Turkey as Diyarbakir. It stands on the left bank of the Tigris. Cf. *EI*², "Diyār Bakr" (M. Canard and C. Cahen).

1081. The son of the Umayyad caliph 'Umar II. For the dismissal of Manṣūr b. Jumhūr and the appointment of 'Abdallāh b. 'Umar b. 'Abd al-'Azīz, cf. Ibn al-Athīr, V, 228–29; *Fragmenta*, 152–53.

1082. *Muta'allimun. Ta'allama:* "to be in pain."

who were in Iraq, for he was afraid that Manṣūr b. Jumhūr would not surrender the post to him. All the commanders submitted to his authority and Manṣūr b. Jumhūr handed over (the post) to him and left for Syria. Then 'Abdallāh b. 'Umar appointed his own agents to office and issued the people with their rations and their stipends. Then the Syrian commanders began to dispute with him and said: "You are distributing our *fay'* to these people, yet they are our enemy." 'Abdallāh said to the people of Iraq: "I wanted to return your *fay'* to you, for I knew that you were more entitled to
[1855] it. (Now) these men have disputed with me and found fault with me." Then the people of al-Kūfah went out to the *jabbānah* and mobilized (there). The Syrian commanders sent messengers to them, making excuses and denying (their own words) outright and swearing that they had not said any of the things that the Kūfans had heard. Then a mixed rabble of men rose up from both sides and began stabbing each other with spears, and a small group of them were killed. These were not identified. 'Abdallāh b. 'Umar was in al-Ḥīrah and 'Ubaydallāh b. al-'Abbās al-Kindī was in al-Kūfah. Manṣūr b. Jumhūr had appointed him as his deputy in the city and the people of al-Kūfah wanted to drive him out of the citadel. So 'Ubaydallāh sent word to 'Umar b. al-Ghaḍbān b. al-Qaba'tharī,[1083] who came to him, kept the people away from him, calmed them down, and rebuked them until they had dispersed peaceably with one another.[1084] When 'Abdallāh b. 'Umar heard about this he sent for Ibn al-Ghaḍbān, gave him a set of clothes and a beast to ride,[1085] rewarded him generously, and put him in charge of his *shurṭah* and the *kharāj* of the Sawād. He also entrusted him with the auditing[1086] and ordered him to assign a portion (in the *dīwān*) to his family, so he assigned (them) sixty or seventy (dirhams).

In this year discord broke out in Khurāsān between the Yamāniyyah and the Nizāriyyah, and al-Kirmānī[1087] rose up in opposition to Naṣr b. Sayyār. A group of supporters rallied to each of them.

1083. 'Umar b. al-Ghaḍbān al-Shaybānī. For a discussion of the activities of his father, al-Ghaḍbān, and himself, cf. Crone, 162.

1084. Literally, "some of them felt safe from others."

1085. *Wa-ḥamalahu.* Cf. Lane, I, 647. Cf. also Qur'ān 9, v. 92.

1086. *Al-muḥāsabāt.*

1087. Juday' al-Kirmānī of the Banū Azd had been the general of Asad al-Qasrī, governor of Khurāsān, who, after al-Ḥārith b. Surayj had been driven back across

The Discord between Naṣr and al-Kirmānī and What Had Caused It

According to ʿAlī b. Muḥammad (al-Madāʾinī)—his *shaykhs*: When ʿAbdallāh b. ʿUmar came to Iraq as its governor on behalf of Yazīd b. al-Walīd, he wrote to Naṣr appointing him as governor of Khurāsān.

According to another report: ʿAbdallāh's letter reached Naṣr after al-Kirmānī had escaped from Naṣr's prison.[1088] The astrologers said to Naṣr: "There will be discord in Khurāsān." So Naṣr gave orders that the remaining funds should be taken from the treasury and he gave the people some of their stipends in silver [1856]
coins and some in gold which originated from the vases[1089] that he had collected to send to al-Walīd b. Yazīd.[1090] The first person to speak up (about all this)[1091] was a man from the Banū Kindah who was eloquent and loquacious. He said: "What about the stipends?" The following Friday Naṣr gave orders to some of the guards; they put on their weapons and he dispersed them through the mosque, fearing that someone would speak up. The man from the Banū Kindah stood up and said: "What about the stipends?" Then a man who was a mawlā of the Banū Azd, whose *laqab* was Abū al-Shayāṭīn, stood up and spoke his piece. Ḥammād al-Ṣāʾigh and Abū al-Salīl al-Bakrī also rose to their feet and said: "What about the stipends?" So Naṣr replied: "Preserve me from disobedience![1092] It is your duty to obey and to remain united. Fear God and heed what is preached to you." Then Salm b. Aḥwaz went up to Naṣr, who was on the *minbar*, and spoke to him, saying: "Your talking to us in this way does not satisfy us one bit." Thereupon the people of the bazaar ran off to their market stalls. Naṣr was

---

the Oxus, and had taken refuge with the Türgesh, was sent by Asad in 118 (736) against some of al-Ḥārith's followers in Badakhshān. Cf. al-Ṭabarī, II, 1589–91; Gibb, 81; Wellhausen, 467–69; Shaban, *ʿAbbāsid Revolution*, 124; Hawting, 86–88.

1088. This is looking forward to events discussed later in detail by al-Ṭabarī (II, 1861–62).

1089. Literally, "gold from the vases." This is ambiguous. It is not clear whether the gold came from the melting down of the vases or whether the vases had been used to store gold coins. The former possibility is more likely.

1090. Cf. n. 574.

1091. As it appears to have been a Friday, the discussion must have taken place in the mosque.

1092. *Iyyāya wa-al-maʿṣiyata:* "preserve me from disobedience (on your part)." Cf. the examples quoted in Wright, II, 82.

furious and declared: "You will not receive any stipends from me after this behavior of yours today." Then he went on: "My position with you is as if one of you[1093] rose up against his brother or his cousin and slapped his face when he was being given a camel or a garment to wear (as presents) and who (then) said: "My lord and my foster-father!" Or I feel as if[1094] some intolerable evil has materialized from under your very feet[1095] and it is as if you are being flung down in the bazaars like slaughtered camels.[1096] Truly people become disenchanted with the rule of anyone who rules for a long time. You, people of Khurāsān, are a garrison in the very heart of the enemy. Beware lest there should be any dissension amongst you."

According to ʿAlī b. Muḥammad (al-Madāʾinī)—ʿAbdallāh b. al-Mubārak: Naṣr said in his oration:

> Verily, I am one who pronounces (people) unbelievers[1097] and, further, who tells (them) when they are doing wrong. That is probably better for me. Indeed, you are striving to attain your ends but deliberately arousing discord in so doing.[1098] May God (therefore) not preserve you. By God, I know you through and through[1099] and I do not have (even) ten of you left on my side. The situation with me and you is
> [1857] as one of your predecessors said:[1100]

> Hold fast, comrades,[1101] and we shall urge on[1102] your

1093. Literally, "it seems to me that a man amongst you . . ." (*ka-annanī bi-rajulin minkum*). Cf. Wright, II, 170.

1094. The text has *ka-annanī bihim*. Ibn al-Athīr changes *bihim* to *bikum* (V, 229). This makes better sense in the context and has been followed in the translation.

1095. Similarly here, Ibn al-Athīr (loc. cit.) has *taḥtā arjulikum* for al-Ṭabarī's *arjulihim*.

1096. *Wa-ka-annanī bikum muṭarraḥīna fī al-aswāqi*. Probably some prophetic allusion to the forthcoming revolution is being attributed here to Naṣr.

1097. *Mukaffir*. Cf. Ullman, 263.

1098. Literally, "you are striving to attain a matter in which you want discord."

1099. Literally, "I have stretched you out and rolled you up and rolled you up and stretched you out."

1100. The meter is *rajaz*. Cf. Ibn al-Athīr, V, 229.

1101. Literally, "our comrade."

1102. The text has *naḥdū*. This is later emended to *naḥdu*. Cf. *Emend.*, p. DCCXIII. *Ḥadā:* "to urge on camels by singing to them"; cf. Lane, I, 532–33.

camels by singing to them,
for we have experienced both your good side and your bad.

Fear God! By God, if there should be any disagreement amongst you, it would be preferable for each of you to be deprived of your money and children than to see what would ensue.[1103] O people of Khurāsān, you have held communal concord in contempt and you have veered toward divisiveness. Is it authority of an unpredictable kind[1104] that you want and expect? Verily, therein lies your destruction, O assembly of Arabs.

Then he quoted the words of al-Nābighah al-Dhubyānī:[1105]

If your evil nature triumphs over you,
I have nevertheless striven for your good.

Al-Ḥārith b. ʿAbdallāh b. al-Hashraj b. al-Mughīrah b. al-Ward al-Jaʿdī said:

I pass the night leaning on my elbow, contemplating the stars;
whenever the last of them depart, the first of them reappear.[1106]
Because discord has become widespread,
encompassing all the people of prayer,
Those in Khurāsān and Iraq, and those
in Syria, are all grieved and troubled about it.
For this reason, the people are in pitch darkness;
their cries of confusion are enmeshed in the darkness.[1107]
In the dark the fool who is rebuked for
his folly is equal to the wise man.
People are in such distress that pregnant women
have almost disowned their children.

1103. Literally, "then each man amongst you would certainly want to be deprived of his money and children and not to have seen it."

1104. *A-sulṭāna al-majhūli turīdūna. . .* ?

1105. The meter is *wāfir.* Al-Nābighah al-Dhubyānī was born in the second half of the sixth century. He enjoyed a high reputation, and the caliph ʿUmar was said to have called him the best poet of the Arabs. Cf. Sezgin, II, 110–13.

1106. Literally, "whenever they depart, their first ones reappear."

1107. Literally, "entangled are its woods."

For this reason, they stray blindly in total confusion;
its dangers slay them unawares.[1108]
The people see in this situation only
all kinds of unknown hazards[1109]
Like the whickering of a young she-camel or the cry
of a woman in labor whose child has become stuck fast,
around whom stand her midwives.[1110]
He has come[1111] into our midst, despised in manner,
with calamitous affairs whose afflictions are red in color.[1112]

[1858] When Naṣr's letter of appointment to govern on behalf of ʿAbdallāh b. ʿUmar reached him, al-Kirmānī announced to his followers: "There is discord among the people, so look for someone to run your affairs." (Now he was only called al-Kirmānī because he was born in Kirmān. His name was Judayʿ b. ʿAlī b. Shabīb b. Bararī b. Ṣunaym al-Maʿnī.) His followers said: "You are the man for us." Then the Muḍariyyah said to Naṣr: "Al-Kirmānī is fomenting discord against you. Send people against him and kill him." Naṣr replied: "No, but I have children, both male and female. I will marry my sons to his daughters and his sons to my daughters." The Muḍariyyah said: "No." Then Naṣr said: "I will send him one hundred thousand dirhams, for he is miserly and gives nothing to his followers. They will get to hear of this and will desert him." The Muḍariyyah rejected that idea, too, saying: "That would only strengthen him." Thereupon Naṣr rejoined: "Leave him as he is, with him on his guard against us and us on

---

1108. Literally, "because of it they are in every blind confusion, tested by its tangled complexities[?]." The text has *fī-kulli mubhamatin.* The Cairo edition (VII, 276) has *fī ẓilli mubhamatin* ("in the shadow of blind confusion"). The text has *tumnā lahum.* The Cairo edition (loc. cit.) has *taghtāluhum,* which makes much better sense.

1109. Literally, "the people do not see in its consequences except that which its speaker does not explain." The text has *yabīnu.* This is later emended to *yubīnu.* Cf. *Emend.*, p. DCCXIII.

1110. *Kaṣayḥati ḥublā ṭarraqat, ḥawlahā qawābiluhā.* The text has *ṭaraqat,* but a reading of *ṭarraqat* makes better sense. Cf. *Lisān,* II, 589.

1111. The text has *fa-jāʾin.* This is later emended to *fa-jāʾa.* Cf. *Emend.*, p. DCCXIII.

1112. Possibly a reference to the newborn child as well as the bloodshed of *fitnah.*

our guard against him." So the Muḍariyyah said: "Send your men to him and imprison him."[1113]

Naṣr received word that al-Kirmānī was saying: "My ultimate aim in obeying the Banū Marwān was that I would be made a commander[1114] and then I would seek vengeance for the Banū Muhallab[1115] as well as for the treatment that we have received at the hands of Naṣr, what with his coarseness and the prolonged restrictions he has imposed on us and his retaliation against us for what Asad did to him."[1116] Then 'Iṣmah b. 'Abdallāh al-Asadī said to Naṣr: "This is the beginning of discord. Accuse al-Kirmānī of some foul deed, announce publicly that he is a dissident, and execute him. Execute Sibā' b. al-Nu'mān al-Azdī and also al-Farāfiṣah[1117] b. Zuhayr al-Bakrī, who continues to be angry at (Asad b. 'Abd) Allāh because he thought himself to be superior to the Muḍar and the Rabī'ah when he was in Khurāsān"(?).[1118] Jamīl b. al-Nu'mān said (to Naṣr): "You have treated al-Kirmānī

1113. Cf. Ibn al-Athīr, V, 230. The Cairo edition interprets this passage differently. The Leiden text is vocalized to read: "They said, 'Send (people) to him and imprison him.'" The Cairo edition (VII, 287) has *qālū [lā, qāla]* [brackets are those of the Cairo editor] *fa-arsala ilayhi fa-ḥabasahu:* "They said 'no.' So he sent (people) to him and he imprisoned him."

1114. *An tuqallidanī al-suyūfu.* The Cairo edition (loc. cit.) has *an yuqallada wuldī al-suyūfa* ("that my sons would be invested with swords (i.e., given command)").

1115. Cf. n. 676.

1116. Probably a reference to Asad's having ordered that Naṣr should be lashed. Cf. Wellhausen, 455.

1117. The form of this name is uncertain. The editor earlier had al-Furāfiṣah (II, 1604) but has al-Farāfiṣah here.

1118. This part of the text is clearly faulty and neither the Leiden nor Cairo editions have satisfactory versions. Ibn al-Athīr omits it altogether and al-Dīnawarī's account sheds no light on the matter (op. cit., 350–51). The Leiden text has *fa-innahu lam yazil muta'aṣṣaban 'alā Allāhi bi-tafaḍḍulihi 'alā Muḍari [wa-bi-tafaḍḍulihi 'alā Rabī'ata kāna bi-Khurāsān.]* By the editor's own admission he guessed at what is between the brackets. The Cairo edition (VII, 287) has *fa-innahu lam yazil mutaghaḍḍaban 'alā Allāhi bi-tafḍīlihi Muḍara 'alā Rabī'ah* (and then, in a new paragraph:) *wa kāna bi-Khurāsān.* It is possible that words may have been omitted here, e.g., part of a name before Allāh (e.g., Asad b. 'Abdallāh, the preceding governor of Khurāsān, who supported a pro-Yemeni and anti-Rabī'ah and Muḍar policy). A possible reconstruction of the sentence might therefore lead to the following translation: "for he continues to be angry (*mutaghaḍḍaban*) against Asad b. 'Abdallāh (?) because of his thinking himself superior (*bi-tafaḍḍulihi*) to Muḍar and to Rabī'ah when (?) he was in Khurāsān." Various textual problems remain unsolved, however.

honorably. If you can't face killing him (yourself), hand him over to me and I will kill him."

It was said that Naṣr became angry with al-Kirmānī only be-
[1859] cause the latter wrote to Bakr b. Firās al-Bahrānī, the governor of Jurjān, telling him about Manṣūr b. Jumhūr, and because he (Bakr?) sent a letter with Abū al-Zaʿfarān, the mawlā of Asad b. ʿAbdallāh, appointing al-Kirmānī. So Naṣr instituted a search for al-Kirmānī but he could not find him. The man who wrote to al-Kirmānī informing him of the killing of al-Walīd and the coming of Manṣūr b. Jumhūr to Iraq was Ṣāliḥ al-Athram al-Ḥirār.

It is said that a group of people came to Naṣr and reported: "Al-Kirmānī is encouraging faction." Aṣram b. Qabīṣah said to Naṣr: "If Judayʿ could achieve power and authority only by means of Christianity or Judaism, he would become a Christian or a Jew."[1119] Naṣr and al-Kirmānī had been on friendly terms and al-Kirmānī had behaved well toward Naṣr during the governorship of Asad b. ʿAbdallāh. Then when Naṣr became governor of Khurāsān he dismissed al-Kirmānī from (his) command[1120] and appointed to it Ḥarb b. ʿĀmir b. Aytham al-Wāshijī. His leadership was not successful[1121] and Naṣr reinstated al-Kirmānī in office; but only a short time later he dismissed al-Kirmānī, appointing in his stead Jamīl b. al-Nuʿmān. Relations between Naṣr and al-Kirmānī became strained and then Naṣr imprisoned al-Kirmānī in the citadel. The man in charge of the citadel was Muqātil b. ʿAlī al-Maraʾī—or according to some sources, al-Murrī.[1122]

When Naṣr had made up his mind to imprison al-Kirmānī, he gave orders to ʿUbaydallāh b. Bassām, the commander of his guards, who brought al-Kirmānī to Naṣr. Naṣr said to him: "Kirmānī, did I not receive a letter from Yūsuf b. ʿUmar ordering me to kill you, and write back to him saying: 'Al-Kirmānī is a *shaykh* and a knight of Khurāsān,' and prevent the shedding of your blood?" Al-Kirmānī said: "Yes." Naṣr went on: "Did I not pay the debts you had incurred and did I not take it equally out of the

---

1119. Cf. Ibn al-Athīr, V, 230.

1120. *Al-riʾāyasah.* Cf. Crone, 31.

1121. *Fa-mā zujirat.* The Cairo edition (VII, 287) has *fa-māta Ḥarb* ("then Ḥarb died").

1122. This last being the form preferred by Nöldeke. Cf. *Emend.*, p. DCCXIII.

people's stipends?" Al-Kirmānī said: "Yes." Naṣr said: "Did I not appoint[1123] your son 'Alī to a position of authority, even though your people were against it?" Al-Kirmānī replied: "Yes." Then Naṣr went on: "And yet you repaid that (kindness) by arousing discord." Then al-Kirmānī said: "There was more to it than what the *amīr* has said.[1124] And I give thanks for that. Just as the *amīr* prevented the shedding of my blood, so too I behaved during the time of Asad b. 'Abdallāh in the way that he knows. So let the *amīr* act without haste and make sure (of the truth), for I am no friend to faction." Then 'Iṣmah b. 'Abdallāh al-Asadī said: "You are lying. Your aim is sedition and that you will not achieve." Salm b. Aḥwaz urged: "Behead him, O *amīr*." Al-Miqdām and Qudāmah, the two sons of 'Abd al-Raḥmān b. Nu'aym al-Ghāmidī, said: "Truly the companions of Pharaoh were better than you when they said 'Put him off (for a while), both him and his brother.'[1125] By God, do not let al-Kirmānī be killed, as Ibn Aḥwaz recommends." So Naṣr gave orders to Salm, who put al-Kirmānī in prison, three days before the end of Ramaḍān, 126 [July 14, 744]. Then the Banū Azd spoke up (about al-Kirmānī) and Naṣr said: "I have sworn that I would imprison him and that no evil will befall him at my hands. If you fear for his safety, then choose a man to keep him company." So the Banū Azd chose Yazīd al-Naḥawī and he remained with al-Kirmānī in the citadel.[1126] Naṣr appointed the Banū Nājiyah, who were the associates of 'Uthmān and Jahm, the two sons of Mas'ūd, to guard al-Kirmānī. The Banū Azd sent al-Mughīrah b. Shu'bah al-Jahḍamī and Khālid b. Shu'ayb b. Abī Ṣāliḥ al-Ḥuddānī to Naṣr and they spoke to Naṣr about al-Kirmānī. Al-Kirmānī remained in prison for twenty-nine days. [1860]

According to 'Alī b. Wā'il, one of the Banū Rabī'ah b. Ḥanẓalah: I went in to see Naṣr and al-Kirmānī was sitting apart and complaining: "What have I done wrong? If Abū al-Za'farān had come,

1123. The text has *a-lam artash*. This is later emended to *a-lam ura''is*. Cf. *Emend.*, p. DCCXIII.

1124. Literally, "the *amīr* did not say anything except there was more than it." In other words, in everything Naṣr said there was more to be added.

1125. Cf. Qur'ān 7, v. 111.

1126. Cf. Ibn al-Athīr, V, 231.

by God, I would never have hidden him; and I do not know where he is."

On the day that al-Kirmānī was imprisoned, the Banū Azd had wanted to snatch him away from his escorts, but al-Kirmānī implored them in God's name not to do that and he went away laughing under escort from the guards of Salm b. Aḥwaz. Then
[1861] when al-Kirmānī was put in prison, ʿAbd al-Malik b. Ḥarmalah al-Yaḥmadī, al-Mughīrah b. Shuʿbah, ʿAbd al-Jabbār b. Shuʿayb b. ʿAbbād, and a group of the Banū Azd talked (over the matter). They went down to Nawsh[1127] and said: "We do not accept that al-Kirmānī should be imprisoned when he has committed no crime or offense." Some *shaykh*s from the Banū al-Yaḥmad[1128] said: "Do not take any action. See what your *amīr* does." The Banū Azd replied: "We are not satisfied. Just let Naṣr keep his hands off us or we will certainly start on you." Then ʿAbd al-ʿAzīz b. ʿAbbād b. Jābir b. Hamā(m)[1129] b. Ḥanẓalah al-Yaḥmadī joined them with one hundred men, and also Muḥammad b. al-Muthannā and Dāwūd b. Shuʿayb. They spent the night in Nawsh with ʿAbd al-Malik b. Ḥarmalah and those men who were with him. The following morning they marched to Ḥawzān and set fire to the house of ʿAzzah, Naṣr's concubine. They remained (there) for three days, proclaiming: "We are not satisfied." Thereupon they (Naṣr's men?) appointed trustworthy men to watch over al-Kirmānī and they put Yazīd al-Naḥawī and others with al-Kirmānī. Then one of the people of Nasaf[1130] came and said to Jaʿfar, the servant of al-Kirmānī: "What would you give me if I got al-Kirmānī out (of prison)?" They replied: "You could have whatever you requested." Then the man went to the water conduit (leading) from the citadel and widened it. Then he made his way to al-Kirmānī's sons and said to them; "Write a letter to your father telling him to be ready to escape tonight." So they wrote to him and they put the letter in the food. Al-Kirmānī called Yazīd al-Naḥawī and Ḥuṣayn[1131] b. Ḥukaym and they ate supper with him

1127. A number of villages in the Marw district bore this name. Cf. Yāqūt, IV, 823–24.
1128. For the Banū al-Yaḥmad, a subgroup of the Azd, cf. Ibn al-Kalbī, II, 589.
1129. The text has Hamā.
1130. For the city of Nasaf in Sughd, cf. Le Strange, *Lands*, 469–71.
1131. Ibn al-Athīr has: Khiḍr b. Ḥukaym. (V, 231).

and then they went out. Al-Kirmānī went in to the (subterranean) conduit and his rescuers pulled him by his arm. Then a serpent wound itself around al-Kirmānī's stomach, but it did not harm him. One of the Banū Azd said: "The snake was Azdī and so it did not harm him." He came finally to a narrow place where they dragged him out; his shoulder and side were grazed. When al-Kirmānī emerged (from the conduit) he mounted his she-mule, Dawwāmah (according to some sources, he mounted his horse, al-Bashīr), with the fetters still on his foot. The men then brought him to a village called Ghalaṭān, where 'Abd al-Malik b. Ḥarmalah was waiting, and al-Kirmānī was cut loose from the fetters. [1862]

According to 'Alī (b. Muḥammad al-Madā'inī) and Abū al-Walīd[1132] Zuhayr b. Hunayd al-'Adawī: Al-Kirmānī had his servant Bassām with him (in prison). Bassām noticed a hole in the citadel and he kept on making it wider until he made it possible to escape through it.[1133] Al-Kirmānī sent a message to Muḥammad b. al-Muthannā and 'Abd al-Malik b. Ḥarmalah, saying: "I am escaping tonight." So al-Kirmānī's supporters assembled. Then when al-Kirmānī had escaped, his mawlā Farqad[1134] came to them and told them the news and they met up with him at the village of Ḥarb b. 'Āmir. Al-Kirmānī was wearing a sheet with a sword around his waist. With him were 'Abd al-Jabbār b. Shu'ayb and the two sons of al-Kirmānī, 'Alī and 'Uthmān, together with his servant Ja'far. Al-Kirmānī gave orders to 'Amr b. Bakr to go to Ghalaṭān, Andagh, and Ushturj[1135] together(?). Al-Kirmānī ordered the people to meet him at the gate of al-Rayyān b. Sinān al-Yaḥmadī in Nawsh, in the meadow, which was the place where they prayed during the *'īd*. So 'Amr went to the people and told them (what al-Kirmānī had said). Then the people left their vil-

---

1132. The name Abū al-Walīd in the text is later emended to Abū al-Dhiyal. Cf. *Emend.*, p. DCCXIII. This is not accepted by the Cairo edition (VII, 289).

1133. Al-Dīnawarī gives a detailed account of al-Kirmānī's escape from prison, giving a longer version of the story involving Bassām (op. cit., 351–52). Cf. also Ibn A'tham, VIII, 146–53.

1134. The text has Farqadu, later emended to Farqadun. Cf. *Emend.*, p. DCCXIII.

1135. Ushturj is a town in the district of Andkhoy in Khurāsān. Cf. *Ḥudūd*, 336, n. 61; al-Iṣṭakhrī, I, 270–71. The text has Ushturj Ma'nan. The Cairo edition (VII, 290) has *ma'an* ("together"). Ma'an is the name of a tribe, but it makes little sense here.

lages, armed with weapons, and al-Kirmānī led them in the morning prayer. They numbered around one thousand. Before sunset, however, their number had increased to three thousand. Then the people of al-Saqādim joined them. Al-Kirmānī marched to Marj Nīrān, getting as far as Ḥawzān. Khalaf b. Khalīfah recited the following lines:[1136]

Go forth to the meadow which most effectually removes
 blindness,
 for the people of the conduit have already departed.[1137]
Truly the meadow of the Azd is extensive,
 and in it the feet stand equal to the knees.

It is said that the Banū Azd gave the oath of allegiance to ʿAbd al-Malik b. Ḥarmalah on the basis of God's Book on the night that al-Kirmānī escaped. Once they had assembled in the meadow at
[1863] Nawsh, prayer began[1138] and ʿAbd al-Malik and al-Kirmānī were in dispute for a while. Then ʿAbd al-Malik conceded al-Kirmānī precedence, handing the command over to him, and al-Kirmānī led the prayer.

When al-Kirmānī had escaped, Naṣr went and camped hard by the gate of Marw al-Rūdh[1139] on the Ibrdānah(?)[1140] side where he remained for a day or two. It is said that when al-Kirmānī escaped, Naṣr appointed as his own deputy ʿIṣmah b. ʿAbdallāh al-Asadī, while he himself made for the five bridges at the gate of Marw al-Rūdh, where he addressed the people and carped at al-Kirmānī, saying: "He was born in Kirmān and was a Kirmānī. Then he came to Harāh (Herat) and was a Harawī. He who falls between two stools[1141] has no firm base nor does he flourish."[1142] Then Naṣr said, referring to the Banū Azd: "If they gather together,

1136. The meter is *ramal.*

1137. Surely a reference to the escape of al-Kirmānī from the conduit (*al-sarab*) and to al-Kirmānī's meeting at the *marj.* In a more general way, the lines could be interpreted as praise of desert instead of city life.

1138. *Uqīmat al-ṣalāt.*

1139. Marw al-Rūdh or Little Marw was thus named to differentiate it from Marw al-Shāhijān. Marw al-Rūdh was situated about 160 miles further up the Murghāb river than Marw al-Shāhijān. Cf. Le Strange, *Lands,* 404–05; Yāqūt, IV, 506; *EI²*, s.v. (C. E. Bosworth).

1140. This place has not been identified and the editor is not sure of the vocalization.

1141. Literally, "two beds."

1142. Literally, "nor is he a growing branch."

they are the most contemptible of people; and if they refuse to do so, they are as al-Akhṭal[1143] said:

(They are) frogs answering one another in the darkness of night;
their voices guide the water-snake toward them."

Then Naṣr regretted his hasty words and added: "Pronounce the name of God, for to pronounce God's name is a sovereign remedy. To pronounce God's name is a blessing, with no tincture of evil, that drives away sin.[1144] To pronounce God's name is to be absolved from hypocrisy." Thereafter many people gathered to Naṣr, and he sent Salm b. Aḥwaz in heavy armor with many men to al-Kirmānī. People mediated between Naṣr and al-Kirmānī and they asked Naṣr to grant al-Kirmānī safe-conduct and not to imprison him, while al-Kirmānī's family would guarantee that he would not oppose Naṣr. Al-Kirmānī placed his hand in Naṣr's hand and Naṣr ordered him to stay in his house. Then al-Kirmānī heard something about Naṣr, so he left (his house) to go to a village that belonged to him. Then Naṣr sallied forth and camped at the bridges (at the gate of Marw), where al-Qāsim b. Najīb came to him. He spoke to Naṣr about al-Kirmānī and Naṣr guaranteed his safety (no matter what he said). Al-Qāsim said to Naṣr: "If you want, al-Kirmānī will go away from Khurāsān for you or, if you so desire, he will stay in his house." Naṣr thought it wise to banish
al-Kirmānī, but Salm said to him: "If you banish him, you will [1864]
make his name and reputation famous and people will say: 'Naṣr banished him because he was afraid of him.'"[1145] Naṣr replied: "What I fear from him if he is banished is less than what I fear from him if he is living (here); for a man who is exiled from his country becomes less powerful." They urged him not to do it, so Naṣr stayed his hand from al-Kirmānī and gave his followers ten (dīnārs) each. Then al-Kirmānī came to Naṣr and entered his tent and Naṣr promised him safe-conduct.

1143. The famous Christian Arab poet (d. probably before 92/710). Cf. *EI*², s.v. (R. Blachère).

1144. Literally, "the mentioning of God is a cure, the mentioning of God is a blessing in which there is no evil."

1145. *Qāla al-nāsu akhrajahu annahu hābahu.* Ibn al-Athīr (V, 232) has *li-annahu,* which has been followed here. The Cairo edition (VII, 291) also has *li-annahu.*

ʿAbd al-ʿAzīz b. ʿAbd Rabbihi joined al-Ḥārith b. Surayj.[1146] Then, in Shawwāl 126 [July 17–August 14, 744], Naṣr received word that Manṣūr b. Jumhūr had been dismissed and that ʿAbdallāh b. ʿUmar b. ʿAbd al-ʿAzīz had been made governor (of Iraq). Then Naṣr addressed the people, mentioning Ibn Jumhūr and saying: "I have found out that he is not a governor of Iraq. God has dismissed him from office and has appointed (in his stead) the Virtuous One (al-Ṭayyib, i.e., ʿAbdallāh), the son of the Virtuous One (al-Ṭayyib, i.e., ʿUmar b. ʿAbd al-ʿAzīz)." Al-Kirmānī was angry about Ibn Jumhūr and began collecting men and taking up arms again. He would attend the Friday prayer, accompanied by about fifteen hundred men, and would perform the prayer outside the *maqṣūrah,* before going in to see Naṣr. He would greet Naṣr but would not sit down. Then al-Kirmānī stopped going in to see Naṣr and began to oppose him publicly.

So Naṣr sent the following message to him by Salm b. Aḥwaz: "By God, I did not want to do you any harm by imprisoning you, but I was afraid that you would cause mischief amongst the people. So come to me." Al-Kirmānī gave Salm the following reply: "Were it not for the fact that you are in my house I would kill you. Were it not for what I know of your foolishness I would teach you how to behave. Go back to Ibn al-Aqṭaʿ[1147] and tell him whatever you like, be it good or bad." So Salm returned to Naṣr and gave him the message.[1148] Then Naṣr said to him: "Go back to him." Salm replied: "No, by God! I am not afraid of him but I would hate him to make me listen to things about you that I do
[1865] not like (to hear)." So Naṣr dispatched ʿIṣmah b. ʿAbdallāh al-Asadī, who said (to al-Kirmānī): "Abū ʿAlī, I fear for your fate in this world and the next as a result of what you have begun. We are going to make certain proposals to you. So go to your *amīr,* who will give you the details.[1149] Our aim in this is only to warn you."

1146. The text has no obvious break between the events occurring with Naṣr and al-Kirmānī and then the reference to al-Ḥārith b. Surayj. This is probably an early allusion to the men who rallied to al-Ḥārith (under the year 127) amongst whom ʿAbd al-ʿAzīz b. ʿAbd Rabbihi was one. Cf. al-Ṭabarī, II, 1890; Wellhausen, 485–86.

1147. Cf. n. 327. Cf. also al-Dīnawarī, 352.

1148. Cf. Ibn al-Athīr, V, 232. Hereafter, Ibn al-Athīr's account omits the details of the various attempts to persuade al-Kirmānī to go to see Naṣr.

1149. Literally, "we are proposing certain proposals to you. So go to your *amīr,* who will suggest them to you."

Al-Kirmānī replied: "I know that Naṣr did not charge you with this message, but that you wanted (what you said) to reach his ears and thereby to gain favor (with him). By God, I will not say another word (to you) after I have finished what I am saying now until you have gone back to your house. So let him send anyone he likes so long as it is not you." Then ʿIṣmah went back and said (to Naṣr): "I have not seen a more undisciplined lout than al-Kirmānī. I do not wonder at him, but I do wonder at Yaḥyā b. Ḥudayn (and his people)—may God curse them![1150]—indeed, they respect him more than his (own) associates do."

Salm b. Aḥwaz said: "I am afraid that this frontier and the people will become corrupted. So send Qudayd to al-Kirmānī." Then Naṣr told Qudayd b. Manīʿ to go to him. Qudayd did so and said to al-Kirmānī: "Abū ʿAlī, you have been stubbornly persistent (in this matter) and I am afraid that the situation will become too difficult, that we will all perish, and that these foreigners[1151] will gloat over us." Al-Kirmānī replied: "Qudayd, I am not suspicious of you; but what has happened has made me mistrustful of Naṣr. The Prophet of God said: 'The Bakrī is your brother, but do not trust him.'" Qudayd said: "If that is what you think, give him some surety." Al-Kirmānī asked: "Who?" Qudayd answered: "Give me ʿAlī and ʿUthmān." Al-Kirmānī rejoined: "Who is he giving me? He has nothing good to offer." Qudayd replied: "Abū ʿAlī, I swear to you, by God, do not let the ruin of this city be on your hands." Then Qudayd went back to Naṣr and he said to ʿAqīl b. Maʿqil al-Laythī: "What I most fear is that disaster will befall this frontier. So speak to your (paternal) cousin." So ʿAqīl said to Naṣr, "O *amīr*, I beseech you, by God, not to cause evil fortune to befall your tribe. Rebels (*khawārij*) are fighting Marwān in Syria. Both the people and the Banū Azd are in a state of dissension.[1152] They are light-headed and foolish; but

---

1150. The text is perhaps faulty here. The editor notes that after Ḥuḍayn there may have been the words *wa-qawmihi*, i.e., Bakr b. Wāʾil. Cf. al-Ṭabarī, II, 1571. This makes good sense with the plural suffix of *laʿanahum*.

1151. *Al- aʿājim:* the non-Arab population of Khurāsān.

1152. There are various ways in which this passage could be punctuated. It could be translated as: "Indeed, Marwān is in Syria (and) the rebels are fighting him, and the people and the Azd are in discord . . ." Alternatively, it could read: "Indeed, Marwān is in Syria (and) the rebels and the people are fighting him, and the Azd are in discord . . ." The punctuation of the Cairo edition (VII, 292) places a comma after "rebels."

they are your neighbors." Naṣr replied: "What am I to do? If you know a way of restoring the people to good order, then go ahead,
[1866] for al-Kirmānī has made up his mind not to trust me."

Then ʿAqīl went to al-Kirmānī and said: "Abū ʿAlī, you have instituted a custom which will be followed by other *amīr*s after you. Indeed, I foresee a situation in which I fear that people will act quite unreasonably." Al-Kirmānī said: "Naṣr wants me to go to him, but I do not feel safe from him. We want him to withdraw. (Then) we ourselves will withdraw and we will choose a man from Bakr b. Wā'il who is satisfactory to all of us to be our governor until a decree comes from the caliph. (But) Naṣr refuses (to do) this." ʿAqīl replied: "Abū ʿAlī, I am afraid that the people of this frontier will perish, so go to your *amīr* and say that whatever he (Naṣr) wants will be agreed to by you. But do not incite the fools amongst your people to action in this affair that they have undertaken." Al-Kirmānī said: "I am not suspicious of you so far as your advice or your reasoning are concerned, but I do not trust Naṣr. Let him take what he wants from the wealth of Khurāsān and go away." ʿAqīl said: "Are you willing to do something that would lead to agreement between you? You can make marriage alliances with his family and he can make marriage alliances with yours." Al-Kirmānī replied: "I don't feel safe from him in any situation." ʿAqīl said: "No good will come of this. I am afraid that tomorrow you will be wiped out and all to no purpose." Al-Kirmānī replied: "There is no power and no strength except in God." ʿAqīl asked him: "Shall I come back to you?" Al-Kirmānī replied: "No, but take him a message from me and tell him: "I fear that people will incite you to do what you do not want (to do) and that you will behave toward us in a way that has irrevocable consequences. But, if you insist, I will go away from you, not out of fear of you but (because) I would hate to be the cause of any disaster to the inhabitants of the province or to cause bloodshed in it." So al-Kirmānī prepared himself to leave for Jurjān.

In this year Yazīd b. al-Walīd granted al-Ḥārith b. Surayj safe-
[1867] conduct and he wrote to al-Ḥārith accordingly. He also wrote to ʿAbdallāh b. ʿUmar ordering him to return to al-Ḥārith such of his money and sons as had been seized from him.

The Reason for Granting Safe-Conduct to al-Ḥārith b. Surayj[1153]

It is reported that when the disagreement between Naṣr and al-Kirmānī occurred in Khurāsān, Naṣr was afraid that al-Ḥārith b. Surayj would muster his followers and the Turks against him, and that the situation would be worse for him than it had been with al-Kirmānī and others. Naṣr therefore was keen[1154] to consult al-Ḥārith. So he sent Muqātil b. Ḥayyān al-Nabaṭī, Tha'labah b. Ṣafwān al-Banānī, Anas b. Bajālah al-'Arajī, Hudbah al-Sha'rāwī, and Rabī'ah al-Qurashī to al-Ḥārith to bring him back from the country of the Turks.

According to 'Alī b. Muḥammad (al-Madā'inī)—his *shaykhs*: Khālid b. Ziyād al-Baddī, who was one of the inhabitants of Tirmidh, and Khālid b. 'Amr, a mawlā of the Banū 'Āmir, went to Yazīd b. al-Walīd to ask for safe-conduct for al-Ḥārith b. Surayj. When they reached al-Kūfah, they met Sa'īd Khudaynah,[1155] who said to Khālid b. Ziyād: "Do you know why people called me Khudaynah?" Khālid said: "No." So Sa'īd said: "They wanted to make me kill the Yamāniyyah and I refused to do so." Then the two men asked Abū Ḥanīfah[1156] to write on their behalf to al-Ajlaḥ, who was one of the close associates of Yazīd b. al-Walīd. So he wrote to al-Ajlaḥ on their behalf and al-Ajlaḥ took them in to

1153. For an analysis of the amnesty granted to al-Ḥārith through the mediation of Naṣr, who hoped that al-Ḥārith would support him against al-Kirmānī, cf. Shaban, *'Abbāsid Revolution*, 136; Hawting, 107–08.

1154. Literally, "desired."

1155. Sa'īd b. 'Abd al-'Azīz, who was an Umayyad and the son-in-law of Maslamah b. 'Abd al-Malik, had been governor of Khurāsān in 102 (720). He preferred a policy of conciliation in Khurāsān but was forced to go out against the Turks and, after initial success, was severely defeated by them. He was recalled in 103 (721) because of his weakness and complaints of tyranny. The father of one of the men in this delegation to Yazīd, Ḥayyān al-Nabaṭī, had vigorously opposed Sa'īd's policies and had intrigued against him. The nickname Khudhaynah ("little lady") was given to him by his enemies in Khurāsān, although some Arab elements called him "a sword held over our heads." The term *khudhaynah* is explained as *dihqanah* ("lady of the house"). Cf. Gibb, 61–62; Shaban, *'Abbāsid Revolution*, 95, 99–101; Barthold, *Turkestan*, 188–89; al-Ṭabarī, II, 1418.

1156. Abū Ḥanīfah al-Nu'mān b. Thābit, born *ca.* 80 (699) and died 150 (767), the eponymous founder of the Ḥanafī *madhhab*. He lived in al-Kūfah and became the foremost authority on religious law there. Cf. *EI*², s.v. (J. Schacht).

see Yazīd. Khālid b. Ziyād said to Yazīd: "O Commander of the Faithful, you killed your cousin in order to establish the Book of God. Yet now your agents are acting unjustly and tyrannically." Yazīd replied: "I can find no helpers other than them, and yet I hate them." Khālid said: "O Commander of the Faithful, appoint as governors people from noble families[1157] and attach to every governor men who are of known piety and knowledgeable in *fiqh* to make them adhere to the terms of your covenant." Yazīd replied: "I will do so." Then the two men asked Yazīd to grant safe-conduct to al-Ḥārith b. Surayj and Yazīd wrote to him as follows:

> Now to our subject matter. We have been angry on God's behalf that His ordinances have been neglected and that His
> [1868] servants have sunk into every kind of excess. Blood has been shed unlawfully and money has been seized illegally. We wanted our actions in this community to be according to the Book of God, may He be praised and glorified, and the *sunnah* of His prophet. There is no power except in God. We have explained this to you ourselves. So come in safety, you and those who are with you, for you are our brothers and our helpers. I have written to ʿAbdallāh b. ʿUmar b. ʿAbd al-ʿAzīz asking him to return such of your wealth and children as were confiscated.

Then the two men (i.e. Khālid b. Ziyād and Khālid b. ʿAmr) came to al-Kūfah and went in to see Ibn ʿUmar. Khālid b. Ziyād said: "May God preserve and prosper the *amīr!* Do you not order your agents to conduct themselves as your father did?" ʿAbdallāh replied: "But isn't ʿUmar's (irreproachable) conduct clear and known to all?" Khālid said: "People don't benefit from it and it has not been put into practice." Then the two men arrived in Marw and they gave Yazīd's letter to Naṣr, who returned as much as he could of what had been taken from al-Ḥārith and his followers.[1158] They then called on al-Ḥārith, where they met Muqātil b. Ḥayyān and his associates, whom Naṣr had sent to al-Ḥārith. Ibn ʿUmar had written to Naṣr saying: "You have granted safe-conduct to al-Ḥārith without my permission and without the permission of the caliph." So Naṣr regretted[1159] what he had

1157. *Ahla al-buyūtāti.* Cf. *Gloss.*, p. CXLV.
1158. Literally, "them."
1159. *Fa-usqiṭa fī yadayhi.* Cf. Lane, I, 1380.

done. He dispatched Yazīd b. al-Aḥmar with orders to kill al-Ḥārith when he had got him onto the boat. When Khālid b. Ziyād and Khālid b. ʿAmr met Muqātil in Āmul, Muqātil himself crossed over to al-Ḥārith and prevented Yazīd from attacking him.

Al-Ḥārith traveled to Marw, after living in the country of the infidels for twelve years, accompanied by al-Qāsim al-Shaybānī and Muḍarris b. ʿImrān, his judge, and ʿAbdallāh b. Sinān. When al-Ḥārith arrived in Samarqand, the governor in charge of the city was Manṣūr b. ʿUmar.[1160] The latter did not receive al-Ḥārith and he said: ("Should I see him) because of his good deeds?"[1161] Then Manṣūr wrote to Naṣr asking his permission to attack al-Ḥārith, and whichever of them killed the other would go to Paradise or the Fire. Manṣur wrote as follows:[1162] "If al-Ḥārith comes to the *amīr*, having already impaired the authority of the Banū Umayyah, lapping up more and more blood, and having severed all [1869] ties with this world, whereas while he was under their rule he had been the most hospitable of them to a guest, the fiercest of them in courage and the most zealous of them against the Turks, then he will cause division among the Banū Tamīm and do you a mischief."[1163]

The Sardarkhudāh was imprisoned with Manṣūr b. ʿUmar because he had killed Baysān. His son Jundah sought vengeance from Manṣūr and Manṣūr imprisoned him.[1164] Al-Ḥārith spoke to Manṣūr about him, so Manṣūr released him. Thereupon al-Ḥārith took over his debt and he paid it for him in full.

According to some sources: In this year the imām Ibrāhīm b. Muḥammad[1165] sent Abū Hāshim Bukayr b. Māhān[1166] to Khurāsān, furnished with a mandate[1167] and injunctions

1160. Manṣūr b. ʿUmar al-Sulamī. Cf. al-Ṭabarī, II, 1677, 1679; Wellhausen, 477.

1161. *A-li-ḥusni balāʾihi!* Presumably a sarcastic comment.

1162. It is not clear from the text whether this is Manṣūr's letter to Naṣr or Naṣr's reply to Manṣūr. The former possibility has been adopted in the translation.

1163. Literally, "to your disadvantage."

1164. *Fa-istaʿadā ibnuhu J.nd.h Manṣūran fa-ḥabasahu.* The vocalization of the name is uncertain, but it appears in the indices, 109, as J.nd.h b. Baysān.

1165. Cf. *EI*², Ibrāhīm b. Muḥammad (F. Omar).

1166. Cf. n. 358.

1167. *Bi-al-sīrati.* I.e., having been given instructions as to how he should proceed.

(*waṣiyyah*). He arrived in Marw and assembled the *naqībs* and those *dāʿīs* who were present there. He announced the death of the imām Muḥammad b. ʿAlī, called on them to support Ibrāhīm, and gave them Ibrāhīm's letter. They accepted what it said and handed over to him such subscriptions to the Shīʿī cause as had come in to them. Bukayr then took these monies to Ibrāhīm b. Muḥammad.

[1870] In this year Yazīd b. al-Walīd had the people give the oath of allegiance to his brother Ibrāhīm and he made him his heir.[1168] He also had the oath of allegiance given to ʿAbd al-ʿAzīz b. al-Ḥajjāj b. ʿAbd al-Malik as the heir of Ibrāhīm b. al-Walīd. According to Aḥmad b. Zuhayr—ʿAlī b. Muḥammad (al-Madāʾinī): The reason for that was that Yazīd b. al-Walīd fell sick in Dhū al-Ḥijjah 126 [September 14–October 12, 744]. People said to him: "Have the oath of allegiance given to your brother Ibrāhīm and to ʿAbd al-ʿAzīz b. al-Ḥajjāj after him." The Qadariyyah kept on pressing him to have the oath of allegiance sworn, and urging him: "It is not lawful for you to neglect the leadership of the community. So have the oath of allegiance taken to your brother." (They did this) until Yazīd had the oath of allegiance taken for Ibrāhīm and ʿAbd al-ʿAzīz b. al-Ḥajjāj after him.

In this year Yazīd b. al-Walīd dismissed Yūsuf b. Muḥammad b. Yūsuf[1169] from the governorship of Medina, appointing in his place ʿAbd al-ʿAzīz b. ʿAbdallāh b. ʿAmr b. ʿUthmān. According to Muḥammad b. ʿUmar (al-Wāqidī): It is alleged that Yazīd b. al-Walīd did not appoint Yūsuf b. Muḥammad as governor but that the latter forged a letter of appointment as governor of Medina. Later, Yazīd dismissed him and appointed ʿAbd al-ʿAzīz to the post and he went there (to Medina) two nights before the end of Dhū al-Qaʿdah (126) [August 15–September 13, 744].

In this year Marwān b. Muḥammad rebelled against Yazīd b. al-Walīd. He left Armenia for the Jazīrah, on the pretext that he was

---

1168. For Yazīd's nomination of his brother Ibrāhīm as his heir, cf. *Fragmenta*, 153; Ibn Khayyāṭ, 387.

1169. Yūsuf b. Muḥammad b. Yūsuf al-Thaqafī, the brother of al-Walīd II's mother, Umm Ḥajjāj, had been sent as governor to Medina by al-Walīd on his accession. Cf. Wellhausen, 354; al-Ṭabarī, II, 1768.

seeking vengeance for the blood of al-Walīd b. Yazīd. But when he reached Ḥarrān,[1170] he gave the oath of allegiance to Yazīd.

The Account of [Marwān's Rebellion] and of the Reason That Prompted Marwān to Oppose (Yazīd) and Then to Give Allegiance to Yazīd

According to Aḥmad b. Zuhayr—ʿAbd al-Wahhāb b. Ibrāhīm b. Khālid b. Yazīd b. Huraym—Abū Hāshim Mukhallad b. Muḥammad b. Ṣāliḥ, the mawlā of ʿUthmān b. ʿAffān: I asked Abū Hāshim how closely he had witnessed the events he related to us and he said: "I was staying in the camp of Marwān b. Muḥammad." (Abū Hāshim's account continues:) When ʿAbd al-Malik b. Marwān b. Muḥammad b. Marwān returned from his summer raiding campaign, he was with al-Ghamr b. Yazīd in Ḥarrān. While ʿAbd al-Malik was there he received the news of al-Walīd's murder. Al-Walīd's agent in the Jazīrah was ʿAbdah b. Rabāḥ al-Ghassānī. When he heard that al-Walīd had been killed, ʿAbdah left the Jazīrah and made for Syria. Then ʿAbd al-Malik b. Marwān b. Muḥammad attacked Ḥarrān and the (other) cities of the Jazīrah; he held on to them and appointed Sulaymān b. ʿAbdallāh b. [1871]
ʿUlāthah to govern them. ʿAbd al-Malik then wrote to his father in Armenia informing him of what he had done and advising him to hasten to join him. Marwān made his preparations for the journey and announced publicly that he was seeking (vengeance for) the blood of al-Walīd. Marwān did not like to leave the frontier unguarded before he had put his affairs in order. He dispatched to the people of al-Bāb[1171] Isḥāq b. Muslim al-ʿUqaylī,[1172] who was the

1170. Ḥarrān is the well-known city in Northern Mesopotamia (now in Turkey). Marwān was to make it his residence when he became caliph. Cf. *EI²*, s.v. (G. Fehérvári).

1171. I.e., Bāb al-Abwāb, Darband on the Caspian. This was a pass and a frontier town at the eastern end of the Caucasus. Yāqūt describes the great wall which lay to the west of it and which had been built in the sixth century A.D. to keep out the barbarians. After the Muslim conquest the Bāb became the base for future Arab operations against the Khazars. In Hishām's reign, Maslamah is said to have established twenty-four thousand Syrians there. Cf. al-Balādhurī, *Futūḥ*, 207; Le Strange, *Lands*, 180; Minorsky, *Sharvān and Darband*, 18–19; *EI²*, s.v. (D. M. Dunlop).

1172. Cf. al-Ṭabarī, II, 1635; al-Balādhurī, *Futūḥ*, 206; al-Yaʿqūbī, *Historiae*, II, 403; Crone, 106.

head of the Banū Qays, and Thābit b. Nu'aym al-Judhāmī,[1173] a man from Palestine who was the head of the Yamāniyyah. The reason why Thābit was in Marwān's company was that Marwān had released him from Hishām's prison at al-Ruṣāfah. Marwān used to visit Hishām once every two years to discuss the affairs of the frontier, its condition, what would be good for his troops, and what he thought should be done against the enemy. The reason that Hishām had imprisoned Thābit was, as we have mentioned above, because of what had happened between him and Ḥanẓalah b. Safwān. Hishām had sent Ḥanẓalah with a *jund* to fight the Berbers[1174] and the people of Ifrīqiyah after they had killed Hishām's agent over them, Kulthūm b. 'Iyāḍ al-Qushayrī. Thābit had turned this *jund* against Ḥanẓalah. Ḥanẓalah then wrote a letter to Hishām complaining about his situation, whereupon Hishām ordered Ḥanẓalah to send Thābit to him in irons. Ḥanẓalah accordingly sent Thābit to Hishām, who put him in prison, where he remained until Marwān b. Muḥammad came to Hishām on one of his visits. We have already said something about Kulthūm b. 'Iyāḍ and his activities in Ifrīqiyah in the relevant section of this book of ours.

While Marwān was visiting Hishām, those leaders of the Yamāniyyah who were with Hishām came to him and sought his help over the matter of Thābit. Amongst the people who spoke to Marwān about Thābit were Ka'b b. Ḥāmid al-'Ansī,[1175] Hishām's chief of police; 'Abd al-Raḥmān b. al-Ḍakhm; and Sulaymān b. Ḥabīb, his judge.[1176] Then Marwān asked Hishām to hand Thābit over to him, so Hishām did so. Thābit went (with Marwān) to

---

1173. For his biography, cf. Crone, 161.

1174. Literally, "The reason for Hishām's imprisoning Thābit was what we have already mentioned of his affair with Ḥanẓalah b. Ṣafwān and his (Thābit's) turning against him (Ḥanẓalah) of the *jund*, which Hishām had sent with him (Ḥanẓalah) to fight the Berbers . . ." Cf. al-Ṭabarī, II, 1716.

1175. The text has al-'Absī. Crone proves convincingly that Ka'b b. Ḥāmid, who had been the head of the *shurṭah* of 'Abd al-Malik, al-Walīd, Sulaymān, Yazīd, and Hishām, is often called al-'Absī. Ibn Ḥabīb, on the other hand, has him as al-'Ansī, and therefore of Yamanī descent, as the passage here suggests. Cf. Crone, 163–64; Ibn Ḥabīb, *Muḥabbar*, 374.

1176. There were two men of this name. One was a judge and was a Qaysī. Cf. Ibn Khayyāṭ, 557; al-Ṭabarī, II, 1226, 1338. The other was a well-known Yamanī leader and is most probably the one mentioned here. Cf. al-Ṭabarī, II, 1946, 1977. Crone argues that the phrase "his judge" is an incorrect gloss (op. cit., 164).

Armenia and Marwān placed him in authority and behaved generously to him. When Marwān sent Thābit with Isḥāq to the people [1872] of al-Bāb, he wrote a letter to them which the two men were to take with them. In it he informed them about the state of their frontier, and what remuneration they would receive if they followed their orders and remained in their posts; by standing firm they would ward off the evil of the enemy from the sons of the Muslims. Marwān also sent the people's stipends with the two men and he appointed as commander over the people of al-Bāb a man from Palestine called Ḥumayd b. ʿAbdallāh al-Lakhmī, who was acceptable to them, who had been their governor before, and whose rule they had praised. The two envoys carried out Marwān's orders amongst the people; they transmitted his message and read out his letter to them. The people agreed to stand firm on their frontier and to remain in their posts.

Then news reached Marwān that Thābit had been plotting with the local commanders[1177] to leave their frontier post and to join their *junds*. When the two men got back to Marwān, he made preparations to leave and inspected his troops. Thābit b. Nuʿaym plotted with those Syrians whom he had with him to break away from Marwān and to join up with himself so that he could take them to their *junds* and be in command of them. Then they broke away from their camp together with (other) people who fled at night[1178] and they pitched camp separately.

Marwān got wind of their activities, so he and his men kept watch, fully armed, throughout the night. The following morning he and his men sallied forth against them. Thābit's followers were twice as many as those of Marwān. They lined the men up in battle order. Then Marwān gave orders to heralds, who shouted between the two lines on the right, on the left, and in the middle. They proclaimed the following announcement to them: "People of Syria, what has prompted you to defect and for what conduct on my part have you conceived a dislike for me? Did I not rule you in a way that won your approval and behave correctly toward you and govern you well? What is it that has prompted you into shedding your own blood?" The rebels gave Marwān the follow-

---

1177. Literally, "their commanders."
1178. *Maʿa man farra laylān.* This is somewhat obscure.

ing reply: "We were obedient to you because of our obedience to
[1873] our caliph. Then our caliph was killed and the Syrians gave the oath of allegiance to Yazīd b. al-Walīd. We are content to be governed by Thābit and we have made him our leader to march with us under our banners until we return to our *junds*." Then Marwān gave orders to his herald to proclaim:[1179] "Truly you have lied! You do not want what you have said you want. Your sole desire has been to act rashly and to seize wrongfully the possessions, food, and fodder of any *dhimmīs* whom you pass. The only thing between you and me will be the sword until such time as you submit to me. I will go with you as far as the Euphrates and then I will take my leave of every commander and his *jund*. Then rejoin your *junds*."

When the rebels had seen how serious Marwān's intentions were, they submitted to him and cast in their lot with him. They then handed over Thābit b. Nuʿaym and his sons to Marwān. Thābit had four sons: Rifāʿah, Nuʿaym, Bakr, and ʿImrān. Marwān gave orders concerning them and they were hauled off their horses and stripped of their weapons. He put chains on their feet and appointed some of his guards to keep watch over them. He took a group of the *jund* from Syria and the Jazīrah and attached them to his troops. He kept a tight rein on them during the journey, so that none of them were able to attack or act tyrannically against any of the villagers or to obtain anything without paying. (This state of affairs prevailed) until he reached Ḥarrān. Then Marwān ordered the Syrians to rejoin their *junds*, but he kept Thābit under his own eye in prison. He then invited the people of the Jazīrah to mobilize and he paid stipends to more than twenty thousand stalwarts. Then Marwān made preparations to march on Yazīd. Yazīd wrote to him saying that if Marwān gave him the oath of allegiance, he would appoint Marwān as governor of the lands over which ʿAbd al-Malik b. Marwān had appointed his father, Muḥammad b. Marwān, in the Jazīrah, Armenia, al-Mawṣil, and Āzarbāyjān. Marwān duly gave the oath of allegiance to him and he sent Muḥammad b. ʿUlāthah and a number of other notables of the Jazīrah to Yazīd.[1180]

1179. Literally, "who proclaimed."

1180. For this episode, cf. Ibn al-Athīr, V, 234–35; al-Yaʿqūbī, *Historiae*, II, 403.

In this year Yazīd b. al-Walīd died. His death was at the end of Dhū al-Ḥijjah 126 [October 12, 744]. According to Abū Ma'shar— [1874]
Aḥmad b. Thābit—his informants—Isḥāq b. 'Īsā: Yazīd b. al-Walīd died after the Feast of the Sacrifice in Dhū al-Ḥijjah 126 [after September 23, 744].

According to all of our informants, his caliphate lasted six months. It is (also) said[1181] that his caliphate lasted five months and two nights. According to Hishām b. Muḥammad (al-Kalbī): Yazīd ruled for six months and several days. According to 'Alī b. Muḥammad (al-Madā'inī): He ruled for five months and twelve days.[1182] Yazīd b. al-Walīd died ten days before the end of Dhū al-Ḥijjah 126 [October 3 or 4, 744][1183] at the age of forty-six.

According to some sources: Yazīd ruled for six months and two nights.

He died in Damascus but there is disagreement as to how old he was when he died. According to Hishām (b. Muḥammad al-Kalbī): Yazīd died when he was thirty-seven. According to some sources: He died when he was thirty-seven. Yazīd's patronymic was Abū Khālid.[1184] His mother was a concubine. Her name was Shāh-i Āfrīd.[1185] She was the daughter of Fīrūz[1186] b. Yazdigird b. Shahriyār b. Kisrā. Yazīd used to say:[1187]

I am the son of Kisrā; my father is Marwān.
One grandfather is a *qayṣar;* the other a *khāqān.*[1188]

It is said that he was a Qadarī.

1181. There is an apparent contradiction here with the preceding sentence.

1182. "'Alī b. Muḥammad said" is repeated here.

1183. The exact date is somewhat uncertain since it is not clear whether this statement includes or excludes the last day of Dhū-al Ḥijjah itself. Al-Mas'ūdī gives the date of Yazīd's death as *hilāl* (new moon) in Dhū al-Ḥijjah, 126. Cf. *Murūj*, VI, 18. Ibn A'tham (VIII, 141) has a date in Muḥarram, 127. Ibn Khayyāṭ (387) has ten days remaining of Dhū al-Ḥijjah 126.

1184. Cf. al-Mas'ūdī, *Murūj*, VI, 32.

1185. She was the daughter of Fīrūz, the son of Yazdigird III. She was taken prisoner in Sughd by Qutaybah and placed in the harem of al-Walīd I. For a discussion of this and other forms of the name, cf. Justi, *Iranisches Namenbuch*, 272.

1186. The editor vocalizes the name as Fayrūz.

1187. For this line, cf. Ibn al-Athīr, loc. cit., and Muir, 417.

1188. Literally, "my grandfather is a *qayṣar* and my (other) grandfather a *khāqān.*"

According to Aḥmad (b. Zuhayr)—ʿAlī b. Muḥammad (al-Madā'inī): In appearance he was brown-skinned, tall, with a small head, and a mole on his face. He was a handsome man. He had quite a wide mouth but not excessively so. According to al-Wāqidī: He was nicknamed Yazīd the Inadequate because he cut back the people's stipends which al-Walīd had increased. According to ʿAlī b. Muḥammad (al-Madā'inī): Marwān b. Muḥammad railed against Yazīd and called him: "The Inadequate (*al-Nāqiṣ*) Son of al-Walīd," so the people called him the "Inadequate."

[1875] According to al-Wāqidī: In this year ʿAbd al-ʿAzīz b. ʿUmar b. ʿAbd al-ʿAzīz b. Marwān led the pilgrimage.[1189] According to some sources: In this year ʿUmar b. ʿAbdallāh b. ʿAbd al-Malik led the pilgrimage. He was appointed by Yazīd b. al-Walīd. ʿAbd al-ʿAzīz, who was in charge of Medina, Mecca, and al-Ṭā'if, went with him.

Yazīd's governor of Iraq in this year was ʿAbdallāh b. ʿUmar b. ʿAbd al-ʿAzīz. The judge of al-Kūfah was Ibn Abī Laylā. In charge of the *aḥdāth*[1190] of al-Baṣrah was al-Miswar b. ʿUmar b. ʿAbbād.[1191] The judge of al-Baṣrah was ʿĀmir b. ʿAbīdah. The governor of Khurāsān was Naṣr b. Sayyār al-Kinānī.

1189. Cf. al-Yaʿqūbī, *Historiae*, II, 402.

1190. From the fourth/tenth century to the sixth/twelfth century the term *aḥdāth* referred to a kind of urban militia, often representing a "municipal opposition" to political authority. It is, however, more difficult to define the term in earlier periods of Islamic history. Cf. *EI²*, s.v. (C. Cahen). Probably the term referred either to some kind of auxiliary police force or auxiliary troops.

1191. Cf. Crone, 109.

The Caliphate of Abū Isḥāq Ibrāhīm b. al-Walīd and the Rise of Marwān II

The Events of the Year

126 (cont'd)

(October 25, 743–October 12, 744)

Then came Ibrāhīm b. al-Walīd b. ʿAbd al-Malik b. Marwān, but his rule was not recognized.[1192]

According to Aḥmad b. Zuhayr—ʿAlī b. Muḥammad (al-Madāʾinī): The rule of Ibrāhīm was not universally recognized. One week he would be recognized as caliph, another week as *amīr*, and another as neither caliph nor *amīr*.[1193] This situation continued until Marwān b. Muḥammad arrived to depose him and kill ʿAbd al-ʿAzīz b. al-Ḥajjāj b. ʿAbd al-Malik. According to Hishām b. Muḥammad (al-Kalbī): Yazīd b. al-Walīd nominated as his successor Abū Isḥāq Ibrāhīm b. al-Walīd. He remained in office for four months and was then deposed in Rabīʿ II 126 [January 22–February 19, 744].[1194] Thereafter he remained alive until he

1192. *Lam yatimm amrun.* Literally, "a command/an affair was not accomplished." Ibn al-Athīr, loc. cit., has *al-amru; Fragmenta,* 154, has *amruhu.*

1193. Cf. the verse of a poet quoted by al-Masʿūdī: "We give the oath of allegiance to Ibrāhīm every Friday" (*Murūj,* VI, 19).

1194. The dating is somewhat uncertain here. According to al-Yaʿqūbī (loc. cit.), Ibrāhīm was deposed by Marwān, who then had the oath of allegiance given to himself on a Monday halfway through Ṣafar 127. For the reign of Ibrāhīm, cf. also Ibn Aʿtham, VIII, 141–42; *Fragmenta,* 154.

was killed in 132 [August 20, 749–August 8, 750]. His mother was a concubine.

According to Aḥmad b. Zuhayr—ʿAbd al-Wahhāb b. Ibrāhīm—Abū Hāshim Mukhallad b. Muḥammad: The rule of Ibrāhīm b. al-Walīd lasted seventy nights.

The Events of the Year 127 [1876]

(October 13, 744 – October 2, 745)

Among the events taking place during this year were the journey of Marwān b. Muḥammad to Syria and the battle that took place between him and Sulaymān b. Hishām at ʿAyn al-Jarr.[1195]

The Account of Marwān's Journey and What Caused The Battle [at ʿAyn al-Jarr][1196]

According to Abū Jaʿfar (al-Ṭabarī): The cause (of the battle) sprang from what I have already mentioned in part:[1197] namely Marwān's going from Armenia to the Jazīrah after the murder of al-Walīd b. Yazīd, his conquering of it (the Jazīrah), professing that he was incensed on account of al-Walīd, out of disapproval of his murder; then his taking of the *baʿyah* for Yazīd b. al-Walīd after Yazīd had appointed him as governor of the province of his father, Muḥammad b. Marwān; and his subsequent behavior and

1195. ʿAyn al-Jarr was an important site in the Biqāʿ and contained a vast enclosure with towers. It is generally held to have been founded by al-Walīd b. ʿAbd al-Malik around 95–96/714–15. Cf. *EI²*, s.v. (J. Sourdel-Thomine); M. Chehab, "The Umayyad palace at ʿAnjar" in *Ars Orientalis*, V (1963): 17–27.

1196. For parallel accounts, cf. Ibn al-Athīr, V, 243–45; *Fragmenta*, 154–56.

1197. Cf. al-Ṭabarī, II, 1870–73.

his sending Muḥammad b. ʿAbdallāh b. ʿUlāthah and a group of notables from the people of the Jazīrah (to Yazīd) while he (Marwān) was in Ḥarrān.

According to Aḥmad (b. Zuhayr)—ʿAbd al-Wahhāb b. Ibrāhīm—Abū Hāshim Mukhallad b. Muḥammad: When Marwān heard about the death of Yazīd he sent a message to Ibn ʿUlāthah and his associates, recalling them from Manbij,[1198] whilst he (himself) set out for Ibrāhīm b. al-Walīd. Marwān departed with the *jund* of the Jazīrah, having appointed his son ʿAbd al-Malik as his deputy with forty thousand men from the garrison in al-Raqqah.[1199] When he reached[1200] Qinnasrīn, where there was a brother of Yazīd b. al-Walīd called Bishr, whom Yazīd had appointed as governor of Qinnasrīn, Bishr sallied forth toward him, drew up his forces (in preparation to fight) against Marwān, and made a proclamation to the people. Marwān called upon them to give the oath of allegiance to him.[1201] Yazīd b. ʿUmar b. Hubayrah, along with the Qaysiyyah, favored Marwān, and they handed over Bishr and a brother of his called Masrūr b. al-Walīd
[1877] who was Bishr's brother on his mother's and father's side. Marwān took him and his brother Masrūr b. al-Walīd and imprisoned them. He (then) departed with those people from the Jazīrah and from Qinnasrīn whom he had with him, making in the direction of the people of Ḥimṣ. When Yazīd b. al-Walīd died, the people of Ḥimṣ had refused to give the oath of allegiance to Ibrāhīm and ʿAbd al-ʿAzīz b. al-Ḥajjāj. So Ibrāhīm dispatched ʿAbd al-ʿAzīz b. al-Ḥajjāj and the *jund* of the people of Damascus, and he laid siege to them in their city. Marwān hastened his pace, and when he came near to the city of Ḥimṣ ʿAbd al-ʿAzīz departed from them (the people of Ḥimṣ).[1202] They all came out to Marwān, gave the oath

1198. For Manbij, cf. *EI*[1], s.v. (E. Honigmann).

1199. For al-Raqqah, the principal city of Diyār Muḍar, cf. *EI*[1], s.v. (E. Honigmann).

1200. The text has *itnahā*. It is later corrected to *intahā* (cf. *Add.*, II, p. DCCXIV). The Cairo edition has the correct form (VII, 300).

1201. *Fa-kharaja ilayhi fa-ṣāffahu fa-nādā al-nās wa-daʿāhum Marwān ilā mubāyaʿatihi.* This is rather ambiguous, but presumably Bishr is performing all the actions here until Marwān is specifically mentioned. Certainly this is the interpretation to be inferred from the punctuation of the Cairo edition (loc. cit.).

1202. Ibn al-Athīr has "departed from it" (i.e., the city; V, 244).

of allegiance to him, and left with him. Ibrāhīm b. al-Walīd sent out contingents with Sulaymān b. Hishām, who went with them and encamped at 'Ayn al-Jarr where Marwān came to him. Sulaymān had one hundred and twenty thousand horsemen and Marwān had eighty thousand with him. They (the two sides) met each other and Marwān called on them to refrain from fighting him and to release the two sons of al-Walīd, al-Ḥakam and 'Uthmān, who were imprisoned in the jail in Damascus. He guaranteed on their behalf (i.e., al-Ḥakam and 'Uthmān) that they would not take reprisals against them (al-Walīd's murderers) because the latter had killed their father (i.e., al-Walīd) and that the two of them would not seek out any of those who had been responsible for his murder. They (Sulaymān's men) refused to accept it (the guarantee) and persisted in fighting Marwān. They fought from the time that the sun was high[1203] until late afternoon, and the slaughter on both sides mounted and was general amongst them. Marwān was experienced and wily, so he called three of his commanders, one of whom was a brother of Isḥāq b. Muslim[1204] called 'Īsā, and he ordered them to go behind his line with his cavalry, which numbered three thousand, sending with them laborers with axes. The two lines of Marwān's men and those of Sulaymān b. Hishām filled the area between the two mountains that enclosed the meadow, whilst between the two armies there flowed a slowly moving river.[1205] Marwān ordered them to cut down the trees when they reached the mountain, to tie the logs together, to cross over to Sulaymān's army, and to make a surprise attack on it.

Sulaymān's cavalry, who were[1207] busy fighting, were aware [1878] only of the horses and swords and of the *takbīr* (being said) by their own men behind them. So when they saw that (i.e., Mar-

1203. *Irtifā' al-nahār*. Cf. Lane, I, 1123.

1204. Isḥāq b. Muslim al-'Uqaylī had served in Armenia and Āzarbāyjān. For his biography, cf. Crone, 106. Little is known of his brother 'Īsā.

1205. *Jarrār*. Cf. *Gloss.*, p. CLXI. Riḍā suggests that the term means "slowly moving on account of its abundance" (I, 507).

1206. *Jusūr*: that on which one crosses over a river or the like (Lane, I, 424).

1207. *Huwa mashghūlūn* is corrected by the editor to *hum mashghūlūn*. Cf. *Add.*, II, p. DCCXIV.

wān's men crossing the river) they fled in disarray and were routed. The people of Ḥimṣ thrust their weapons into them because of their anger toward them, and they killed about seventeen thousand of them. The people of the Jazīrah and Qinnasrīn (on the other hand) recoiled from slaughtering them, and they did not kill a single one of them. They brought to Marwān prisoners from amongst them who were as many as those killed or even more, and Marwān's men were permitted to plunder Sulaymān's army.[1208] Marwān took the *ba'yah* from them in favor of the two boys, al-Ḥakam and 'Uthmān; he released them (the prisoners) after he had provided them[1209] with a *dīnār* each, and he allowed them to rejoin their families. He killed only two men from their number, one of whom was called Yazīd b. al-'Aqqār and the other al-Walīd b. Maṣād, both of them Kalbīs. They were among those who had gone after al-Walīd and compassed his murder. Yazīd b. Khālid b. 'Abdallāh al-Qasrī was with them, and he took flight with those who escaped with Sulaymān b. Hishām to Damascus. One of the two, i.e, the two Kalbīs, had been in command of the guards of Yazīd (b. al-Walīd), and the other had been in charge of his police.[1210] Marwān beat them with whips then and there.[1211] He subsequently gave orders concerning them, and they were thrown into prison, where they perished.[1212]

Sulaymān and those men who were with him kept going until they reached Damascus, where the leaders of the people[1213]—Yazīd b. Khālid al-Qasrī, Abu 'Ilāqah al-Saksakī,[1214] al-Aṣbagh b. Dhu'ālah al-Kalbī,[1215] and the likes of them—gathered to him, Ibrāhīm, and 'Abd al-'Azīz b. al-Ḥajjāj. They said to one another: "If the two boys, the sons of al-Walīd, survive until Marwān

1208. Lit. "their *'askar* was made lawful."
1209. *Fragmenta*, 156, has "after he had given them stipends."
1210. I.e., *ṣāḥib al-ḥaras* and *ṣāḥib al-shurṭah*.
1211. Lit. "in that stopping place of his."
1212. Lit. "they were imprisoned, and they perished in his prison."
1213. *Ru'ūs min ma'ahum. Fragmenta*, 156, is less ambiguous: *ru'ūs al-nās*.
1214. The text has Abū 'Ilāqah. Crone vocalizes this name as 'Ulāqah (op. cit., 96 and 294). This person is Sarī b. Ziyād, one of the conspirators against al-Walīd II (cf. al-Ṭabarī, II, 1778, 1800).
1215. Cf. his biography in Crone, 156.

arrives and gets them out of prison and authority devolves onto them, they will not spare any of their father's murderers. The best thing for us is to kill them both." So they appointed Yazīd b. Khālid to do that. In prison with the two of them were Abū Muḥammad al-Sufyānī and Yūsuf b. ʿUmar. Yazīd sent a mawlā affiliated to Khālid (al-Qasrī) called Abū al-Asad with a number of [1879] his associates. Abū al-Asad went into the prison and broke the skulls of the two young boys with clubs.[1216] He brought out Yūsuf b. ʿUmar in order that they should kill him, and he was (accordingly) beheaded. They (also) wanted to kill Abū Muḥammad al-Sufyānī.[1217] He went into one of the rooms of the prison, locked the door,[1218] threw carpets and cushions behind it,[1219] and leant against it, so that nobody could open it.[1220] They called for fire to burn him out,[1221] but it was not brought before news came that Marwān's cavalry had entered the city.[1222] Ibrāhīm b. al-Walīd fled and hid himself. Sulaymān plundered[1223] what was in the treasury, distributed it amongst those contingents he had with him, and left the city.

In this year[1224] ʿAbdallāh b. Muʿāwiyah b. ʿAbdallāh b. Jaʿfar b. Abī Ṭālib[1225] summoned people in al-Kūfah to his cause and fought ʿAbdallāh b. ʿUmar b. ʿAbd al-ʿAzīz b. Marwān[1226] there. ʿAbdallāh b. ʿUmar defeated ʿAbdallāh b. Muʿāwiyah, who made for al-Jibāl[1227] and took possession of it.

1216. For a previous account of this murder, cf. al-Ṭabarī, II, 1841–42.

1217. For this person, cf. al-Ṭabarī, II, 1828, 1830–31.

1218. *Fa-aghlaqahu.*

1219. *Khalfahu.* Presumably the door is meant here, although it could be translated as "behind him."

1220. *Fa-lam yaqdir ʿalā fatḥihi.* Both the Cairo edition (VII, 302) and Ibn al-Athīr (V, 245) have *yaqdirū.*

1221. *Li-yuḥriqūhu.* It is possible that the prison is meant here, rather than al-Sufyānī.

1222. Here Ibn al-Athīr adds: "and they (Yazīd's associates) fled" (loc. cit.).

1223. *Wa-anhaba.* Ibn al-Athīr has the more appropriate usage of *intahaba* (loc. cit.). *Fragmenta* (156) has *nahaba.*

1224. The apparatus has the variant "Abū Jaʿfar said" before the account begins.

1225. This man was a Shīʿite, the great-grandson of ʿAlī's brother Jaʿfar. Cf. Shaban, *Islamic History,* 161; Wellhausen, 384.

1226. Cf. al-Ṭabarī, II, 1854–55, 1858, 1864, 1867–68, and subsequent accounts.

1227. For the province of Jibāl, cf. Le Strange, *Lands,* 185–231; *EI²,* s.v. (L. Lockhart).

The Account of the Cause of the Uprising of ʿAbdallāh (b. Muʿāwiyah) and of His Summoning the People to Himself

According to Hishām (b. Muḥammad al-Kalbī)—Abū Mikhnaf: ʿAbdallāh b. Muʿāwiyah rebelled against ʿAbdallāh b. ʿUmar and declared war on him in Muḥarram 127 (October 13, 744–November 11, 744).[1228]

According to Aḥmad—ʿAlī b. Muḥammad—ʿĀṣim b. Ḥafṣ al-Tamīmī and other knowledgeable people: The reason for the uprising of ʿAbdallāh b. Muʿāwiyah b. ʿAbdallāh b. Jaʿfar against ʿAbdallāh b. ʿUmar b. ʿAbd al-ʿAzīz was that the former came to al-Kūfah on a visit to the latter seeking remuneration from him[1229]
[1880] and not intending to rebel, and he married the daughter of Ḥātim b. al-Sharqī b. ʿAbd al-Muʾmin b. Shabath b. Ribʿī.[1330] When tribal discord surfaced, the Kūfans said to him: "Call on people to join you, for the Banū Hāshim are more entitled to rule than the Banū Marwān." Then ʿAbdallāh b. Muʿāwiyah summoned people secretly in al-Kūfah whilst Ibn ʿUmar was in al-Ḥīrah, and Ibn Ḍamrah al-Khuzāʿī gave him the oath of allegiance. Then Ibn ʿUmar got in touch with Ibn Ḍamrah secretly and gave him a bribe.[1331] Then Ibn Ḍamrah[1232] sent a message to Ibn ʿUmar saying, "When we meet the people I will retreat with them." This message reached Ibn Muʿāwiyah and when the people assembled he said: "Ibn Ḍamrah has acted treacherously, and he has promised Ibn ʿUmar that he will retreat with the people. So do not be alarmed when he retreats,[1233] for he will be doing so out of treachery." When they assembled, Ibn Ḍamrah retreated, and the people retreated (too), and nobody remained with Ibn Muʿāwiyah. He recited:

1228. For other accounts of the revolt of ʿAbdallāh b. Muʿāwiyah, cf. al-Iṣfahānī, *Aghānī*, XII, 228–32; Ibn al-Athīr, V, 246–48; Ibn Khayyāṭ, II, 394–95.

1229. *Yaltamisu ṣilatahu*. The *Aghānī* (XII, 228) has *mustamīhan* "asking for a stipend."

1230. For the family of this man, cf. Crone, 118. He must have been a local notable.

1231. *Fa-arḍāhu*: lit: "gave him what satisfied him."

1232. The *Aghānī* calls him Ibn Ḥamzah (XII, 229).

1233. Lit: "do not let his running away alarm you." And yet, as the sequel shows, the people did do exactly as Ibn Ḍamrah wanted, leaving Ibn Muʿāwiyah in the lurch.

The gazelles have departed from Khidāsh,[1234]
so Khidāsh does not know what to hunt.

Ibn Muʿāwiyah returned to al-Kūfah—they had met at a place between al-Ḥīrah and al-Kūfah—and then he went to Ctesiphon (al-Madā'in), and the people gave the oath of allegiance to him. A group of Kūfans joined him, and he departed and took possession of Ḥulwān[1235] and al-Jibāl.

It is said: ʿAbdallāh b. Muʿāwiyah came to al-Kūfah and collected a group of people, and ʿAbdallāh b. ʿUmar did not know (about it) until ʿAbdallāh b. Muʿāwiyah went out to the *jabbānah*, assembling (his men) for battle. When they met, Khālid b. Qaṭan al-Ḥārithī[1236] was in charge of the Yemenis. Al-Aṣbagh b. Dhu'ālah al-Kalbī with the Syrians pressed Khālid, and he and the Kūfans fled. (One group of) Nizār held back from (attacking another group of) Nizār, and they returned (to al-Kūfah). Fifty men of the Zaydiyyah came to the house of Ibn Muḥriz al-Qurashī intending to fight, and they were killed. None of the Kūfans apart from them were killed.

Ibn Muʿāwiyah left al-Kūfah for Ctesiphon in the company of ʿAbdallāh b. ʿAbbās al-Tamīmī. Then he left there and took possession of al-Māhān,[1237] Hamadhān, Qūmis, Iṣfahān, and al-Rayy.[1238] The slaves of the Kūfans joined him and he recited (the [1881]
following):[1239]

Do not embark on an action[1240]
for the like of which you blame your brother.
Of no pleasure to you will be the saying of a man
who contradicts what he says in what he does.

1234. For Khidāsh, cf. al-Ṭabarī, II, 1503, 1588, 1593; Wellhausen, 504, 509–11, 514–17; *EI*², s.v. (M. Sharon).

1235. For the city of Ḥulwān in the province of Jibāl, cf. Le Strange, *Lands*, 191; *EI*², s.v. (L. Lockhart).

1236. For this man's family, cf. Crone, 111–12.

1237. For the city of Māhān in the province of Kirmān, cf. Le Strange, *Lands*, 307.

1238. Ibn al-Athīr has a slightly different list of places in his account—Ḥulwān, al-Jibāl, Hamadhān, Iṣfahān, and al-Rayy (V, 248).

1239. Those lines are found, along with others not included here, in the *Aghānī* (XII, 232).

1240. *Al-ṣanī*. Cf. Lane, I, 1734.

As for Abū ʿUbaydah Maʿmar b. al-Muthannā, he asserted that the reason for that (i.e., the rebellion of Ibn Muʿāwiyah) was that ʿAbdallāh, al-Ḥasan, and Yazīd b.[1241] Muʿāwiyah b. ʿAbdallāh b. Jaʿfar came to ʿAbdallāh b. ʿUmar, and they lodged amongst the (Banū) Nakhʿ[1242] in the house of a mawlā of theirs called al-Walīd b. Saʿīd. Ibn ʿUmar treated them kindly, gave them presents, and spent three hundred dirhams on them every[1243] day. Their situation remained like this until Yazīd b. al-Walīd died and the people gave the oath of allegiance to his brother Ibrāhīm b. al-Walīd and after him to ʿAbd al-ʿAzīz b. al-Ḥajjāj b. ʿAbd al-Malik. (News of) the *baʿyah* in their names came to ʿAbdallāh b. ʿUmar in al-Kūfah. So the people gave the oath of allegiance to the two of them, and he increased the people's stipends by a hundred (dirhams) each. He wrote to the outlying districts (announcing) that the oath of allegiance had been given to them, and (news of) the oath (being taken there) reached him. While he was thus engaged, he heard that Marwān b. Muḥammad had gone with the people of al-Jazīrah to Ibrāhīm b. al-Walīd and that Marwān had held back from giving Ibrāhīm the oath of allegiance. ʿAbdallāh b. ʿUmar kept ʿAbdallāh b. Muʿāwiyah close by him; he increased what he was spending on him and prepared him to face up to Marwān b. Muḥammad, so that, if Marwān was victorious over Ibrāhīm, ʿAbdallāh b. Muʿāwiyah would give him (ʿAbdallāh b. ʿUmar) the oath of allegiance and would fight Marwān with him. The people were in an uproar about what was going on. As Marwān came near to Syria, Ibrāhīm sallied forth to him and fought him. When Marwān had defeated and routed him, Ibrāhīm fled.[1244] ʿAbd al-ʿAzīz b. al-Ḥajjāj stood firm in the battle until he was killed. Ismāʿīl b. ʿAbdallāh, the brother of Khālid b. ʿAbdallāh al-Qasrī,
[1882] fled until he reached al-Kūfah. He had been in Ibrāhīm's army. He

1241. The editor rightly notes that it would be more accurate to say "Banū" (Notes, 1881).

1242. The Banū Nakhʿ were brought from Yemen to al-Kūfah at the time of the wars of conquest (cf. Ibn al-Kalbī, II, 444).

1243. Ibn al-Athīr has "on him and his brothers" (V, 246).

1244. *Wa-kharaja ilayhi Ibrāhīm fa-qātalahu fa-hazamahu Marwān wa-ẓafara bihi wa-kharaja hāriban.* The Cairo edition has a version of the text that is different in some places, although its apparatus makes no reference to this: *wa-kharaja ilayhi Ibrāhīm fa-qātalahu Marwān fa-hazamahu wa-ẓafara bi-ʿaskarihi wa-kharaja hāriban* (VII, 304).

fabricated a letter allegedly from Ibrāhīm about the governorship of al-Kūfah. Then he sent a message to the Yamāniyyah and secretly informed them that Ibrāhīm b. al-Walīd had appointed him governor of Iraq, and the Yamāniyyah accepted that from him. When ʿAbdallāh b. ʿUmar heard about this, he came for Ismāʿīl at the daybreak prayer, accompanied by ʿUmar b. al-Ghaḍban,[1245] and attacked him straightaway. When Ismāʿīl saw that—having no letter of contract with him and (knowing that) his master, in whose name he had counterfeited the appointment, was fleeing in disarray—he became afraid that his doings might be made public and that he would be disgraced and killed. So he said to his companions: "I dislike the shedding of blood, and I did not realize that the matter would end like this. So hold back your hands (from fighting)." Then the group left him, and he said to the people of his family: "Ibrāhīm has fled, and Marwān has entered Damascus." This was related by the people of Ismāʿīl's family, and the news spread. Strife became general, and tribal discord broke out amongst the people. The cause of that was as follows: ʿAbdallāh b. ʿUmar had given Muḍar and Rabīʿah very large stipends and had not given anything to Jaʿfar b. Nāfiʿ b. al-Qaʿqāʿ b. Shawr al-Dhuhlī and ʿUthmān b. al-Khaybarī, the brother of[1246] Banū Taym al-Lāt,[1247] and had not treated them equally with their peers. So the two of them went to see ʿAbdallāh b. ʿUmar and spoke rudely to him. ʿAbdallāh b. ʿUmar became angry and gave orders concerning them. ʿAbd al-Malik al-Ṭāʾī, who was in charge of his police force (and) who was standing at his head, went up to them. He pushed them away, and they pushed him and went out angrily. Thumāmah b. Ḥawshab b. Ruwaym al-Shaybānī[1248] was present, and he left in angry protest because of his two friends. Then they all departed for al-Kūfah. This occurred while Ibn ʿUmar was in al-Ḥīrah. When they came to al-Kūfah, they shouted: "O family of Rabīʿah!" Then the Rabīʿah rose up on their behalf; they assembled and were in an angry mood. When Ibn ʿUmar heard the news, he sent his brother ʿĀṣim against them. When he reached

---

1245. For this head of the *shurṭah* for ʿAbdallāh b. ʿUmar, cf. Crone, 162.

1246. Ibn al-Athīr has "from," rather than "the brother of" (V, 246).

1247. For this branch of the Bakr, cf. Ibn al-Kalbī, II, 543.

1248. Thumāmah had been head of police for Manṣūr b. Jumhūr, apparently in Wāṣit (cf. Crone, 119).

them they were in Dayr Hind,[1249] where they had gathered together.[1250] He precipitated himself among them and said, "This is my hand (as a pledge) for you, so make your decision." They felt
[1883] ashamed and honored and thanked ʿĀṣim. ʿĀṣim went up to their two leaders, but they remained silent and held back. In the evening, under cover of night, Ibn ʿUmar sent to ʿUmar b. al-Ghaḍbān with one hundred thousand (dirhams), and he distributed them amongst his tribe, the Banū Hammām b. Murrah b. Dhuhl b. Shaybān.[1251] He sent to Thumāmah b. Ḥawshab b. Ruwaym with one hundred thousand (dirhams), and the latter distributed them amongst his tribe. He sent to Jaʿfar b. Nāfiʿ b. al-Qaʿqāʿ with ten thousand (dirhams)[1252] and to ʿUthmān b. al-Khaybarī with ten thousand.

According to Abū Jaʿfar (al-Ṭabarī): When the Shīʿites saw his[1253] weakness, they censured him, became enboldened against him, sought to overcome him, and called for ʿAbdallāh b. Muʿāwiyah b. Jaʿfar—the person who was in charge of that was Hilāl b. Abī al-Ward, the mawlā of the Banū ʿIjl. The Shīʿites rose up with the rabble from the people and reached the mosque where they assembled. Hilāl was the one in charge of matters. The Shīʿites joined him in giving the oath of allegiance to ʿAbdallāh b. Muʿāwiyah. Then they went immediately to ʿAbdallāh (b. Muʿāwiyah), removed him from the house of al-Walīd b. Saʿīd, brought him into the citadel, and prevented ʿĀṣim b. ʿUmar from entering the citadel. So ʿĀṣim joined his brother ʿAbdallāh in al-Ḥīrah. The Kūfans came to Ibn Muʿāwiyah and gave the oath of allegiance to him; amongst them were ʿUmar b. al-Ghaḍbān b. al-Qabaʿtharī, Manṣūr b. Jumhūr, Ismāʿīl b. ʿAbdallāh al-Qasrī, and those Syrians who had family connections[1254] in al-Kūfah. He remained in al-Kūfah for a few days, and the people gave the oath of allegiance to him. The oath of allegiance was (also) given to him in Ctesiphon (al-Madāʾin) and Fam al-Nīl,[1255] and the people

---

1249. There were two sites known as Dayr Hind in al-Ḥīrah (Yāqūt, II, 707 and 709).

1250. Lit: "they had assembled and collected."

1251. Cf. Ibn al-Kalbī, II, 278.

1252. Ibn al-Athīr has simply "money" (V, 247).

1253. Presumably Ibrāhīm is meant here, although it could equally apply to Ibn ʿUmar.

1254. Lit: "who had family and stock."

1255. Cf. Wellhausen, 541.

flocked to him. Then he left, making for ʿAbdallāh b. ʿUmar in al-Ḥīrah. ʿAbdallāh b. ʿUmar came out to (meet) him with those Syrians who were with him. One of the Syrians sallied forth demanding single combat. So al-Qāsim b. ʿAbd al-Ghaffār al-ʿIjlī came out against him. The Syrian said to him: "I issued my challenge when I did, but I did not think that a man from the Bakr [1884]
b. Wā'il would come out to me. By God, I do not want to fight against you—but I would like to tell you what (information) has reached us. I should tell you that there is no Yemeni with you, neither Manṣūr nor Ismāʿīl nor any other, who has not written to ʿAbdallāh b. ʿUmar, and letters have (also) come to him from the Muḍar. (Yet) I have seen, O tribe of Rabīʿah, no letter or messenger on your behalf. They are not fighting you today, but in the morning they will do so.[1256] Therefore, if you can see to it that no blow is struck amongst you,[1257] then do so, for I am a man of Qays, and we shall be ranged opposite you tomorrow. If you want to write a letter to our master, then I will deliver it (to him); and if you want to keep faith with those in whose company you have rebelled, I have told you how matters stand with the people." Then al-Qāsim called men from his tribe, and he told them what the man had said to him and that the right wing of Ibn ʿUmar, Rabīʿah and Muḍar, would be drawn up opposite his (Ibn Muʿāwiyah's) left wing, in which Rabīʿah[1258] would (also) be. ʿAbdallāh b. Muʿāwiyah said: "This is a matter that will become clear to us if we wait until the morning.[1259] If ʿUmar b. al-Ghaḍbān wishes, then let him meet me tonight; and, if some activity in which he is involved prevents him, it is (only) an excuse.[1260] Tell him that I think that the Qaysī has been lying." The messenger brought ʿUmar that (news), and he sent him back to Ibn Muʿāwiyah with a letter informing him that its bearer had some standing with him

1256. Lit: "they are not fighting you today until you get up in the morning and they will fight you." Ibn al-Athīr has: "Tomorrow we will be opposite you, for today they are not fighting you" (loc. cit.).

1257. *In istataʿtum an lā takūna bikum al-ḥazzata.* Cf. *Gloss.*, p. CLXCI.

1258. The Cairo edition has *min Rabīʿah*, and its punctuation yields the translation: "that the left wing of Ibn ʿUmar is from Rabīʿah, and Muḍar will be standing opposite his (Ibn Muʿāwiyah's) right wing, in which is Rabīʿah" (VII, 306). This is less satisfactory.

1259. Lit: "This is a sign that will appear to us if we get up in the morning."

1260. *Fa-huwa ghadara.* The Cairo edition prefers the reading *fa-huwa ʿudhrun*: "it is an excuse" (loc. cit.). This latter reading has been followed in the translation.

('Umar) and ordering him to obtain assurances from Manṣūr and Ismāʿīl—'Umar wanted no more than to let the two of them know what was happening.[1261] Ibn Muʿāwiyah refused to comply. The following morning the people began to fight. Ibn Muʿāwiyah had put the Yamāniyyah on the right wing and Muḍar and Rabīʿah on the left. A herald announced: "Anyone who brings a head will have such and such or (anyone who brings) a prisoner will have such and such, and the money is with 'Umar b. al-Ghaḍbān." The people met (in battle) and began fighting. 'Umar b. al-Ghaḍbān attacked the right flank of Ibn 'Umar, and they withdrew in disor-
[1885] der. (Thereupon) Ismāʿīl and Manṣūr departed straightaway to al-Ḥīrah. The rabble from among the people attacked the Yamāniyyah with the Kūfans, and they killed more than thirty of them. The Hāshimite al-ʿAbbās b. ʿAbdallāh, the husband of the daughter of al-Malāt, was killed.

According to 'Umar—Muḥammad b. Yaḥyā—his father—ʿĀtikah, daughter of al-Malāt: "I married a number of husbands amongst whom was al-ʿAbbās b. ʿAbdallāh b. ʿAbdallāh b. al-Ḥārith b. Nawfal, who was killed with ʿAbdallāh b. 'Umar b. al-ʿAzīz in the tribal discord in Iraq." Mubakkir b. al-Ḥawārī b. Ziyād and others of them (the Kūfans) were killed. Then they (the rest), including ʿAbdallāh b. Muʿāwiyah, withdrew, and he entered the citadel of al-Kūfah. The left wing, consisting of the Muḍar and Rabīʿah, remained (on the battlefield), with the Syrians opposite them. Those Syrians who were stationed amongst the people in the center launched an attack on the Zaydiyyah, and they fled and entered al-Kūfah. The left wing, numbering some five hundred men, remained (firm). ʿĀmir b. Ḍubārah, Nubātah b. Ḥanẓalah b. Qabīṣah, 'Utbah b. ʿAbd al-Raḥmān al-Thaʿlabī, and al-Naḍr b. Saʿīd b. ʿAmr al-Ḥarashī came along and stopped at the Rabīʿah. They said to 'Umar b. al-Ghaḍbān: "As for us, O tribe of Rabīʿah, we do not feel that you are safe against what the people did with the Yamāniyyah, and we are afraid that you will receive similar treatment, so go away." 'Umar said: "I will not leave until I

1261. *Wa-innamā arāda an yuʿallamahumā bi-dhālika.* This is a little obscure. Presumably 'Umar wanted by the ploy of seeking guarantees from Manṣūr and Ismāʿīl to inform them of the forthcoming conflict, which would involve fellow-tribesmen fighting each other. This sentence is omitted from Ibn al-Athīr's account (V, 248).

die."[1262] They retorted: "This will avail you and your companions nothing." So they took the reins of his horse and brought him into al-Kūfah.

According to ʿUmar—ʿAlī b. Muḥammad—Sulaymān b. ʿAbdallāh al-Nawfalī—his father—Khirāsh b. al-Mughīrah b. ʿAṭiyah, a mawlā of the Banū Layth—his father: "I was the scribe of ʿAbdallāh b. ʿUmar. By God, I was with him one day, when he was in al-Ḥīrah, and somebody came to see him and said: "That man[1263] [1886]
ʿAbdallāh b. Muʿāwiyah has arrived with the people." ʿAbdallāh b. ʿUmar remained silent for a while, and his head baker came to him and stood in front of him as if notifying him that his food was ready, so ʿAbdallāh made a sign to him that he should bring it in and he brought in the food. We were anxious,[1264] fearful that Ibn Muʿāwiyah would attack us while we were with Ibn ʿUmar. I began to scrutinize Ibn ʿUmar to see whether he had changed in any aspect of his eating or drinking or appearance or the instructions[1265] (he was giving). But no, by God! I failed to see any change either great or small in his mien. When his food was brought in, a bowl was placed in front of each pair of us. A bowl was put between me and so and so and another bowl between so and so and so and so until (all) those who were at his table were included. When he had finished his breakfast and his ablutions, he ordered (that) money (should be brought), and it was (duly) brought, together with vessels of gold and silver and clothes. He distributed most of that amongst his commanders. Then he summoned a mawlā of his, or (perhaps it was) a *mamlūk*, who used to bring him luck and good fortune because of his name; he was called either Maymūn or Fatḥ or one of the names of good augury.[1266] Ibn ʿUmar said to him: "Take your standard, go to such and such a hill, stick it in the ground, call your companions, and

---

1262. *Ḥattā amartu*: "until I give the command." The Cairo edition has *amūta* (VII, 307). This has been followed in the translation, especially in view of the version of Ibn al-Athīr: *ḥattā uqtala*, "until I am killed" (V, 248).

1263. Presumably the word *hādhā* forms part of the sentence that forms part of the sentence that contains "ʿAbdallāh." This is certainly the interpretation of the Cairo editor (VII, 307).

1264. Lit: "our hearts became swelled" (disquieted).

1265. Lit: "in any thing of his affair consisting of his place of eating or drinking or outward appearance or ordering or forbidding."

1266. Lit: "from whom he used to look for a blessing (*yatabarraku bihi*) and

remain until I come to you." So he did that. ʿAbdallāh (b. ʿUmar) set out, accompanied by us, and he reached the hill, where the ground was white with the companions of Ibn Muʿāwiyah. Then ʿAbdallāh (b. ʿUmar) gave orders to a herald, and he announced that anyone who brought a head would have five hundred (dirhams). By God, it was not long before a head was brought and placed in front of him. He ordered five hundred (dirhams) for it, and they were given to the person who had brought it. When his companions saw the way he had kept faith with the person who had brought the head,[1267] they spread (the news) amongst the people,[1268] and by God it was only a short while before I saw around five hundred heads that had been thrown in front of him. Ibn Muʿāwiyah and those with him withdrew in disarray. The first of his followers who entered al-Kūfah in flight was Abū al-
[1887] Bilād, the mawlā of the Banū ʿAbs, accompanied by his son Sulaymān. Abū al-Bilād was a Shīʿite supporter. Every day the Kūfans began (afresh) to yell at them as if rebuking them for the defeat of Ibn Muʿāwiyah. Abū al-Bilād began shouting to his son Sulaymān: "Go and let the camels die."[1269] ʿAbdallāh b. Muʿāwiyah passed by. He hurried through al-Kūfah and did not remain there but went as far as the mountain.[1270]

According to Abū ʿUbaydah: ʿAbdallāh b. Muʿāwiyah and his brothers entered the citadel. When evening came, they said to ʿUmar b. al-Ghaḍbān and his associates: "O company of Rabīʿah, you have seen what the people have done to us. We have made you responsible for our lives with your own[1271] (lives as surety). If you fight together with us, we will fight together with you, and, if you see the people forsaking both us and you, then take a pledge

---

from whose name he would seek a good augury (*yatafāʾalu bi-ismihi*), being called Maymūn or Fatḥ or one of the names through which blessing is sought by uttering the name of God (*al-mutabarrak bihā*)." Ibn al-Athīr adds "Riyāḥ . . . or another auspicious name" (V, 247). Cf. *EI*², "faʾl" (T. Fahd).

1267. Lit: "the owner of the head," a phrase that might be misinterpreted as it stands!

1268. The Cairo edition has *thārū bi-al-qawm*: "they rose up with the people" (VII, 308).

1269. *Al-nawāḍiḥ*, plural of *nāḍiḥ*: "a camel or ass or bull upon which water is drawn"; cf. Lane, I, 2807.

1270. This is possibly a reference to al-Jibāl, since preceding accounts in al-Ṭabarī mention that area as the destination of Ibn Muʿāwiyah.

1271. Cf. *Gloss.*, p. CCCLXXIII.

of safe-conduct both on our behalf and on your own, for whatever you take in respect to yourselves we will (also) be satisfied with for ourselves." ʿUmar b. al-Ghaḍbān assured them: "We will not leave you without fulfilling one of two conditions:[1272] either that we will fight together with you or that we will take a pledge of safe-conduct for you as we take for ourselves. So calm yourselves." So they stayed in the citadel, whilst the Zaydiyyah were at the entrances of the streets with the Syrians hastening[1273] out to them (the Zaydiyyah) and embarking on fighting them (and beginning a conflict that lasted) for several days. Then the Rabīʿah took a pledge of safe-conduct for themselves, the Zaydiyyah, and ʿAbdallāh b. Muʿāwiyah; (this specified) that they would not pursue[1274] them and that they (Ibn Muʿāwiyah's men) might go wherever they wanted. ʿAbdallāh b. ʿUmar sent a message to ʿUmar b. al-Ghaḍbān ordering him to attack the citadel and to bring out ʿAbdallāh b. Muʿāwiyah. So Ibn al-Ghaḍbān sent a message to him and removed Ibn Muʿāwiyah and those of his party and his followers from amongst the people of Ctesiphon, the Sawād, and al-Kūfah who were with him. The envoys of ʿUmar accompanied them until they had driven them from the bridge, and then ʿUmar came down from the citadel.

In this year al-Ḥārith b. Surayj came to Marw,[1275] making his way there from the land of the Turks with the safe-conduct that [1888] Yazīd b. al-Walīd had written for him. He came to Naṣr b. Sayyār; then he opposed Naṣr and displayed hostility toward him, and a large group of people gave the oath of allegiance to him on that basis.

The Account of the Affair of al-Ḥārith and Naṣr after al-Ḥārith Came to See Him

According to ʿAlī b. Muḥammad (al-Madāʾinī)—his *shaykh*s: Al-Ḥārith went to Marw on his departure from the land of the

1272. *Min iḥdā khallatayn*: lit: "from one of two qualities."
1273. The text has *yaghdūna*. This is later corrected to *yaghdū*. Cf. *Add.*, II, p. DCCXIV. The Cairo edition has the corrected form (VII, 308).
1274. The text has *lā yamnaʿūnahum*. Nöldeke suggests *allā yatbaʿūhum*. Cf. *Add.*, II, p. DCCXIV. The Cairo edition follows Nöldeke (loc. cit.).
1275. Cf. al-Ṭabarī, II, 1866–69.

Turks.[1276] He reached Marw on the last Sunday of Jumādā II 127 (Sunday, April 4, 745), when the month had three days left to run. Salm b. Aḥwaz and the people met al-Ḥārith at Kushmāhan.[1277] Muḥammad b. al-Faḍl[1278] b. ʿAṭiyah al-ʿAbsī proclaimed: "Praise be to God who has caused us to rejoice at your coming and who has handed you back to the ordinance to Islam and the community." Al-Ḥārith announced: "O my people, did you not know that the many, when they are in disobedience to God, are few and that the few, when they are in obedience to God, are many? I have not been happy from the time I rebelled until today, and there is no happiness for me unless God is obeyed." When he entered Marw, he said: "O God, I have had no purpose in anything (that has transpired) between them and me other than to keep faith. If they want to act treacherously, then help me against them." Naṣr met him and lodged him in the citadel of the Bukhār Khudāh. Naṣr set aside fifty dirhams for his daily expenses, and he used to restrict himself to one dish. Naṣr released those of al-Ḥārith's family who were in his custody. He set free Muḥammad b. al-Ḥārith and al-Alūf, the daughter of al-Ḥārith and Umm Bakr. When his son Muḥammad came to him, he (al-Ḥārith) said: "O God, make him pious and God-fearing."

Al-Waḍḍāḥ b. Ḥabīb b. Budayl came to Naṣr b. Sayyār on behalf of ʿAbdallāh b. ʿUmar. A sharp cold had afflicted him, so Naṣr wrapped him in garments and ordered hospitality and two slave girls for him. Then al-Waḍḍāḥ went in to see al-Ḥārith, who had a group of his companions standing at his head. Al-Waḍḍāḥ said:
[1889] "We in Iraq have heard a lot about the size and weight of your mace, and I would like to see it." Al-Ḥārith replied: "It is like one of those (maces) that you see wielded by those (men)" and pointed to his followers. "But whenever I strike with it, my blow becomes well known."[1279] His mace weighed eighteen Syrian *raṭl*s.

Al-Ḥārith b. Surayj came in to see Naṣr wearing the coat of mail

---

1276. Cf. Ibn al-Athīr, V, 249.

1277. For Kushmayhan, one march from Marw on the road to Bukhārā, cf. Le Strange, *Lands*, 400. According to al-Yaʿqūbī, it was called Kushmāhan (ibid.).

1278. The text has al-Fuḍayl. This is later corrected to al-Faḍl. Cf. *Add.*, II, p. DCCXIV.

1279. The text seems unsatisfactory here: *walākinnanī idhā ḍarabtu bihi ḍarbatī*. The Cairo edition has: *walākinnanī idhā ḍarabtu bihi shuhirat ḍarabatnī* (V, 309). The translation given is very tentative and is based on the reading *idhā ḍarabtu bihi shuhirat ḍarbatī*.

that he had obtained from a *khāqān*. The *khāqān* had made al-Ḥārith choose between one hundred thousand Danbakāniyyah *dīnār*s and the coat of mail, and he had chosen the coat of mail. Al-Marzubānah, the daughter of Qudayd and the wife of Naṣr b. Sayyār, caught sight of it. She sent al-Ḥārith a sable garment of hers with a slave girl who (also) belonged to her with the message: "Greet my cousin and say to him that it is cold today, so warm yourself up with this sable garment, and praise be to God who has brought you safely (here)." Al-Ḥārith said to the slave girl: "Greet my cousin and say to her: 'Is this a loan or a gift?' " She said: "It's a gift." Then al-Ḥārith sold it for four thousand *dīnār*s and distributed them amongst his companions. Naṣr sent al-Ḥārith many carpets and a horse. Al-Ḥārith sold all that and distributed the proceeds equally amongst his companions. Al-Ḥārith used to sit on a saddle with a rough cushion folded for him. Naṣr suggested to al-Ḥārith that he (Naṣr) should entrust him with authority and give him one hundred thousand dīnārs. Al-Ḥārith refused to accept and sent a message to Naṣr saying: "I have no liking at all for this world nor for its (lit: 'those') pleasures nor for marriage with the most excellent of the Arabs. I ask only for the Book of God, may He be praised and glorified, and for conduct in accordance with the *sunnah* and for fair treatment of the people who are good and have merit. If you act accordingly, I will help you against your enemy." Then al-Ḥārith sent to al-Kirmānī saying: "If Naṣr deals with me by the Book of God and fair treatment of the people who are good and have merit, as I have asked him, I will support him and will fulfill God's command. If he does not do so, I will call on God's help against him, and I will help you if you guarantee to me what I want in the way of conduct in accor- [1890]
dance with justice and the *sunnah*." Whenever the Banū Tamīm came in to see him, he would summon them to himself—and Muḥammad b. Ḥumrān, Muḥammad b. Ḥarb b. Jirfās al-Minqariyyān, al-Khalīl b. Ghazwān al-ʿAdawī, ʿAbdallāh b. Mujjāʿah, Hubayrah b. Sharāḥīl al-Saʿdiyyān, ʿAbd al-ʿAzīz b. ʿAbd Rabbihi al-Laythī, Bishr b. Jurmūz al-Ḍabbī, Nahār b. ʿAbdallāh b. al-Ḥutāt al-Mujāshiʿī, and ʿAbdallāh al-Nubātī took the oath of allegiance to al-Ḥārith. Al-Ḥārith said to Naṣr: "I left this city thirteen years ago in disgust at tyranny, and (now) you want to incite me to that." Then three thousand men joined al-Ḥārith.

Appendix I

Problems of Translation

i. Al-Walīd's letter to Hishām (al-Ṭabarī, II, 1746–47)

(a) *1746, l.6: min . . . maḥwi mā maḥā min aṣḥābī wa-ḥuramī wa-ahlī.* Al-Iṣfahānī (*Aghānī*, VI, 107) has *min . . . maḥwi mā maḥā min aṣḥābī wa-annahu ḥarramanī wa ahlī* ("how he has ruined my friends and has ostracized me and my dependents").

(b) *1746, ll.7–8: wa-lam akun akhāfu an yabtaliya Allāhu amīra al-mu'minīna bi-dhālika wa-lā ubālī bi-hi minhu.* For both the literal and more elegant Latin translations of this passage and a detailed discussion, cf. *Gloss.*, CXLI. Al-Iṣfahānī has *wa-lam akun akhāfu an yabtaliya Allāhu amīra al-mu'minīna bi-dhālika fiyya wa-lā yunālunī mithlahu minhu* (lit., "I would never have thought that God would thus test the Commander of the Faithful through me and that he (Hishām) would defame me like that"). Cf. *Aghānī*, loc. cit. This version, as suggested in the Ṭabarī apparatus, is much better and has been adopted here.

Cf. also al-Balādhurī's version: "I did not fear that God would thus test the Commander of the Faithful nor that He would test me thereby" (*Ansāb* (Derenk), 13).

(c) *1746, l.10:* The text has *istiṣlāḥihi.* The apparatus has the variant *istiṣḥābī*, which makes good sense, especially with the suggested amendment *lahu* (II, 1746, n. 1.) The translation given is based on the variant. Cf. al-Iṣfahānī's version: *istiṣḥābī li-Ibni Suhayl.* Cf. *Aghānī,* loc. cit.

(d) *1746, l.16–1747, l.1: fa-al-nāsu bayna dhālika yaqtarifūna al-āthāma ʿalā nufūsihim min Allāhi aw yastawjibūna al-ujūr ʿalayhi* ("in such a situation men commit sin against themselves before God or deserve punishments on that basis"). The Cairo edition (VII, 213) has a very significant change in the text, a change for which no textual justification is given: *wa-lā yastawjibūna al-ʿuqūbata ʿalayhi* ("they do not deserve punishment on that basis").

A more satisfactory reading is that in the *Aghānī,* 107: *wa-yaqtarifūna al-āthamā ʿalā anfusihim min Allāhi bi-mā yastawjibūna al-ʿuqūbata ʿalayhi* ("They commit sins against themselves before God for which they deserve punishment"). This version has been used in the translation.

For al-Walīd's views on the *Qadariyyah,* cf. n. 641.

ii. *Hishām's letter to al-Walīd (al-Ṭabarī, II, 1747–49)*

(a) *1747, ll.11–13*

The text is rather problematical. It reads: *wa-amīr al-mu'minīn akhwafu ʿalā nafsihi min iqtirāfi al-ma'thami ʿalayhā fī alladhī kāna yujrī ʿalayka minhu fī alladhī aḥdatha min qaṭʿi mā qaṭaʿa wa-maḥwi mā maḥā min saḥābatika li-amrayni.*

Al-Iṣfahānī's version of the same part of the letter is as follows: *wa-lā yatakhawwafu ʿalā nafsihi iqtirāfa al-ma'thami fī alladhī aḥdatha min qatʿi mā qaṭaʿa wa-maḥwi maḥā min ṣaḥābatika li-amrayni* ("but he (the caliph) does not fear that he has committed wrong in the matter of the cuts he has made and the way in which he has ruined those of your friends whom he has ruined. (This absence of fear is) for two reasons"). Cf. *Aghānī,* VI, 107.

The version in the *Aghānī* is adopted without comment by the Cairo al-Ṭabarī edition (VII, 213).

The version given by al-Balādhurī is of some help in clarifying the Leiden al-Ṭabarī text: *wa-amīru al-muʿminīn yastaghfiru Allāha min ijrā'ihi mā kāna yujrī ʿalayka fa-inna al-ma'thama fī dhālika akhwafu minhu ʿalā nafsihi fī qatʿihi mā qaṭaʿa li-amraynī.* Cf. *Ansāb* (Derenk), 14. A possible translation would be: "The Commander of the Faithful asks God's forgiveness for his having given you the allowance that he gave you, for the wrong in (doing) that is more frightening (to him) than the wrong (lit., what) he has (done) against his soul by making the cuts he has made. (This is) for two reasons".

Appendix II

Al-Walīd's Letter Appointing His Two Sons, al-Ḥakam and ʿUthmān, as His Successors: al-Ṭabarī, II, 1756–64

The notes in the commentary itself deal with small points of clarification raised by the text of al-Walīd's letter. The purpose of this appendix is to consider at greater length the manifold problems of translating the letter. Its style is tortuous and full of rhetorical devices. On a number of occasions the text is clearly corrupt. Throughout, it presents the translator with the problem of striking the right balance between a literal English version which adheres as closely as possible to the Arabic (however convoluted that may be) and a more elegant rendering which might invite the charge of straying too far from the original and thus becoming more of a paraphrase than a proper translation.

The translation offered here took many weeks because of the inherent difficulty of the text. Fortunately, Patricia Crone and Martin Hinds have also been working on this letter (cf. their recent book, *God's Caliph*, 116–26). As well as a literal translation, they provide a detailed discussion of the background and significance of the letter, concluding that it is authentic.

The translation presented here was made before I saw that of Drs. Crone and Hinds. However, the notes have been adjusted slightly in the light of their comments, and I have made one major emendation in my translation (specified later in this appendix) on the basis of their version. I am very grateful to them for most generously allowing me access to their work just before I completed this volume.

(a) *1757, l.14–1758, l.2.*

The decision to omit the extremely problematic phrase *fa-lam yabqa kāfirun,* supported by the apparatus (BM and O), was made after reading the version of Crone and Hinds (cf. *God's Caliph,* 119), which makes much better sense. The Leiden text as it stands would require the translation: "there remained no infidel whose blood was not licit thereby and the cutting of ties which were between them [lit., him (the member of the *ummah*) and him (the infidel)] even if he [lit., they] were his father, son, or tribesman [lit., their fathers, sons, or kinsmen]". For this change from singular to plural, cf. Crone and Hinds, op. cit., 119, n.16.

(b) *1759, l.17–1760, l.1.*

The text here is extremely corrupt. The text as it stands reads *wa-fī-al maʿṣiyati mimmā yuḥillu bi-ghayrihim min naq-mātihi wa-tuṣībuhum ʿalayhi wa-yuḥiqqu min sukhtihi wa-ʿadhābihi.* Crone and Hinds (loc. cit.) make drastic but convincing emendations to the text and give better balance to the different elements of the sentence.

In this translation, the following more modest changes and additions are suggested: *wa-fī-al maʿṣiyati nāla ghayruhum mā yuḥillu bi-him min naqmātihi wa-yusībuhum ʿalayhi wa-yuḥiqqu min sukhtihi wa-ʿadhābihi* ("by disobedience others obtain those punishments with which He assails (them) and by which He strikes them and that which befalls them of His displeasure and chastisement").

(c) *1760, ll.1–3*

The text has *wa-yunzalu bi-al-ṭāʿati.* The reading of the Cairo edition (221), *wa-bi-tarki al-ṭāʿati* (which is partly based on the apparatus), has been preferred in the translation. Even so, it is difficult to decide whether the whole phrase *wa-bi-tarki al-ṭāʿati . . . wa-al-tabadduli bi-hā* should belong to the preceding sentence or to the following one. Crone and Hinds consider it to belong to the following sentence, thus: "In abandonment and neglect of obedience, in departure from it, lack of attention to it and carelessness of it, God destroys [all] those who stray and disobey. . ." (loc. cit.). There is here, however, a slight non sequitur in the shift of subject from the miscreants to God. If, on the other hand, the phrase *bi-tarki al-ṭāʿati . . . al-tabadduli bi-hā* is taken with the preceding sentence, the result is perhaps more coherent (if a period is placed after *bi-hā.*) This alternative has been followed in the translation but with the full awareness that the result is still slightly unsatisfactory. The text would read better with a *wa* or *fa* before *ahlaka.*

(d) *1760, ll.13–14*

Once again there is a problem of punctuation. The Cairo edition (VII, 222) makes a break in the sentence after *dahmāʾihā,* whereas Crone and Hinds make the next phrase *dhukhru al-niʿmati* part of the preceding sentence. Neither solution is entirely satisfactory. In this translation, the former alternative has been followed and the text is read as *wa-dhukhru al-niʿmati ʿalayhā . . . huwa al-ʿahdu. . .* Here *ʿalayhā* refers to the community and the *wa* before *huwa* has been omitted.

(e) *1761, ll.1–4*

Literally, "a cutting of the enticements of the Devil in that for which his followers long and to which he (the Devil) incites them, concerning the destruction of this religion, the splitting of the unity of its people, and their disagreeing about that in which God united them through it (His religion)".

(f) *1762, l.3*

Tastaẓillūna fī afnānihi. There is a variant reading, *afnāʾihi.* Crone and Hinds read *afyāʾihi* (op. cit., 123), rejecting *afnānihi* because of the following preposition *fī. Afyāʾihi* ("shades") is certainly very plausible. Reading the text as it stands with *afnānihi* still makes quite good sense. Perhaps there is here an indirect allusion to Qurʾān 55, v.48. This sūrah enumerates the favors of God toward men.

Bibliography of Cited Works

I. Primary Sources: Text and Translations

Anon. *Ḥudūd al-ʿālam.* Translated with commentary by V. Minorsky. London, 1937.

al-Balādhurī, Abū al-Ḥasan Aḥmad b. Yaḥyā. *Futūḥ al-buldān.* Edited by M. J. de Goeje under the title *Liber expugnationis regionum.* Leiden, 1866.

———. *Ansāb al-ashrāf.* Parts transcribed by D. Derenk in *Leben und Dichtung des Omaiyadenkalifen al-Walīd ibn Yazīd.* Freiburg im Breisgau, 1974.

———. *Ansāb al-ashrāf.* Edited by Muḥammad Bāqir al-Maḥmūdī. Beirut, 1977.

Balʿamī, Abū ʿAlī Muḥammad, *Taʾrīkh-i Ṭabarī.* Translated by H. Zotenberg under the title *Chronique de Abou-Djafar Moʿhammed-ben-Djarir-ben-Yezid Tabari.* 4 vols. Nogent-Le-Rotrou, 1874.

al-Dīnawarī, Abū Ḥanīfah Aḥmad b. Dāwūd. *Kitāb al-Akhbār al-ṭiwal.* 2 vols. Edited by V. W. Guirgass and I. Kratchkovsky. Leiden, 1888–1912.

Ibn ʿAbd Rabbihi, Abū ʿUmar Aḥmad b. Muḥammad. *Al-ʿiqd al-farīd.* 3 vols. Cairo, 1321.

Ibn Aʿtham, Abū Muḥammad Aḥmad al-Kūfī al-Kindī. *Kitāb al-Futūḥ.* Vol. VIII. Hyderabad, 1978.

Ibn al-Athīr, ʿIzz al-Dīn Abū al-Ḥasan ʿAlī b. Muḥammad. *al-Kāmil fī al-taʾrīkh.* Edited by C. J. Tornberg. Vol. V. Leiden, 1871.

Ibn Durayd, Abū Bakr Muḥammad b. al-Ḥasan al-Azdī. *Kitāb al-Ishtiqāq.* Baghdad, 1958.

Ibn Ḥajar, Shihāb al-Dīn Abū al-Faḍl Aḥmad b. Nūr al-Dīn ʿAlī b. Muḥammad. *Tahdhīb al-Tahdhīb.* Hyderabad, 1325–27.

Ibn Ḥawqal, Abū al-Qāsim b. ʿAlī al-Naṣībī. *Kitāb Ṣūrat al-arḍ.* Translated by J. H. Kramers and G. Wiet under the title *Configuration de la terre.* 2 vols. Paris and Beirut, 1964.

Ibn Hishām, *Sīrat Rasūl Allāh.* Translated by A. Guillaume under the title *The life of Muḥammad.* Oxford, 1955.

Ibn al-Kalbī, Hishām b. Muḥammad. *Ǧamharat an-nasab, das genealogische Werk des Hišām b. Muḥammad al-Kalbī.* Translated and rearranged with a commentary by W. Caskel and G. Strenziok. Leiden, 1966.

Ibn Khallikān, Abū al-ʿAbbās Aḥmad b. Muḥammad al-Irbilī. *Wafayāt al-aʿyān wa-anbāʾ abnāʾ al-zamān.* Translated by Baron McGuckin de Slane under the title *Ibn Khallikan's Biographical Dictionary.* 4 vols. Paris, 1842–71.

Ibn Manẓūr, Jamāl al-Dīn Abū al-Faḍl Muḥammad b. Mukarram al-Anṣārī. *Lisān al-ʿarab al-muḥīṭ.* Revised and completed by Yūsuf Khayyāṭ. 3 vols. Beirut, n.d.

Ibn al-Marzubān, Abū Bakr Muḥammad b. Khalaf. *Kitāb Faḍl al-kilāb ʿalā kathīr mimman labisa al-thiyāb.* Translated and edited by G. R. Smith and M. A. S. Abdel Haleem. Warminster, 1978.

Ibn al-Nadīm, Abū al-Faraj Muḥammad b. Isḥāq al-Warrāq. *Kitāb al-Fihrist.* Translated by B. Dodge under the title *The Fihrist of al-Nadim, a Tenth Century Survey of Muslim Culture.* 2 vols. New York and London, 1970.

Ibn Qutaybah, Abū Muḥammad ʿAbdallāh b. Muslim al-Dīnawarī. *Kitāb al-Maʿārif.* Edited by F. Wüstenfeld. Göttingen, 1850.

Ibn Rustah, Abū ʿAlī Aḥmad b. ʿUmar. *Kitāb al-Aʿlāq al-nafīsah.* Translated by G. Wiet under the title *Les Atours précieux.* Cairo, 1955.

Ibn Saʿd, Abū ʿAbdallāh Muḥammad b. Saʿd b. Manī al-Baṣrī al-Hāshimī. *Kitāb al-Ṭabaqāt al-Kabīr.* Edited by E. Sachau, et al. 9 vols. Leiden, 1904–40.

Ibn al-Ṭiqṭaqah, Ṣafī al-Dīn Muḥammad b. ʿAlī. *al-Fakhrī.* Translated by C. E. J. Whitting. London, 1947.

al-Iṣfahānī, Abū al-Faraj ʿAlī b. Ḥusayn. *Kitāb al-Aghānī.* 20 vols. Būlāq, 1285–86 (1868–70).

———. *Kitāb Maqātil al-Ṭalibiyyīn.* Najaf, 1353 (1934).

al-Iṣfahānī, Hamzah b. al-Ḥasan [b.] al-Muʾaddib. *Taʾrīkh Sinī mulūk al-arḍ wa-al-anbiyāʾ.* Beirut, 1961.

al-Jāḥiẓ, Abū ʿUthmān ʿAmr b. Baḥr al-Fuqaymī al-Baṣrī. *Kitāb al-Bayān wa-al-tabyīn.* 4 vols. Cairo, 1948–50.

al-Jahshiyārī, Abū ʿAbdallāh Muḥammad b. Abdūs. *Kitāb al-Wuzarāʾ wa-al-kuttāb.* Edited by ʿAbdallāh Ismāʿīl al-Sāwī. Baghdad, 1357 (1938).

Khalīfah, Abū ʿAmr b. Khayyāṭ. *Taʾrīkh.* 2 vols. Najaf, 1967.

Kitāb al-ʿUyūn wa-al-ḥadāʾiq fī akhbār al-ḥaqāʾiq. Edited by M. J. de

Goeje and P. de Jong in *Fragmenta Historicorum Arabicorum.* Leiden, 1869.
al-Mas'ūdī, Abū al-Ḥasan 'Alī b. al-Ḥusayn. *Murūj al-dhahab wa-ma'ādin al-jawhar.* Edited and translated by C. Barbier de Meynard and Pavet de Courteille under the title *Les prairies d'or.* 9 vols. Paris, 1861–77.
———. *Kitāb al-tanbīh wa-al-ishrāf.* Beirut, 1981.
al-Maydānī, Abū al-Faḍl Aḥmad b. Muḥammad. *Majma' amthāl al-'Arab.* 3 vols. Translated by G. W. Freytag under the title *Arabum proverba.* Bonn, 1838–43.
Narshakhī. *The History of Bukhārā.* Translated by R. N. Frye. Cambridge, Mass., 1954.
Rasā'il al-bulaghā'. Edited by M. Kurd 'Alī. Cairo, 1953.
Shaykh al-Mufīd. *Kitāb al-Irshād. The Book of Guidance into the Lives of the Twelve Imams.* Translated by I. K. A. Howard. London, 1981.
al-Ṭabarī. *Ta'rīkh al-Ṭabarī.* Edited by M. Abū al-Faḍl Ibrāhīm. Vol. VII. Cairo, 1966.
al-Ṭabarī, Abū Ja'far Muḥammad b. Jarīr. *Ta'rīkh al-Rusul wa-al-mulūk.* Edited by M. J. de Goeje et al. Leiden, 1879–1901.
al-Ya'qūbī, Abū al-'Abbās Aḥmad b. Isḥāq. *Les Pays.* Translated by G. Wiet. Cairo, 1937.
———. *Ta'rīkh.* Edited by M. T. Houtsma under the title *Historiae.* 2 vols. Leiden, 1883.
Yāqūt, Abū 'Abdallāh Ya'qūb b. 'Abdallāh al-Ḥamawī al-Rūmī. *Mu'jam al-buldān.* 5 vols. Beirut, 1374–76 (1955–57).

II. Secondary Sources and Reference Works

'Atwān, H. *Al-Walīd b. Yazīd, 'arḍun wa-naqdun.* Beirut, 1981.
Barthold, W. *Turkestan down to the Mongol Invasion.* 3rd ed. London, 1968.
———. *An Historical Geography of Iran.* Translated by S. Soucek. Edited by C. E. Bosworth. Princeton, 1984.
Bosworth, C. E. *Al-Maqrīzī's Book of Contention and Strife Concerning the Relations between the Banū Umayya and the Banū Hāshim.* Manchester, 1980.
———. "The Rulers of Chaghāniyān in Early Islamic Times," *Iran* XIX (1981): 1–20.
Braslavski, I. "Hat Welīd II den Jordan ablenken wollen?" *Journal of the Palestine Oriental Society* XIII/1–2 (1933): 97–100.
Brockelmann, C. *Geschichte der arabischen Literatur.* 5 vols. Leiden, 1937–42.

Brooks, E. W. "The Arabs in Asia Minor (641–750) from Arabic Sources," *Journal of Hellenic Studies* XVIII (1898): 182–208.

Cahen, C. "Points de vue sur la 'revolution ʿabbāside,'" *Revue historique* CCXXX (1963): 295–338.

Cook, M. A. *Early Muslim Dogma.* Cambridge, 1981.

Creswell, K. A. C. *Early Muslim Architecture.* 2d ed. Oxford, 1969.

Crone, P. *Slaves on Horses. The Evolution of the Islamic Polity.* Cambridge, 1980.

Crone, P., and M. Hinds. *God's Caliph. Religious Authority in the First Centuries of Islam.* Cambridge, 1986.

De Goeje, M. J. *Annales . . . al-Tabari. Introductio, glossarium, addenda et emendanda.* Leiden, 1901.

Dennett, D. *Marwān b. Muḥammad. The Passing of the Umayyad Caliphate.* Ph.D. thesis. Harvard, 1939.

———. *Conversion and the Poll-tax in Early Islam.* Cambridge, Mass., 1950.

Derenk, D. *Leben und Dichtung des Omaiyadenkalifen al-Walīd ibn Yazīd.* Freiburg im Breisgau, 1974.

Dixon, A. A. *The Umayyad Caliphate 65–86/684–705.* London, 1971.

Djaït, H. "Les Yamanites à Kufa au 1er siècle de l'hégire," *JESHO* (1976): 148–81.

Duri, A. A. *The Rise of Historical Writing among the Arabs.* Edited and translated by L. I. Conrad. Princeton, 1983.

Dussaud, R. *Topographie historique de la Syrie antique et médiévale.* Paris, 1927.

Encyclopaedia of Islàm. First edition. 4 vols. and Supplement. Leiden, 1913–42.

Encyclopaedia of Islâm. New edition. 5 vols. and Supplement. Leiden and London, 1960–.

Endres, F. C., and A. M. Schimmel. *Das Mysterium der Zahl.* Cologne, 1984.

Flügel, G. *Concordantiae Corani Arabicae.* Leipzig, 1842.

Freytag, G. W. *Lexicon Arabico-Latinum.* Halle, 1837.

Gabrieli, F. *Il Califfato di Hisham.* Alexandria, 1935.

———. "Al-Walīd b. Yazīd, il califfo e il poeta". *RSO* 15 (1935): 1–64.

Gibb, H. A. R. *The Arab Conquests in Central Asia.* New York, 1970.

———. *Studies on the Civilisation of Islam.* Edited by S. J. Shaw and W. R. Polk. Princeton, 1982.

Goldziher, I. *Muhammedanische Studien.* 2 vols. Halle, 1889–90. Translated by C. R. Barber and S. M. Stern and edited by Stern under the title *Muslim Studies.* 2 vols. London, 1967–71.

Grabar, O. "Al-Mushatta, Baghdād, and Wāsiṭ," *The World of Islam (Studies in Honour of P. K. Hitti)*, edited by R. B. Winder, 99–108. London, 1959.

Grabar, O. and M. Carter. *Sasanian Silver. Late Antique and Early Mediaeval Arts of Luxury from Iran.* Ann Arbor, 1967.

Grignaschi, M. "Les 'Rasā'il Arisṭaṭālīsa ilā l-Iskandar' de Sālim Abū l-'Alā et l'activité culturelle à l'époque umayyade," *BEO* XIX (1965–66): 7–83.

Grunebaum, G. E. von. *Muslim Festivals.* New York, 1951.

Guidi, I. *Tables Alphabétiques du Kitāb al-Aġānī.* 2 vols. Leiden, 1900.

Hawting, G. R. *The First Dynasty of Islam.* London and Sydney, 1986.

Hell, J. *Das Leben des Farazdaḳ nach seinen Gedichten und sein Loblied auf al-Walīd ibn Jazīd.* Leipzig, 1903.

Hillenbrand, R. "*La Dolce vita* in early Islamic Syria: The Evidence of Later Umayyad Palaces," *Art History* 5/1 (1982): 1–35.

Hinz, W. *Islamische Masse und Gewichte umgerechnet ins metrische System.* Handbuch der Orientalistik, Ergänzungsband I, Heft I. Leiden, 1955.

Hitti, P. *History of Syria.* London, 1951.

Honigmann, E. *Die Ostgrenze des byzantinischen Reiches von 363 bis 1071 nach griechischen, arabischen, syrischen und armenischen Quellen.* In *Byzance et les Arabes,* vol. III, edited by A. A. Vasiliev. Brussels, 1935.

Howard, I. K. A. "The Development of the *Adhān* and *Iqāma* of the *Ṣalāt* in Early Islam," *JSS* 26/2 (1981): 219–28.

Hrbek, I. "Muḥammads Nachlass und die Aliden," *Arch. Or.* XVIII/3 (1950): 143–49.

Huart, C. *Histoire des Arabes.* Paris, 1911.

Justi, F. *Iranisches Namenbuch.* Marburg, 1895.

Kazimirski, A. de Biberstein, *Dictionnaire Arabe-Français,* Paris, 1860.

Lane, E. W. *An Arabic-English Lexicon Derived from the Best and Most Copious Eastern Sources.* 8 vols. London, 1863–93.

Le Strange, G. *Palestine under the Moslems, a Description of Syria and the Holy Land from A.D. 650 to 1500.* London, 1890.

———. *The Lands of the Eastern Caliphate, Mesopotamia, Persia and Central Asia from the Moslem Conquest to the Time of Timur.* Cambridge, 1905.

Løkkegaard, F. *Islamic Taxation in the Classic Period.* Copenhagen, 1950.

Makdisi, G., D. Sourdel, and J. Sourdel-Thomine. *Prédication et propagande au Moyen Age: Islam, Byzance, Occident.* Paris, 1983.

Marquart, J. *Ērānšahr nach der Geographie des Ps. Moses Xorenacʻi.* In *Abhandlungen der Königl. Gesell. der Wiss. zu Göttingen* n.s. III, 2. Berlin, 1901.

Massignon, L. "Explication du plan de Kufa (Irak)," *Mélanges Maspero, III. Mémoires de l'Institut français d'archéologie orientale du Caire* 68. (Cairo, 1935–40): 336–70.

Minorsky, V. *A History of Sharvān and Darband in the 10th—11th Centuries.* Cambridge, 1958.

Morony, M. *Iraq after the Muslim Conquest.* Princeton, 1984.

Muir, W. *The Caliphate: Its Rise, Decline and Fall.* Beirut, 1963.

Petersen, E. L. *ʻAlī and Muʻāwiya in Early Arabic Tradition.* Copenhagen, 1964.

Riḍā, A. *Muʻjam matn al-lughah,* Beirut, 1965.

Rogers, J. M. *The Spread of Islam.* Oxford, 1976.

Rosenthal, F. *A History of Muslim Historiography.* Leiden, 1968.

Rotter, G. *Die Umayyaden und der zweite Bürgerkrieg (688–692).* Wiesbaden, 1982.

Sadan, J. *Le mobilier au Proche Orient mediéval.* Leiden, 1976.

Sauvaget, J. "Remarques sur les monuments omeyyades," *JA* 231 (1939): 1–59.

Schönig, H. *Das Sendschreiben des ʻAbdalḥamīd b. Yaḥyā (gest. 132/750) an den Kronprinzen ʻAbdallāh b. Marwān II.* Stuttgart, 1985.

Schwarz, P. *Iran im Mittelalter nach den arabischen Geographen.* 9 parts. Leipzig, Stuttgart, and Berlin, 1896–1936.

Sezgin, F. *Geschichte des arabischen Schrifttums.* Vol. 1, Leiden, 1967; Vol. 2, Leiden, 1975.

Sezgin, U. *Abū Mihnaf.* Leiden, 1971.

Shaban, M. A. *The ʻAbbāsid Revolution.* Cambridge, 1970.

———. *Islamic History. A New Interpretation. I. AD 600–750 (AH 132).* Cambridge, 1971.

Smith, G. R. and M. A. S. Abdelhaleem, *The Book of the Superiority of Dogs over many of Those who wear Clothes,* Warminster, 1978.

Sprenger, A. *Die Post- und Reiserouten des Orients.* Leipzig, 1864.

Ullmann, M. *Wörterbuch der klassischen arabischen Sprache.* Wiesbaden, 1957–74.

Van Arendonk, C. *Les débuts de l'imāmat zaidite au Yémen.* Leiden, 1960.

Van Ess, J. "La Qadarīya et la Ģailanīya de Yazīd III," *SI* 31 (1970), 269ff.

———. *Anfänge muslimischer Theologie.* Beirut, 1977.

Van Vloten, G. *Recherches sur la domination arabe, le Chiitisme, et les croyances messianiques sous le Khalifat des Umaiyades.* Amsterdam, 1894.

Von Kremer, A. *Culturgeschichte des Orients unter den Chalifen.* 2 vols. Vienna, 1875.

Watson, W. *The Genius of China.* London, 1977.

Watt, W. M. *The Formative Period of Islamic Thought.* Edinburgh, 1973.

Wellhausen, J. *The Arab Kingdom and its Fall.* Translated by M. G. Weir. Calcutta, 1927.

Wensinck, A. J., et al. *Concordance et indices de la tradition musulmane.* 6 vols. Leiden, 1936–69.

Wright, W. *A Grammar of the Arabic Language.* 2 vols. London and Edinburgh, 1874–75.

Zambaur, E. von. *Manuel de généalogie et de chronologie pour l'histoire de l'Islam.* Hanover, 1927.

Index

The index contains all proper names of places, persons, and tribal and other groups that occur in the introduction, the text, and the footnotes, as well as some technical terms, except that only names belonging to the medieval or earlier periods have been included from the footnotes.

The definite article and the abbreviation b. (for ibn, son) have been disregarded for the purposes of alphabetization. When there may be ambiguity over names (as with some of the Umayyads), a longer genealogical chain has been provided.

A

Abān b. ʿAbd al-Raḥmān al-Numayrī 131, 176
Abān b. al-Ḥakam al-Zahrānī 210
Abārākharrah 31
ʿAbbād b. Ziyād 141
al-ʿAbbās b. ʿAbd al-Muṭṭalib 46, 74
al-ʿAbbās b. ʿAbdallāh al-Hāshimī 260
al-ʿAbbās b. Muḥammad b. ʿAlī b. ʿAbdallāh, ʿAbbāsid 4
al-ʿAbbās b. Saʿīd al-Murrī 41, 45–46, 49
al-ʿAbbās b. al-Walīd b. ʿAbd al-Malik b. Marwān xix, 100, 137–38, 140–41, 150–52, 154, 157–59, 163, 184, 198, 216–17
ʿAbbāsid(s) xiii–xiv, 15, 66–68, 74, 120, 122, 136
al-ʿAbbāsiyyah 47
ʿAbd al-ʿAzīz b. ʿAbbād b. Jābir al-Yaḥmadī 228
ʿAbd al-ʿAzīz b. ʿAbd Rabbihi al-Laythī 232, 265
ʿAbd al-ʿAzīz b. ʿAbdallāh b. ʿAmr b. ʿUthmān 238
ʿAbd al-ʿAzīz b. al-Ḥajjāj b. ʿAbd al-Malik 68, 148–53, 155–61, 184, 186, 188–89, 206, 238, 247, 250, 256
ʿAbd al-ʿAzīz b. Hārūn b. ʿAbdallāh al-Kalbī 196
ʿAbd al-ʿAzīz b. ʿUmar b. ʿAbd al-ʿAzīz 244
ʿAbd al-ʿAzīz b. al-Walīd b. ʿAbd al-Malik 150
ʿAbd al-Ḥamīd, *kātib* 75
ʿAbd al-Jabbār b. Shuʿayb b. ʿAbbād 228–29
ʿAbd al-Malik b. ʿAbdallāh al-Sulamī, governor of Khwārazm 212
ʿAbd al-Malik b. Bishr b. Marwān, Umayyad 51–52
ʿAbd al-Malik b. Ḥarmalah al-Yaḥmadī 228–30
ʿAbd al-Malik b. Marwān, Umayyad caliph xix, 73, 75, 78, 90, 127, 240, 242, 250

'Abd al-Malik b. Marwān b. Muḥammad b. Marwān, Umayyad xix, 219, 239
'Abd al-Malik b. Muḥammad b. al-Ḥajjāj 130–31, 142, 144, 147
'Abd al-Malik b. Nu'aym al-Qaynī 104, 106
'Abd al-Malik b. al-Qa'qā' 136
'Abd al-Malik al-Ṭā'ī 257
'Abd al-Raḥmān b. Abī al-Janūb al-Bahrānī 156
'Abd al-Raḥmān b. 'Ajlān, mawlā of Yazīd b. 'Abd al-Malik 154
'Abd al-Raḥmān b. 'Anbasah b. Sa'īd b. al-'Āṣ 167
'Abd al-Raḥmān b. al-Ḍakhm 240
'Abd al-Raḥmān b. Maṣād 144, 147–48
'Abd al-Raḥmān b. Thuwayb al-Dinnī 172–73
'Abd al-Salām b. Bukayr b. Shammākh al-Lakhmī 154, 160
'Abd al-Ṣamad b. 'Abd al-'Alā al-Shabbānī, 88, 92–93
'Abd al-Ṣamad b. Abī Mālik b. Masrūḥ 46
'Abd al-Wahhāb b. Ibrāhīm b. Yazīd b. Huraym 201–2, 239, 248, 250
'Abdāh b. Rabāḥ al-Ghassānī 239
'Abdallāh b. 'Abbās al-Tamīmī 255
'Abdallāh b. 'Abd al-'Alā 88
'Abdallāh b. Abī al-'Anbas al-Azdī 21
'Abdallāh b. 'Alī 75
'Abdallāh b. 'Anbasah b. Sa'īd b. al-'Āṣ 148–49
'Abdallāh b. 'Awf 43
'Abdallāh b. 'Ayyāsh, *muḥaddith* 4
'Abdallāh al-Baṭṭāl b. al-Ḥusayn 55
'Abdallāh b. al-Ḥasan b. al-Ḥasan b. 'Alī 8–11, 17
'Abdallāh b. Kinānah, tribal group 157
'Abdallāh b. Mu'āwiyah b. 'Abdallāh 253–56, 258–63
'Abdallāh b. al-Mubārak 222
'Abdallāh b. Mujjā'ah 265
'Abdallāh al-Nawfalī 261
'Abdallāh al-Nubātī 265
'Abdallāh b. Qays b. 'Ubbād, governor of Sarakhs 122–23
'Abdallāh b. Sinān 237
'Abdallāh b. 'Umar b. 'Abd al-'Azīz 219–21, 224, 232, 234, 236, 244, 253–62, 264
'Abdallāh b. Wāqid b. 'Abdallāh 9, 11
al-Abrash Sa'īd b. al-Walīd al-Kalbī 12, 57, 71, 78–80, 149, 159, 168, 172–73
Abrashahr (Nīshāpūr) 122–23
'Abs, tribal group 22, 45, 63, 134, 146, 171
Abū al-'Āj Kathīr b. 'Abdallāh al-Sulamī, governor of al-Baṣrah 142–43
Abū al-'Ajlān al-Ḥanīfī 124
Abū al-Asad, mawlā of Khālid b. 'Abdallāh al-Qasrī 160, 202, 253
Abū 'Āṣim al-Ḍabbī 81
Abū 'Āṣim al-Ziyādī 163
Abū Bakr, caliph, 9, 11, 37–38
Abū al-Bilād, mawlā of the Banū 'Abs 262
Abū al-Halbā' al-Bahrānī 187–88
Abū Ḥanīfah al-Nu'mān b. Thābit 235
Abū Hāshim Mukhallad b. Muḥammad b. Ṣāliḥ, mawlā of 'Uthmān b. 'Affān 202, 239, 248, 250
Abū 'Ilāqah al-Quḍā'ī 154
Abū 'Ilāqah b. Ṣāliḥ al-Salāmānī 147
Abū Isḥāq b. Rabī'ah 17, 34
Abū Ja'dah, mawlā of Quraysh 187
Abū al-Juwayriyah, poet 49
Abū Kāmil al-Ghuzayyil al-Dimashqī 162
Abū Khālid 78
Abū al-Khaṭṭāb 171, 213
Abū Khaythamah Zuhayr b. Mu'āwiyah 51
Abū Ma'shar Nājiḥ b. 'Abd al-Raḥmān al-Sindī al-Madanī, *muḥaddith* 35, 55, 65, 68, 70, 120, 164, 243
Abū Miḥjan, mawlā of Khālid al-Qasrī 179
Abū Mikhnaf, historian, xiv, xv, 5, 13–14, 21, 36, 54, 121, 196–97, 254

Abū Muḥammad b. ʿAbdallāh b. Yazīd b. Muʿāwiyah 148
Abū Muḥammad al-Sufyānī 99, 100, 162, 185–86, 188, 190, 253
Abū Muslim, 66–68, 118, 120
Abū al-Najm al-Faḍl b. Qudāmah al-ʿIjlī, poet 81
Abū Nuʿaym 177
Abū Numaylah Ṣāliḥ b. ʿAbbār, mawlā of Banū ʿAbs 29, 63–65
Abū Quḥāfah al-Murrī 176
Abū al-Ṣabbār al-ʿAbdī 48
Abū al-Salīl al-Bakrī 221
Abū al-Shaghb al-ʿAbsī 171
Abū Sharīk 81
Abū ʿUbaydah Maʿmar b. al-Muthannā, scholar 7, 14, 15, 51, 167, 219, 256, 262
Abū ʿUbaydah b. al-Walīd 216
Abū al-ʿUmarras 169–70
Abū al-Walīd Zuhayr b. Hunayd al-ʿAdawī 229
Abū al-Zaʿfarān, mawlā of Asad b. ʿAbdallāh 226–27
Abū Zayd 171, 177
Abū al-Zinād ʿAlī b. Dhakwān al-Qurashī, *muḥaddith* 164–66
Abū al-Zubayr al-Mundhir b. Abī ʿAmr 99
al-Abyaḍ 198
ʿAdhrāʾ xxiii, 186, 189
ʿAdī, tribal group 41
al-Aghdaf 91–92, 148
aḥdāth 244
ahl al-ʿāliyah 62
ahl al-bayt 23, 50, 58
ahl al-dhimmah 146
Aḥmad b. Muʿāwiyah 171, 213
Aḥmad b. Thābit b. ʿAttāb al-Rāzī, *muḥaddith* 35, 55, 65, 68, 70, 120, 164, 243
Aḥmad b. Zuhayr, jurist 71–73, 75–78, 80–82, 88, 106, 127, 129, 132, 135, 137, 141, 144, 147–48, 155, 161–62, 180, 183–85, 188–89, 191–92, 201, 204, 214, 216, 238–39, 244, 247–48, 250, 254
al-Aḥnaf al-Kalbī 137
al-Aḥwal, mawlā of al-Ashʿariyyīn 49
Ahwāz 166
Al-Ajlaḥ 235
al-Akhram 29
Akhsīkath (see Farghānah)
al-Akhṭal, poet 231
ʿAlī b. ʿAbdallāh b. al-ʿAbbās 74, 83, 120
ʿAlī b. Abī Ṭālib 11, 16, 18
ʿAlī b. Judayʿ al-Kirmānī 227, 229, 233
ʿAlī b. Wāʾil 227
ʿAlī Zayn al-ʿĀbidīn 10
al-Alūf bint Ḥārith b. Surayj 264
Āmid 219
ʿāmil 15, 24, 29, 31, 35, 59, 62–63, 136
ʿĀmir, a Kūfan 36
ʿĀmir, tribal group 63, 149, 155, 159, 217, 235
ʿĀmir b. ʿAbīdah 244
ʿĀmir b. al-Aswad 88
ʿĀmir b. Ḍubārah 260
ʿĀmir of Kalb, tribal group 132, 156, 185, 188–89, 196, 217
ʿĀmir b. Sahlah al-Ashʿarī 177
ʿĀmir b. ʿUbaydah al-Bāhilī 35
ʿAmmān 127, 148, 183, 200
ʿAmr b. ʿAbd al-Raḥmān 37, 41
ʿAmr b. Abī Badhl al-ʿAbdī 40
ʿAmr b. ʿAlī 82
ʿAmr b. al-ʿĀṣ 31
ʿAmr b. Bakr 229
ʿAmr b. Ḥārithah al-Kalbī 216–17
ʿAmr b. Ḥazm 11
ʿAmr b. Ḥurayth al-Makhzūmī 44
ʿAmr b. Ḥuwayy al-Saksakī 151
ʿAmr b. Kalīʿ 71
ʿAmr b. Marwān b. Bashshār 186
ʿAmr b. Marwān al-Kalbī 144, 147–48, 155, 161–62, 185–92, 216
ʿAmr b. Muḥammad b. al-Qāsim, governor of Sind 199–200
ʿAmr b. Muḥammad b. Saʿīd b. al-ʿĀṣ 200–1
ʿAmr b. Murrah 156
ʿAmr b. Qays b. Thawr al-Sakūnī 155, 160, 185, 189
ʿAmr b. Saʿīd al-Thaqafī 128

'Amr b. Sharāḥil 129
'Amr b. Yazīd al-Ḥakamī 137
'Amr b. Zurārah 122, 124
'Āmul (Amū or Amūyah) xxii, 118, 237
Anas b. 'Amr 41–42
Anas b. Bajālah al-'Arajī 235
'Anazah, tribal group 124
Anbār 198
'Anbar b. Bur'umah al-Azdī 28
'Anbasah, tribal group 13
Andagh 229
Andkhoy 229
Anṣār 9, 11, 52
'Aqīl b. Ma'qil al-'Ijlī 121
'Aqīl b. Ma'qil al-Laythī 233–34
Aqiva, Jew 24
'Aqqāl b. Shabbah al-Tamīmī al-Khaṭīb 72–73, 104–5, 175
Arabia 17
Arghūnah 124
Arḥab, tribal group 47
Armenia xiii, 3–4, 35, 39, 101, 136, 139, 238–39, 241–42, 249, 251
al-Arzah 145
Asad, tribal group 40–41, 51
Asad b. 'Abdallāh al-Qasrī, Umayyad governor of Khurāsān 56, 67, 91, 220–21, 225–27
al-Aṣbagh b. Dhu'ālah al-Kalbī 129, 252, 255
Ash'arīs 133
al-Ash'ath b. al-Qīnī 171
Ashbdād son of Gregory 24
'Āṣim b. Ḥafṣ al-Tamīmī 254
'Āṣim b. Hubayrah al-Mu'āfirī, deputy *ṣāḥib al-shurṭah* 158
'Āṣim b. 'Umar b. 'Abd al-'Azīz 257–58
'Āṣim b. 'Umayr al-Sughdī 26–28
'Āṣim b. Yūnus al-'Ijlī 67
Aṣram b. Qabīṣah 226
al-Aswad b. Bilāl al-Muḥāribī 119–20, 192
'Aṭā' b. Muslim al-Khaffāf 7, 14, 16
'Ātikah bint Khālid al-Qasrī 170
'Ātikah bint al-Malāt 260
'Atīq b. 'Abd al-'Azīz b. al-Walīd b. 'Abd al-Malik 128
Avars 3
'Awf b. Kalb, tribal group 156
'Ayn al-Jarr 249, 251
'Ayn al-Tamr 167, 198
Ayyūb b. Salmah b. 'Abdallāh al-Makhzūmī 5–6
Ayyūb b. 'Umar b. Abī 'Amr 12
Āzarbāyjān 3, 35, 242, 251
Azd, tribal group 22, 28, 41, 146, 209, 213, 220–21, 227–30, 233
al-Azraq xxiii, 91–92
al-Azraq b. Qurra al-Mismā'ī 117, 148
'Azzah, concubine of Naṣr b. Sayyār 228

B

al-Bāb (Darband) 239, 241
Bāb (al-) Farādīs (in Damascus) 143, 145
Bāb al-Fīl (in al-Kūfah) xxiv, 44
Bāb al-Ḥadīd 24
Bāb al-Ṣaghīr (in Damascus) 145
Badakhshān 63, 221
Bādghīs 32
Bāhilah, tribal group 117
Bahrāmsīs 24
Bajīlah, tribal group 167, 171, 173
al-Bakhrā' 149, 150–51, 156, 158, 160, 162, 196, 206
Bakr, tribal group 14, 210, 257
Bakr b. Firās al-Bahrānī, governor of Jurjān 226
Bakr b. Thābit 242
Bakr b. Wā'il, tribal group 28, 200, 234, 259
Ba'labakk 144
Balkh xxi, xxii, 24, 63, 117, 120, 123
al-Balqā' 103, 137, 200–3
Balqayn, tribal group 91, 190, 213
Bāmiyān 32
Banjīkath 25
Bāriq, tribal group 46

Bāriq al-Tamīmī 36
al-Baṣrah xxiv, 21, 35, 62, 71, 143, 146, 166, 196, 244
Bassām, servant of al-Kirmānī 229
al-Baṭīḥah 192
Bayhaq xxi, 60, 116, 123
Bayhas b. Zumayl al-Kilābī 148, 150
Baysān 237
bayt al-māl (in Damascus) 144, 169
Berbers 54, 116, 240
Bint Ismā'īl b. Jarīr 82
Biqā' 249
Bishr, mawlā of Hishām 76
Bishr, mawlā of the Kinānah b. 'Awf of Kalb 163
Bishr b. Halbā' al-'Āmirī 162
Bishr b. Jurmūz al-Ḍabbī 265
Bishr b. Nāfi', mawlā of Sālim al-Laythī 207–8
Bishr b. 'Ubaydah 32
Bishr b. 'Umayr 160
Bishr b. al-Walīd, Umayyad 141, 250
Biṭāniyyah 15
Bukayr b. Māhān 66–67, 237–38
Bukhār Khudāh xvi, 29–30, 264
Bukhārā xvi, xxii, 26, 29, 31, 46, 264
Bukhāriyyah 46
Byzantium 3, 55, 81, 120, 169

C

Cappadocia 3
Caspian Sea 33, 239
Caucasus 4, 239
China 23, 78
Christian(s) 24, 68, 73, 146, 226, 231
Cilician Gates 169
Ctesiphon (al-Madā'in) 255, 258, 263
Cyprus xxiii, 119–20

D

Daghestan 3
al-Ḍaḥḥāk b. Ayman 156
al-Ḍaḥḥāk b. Qays al-Fihrī 150
al-Ḍaḥḥāk b. Qays b. al-Ḥusayn 39
Dahlak 129
dā'īs 238
Damascus xxiii, 51, 93, 129, 134, 141–45, 148–51, 155, 157, 161–62, 167, 169–75, 179, 183, 185–90, 195, 200, 202, 217, 243, 250–52, 257
Damghān 123
dār al-imārah (in Marw) 117
dār al-rizq (in al-Kūfah) xxiv, 45
Dārayyā 145
Darb al-Salāmah 169
Darband 239
da'wah 66
Dawrīn 77–78
Dāwūd b. 'Alī b. 'Abdallāh b. al-'Abbās, 'Abbāsid 4–5, 7–8, 15–16, 50, 74
Dāwūd b. Shu'ayb 228
Dayr Hind (in al-Ḥīrah) 258
Dayr al-Murrān 145
Dayr Zakkā 146
Dhakwāniyyah 68, 188, 192
Dhanabah 148, 150, 162
dhubaḥah 72
Dhubyān 91
Dhuwayd, *kātib* 77–78
Ḍib'ān b. Rawḥ 190–91, 193
Diḥyah b. Khalīfah 148
Dinnah of Sa'd, tribal group 172
dīwān al-rasā'il 13, 71
Diyār Bakr 219
Diyār Muḍar 250
Dukayn b. al-Shammakh al-Kalbī al-'Āmirī 147, 162
Dūma 146
Dūrān 167

E

Eritrea 129
Euphrates xxiii–xxiv, 15, 45, 48, 81, 125, 168, 242

F

al-Faḍl, mawlā of ʿAbd al-Qays 121
al-Faḍl b. Ṣāliḥ b. ʿAlī, ʿAbbāsid governor of Cairo 55
Fam al-Nīl 258
Fārāb 31
al-Farāfiṣah b. Zuhayr al-Bakrī 225
al-Farazdaq, poet 92, 177
Farghānah xxii, 25, 28, 31–33, 59
Farqad, mawlā of al-Kirmānī 229
Farqad, tribal group 21
Fāryāb xxi, 31, 58
Fāṭimah bint al-Ḥusayn b. ʿAlī 10
al-Fayḍ b. Muḥammad b. al-Qāsim al-Thaqafī 132
al-Fayyūm 48
Fazārah, tribal group 91, 212
Fīrūz b. Yazdigird b. Shahriyār 243

G

Ghalaṭān 229
Ghālib, mawlā of Hishām 100
Ghamr b. Yazīd b. ʿAbd al-Malik, Umayyad xix, 119, 214, 239
Ghanī, tribal group 76
Gharshistān xxi, 32
Ghassān, tribal group 146
Ghassān b. ʿAbd al-Ḥamīd 75
Ghassān b. Qiʿās al-ʿUdhrī 201
al-Ghawr 92
Ghaylān, chief of guards for al-Walīd II 176
Ghaylān b. Muslim al-Qibṭī al-Dimashqī 75–76, 129, 197
Ghaznah 32
Ghubar, tribal group 22
Ghūr xxi, 32
al-Ghūṭah 142, 146, 186
al-Ghuwayr 156

H

Ḥabībah bint ʿAbd al-Raḥmān b. Jubayr 128
Ḥadath 169
al-Ḥadīthah 146
al-Ḥajjāj b. ʿAbdallāh al-Baṣrī 198
al-Ḥajjāj b. Arṭāh al-Nakhaʿī 214
al-Ḥajjāj b. Bishr b. Fayrūz al-Daylamī 129
al-Ḥajjāj b. Hārūn b. Mālik 62
al-Ḥajjāj b. al-Qāsim b. Muḥammad 49
al-Ḥajjāj b. Qutaybah 34–35
al-Ḥajjāj b. Yūsuf 166
al-Ḥakam b. Ḥazn al-Qaynī 168
al-Ḥakam b. Jirʾ al-Qīnī 190–91
al-Ḥakam b. al-Nuʿmān, mawlā of al-Walīd b. ʿAbd al-Malik 130, 163
al-Ḥakam b. Numaylah b. Mālik 62–63
al-Ḥakam b. al-Ṣalt al-Thaqafī 37, 39, 40–41, 49–50, 57–60
al-Ḥakam b. al-Walīd b. Yazīd, Umayyad xix, 104–5, 114, 128, 155, 160, 251–53, 271
Ḥakīm b. Sharīk al-Muḥāribī 51, 54
Ḥalāl 134
Hamadhān 27, 255
Ḥamāh 187
Hamdān, tribal group 14, 40, 43
Ḥamlah b. Nuʿaym al-Kalbī 60–63
Ḥammād al-Abaḥḥ 75
Ḥammād b. ʿAmr al-Sughdī 124
Ḥammād al-Ṣāʾigh 221
Hammām b. Murrah b. Dhuhl b. Shaybān, tribal group 258
Ḥamzah b. Ṭalḥah al-Sulamī 66
Ḥanafī 235
Ḥanbalī 71
Hāniʾ b. Bishr 203
Ḥanīfah, tribal group 124
Ḥanẓalah b. Safwān 240
Ḥarastā 145
Ḥarb b. ʿAbdallāh b. Yazīd b. Muʿāwiyah 187
Ḥarb b. ʿĀmir b. Aytham al-Wāshijī 226, 229
Harim b. ʿAbdallāh b. Diḥyah 152
al-Ḥarīsh b. ʿAmr b. Dāwūd 121
al-Ḥārith b. al-ʿAbbās b. al-Walīd, Umayyad 159, 198, 200

al-Ḥārith b. 'Abdallāh b. al-Hashraj 223
al-Ḥārith b. Aflaḥ b. Mālik 62
al-Ḥārith b. Surayj 25, 28–31, 58–59, 158, 220–21, 232, 234–37, 263–65
al-Ḥārith b. Yazīd 77
Ḥārithah b. Janāb, tribal group 157
Ḥarrān 239, 242, 250
Ḥarrān b. Karīmah 47
Hārūn b. al-Siyāwush 30, 62
al-Ḥasan b. 'Alī b. Abī Ṭālib 5, 16
al-Ḥasan b. al-Ḥasan b. al-Ḥasan, 'Alid 8
al-Ḥasan b. Mu'āwiyah b. 'Abdallāh b. Ja'far 256
al-Ḥasan b. Zayd al-Tamīmī, governor of Ṭūs 122–23
al-Ḥasḥās al-Azdī 124
Hāshimiyyah (also Hāshimī) 15, 27, 34, 66, 68, 168, 254
Hāshimjird 24
Ḥassān al-Asadī, governor of Samarqand 118
Ḥassān b. Ja'dah al-Ja'farī 178
Ḥassān al-Nabaṭī 131
al-Ḥatīm 65
Ḥātim b. al-Sharqī b. 'Abd al-Mu'min 254
al-Hawn b. Khuzaymah, tribal group 37
Ḥawshab 53
Ḥawzān 228, 230
al-Haytham b. 'Adī, historian 4, 132, 168, 177
Ḥayyah b. Salāmah al-Kalbī 187
Ḥayyān al-Nabaṭī 235
Hazārmard 27
al-Hazīm 149
Herat 32, 124, 230
Ḥibāl b. 'Amr al-Kalbī 129, 154
Ḥijāz xiii, 18, 22, 65
Hilāl b. Abī al-Ward, mawlā of Banū 'Ijl 258
Ḥimṣ xxiii, 136, 148, 150, 155–56, 159, 170, 183–90, 250, 252
Ḥimyar, tribal group 134, 146
al-Ḥīrah xxiv, 15, 37, 40, 45, 148, 166–67, 177, 196, 198–99, 220, 254–55, 257–61
Hishām b. 'Abd al-Malik, Umayyad caliph xiii–xvi, xix, 5–8, 10–14, 16–20, 23, 35, 50–51, 54, 57–62, 68, 70–83, 87–101, 103, 117, 121, 127–30, 136, 138, 152, 156, 165–68, 170–73, 175, 180, 185, 205, 239–40, 267–68
Hishām b. Ismā'īl b. Hishām al-Makhzūmī 6, 89, 119
Hishām b. Khālid al-Qasrī 169
Hishām b. Maṣād 186–87
Hishām b. Muḥammad al-Kalbī, historian xiv–xv, 4–5, 13, 21, 36, 70–71, 83, 121, 124, 164, 196, 243, 247, 254
Hīt 48, 168
Hizām b. Murrah al-Muzanī 42
Hubayrah b. Sharāḥil al-Sa'diyyān 265
Ḥubaysh 157
Hudbah al-Sha'rāwī 235
Ḥudhayfah b. Sa'īd 190
Ḥujayyah b. al-Akhlaj al-Kindī 15
Ḥulwān 255
Ḥumayd, mawlā of Naṣr 208, 213
Ḥumayd b. 'Abdallāh al-Lakhmī 241
Ḥumayd b. Ḥabīb al-Lakhmī 145, 148
Ḥumayd b. Naṣr al-Lakhmī 129, 154
Ḥurayth 129
Ḥurayth b. Abī al-Jahm al-Kalbī, governor of Wāsiṭ 196, 199
al-Ḥusayn b. 'Alī 11, 16–17, 42–43, 48, 53
Ḥuṣayn b. Ḥukaym 228
Ḥusayn b. Yazīd 82
Ḥusaynids 5, 8
Ḥuwwārayn 185

I

Ibn Abī Laylā Muḥammad b. 'Abd al-Raḥmān, *qāḍī* 55, 244
Ibn Abī Nuhaylah 72
Ibn Abī al-Zinād 164

Ibn al-Ash'ath 135
Ibn Bīḍ al-Ḥanafī, poet 136
Ibn Bishr b. al-Walīd b. 'Abd al-Malik 141
Ibn Ḍamrah al-Khuzā'ī 254
Ibn al-Ḥakam b. al-Ṣalt 49
Ibn Ḥuwayy 189
Ibn 'Iṣām 144
Ibn Kāmil 47
Ibn Khāzim, 'Abdallāh al-Sulami, governor of Khurāsān 119
Ibn Muḥriz al-Qurashī 255
Ibn al-Naṣrāniyyah, see Khālid b. 'Abdallāh al-Qasrī
Ibn Shaqqī al-Ḥimyarī 173
Ibn Shubrumah, 'Abdallāh al-Ḍabbī 35, 55
Ibn Suhayl 93–95, 97
Ibn Surāqah, governor of Palestine 192
Ibn al-Zubayr 158
Ibrāhīm b. 'Abdallāh b. Jarīr al-Bajalī 40
Ibrāhīm b. Bassām 60
Ibrāhīm b. Hishām b. Ismā'īl al-Makhzūmī, Umayyad governor of Medina 5, 8, 9, 89, 119, 177
Ibrāhīm b. Muḥammad, 'Abbāsid imām 27, 67, 120, 237–38
Ibrāhīm b. al-Mundhir al-Hizāmī, *muḥaddith* 82
Ibrāhīm b. Sa'd b. 'Abd al-Raḥmān b. 'Awf al-Zuhrī 5
Ibrāhīm b. al-Walīd b. 'Abd al-Malik, Umayyad xix, 193, 202, 238, 244, 247–48, 250–51, 253, 256–57
Ibrāhīm b. Ziyād 60
Idrīs b. Ma'qil 67–68
Ifrīqiyah 54, 169, 240
'Ilbā' b. Manẓūr al-Laythī 79–80
imāmat al-fāḍil 37
imāmat al-mafḍūl 37
'Imrān b. Halbā' al-Kalbī 133
'Imrān b. Thābit 242
India 24
Īrāk al-Sughdī 188
Iraq xiii–iv, 7–8, 15, 21, 35, 48, 58–59, 61, 74, 104, 118–19, 121, 125, 129–31, 166, 168–69, 176, 195–98, 204, 207–8, 210–11, 213–14, 219–21, 223, 226, 232, 244, 257, 260, 264
'Īsā, mawlā of 'Īsā b. Sulayman al-'Anazī 124
'Īsā b. 'Alī b. 'Abdallāh, 'Abbāsid 74
'Īsā b. Ma'qil al-'Ijlī 66–67, 120
'Īsā b. Muslim al-'Uqaylī 251
'Īsā b. Shabīb al-Taghlibī 145
'Īsā b. Sulaymān al-'Anazī 124
Iṣfahān 17, 67, 255
Isḥāq b. Ayyūb 88
Isḥāq b. 'Īsā, *muḥaddith* 35, 55, 65, 68, 70, 120, 164, 243
Isḥāq b. Muslim al-'Uqaylī 239, 241, 251
'Iṣmah b. 'Abdallāh al-Asadī 118, 213, 225, 227, 230, 232–33
Ismā'īl (Ishmael) 9, 12–13
Ismā'īl b. 'Abdallāh al-Qasrī 166–67, 169–70, 172, 256–60
'Iyāḍ b. Muslim, mawlā of 'Abd al-Malik b. Marwān 92–93, 100

J

Jabal 'Ajlūn 146
Jabal al-Sharāh 198
jabbānah 22, 40–42, 220, 255
Jabbānat Kindah (in al-Kūfah) xxiv, 42
Jabbānat Mikhnaf b. Sulaym (in al-Kūfah) xxiv, 42
Jabbānat al-Sabī' (in al-Kūfah) xxiv, 48
Jabbānat Ṣā'idiyyīn (in al-Kūfah) xxiv, 41
Jabbānat Sālim al-Salūlī (in al-Kūfah) xxiv, 22, 40–41, 44, 49
al-Jābiyah xxiii, 145, 151
al-Jābiyah (gate of Damascus) 145, 147, 155
Ja'far, servant of al-Kirmānī 228–29
Ja'far b. al-'Abbās al-Kindī, governor of Armenia 39–40
Ja'far b. al-Ḥasan b. al-Ḥasan, 'Alid 8, 10

Ja'far b. Nāfi' b. al-Qa'qā' al-Dhuhlī 257–58
Ja'far al-Ṣādiq b. Muḥammad b. 'Alī 38
Ja'far b. Sulaymān b. 'Alī al-Hāshimī 75
Jahm b. Mas'ūd 227
Jāmi' al-Kūfah (Great Mosque) xxiv, 39–41, 43–45
Jamīl b. al-Nu'mān 225–26
Jarash 146
Jardabah 99
Jarīr b. Yazīd b. Jarīr, governor of al-Baṣrah 196
Jarūd 141
Jaxartes xxii, 25, 28, 31
al-Jaysh 31
al-Jazīrah 3, 75, 144, 218–19, 238–39, 242, 249–50, 252, 256
Jerusalem xxiii, 190
Jews 24, 226
al-Jibāl 123, 208, 253, 255, 262
jizyah 4, 24, 25
Jordan 92, 157, 159, 189–93
Judhām, tribal group 135
Juhaynah, tribal group 41, 49, 146
al-Jum' 198
Junaḥ b. Nu'aym al-Kalbī 151
al-Junayd b. 'Abd al-Raḥmān, governor of Sind 66
al-Junayd b. 'Abdallāh al-Murrī, governor of Khurāsān 58, 63, 78, 136
Jundah 237
Jurjān xxi, 226, 234
Juwayriyah b. Asmā' b. 'Ubayd al-Baṣrī, *muḥaddith* 8, 88
Jūzjān (al-Jūzajān) 62–63, 124
al-Jūzjān b. al-Jūzjān 30

K

Ka'b b. Ḥāmid al-'Ansī, *ṣāḥib al-shurṭah* of Hishām 240
Ka'bah 88, 89
Kabul 32
Kalb, tribal group 129, 134, 146, 157, 178, 203, 213
Kalbiyyīn alley (in Damascus) 145
al-Karak 190
Karbalā' 16, 48, 198
Kardar 209
al-Khaḍrā' (the Green Palace at Damascus) 189, 203
Khalaf b. Khalīfah, mawlā of Qays b. Tha'labah 178, 230
Khālid b. 'Abd al-Malik b. al-Ḥārith, Umayyad governor of Medina 9–11
Khālid b. 'Abdallāh al-Qasrī, Ibn al-Naṣrāniyyah, Umayyad governor in Iraq xiii–xiv, 4–5, 8, 14, 67, 74, 81–82, 90–91, 128–33, 135, 137, 151, 160, 162, 166–80, 197, 202, 256
Khālid b. 'Amr, mawlā of Banū 'Āmir 235–37
Khālid b. Qaṭan al-Ḥārithī 255
Khālid b. Shu'ayb b. Abī Ṣāliḥ al-Ḥuddānī 227
Khālid b. 'Urfuṭah 43
Khālid b. 'Uthmān al-Mikhrāsh, *ṣāḥib al-shurṭah* 156, 158
Khālid b. Yazīd b. Mu'āwiyah 185, 219
Khālid b. Ziyād al-Baddī 235–37
al-Khalīl b. Ghazwān al-'Adawī 265
khāqān 56, 265
kharāj 24–25, 58–59, 118, 167, 170, 191, 220
Khārijite 39, 43
Kharistān, battle 56
Khashabiyyah 151
Khazars 239
Khidāsh 30, 67, 255
Khilāṭ 216
Khirāsh b. Ḥawshab b. Yazīd al-Shaybānī 53, 125
Khirāsh b. al-Mughīrah b. 'Aṭiyah, mawlā of Banū Layth 261
Khurāsān xiii–xvi, xxi, 24–26, 31, 34–35, 50–52, 55–62, 66–68, 73, 115–18, 120, 122–23, 136, 166, 175, 207–10, 213, 220–23, 225–26, 229, 231, 233–35, 237, 244

Khuttal xxii, 31–32
Khuzaymiyyah 15
Khwārazm 209
Kilāb, tribal group 201
Kinānah, tribal group 59, 213
Kinānah b. 'Awf, tribal group 163
Kinānah b. 'Umayr 160
Kindah, tribal group 46, 133, 145, 213, 227
Kirmān xxi, 224, 230, 255
al-Kirmānī, Juday' b. 'Alī xvi, 56, 220–21, 224–35, 265
Kish xxii, 26
al-Kūfah xiii–xiv, xvii, xxiv, 7–8, 12–17, 21–22, 35, 37, 39–40, 42–43, 46, 48, 50–52, 54–55, 63, 66–67, 121, 132, 145, 149, 151, 166, 198, 201, 213–14, 220, 235–36, 244, 253–58, 260–63
Kūfans 15–19, 22, 40, 43–45, 49–50, 52, 54, 220, 254–55, 260, 262
Kulthūm b. 'Iyāḍ al-Qushayrī, Umayyad governor of Ifrīqiyah 54, 169–72, 240
Kulthūm b. 'Umayr 203
al-Kumayt b. Zayd al-Asadī, poet 90
al-Kunāsah (quarter of al-Kūfah) xxiv, 42, 49
Kurds 145
Kūrṣūl 23, 25–28
Kurz, tribal group 179
Kushmāhan 264

L

Lāhiz b. Qurayẓ 67, 120
Lakhm, tribal group 135, 146
Layth, tribal group 64, 118
Leo (III), emperor of Byzantium 68
al-Lu'lu'ah (quarter of Damascus) 155–57

M

Ma'arrat al-Nu'mān 149
al-Madā'inī, 'Alī b. Muḥammad, historian xiv–xv, 10, 24, 56, 58, 62, 67, 70–78, 80–83, 88, 106, 116, 127, 129–30, 132–33, 135, 137, 141, 144, 147–48, 155, 161–62, 164, 180, 183–86, 188–92, 201, 204, 207, 214, 216, 221–22, 229, 235, 238, 243–44, 247, 254, 261, 263
Madhḥij, tribal group 14, 40, 178
Maghrā' b. Aḥmar al-Numayrī 59–65
Magians 24
al-Māhān 255
Mājān 118, 208
Mālik b. Abī al-Samḥ al-Ṭā'ī, singer 163–64
Mālik b. al-Haytham 67, 120
Mālik b. Sāriyah al-Numayrī 62
Ma'lūlā 141
Manbij 250
al-Manṣūr, 'Abbāsid caliph 75, 214
Manṣūr b. Jumhūr al-Kalbī 118, 129, 147–48, 151–52, 154, 157–58, 163, 195–202, 204, 207–8, 213–14, 219–20, 226, 232
Manṣūr b. Naṣīr 198
Manṣūr b. 'Umar b. Abī al-Kharqā 24
Manṣūr b. 'Umar al-Sulamī 237
Manẓūr b. Jumhūr 208–9, 257–60
maqṣūrah 143, 217, 232
Marj Nīrān 230
Marj Rāhiṭ 134, 145, 150–51
Marw (al-Shāhijān) xxi, 24–25, 67, 118, 122, 230, 236–38, 263–64
Marw al-Rūdh xxi, 230–31
Marwān b. 'Abdallāh b. 'Abd al-Malik, Umayyad 184–86
Marwān b. al-Ḥakam, known as Marwān I, Umayyad caliph xxi, 73–74, 134, 151–52, 216
Marwān b. Muḥammad, known as Marwān II, Umayyad caliph, xiii, 3–4, 35, 68, 101–3, 138–40, 154, 180, 195, 202, 214, 217–19, 233, 238–42, 244, 247, 249–53, 256–57
Marwān b. Shujā', mawlā of Marwān b. al-Ḥakam 73
Marwānids 74–75, 78, 134–35, 137–38, 141, 179, 183–84, 218, 225, 254

al-Marzubānah bint Qudayd, wife of Naṣr b. Sayyār 265
Mas'adah b. 'Abdallāh al-Yashkirī 209–10
Masjid Banī Hilāl b. 'Āmir (in al-Kūfah) 22
Maslamah b. 'Abd al-Malik, Umayyad xix, 3, 73, 78, 87, 136, 155, 235, 239
Maslamah b. Hishām b. 'Abd al-Malik, Abū Shākir xix, 72, 89–91, 100
Masrūḥ al-Sa'dī 46
Masrūr b. al-Walīd b. 'Abd al-Malik xix, 185, 187, 193, 250
Maṭāmīr 3
al-Mawṣil (Mosul) 21, 60, 67, 176, 242
Maymūn b. Mihrān 75–76
Mazyad 53
Mecca 13, 15, 35, 42, 55, 66–67, 90, 119, 120, 244
Medina 5, 7, 8, 10, 15, 35, 51–52, 71, 75, 90, 119, 137, 238, 244
al-Minhāl b. 'Abd al-Malik 127
al-Miqdām b. 'Abd al-Raḥmān b. Nu'aym al-Ghāmidī 227
al-Miswar b. 'Umar b. 'Abbād 244
al-Mizzah 142, 144–45, 147, 217
al-Mu'ammal b. al-'Abbās 155
Mu'āwiyah I, Umayyad caliph 16, 75, 150–51, 155, 189
Mu'āwiyah b. Abī Sufyān b. Yazīd b. Khālid 159–60
Mu'āwiyah b. 'Amr b. 'Utbah 138
Mu'āwiyah b. Hishām b. 'Abd al-Malik xix, 81–82
Mu'āwiyah b. Isḥāq b. Zayd al-Ansārī 15, 22, 39, 45, 47, 49–50
Mu'āwiyah b. Maṣād al-Kalbī 142
Mu'āwiyah b. Yazīd b. al-Ḥusayn al-Sakūnī 184–86, 189, 193
Mubakkir b. al-Ḥawārī b. Ziyād 260
Muḍar (Muḍariyyah) 134, 179, 198, 224–25, 257, 259–60
Muḍarris b. 'Imrān 237
Mughallis b. Ziyād al-'Āmirī 124
al-Mughīrah b. 'Aṭiyah 261
al-Mughīrah b. Sa'īd al-'Ijlī 38
al-Mughīrah b. Shu'bah al-Jahḍamī 210, 227–28
Muhallab, Banū 225
al-Muhallab b. Iyās al-'Adawī 118
Muḥammad, the Prophet xiv, 4, 9, 11, 13, 16–17, 19, 23, 37–39, 42, 46, 53, 83, 106–8, 148–49, 151, 173, 193, 216
Muḥammad b. 'Abbād 49
Muḥammad b. 'Abd al-'Azīz al-Zuhrī 12
Muḥammad b. 'Abd al-Malik, Umayyad xix, 190–92
Muḥammad b. 'Abdallāh b. 'Ulāthah 250
Muḥammad b. 'Alī b. 'Abdallāh b. al-'Abbās, 'Abbāsid imām 68, 74, 82–83, 120, 170–71, 238
Muḥammad b. 'Azīz al-Kindī 124
Muḥammad al-Bāqir b. 'Alī, Abū Ja'far 5, 38
Muḥammad b. al-Faḍl b. 'Aṭiyah al-'Absī 264
Muḥammad b. Ghazzān (or 'Izzān) al-Kalbī 199–200
Muḥammad b. Ḥarb b. Jirfās al-Minqariyyān 265
Muḥammad b. al-Ḥārith b. Surayj 264
Muḥammad b. Hishām b. 'Abd al-Malik xix, 73
Muḥammad b. Hishām b. Ismā'īl al-Makhzūmī, Umayyad governor of Medina 35, 55, 68, 89, 119, 177
Muḥammad b. Ḥumrān 265
Muḥammad b. Ibrāhīm b. Muḥammad, 'Abbāsid governor of Mecca 55
Muḥammad b. Khālid al-Azdī 31
Muḥammad b. Khālid al-Qasrī 169
Muḥammad b. Mālik al-Hamdānī, later called al-Khaywānī 40
Muḥammad b. Marwān, Umayyad xix, 242, 249
Muḥammad b. Muḥammad b. al-Qāsim al-Thaqafī 131
Muḥammad b. al-Muthannā al-Azdī 32, 228–29

Muḥammad b. Rashīd al-Khuzā'ī 190, 203–4
Muḥammad b. Sa'īd al-'Amirī 132
Muḥammad b. Sa'īd Ḥassān al-Urdunnī 191–92
Muḥammad b. Sa'īd b. Muṭarrif al-Kalbī 202–3
Muḥammad b. 'Ubaydah, mawlā of Sa'īd b. al-'Āṣ 144
Muḥammad b. 'Ulāthah 242
Muḥammad b. 'Umar b. 'Alī, 4–6, 21
Muḥammad b. Yaḥyā 260
Muḥammad b. Zayd b. 'Abdallāh 80
al-Muḥdathah 176
al-Mukhtār 10, 151
al-Mulaykah 155–57
al-Mundhir b. Asad b. 'Abdallāh al-Qasrī 166, 169
al-Mundhir b. Muḥammad b. al-Ash'ath al-Kindī 40
Muqātil b. 'Alī al-Mara'ī (or al-Murrī) 226
Muqātil b. 'Alī al-Sughdī 58, 118
Muqātil b. Ḥassān 167
Muqātil b. Ḥayyān al-Nabaṭī 235–37
Murghāb (river) xxi, 32, 62, 230
Mūsā b. Ḥabīb 124
Mūsā b. Warqā' al-Nājī, governor of al-Shāsh 118
Muṣallā Khālid b. 'Abdallāh (in al-Kūfah) xxiv, 42
Muslim b. 'Abd al-Raḥmān b. Muslim al-Bāhilī 61, 63
Muslim b. Dhakwān 203, 216–19
Muslim b. Sa'īd al-Kilābī 24, 27
al-Muṣṭaliq, tribal group 39
al-Muthannā b. Mu'āwiyah 155–56, 160

N

Nabateans 212
al-Nābighah al-Dhubyānī, poet 144, 223
al-Naḍr, *kātib* 105
al-Naḍr b. Sa'īd b. 'Amr al-Ḥarashī 260
al-Naḍr b. 'Umar al-Jarashī 145–46
Nahār b. 'Abdallāh b. al-Ḥutāt al-Mujāshi'ī 265
Nahd, tribal group 22
Nahd b. Kahmas b. Marwān al-Najjārī, tribal group 41
al-Nahrayn 48
Nā'il b. Farwah 45–46
Najaf 15
Nājiyah, tribal group 157, 227
Nakh', tribal group 256
Nasaf xxii, 228
Naṣr b. Khuzaymah al-'Absī 15, 22, 41–46, 49
Naṣr b. Sa'īd al-Anṣārī, poet 179
Naṣr b. Sayyār al-Kinānī, governor of Khurasān xiv, 23–35, 56–65, 104, 106, 115–19, 121–24, 207–14, 220–28, 230–37, 244, 263–66
Nasṭās, Abū Zubayr, freedman of Ṣafwān b. Umayyah 96, 172
Nawfal al-Ḥimyarī, poet 91
Nawsh 228–30
Nayrāb 142
Nihāwand 27
Nihyā 157–58
Nineveh 48
Nīshāpūr xxi, 60, 122–23, 208, 210, 213
Nīzak b. Ṣāliḥ 31
Nizār (Nizāriyyah), tribal group 134–35, 180, 220, 255
Nu'aym b. Thābit 242
Nubātah b. Ḥanẓalah b. Qabīsah 260
Nūḥ b. 'Amr b. Ḥuwayy al-Saksakī 152, 155
al-Nukhaylah xxiv, 43, 48
al-Nu'mān b. Bashīr 149, 156
al-Nu'mān b. Yazīd b. 'Abd al-Malik xix, 70
Numayr, tribal group 62, 64, 202

O

Oxus (river) xxi–xxii, 31, 62–63, 78, 117–18, 209, 221

P

Palestine 90, 189–93, 240–41
Palmyra (see Tadmur)
Panj, river 31
Persians 43, 150
Petra 198

Q

qabālah 57
Qadariyyah (Qadarī) 75, 129, 142, 186, 191, 216, 238, 243
Qadīr 31
al-Qādisiyyah 13, 15–16, 43
Qaḥdam, *kātib* 82
Qaḥṭabah b. Shabīb al-Ṭā'ī 27, 67, 120
Qaḥṭān 9, 11
al-Qa'qā' b. Khulayd al-'Absī 89
Qar'ah, physician 30
Qārah, tribal group 37
al-Qaryah 149, 168
al-Qaryatayn 149
al-Qāsim b. 'Abd al-Ghaffār al-'Ijlī 259
al-Qāsim b. Najīb 231
al-Qāsim al-Shaybānī 237
al-Qāsim al-Tin'ī, later called al-Ḥaḍramī 39–40
Qaṣr Banī Muqātil 167–68
Qaṣr al-Ḥayr al-Sharqī 81
Qaṣr al-Ṭūbah 92
al-Qaṣṭal xxiii, 137
Qaṭan, mawlā of Yazīd III 137–38, 151
Qaṭan b. Qutaybah 61
Qaṭāna 142, 147
Qaṭarī, mawlā of al-Walīd 151
Qays (Qaysiyyah), tribal group 59, 62–63, 65, 129, 133–34, 146, 150, 197, 213, 240, 250, 259
Qays b. Hāni' al-'Absī 195
Qays b. Tha'labah 178
Qays b. Thawr al-Sakūnī 155
Qinnasrīn xxiii, 62, 80, 136, 193, 250, 252
Qīqān 41
Qīqāniyyah 41, 46
Qubā 31
Quḍā'ah, tribal group 9, 91, 129, 134
Qudāmah b. 'Abd al-Raḥmān b. Nu'aym al-Ghāmidī 227
Qudāmah b. Muṣ'ab al-'Abdī 213–14
Qudayd b. Manī' 233
Quhistān xxi, 210
Qūmis xxi, 123, 255
Quraysh 7, 9, 11, 40, 118, 134, 187, 200, 211
Quraysh b. al-Ḥarīsh 121
Qusaym b. Ya'qūb 147
Quṣayr 'Amrah 92
Qusṭanīn 152
Qutaybah b. Muslim al-Bāhilī 34–35, 63, 243

R

al-Rabī' 71
Rabī'ah, tribal group 40, 121, 134, 146, 209, 213, 225, 257, 259–60, 262–63
Rabī'ah b. Ḥanẓalah 227
Rabī'ah al-Qurashī 235
Rāfiḍīs 38
al-Rāhib 147
al-Rā'iqah, slave girl of Khālid al-Qasrī 82, 169
Rajā' b. Rawḥ b. Salāmah 189
al-Ramlah 193
al-Raqqah 250
Rashīd b. Jir' 190
Rawḥ b Muqbil 154, 163
al-Rayy 208, 255
al-Rayyān b. Salāmah al-Arāshī 41–42, 45
al-Rayyān b. Sinān al-Yaḥmadī 229
Razīn b. Mājid 144, 147
Red Sea 129
Ribi'ī b. Hāshim al-Ḥārithī 146
Rifā'ah b. Thābit al-Judhāmī 208, 242
Ru'ās, tribal group 46
al-Ruṣāfah xxiii, 5, 71, 80–81, 92, 100, 168, 171–72, 189, 240

S

al-Saba' 190
Sābiq, mawlā of Bishr b. 'Abd al-Malik b. Bishr 48
Sabsavār 60
Sa'd b. Ibrāhīm, *qāḍī* 119
Sa'd b. Zayd, tribal group 46
Ṣadaqah b. Waththāb, astrologer 117
ṣadaqat rasūl Allāh 5
al-Ṣafāh 65
al-Saffāḥ, 'Abbāsid caliph 154
Ṣafiyyah bint al-'Abbās b. 'Abd al-Muṭṭalib 46
Ṣaghāniyān xxii, 117–18
Sa'īd b. 'Abd al-'Azīz Khudaynah 235
Sa'īd b. 'Abd al-Malik b. Marwān, governor of Palestine xix, 139–40, 189–90
Sa'īd b. al-'Āṣ, governor of Ba'labakk 144
Sa'īd b. Bayhas b. Suḥayb 128
Sa'īd b. Khālid al-Qasrī 169–70
Sa'īd b. Rawḥ b. Zinbā' 190
Sa'īd b. al-Walīd (Umayyad) xix, 105–6
Sakāsik, tribal group 145–46, 153
Sakūn, tribal group 133–34
al-Salāmah 187
Salamah b. Kuhayl 15–17
Salamah b. Thābit al-Laythī 47–48
Salāmān, tribal group 146
Sāliḥ al-Athram al-Ḥirār 226
Sālim b. 'Abd al-Raḥmān, *kātib* 13, 18, 99
Sālim Abū al-'Alā', *kātib* 71–74
Sālim al-Laythī 207
Sālim al-Naffāṭ 177
Salm b. Aḥwaz 118–19, 124, 208, 221, 227–28, 231–33
Salm b. Qutaybah 61
Salmān, mawlā of 'Ubaydallāh b. al-'Abbās al-Kindī 43–44
Samāl 115
Samarqand xxii, 24–26, 29, 118, 237
al-Samāwah 149, 200
al-Ṣannabrah 192
al-Saqādim 230
al-Ṣaqr b. Ṣafwān 189
Sar-i Asyā 118
Sarakhs xxi, 121–22
Sardarkhudāh 237
al-Sarī b. Ziyād b. Abī Kabshah al-Saksakī 129, 154, 252
Sarīr 3
al-Sarrājīn (in Marw) 62, 67–68
Sasanian 15, 78, 82
Saṭrā 145
al-Sawād 21, 220, 263
Sawrah b. Muḥammad b. 'Azīz al-Kindī 124
al-Sayyid, Ismā'īl b. Muḥammad al-Ḥimyarī 53
Sergiopolis 81
Sha'bān, tribal group 146
Shabbah b. 'Aqqāl 175
Shabīb b. Abī Malik al-Ghassānī 129
Shāh-i Āfrīd, mother of Yazīd III 243
Shākir, tribal group 47
al-Sharāh 175
Sharqī al-Qurā 157
Shāsh xxii, 25, 28, 31, 56, 118
Shaybah b. 'Uthmān 71
al-Shi'b 152
Shihāb b. 'Abd Rabbihi 82
Shī'īs (Shī'ites) 13, 15, 21, 44, 50, 258, 262
Shiqq b. Sa'b al-Kāhin 167
Shubayl b. 'Abd al-Raḥmān al-Māzinī 60
Shuqayr, mawlā of Banū Ru'ās, physician 47
shūrā 158, 206
Sibā' b. al-Nu'mān al-Azdī 225
Ṣiffīn 151
Sijistān xxi, 55, 199
al-Simṭ b. Thābit b. Yazīd 185–86, 189
Sind 60, 66, 199
Sirḥān b. Farrukh b. Mujāhid al-'Anbarī, Abū al-Faḍl 122–23
Soghdians 25, 27, 56–57
Su'dā, tribal group 132

Sufyān b. Salāmah b. Sulaym b. Kaysān 201
Sughd 58, 188, 243
Ṣūl, Turkish leader 32
Sulaym, tribal group 30, 46
Sulaym b. Kaysān 156
Sulaymān b. ʿAbd al-Malik, caliph xix, 34, 186, 240
Sulaymān b. ʿAbdallāh b. Diḥyah 159
Sulaymān b. ʿAbdallāh al-Nawfalī 261
Sulaymān b. ʿAbdallāh b. ʿUlāthah 239
Sulaymān b. Abī al-Bilād 262
Sulaymān b. Ḥabīb 240
Sulaymān b. Hishām, Umayyad xix, 68, 76, 127, 144, 183, 185–93, 249, 251–53
Sulaymān b. Kathīr 67, 120
Sulaymān b. Muḥammad b. ʿAbdallāh 155
Sulaymān b. Ṣūl 32–33
Sulaymān b. Sulaym b. Kaysān al-Kalbī 46, 198–201, 203
Sulaymān b. Surāqah al-Bāriqī 36
Sulaymān b. Yazīd b. ʿAbd al-Malik, Umayyad xix, 161–62
Sulaymān b. Ziyād al-Ghassānī 188
al-Sulaymāniyyah 186–87
Sumayy b. al-Mughīrah 158
Syria xiii–xiv, 8, 62, 77–79, 81, 103, 120, 137, 146, 149, 167–68, 185, 198, 200–1, 220, 223, 233, 239–40, 242, 249, 256
Syrians 14, 16, 25–26, 37, 40–47, 49, 54, 63, 103, 127, 130, 136, 196–200, 214, 219, 239, 241–42, 255, 258–60, 263–64

T

Ṭabaristān 33, 118
Ṭabariyyah 191–92
Tadmur (i.e., Palmyra) xxiii, 149–50, 157
Taghlib, tribal group 22, 146
al-Ṭāʾif 35, 119, 167, 244
Ṭalḥah b. Saʿīd 146
Ṭalḥah al-Sulamī 66
Ṭalḥah b. ʿUbaydallāh, Companion of the Prophet 15
Tamīm, tribal group 14, 25, 28, 32, 36, 40, 122, 213, 237, 265
Tamīm b. Naṣr 33–34
Ṭarsūs 169
Tashkent 25
Taym al-Lāt, tribal group 257
Ṭayy, tribal group 167
Thābit b. Nuʿaym al-Judhāmī 240–42
Thābit b. Sulaymān b. Saʿd al-Khushanī 142, 204
Thaʿlabah b. Ṣafwān al-Banānī 235
al-Thaʿlabiyyah 15–16
Thaniyyat al-ʿUqāb 144
Thaqīf, tribal group 37, 171
Thubayt b. Yazīd al-Bahrānī 188
Thumāmah b. Ḥawshab b. Ruwaym al-Shaybānī 214, 257–58
Tigris xxiii, 219
Tirmidh xxi, xxii, 117, 235
Transjordan 146
Transoxiana xiii, xv–xvi, xxii, 23–24
al-Ṭufayl b. Ḥārithah al-Kalbī 129, 187–88, 216–17
al-Ṭufayl b. Zurārah al-Ḥabashī 187
Ṭughshādah (see Bukhār Khudāh)
Tukhāristān xxi, 63, 209
Tūmā gate (in Damascus) 145–46
Tuʿmah al-Tamīmī 36
Türgesh 25, 27, 56, 221
Turkestan 62
Turks 25–27, 29, 32, 55–56, 58, 118, 235, 237, 263–64
Ṭūs xxi, 34, 122

U

ʿUbayd b. Jannād 7, 14, 16
ʿUbaydallāh b. al-ʿAbbās al-Kindī 37, 43–44, 214, 220
ʿUbaydallāh b. Bassām 63–64, 208, 226
ʿUbaydallāh b. Ziyād 46
al-ʿUjayf, tribal group 88

'Ukabah b. Numaylah 63
'Umān 132
'Umar I, caliph 9, 11, 37–38, 80, 223, 236
'Umar b. 'Abd al-'Azīz, known as 'Umar II, caliph xix, 75, 136, 165, 195, 219, 232
'Umar b. 'Abdallāh b. 'Abd al-Malik 244
'Umar b. al-Ghaḍbān b. al-Qaba'tharī 220, 257–63
'Umar b. Hubayrah al-Fazārī, governor of al-Jazīrah 136
'Umar b. Sa'd b. Abī Waqqāṣ 43
'Umar b. Shabbah al-Numayrī, *muḥaddith* 12, 17, 213, 260–61
'Umar b. Shajarah 199
'Umar al-Wādī b. Dāwūd b. Zādhān, singer 163–64
'Umar b. al-Walīd b. 'Abd al-Malik 18, 129
'Umārah b. Abī Kulthūm al-Azdī 151, 174
'Umayr b. Hānī al-'Absī 145
'Umayr b. Yazīd 78
Umayyad mosque (in Damascus) 143–45, 195
Umayyads xiii–xiv, xvi–xvii, 13, 15, 25, 37, 50, 74–75, 81, 83, 89, 101, 119, 122, 126, 128–29, 134–37, 141, 144–46, 150, 155, 158, 189, 215, 235, 237
Umm 'Amr bint al-Ṣalt 21–22
Umm Bakr 264
Umm al-Ḥajjāj, Zaynab bint Muḥammad b. Yūsuf al-Thaqafī, mother of al-Walīd II 164, 238
Umm Ḥakīm, wife of the caliph Hishām 90
Umm Hishām bint Hishām b. 'Abd al-Malik 185
Umm Jarīr bint Khālid al-Qasrī 169
Umm Kulthūm bint 'Abdallāh b. Yazīd b. 'Abd al-Malik 156
Umm Salamah bint Hishām b. 'Abd al-Malik 68
'Uqāb pass 186, 188
Ushrūsanah xxii, 26, 31
Ushturj 229
'Utbah b. 'Abd al-Raḥmān al-Tha'labī 260
'Uthayb 13
'Uthmān, caliph 153
'Uthmān b. Dāwūd al-Khawlānī 190, 192
'Uthmān b. Ḥayyān al-Murrī, governor of Medina 80
'Uthmān b. Juday' al-Kirmānī 229, 233
'Uthmān al-Khashabī 151, 158
'Uthmān b. al-Khaybarī 257–58
'Uthmān b. Mas'ūd 227
'Uthmān b. Ṣadaqah b. Waththāb 63
'Uthmān b. al-Walīd b. Yazīd xix, 104–5, 114, 128, 189, 251–53, 271
'Uthrah, tribal group 146
'Uthrah b. Sa'd 172
Utrār (see Fārāb)

W

al-Waḍḍāḥ b. Ḥabīb b. Budayl 264
Wādī Sirḥān 92
Wajh al-Fals, 'Abd al-Raḥmān 163
Wakhshāb, river 31, 118
al-Walīd b. 'Abd al-Malik b. Marwān, known as al-Walīd I, caliph xix, 127–28, 136, 138, 147, 243, 249
al-Walīd b. 'Abd al-Raḥmān 169–70
al-Walīd b. 'Alī 186
al-Walīd b. Khālid al-Qasrī 155–56, 159, 167
al-Walīd b. Khulayd 78
al-Walīd b. Maṣād al-Kalbī 252
al-Walīd b. al-Qa'qā' 136
al-Walīd b. Rawḥ b. al-Walīd 142, 147, 185
al-Walīd b. Sa'īd, mawlā of Banū Nakh' 256, 258
al-Walīd b. Talīd, governor of al-Mawṣil 176

al-Walīd b. Yazīd b. ʿAbd al-Malik, known as al-Walīd II, Umayyad caliph xiii–xvi, xix, 51, 83, 87–119, 121–22, 124, 126–32, 135–39, 143, 145, 147–66, 174–80, 183–85, 189–90, 193–94, 196–99, 201–2, 204–9, 214–15, 218–19, 221, 226, 238–40, 242, 244, 251, 267–68, 271
al-Walīd b. Yūsuf 208
al-Wāqidi, Muḥammad b. ʿUmar, historian 4, 35, 55, 65, 68, 70–71, 83, 164, 238, 244
Waraghsar xxii, 25
Wāṣil b. ʿAmr al-Qaysī 29–30
Wāṣil al-Ḥannāṭ 44
Wāsiṭ 166, 189, 196, 199
Wasnān al-ʿArajī 72
wuqūf ʿAlī 5, 8–9

Y

al-Yaḥmad, tribal group 228
Yaḥyā b. ʿAbd al-Raḥmān al-Bahrānī 186
Yaḥyā b. al-Ḥakam b. Abī al-ʿĀṣ 90
Yaḥyā b. Ḥudayn al-Bakrī 28, 233
Yaḥyā b. Saʿīd al-Anṣārī 119
Yaḥyā b. Zayd b. ʿAlī xiv, xvi, xx, 7, 47–48, 51–52, 63, 120–25, 174–75
al-Yamāmah 17
Yamāniyyah 127, 129, 132, 137, 197–98, 202, 209, 213, 220, 235, 240, 255–57, 260
Yaʿqūb 50
Yaʿqūb, mawlā of Hishām 74
Yaʿqūb b. ʿAbd al-Raḥmān 129, 148, 152
Yaʿqūb b. ʿAbdallāh al-Sulamī 21
Yaʿqūb b. Hānī' 184–85
Yaʿqūb b. Ibrāhīm b. al-Walīd 148
Yaʿqūb b. ʿUmayr b. Hānī al-ʿAbsī 145, 185
Yaʿqūb b. Yaḥyā b. Ḥudayn, governor of Ṭukhāristān 209
Yawm al-ʿAtash (Day of Thirst) 27
Yazdigird III 243
Yazīd, mawlā of Abū al-Zinād 68
Yazīd b. ʿAbd al-Malik, known as Yazīd II, caliph xix, 87, 105, 129, 136, 154, 240
Yazīd b. al-Aḥmar 237
Yazīd b. ʿAnbasah al-Saksakī 137, 143, 153–54
Yazīd b. al-ʿAqqār al-Kalbī 252
Yazīd b. Farwah, mawlā of Banū Marwān 161–62
Yazīd b. Ḥajarah al-Ghassānī 197
Yazīd b. Hishām b. ʿAbd al-Malik, al-Afqam 65, 128, 195
Yazīd b. Khālid al-Qasrī 5–7, 160, 166–67, 169–72, 175–76, 179, 188, 202, 252–53
Yazīd b. Khālid b. Yazīd 148, 188
Yazīd b. Maṣād al-Kalbī 129, 162, 187
Yazīd b. Muʿāwiyah, Umayyad caliph 16
Yazīd b. Muʿāwiyah b. ʿAbdallāh b. Jaʿfar 256
Yazīd b. Muhallab 32, 135
Yazīd al-Naḥawī 227–28
Yazīd b. Qays 47
Yazīd b. Qurran al-Ḥanẓalī 27
Yazīd b. Sulaymān b. ʿAbd al-Malik 189–90, 192
Yazīd al-ʿUlaymī Abū al-Baṭrīq b. Yazīd 160
Yazīd b. ʿUmar b. Hubayrah 121, 136, 250
Yazīd b. ʿUthmān b. Muḥammad b. Abī Sufyān 189
Yazīd b. al-Walīd, known as Yazīd III, al-Nāqiṣ, Umayyad caliph xiii–xiv, xix, 126, 129, 137–45, 147–48, 150–52, 154, 157–58, 160–63, 180, 184–86, 188–207, 215–19, 221, 234–36, 238–40, 242–44, 247, 249–50, 252, 256, 263
Yūnus b. ʿAbd Rabbihi, mawlā of Naṣr b. Sayyār 208

Yūsuf b. Muḥammad b. Yūsuf al-Thaqafī 119–20, 131, 238
Yūsuf b. ʿUmar, Umayyad governor of Iraq xiv, 5–8, 13–18, 28, 35–38, 40–42, 45–46, 49–55, 57–62, 67–68, 82, 93, 104, 115–19, 121–25, 128–32, 166–68, 171–72, 174, 176–77, 195–204, 208, 213, 226, 253

Z

Zamīl, river 117
Zamzam b. Sulaym al-Thaʿlabī 42
Zaranj 55
Zayd b. ʿAlī xiv, xvi, xx, 4–23, 36–54, 168
Zayd b. Tamīm al-Qaynī 177
Zaydiyyah 255, 260, 263
Zaynab bint ʿAbd al-Raḥmān 90
Zaynab bint Khālid al-Qasrī 170
Ziyād b. Ḥusayn al-Kalbī 151
Ziyād al-Nahdī 49
Zīzāʾ xxiii, 130
Zoroastrian (see also Magians) 31
al-Zubayr b. Abī Ḥakīmah 41
al-Zuhrī, Abū Bakr Muḥammad b. Muslim al-Zuhrī *muḥaddith* 171

www.ingramcontent.com/pod-product-compliance
Lightning Source LLC
Chambersburg PA
CBHW021214240426
43672CB00026B/69